Praise for MOMENTS TOGETHER FOR COUPLES

In reading *Moments Together for Couples*, it is Dennis and Barbara's example of open and honest sharing with one another that helps motivate us to do the same.

Brian and Wetonnah McCoy
BOARD MEMBERS, INTIMATE LIFE MINISTRIES

....

Moments Together for Couples is another home run for the Raineys. Today's lifestyle is about pulling families apart, while the Raineys bring our focus back to God's Word and keeping families together under stress. A real encouragement to couples who seek true intimacy in marriage.

Mike and Myra McCoy
CAMPUS CRUSADE FOR CHRIST BOARD OF DIRECTORS

....

If you are like me, *Moments Together for Couples* will touch something deep inside you. Dennis and Barbara's warmth and personal vulnerability plucked my heart-strings. Their stories will fill your daily cup to overflowing with useful, down-to-earth insights. You will see yourself and your family mirrored on these encouraging pages. I promise—if you grab hold of this book, it will grab hold of you!

Patrick M. Morley
AUTHOR AND SPEAKER TO MEN AND LEADERS

....

Dennis and Barbara Rainey have done it again! With down-to-earth, inviting and genuine hearts, they have welcomed us into their home and lives to experience God in a personal and intimate way. This collection of daily moments together will be on the Rosbergs' coffee table to "drink in" during our intimate times of seeking the Father together.

Dr. Gary and Barbara Rosberg
PRESIDENT, CROSSTRAINER MINISTRIES AND AUTHOR OF *GUARD YOUR HEART*

....

A timely collection of devotional thoughts for busy couples—practical words for husbands and wives who want to keep their trust in the Lord a daily focus and their commitment to each other a lifelong reality.

Dr. Tim Kimmel
AUTHOR OF *LITTLE HOUSE ON THE FREEWAY*

MOMENTS TOGETHER FOR COUPLES

Dennis and Barbara Rainey

Regal Books
A Division of Gospel Light
Ventura, California, U.S.A.

Published by Regal Books
A Division of Gospel Light
Ventura, California, U.S.A.
Printed in U.S.A.

Regal Books is a ministry of Gospel Light, an evangelical Christian publisher dedicated to serving the
local church. We believe God's vision for Gospel Light is to provide church leaders with biblical, user-
friendly materials that will help them evangelize, disciple and minister to children, youth and families.

It is our prayer that this Regal book will help you discover biblical truth for your own life and help
you meet the needs of others. May God richly bless you.

For a free catalog of resources from Regal Books/Gospel Light please contact your Christian suppli-
er or call 1-800-4-GOSPEL.

All Scripture quotations, unless otherwise indicated, are from the New American Standard Bible, © 1960,
1962, 1963, 1968, 1971, 1972, 1973, 1975, 1977 by The Lockman Foundation. Used by permission.

The following Bible versions are also used:
NCV—Scriptures quoted from The Everyday Bible, New Century Version, copyright © 1987 by Worthy
Publishing, Fort Worth, Texas 76137. Used by permission.
NIV—Scripture quotations are taken from the Holy Bible, New International Version®. NIV®.
Copyright © 1973, 1978, 1984 by International Bible Society. Used by permission of Zondervan
Publishing House. All rights reserved.
KJV—King James Version. Authorized King James Version. Public Domain.
TLB—Verses marked (TLB) are taken from The Living Bible © 1971. Used by permission of Tyndale
House Publishers, Inc., Wheaton, IL 60189. All rights reserved.

Some material taken from Staying Close by Dennis Rainey, Word Publishing,1989. Used by permission
from Word Publishing.
Some material taken from The New Building Your Mate's Self-Esteem by Dennis and Barbara Rainey,
Thomas Nelson Publishers, 1995. Used by permission from Thomas Nelson Publishers.
Some material taken from The Tribute by Dennis Rainey with David Boehi, Thomas Nelson Publishers,
1994. Used by permission from Thomas Nelson Publishers.

Any omission of credits is unintentional. The publisher requests documentation for future printings.

Library of Congress Cataloging-in-Publication Data
Rainey, Dennis, 1948-
      Moments together for couples / by Dennis and Barbara Rainey.
      p. cm.
      Includes bibliographical references (p.).
      ISBN 0-8307-1754-4 (hardcover)
      1. Married people—Prayer-books and devotions—English.
      2. Marriage —Religious aspects—Christianity. 3. Devotional calendars. I. Rainey, Barbara. II. Title.
      BV4596.M3R35 1995   95-37061
      242'.2—dc20   CIP

1 2 3 4 5 6 7 8 9 10 11 12 13 14 15 16 17 / 02 01 00 99 98 97 96 95

Rights for publishing this book in other languages are contracted by Gospel Literature International
(GLINT). GLINT also provides technical help for the adaptation, translation and publishing of Bible study
resources and books in scores of languages worldwide. For further information, contact GLINT, P.O. Box
4060, Ontario, CA 91761-1003, U.S.A., or the publisher.

ACKNOWLEDGMENTS

*L*ife was never meant to be lived solo, and certainly writing a book would not occur if it depended on a single person. *Moments Together for Couples* has seen many skilled men and women touch its pages. Barbara and I want to say thanks to the great FamilyLife team who made this book possible.

Julie Denker, you deserve kudos! Over the past decade, you have searched, researched, edited and re-edited. And recently you have been a master coordinator of the transcription of myriad messages that have become part of *Moments Together for Couples*. Thank you for your faithfulness as a single woman. Thank you for your impact on tens of thousands of families who owe you a great deal. You are a woman of incredible value!

And to Dave Boehi, once again you have proven yourself to be of inestimable value not only to this ministry, but also to families around the world. Thanks for caring enough to hole up on Lake Hamilton and for becoming a celibate hermit for stretches of time. Your involvement had its definite mark of excellence on *Moments Together for Couples*. Thanks for your commitment not only to this project, but more importantly to me personally. I appreciate you.

A special thanks to Ron Durham. You were the right man at the right time to ease the burden of beginning this project. I appreciate your painstaking care in crafting many of these devotions for couples. Thanks for your dedication to marriages and families. You truly are a difference maker.

Mary Larmoyeux, no doubt there will be extra stars in your crown when you get to heaven for not only putting up with me as your boss, but also for all of the proofreading you have done during your four faithful years at FamilyLife. Thanks for catching those pesky grammatical errors that would have easily convicted me to a life sentence! You have been tremendous help from day one at FamilyLife. Not only does the entire ministry run better because of you, but most certainly my life and family have been dramatically affected because of your servant spirit.

Many thanks also go to Sharon Hill for faithfully running interference with my schedule so I could slay the beast and feed it to the public. You have done a great job of protecting me not only with the calendar, phone calls and transcription, but also from the numerous gnats that surround our ministry and office. Kathy Horton, you have been a choice angel sent by God to work on our team. I appreciate all you have done in your brief time at FamilyLife. You've been a tremendous addition to the team. And finally, thanks to Fran Taylor who makes up the fourth member of the rescue squad that keeps our area going. I appreciate how you fill in and plug the gaps virtually without notice. Your steady spirit and pleasant smile have earned you the respect of the entire FamilyLife team.

Special thanks go to Cristi Mansfield and Lee Walti for the material you edited for this book. Thanks for rolling up your sleeves and pitching in on a project that needed your touch. I know your busy schedules, and I appreciate your help on *Moments Together for Couples*. Linda Treadway and Pat Claxton, you both deserve a tremendous note of appreciation for tirelessly transcribing endless mounds of tapes and countless chapters of books. Thanks for your service and team spirit. You are both a great encouragement.

I also want to say thanks to Betty Dillon. You've bailed me out with research and synthesized material when I got into deep water. You are a real sleuth as you track down various articles. It is amazing how you can find virtually any magazine I need. I may get to heaven and find out you are bionic. Thanks for your efforts at FamilyLife and for being a difference maker. You work diligently behind the scenes and without recognition. Thank you, Betty, for your commitment to families and for the gracious servant spirit you have demonstrated at FamilyLife. You are a valued teammate.

Special appreciation goes to the entire materials marketing team, especially to Blair Wright, Kevin Hartman and Rick Ferguson. Thanks for believing in this project and for wanting to see *Moments Together for Couples* become a reality. I am grateful for how you diligently prepared for this book's release. You guys are truly a dynamic trio, and I really do appreciate all you do. And to Merle Engle (I know I'm beginning to sound like a broken record), thanks so much for rolling up your sleeves and making this ministry happen. I appreciate the leadership you have given to this book and to FamilyLife.

Books need publishers, and without question, one of the finest in the country is Gospel Light. Many thanks to Bill Greig Jr. and Bill Greig III. I appreciate all you do at Gospel Light to build families. Undoubtedly, you and your team would have been a part of "David's mighty men." Kyle Duncan, you are first-class all the way, and I really am grateful for what you have done to make this a quality book. Thanks for putting the rubber on the road and pouring out a deep commitment to this project. And Virginia Woodard, you performed a yeoman's job as you coordinated mountains of editing.

Finally, Mark Crull, you were such an integral part of making *Moments Together for Couples* possible. I appreciate how you kept me going in the midst of car problems, phone calls, press releases and a jillion other projects that no one else could appreciate as much as I do. I am grateful to God for you and deeply appreciate the privilege of working alongside you over these past three years.

Once again, thanks to the great team who made *Moments Together for Couples* a reality!

INTRODUCTION

There are many encouraging signs that our culture still recognizes the value and the power of the family. Just in the last year, major newspapers, magazines and television news shows have begun running a steady stream of reports about the need for strong marriages and strong families. We've adopted and popularized a phrase called "Family Values."

While our culture recognizes the need for strong families, few people seem to know how to build them. That's why we helped form the ministry of FamilyLife nearly 20 years ago, and that's why we put together this book—to help you learn and apply biblical principles for building a godly home.

While you can use this devotional for your personal times with Jesus Christ, you will receive the greatest impact if you work through it day-by-day with your mate. In our experience, most Christian couples wish they spent time together praying and encouraging each other from the Bible—but they just don't do it. They let other priorities crowd out what should be the most important aspect of their marriage relationship.

We'd like to challenge you to set yourself apart from the norm. Use this devotional to seek God together. Use these pages to grow closer together spiritually. Perhaps you could set aside a few minutes each night before you go to bed to read that day's selection, answer the discussion question and then pray together. If you do this for the next year, we guarantee your marriage relationship will reach a totally new dimension of oneness and intimacy. It will be the best investment you could make.

Dennis and Barbara Rainey

TRUTH DEMANDS A RESPONSE

Teach me Thy way, O Lord; I will walk in Thy truth.

PSALM 86:11

*O*ne foggy night, the captain of a large ship saw what appeared to be another ship's lights approaching in the distance. This other ship was on a course that would mean a head-on collision. Quickly, the captain signaled to the approaching ship: "Please change your course 10 degrees west."

The reply came blinking back through the thick fog: "You change your course 10 degrees east."

Indignantly, the captain pulled rank and shot a message back to the other ship: "I am a sea captain with 35 years of experience. Change your course 10 degrees west!"

Without hesitation, the signal flashed back: "I am a seaman, fourth class. You change your course 10 degrees east!"

Enraged, the captain realized they were approaching each other quickly and would crash within minutes. So he blazed his final warning: "I am a 50,000-ton freighter. Change your course 10 degrees west!"

A simple message winked back: "I am a lighthouse. You change your course!"

Like the sea captain, we may need to change course when confronted with the truth. That's what happens when we make it a priority to spend time reading and applying God's Word. It is eternal truth. It doesn't change, so we need to adjust our lives to walk in that truth.

So many of us spend our lives avoiding the truth of God's Word because we don't want to walk in it. Christ said in John 8:32 that "the truth shall make you free," but as Herbert Agar wrote in *A Time for Greatness*, "The truth that makes men free is for the most part the truth which men prefer not to hear."

What is the Bible to you? A collection of nice stories? The foundation of a conservative worldview? Or is it God's Word, "living and active and sharper than any two-edged sword?" (Heb. 4:12). Does anything keep you from obeying God's Word in every area of your life—your business, your marriage, your family? Do you need to adjust the course on which you are heading today?

....

Discuss:
Is there a truth you have been avoiding in your life—an area of your relationship you have been unwilling to confront?

Pray:
That God's Word will be your guide in decision making and your rock in establishing family values and priorities.

MAKING THE MOST OF IT ALL

*Therefore be careful how you walk, not as unwise men, but as wise,
making the most of your time.*

EPHESIANS 5:15,16

*S*omeday, when the kids are gone, there will be plenty of ice cream just for Barbara and me. I won't find the can of Hershey's chocolate on the lower shelf...empty and with a sticky bottom. We will return to a small refrigerator and eat on the antique table we used when we were first married.

Cars will be clean again. The floorboard won't be covered with Sunday School papers or petrified McDonald's french fries. And gum, Legos, Matchbox cars, doll combs and even fishhooks won't be smushed into the carpet.

Doors will be shut, and I won't have to go through the house turning off every light. We won't stumble over herds of teddy bears, dolls and stuffed animals grazing or napping on the carpet.

Fewer tools will be lost. No frantic search parties at bedtime for lost blankets. Socks will miraculously find their mates, and the car keys will be right where I left them.

But of course other things will have changed, too.

When the kids are gone, we won't hear the pitter-patter of little feet running down the hallway, then feel a warm, wiggly body crawling into bed and snuggling with us early on Saturday morning.

No more little-girl, frilly Easter dresses or first days of school. No winter picnics or log cabin playhouses. No more fishing and hunting trips or wiener roasts or just goofing around with a childish hand in mine.

Someday there will be no more handmade Father's Day cards or wooden plaques titled "World's Best Mom." No more crayon drawings, verses and stick people drawn on construction paper and displayed on the refrigerator.

So until someday arrives, we're going to cherish our moments together. We're going to try to take seriously—but happily—the apostle Paul's counsel: "Making the most of your time."

Sticky or not.

....

Discuss:
What "season of life" are you in right now? Are you making the most of this time, fulfilling your responsibilities with contentment, joy and appreciation?

Pray:
For contentment and for the ability to focus on what
God has called you to presently do.

RESISTING CROWDED LONELINESS

And Jesus said, "Who is the one who touched Me?" And while they were all denying it,
Peter said, "Master, the multitudes are crowding and pressing upon you."
But Jesus said, "Someone did touch Me."

LUKE 8:45,46

With the world's population racing toward five billion inhabitants, it may seem strange that many observers see loneliness as society's number one need. This widespread disorder has been described as being lonely in a crowd or "crowded loneliness."

Although it would seem that families are a natural antidote for loneliness, we all know they don't always work that way. In large and small families among children, and between husband and wife, individual needs for "belonging" are often ignored and loneliness looms. Here are some symptoms: declaring some topics off-limits for discussion; substituting television, small talk or silence for meaningful conversation; allowing the calendar to become too crowded for time together; the wife immersing herself in the children and the husband in his work in order to avoid intimacy; refusing to confront each other on important issues and covering them up with an attitude of "peace at any price."

Jesus lived in a tiny, crowded portion of Palestine. It was incredible that in the midst of a mob, all jostling each other, He should take note of a lonely woman's personal touch. But that's just what He did.

Your family can be just such a gathering—a place where each family member can experience both the security of togetherness and the meeting of individual needs.

One of Satan's greatest strategies is to isolate people from each other. Is his demonic strategy working in your home?

....

Discuss:

Which path does your family seem to be on—toward greater intimacy or isolation? What schedule pressures could you adjust to give your family more opportunities for interaction?

Pray:

That God will give each family member some of Jesus' ability to overcome the threat of "crowded loneliness."

GOD'S "BOX TOP" FOR THE FAMILY

Unless the Lord builds the house, they labor in vain who build it.

PSALM 127:1

Each fall I divide my sixth grade Sunday School class into three groups to compete in putting together a jigsaw puzzle. As these 12-year-olds scatter into three circles on the floor, I explain that there is only one rule in our competition: to put together the puzzle *without talking.*

The contents of one puzzle are deposited on the floor and Group One immediately goes to work. The group promptly sets up the box top that depicts the picture of the puzzle it is completing.

Then I move to the second group, dump the pieces on the floor and quickly give the group a box top. What the group doesn't know is that the box top is for another puzzle!

The third group is given the same puzzle pieces, but it doesn't receive a box top. Usually the kids in the group start to protest, but I quickly remind them there is to be no talking!

What follows is fascinating.

Group One is somewhat frustrated by not being allowed to talk, but it still makes steady progress. Group Two keeps trying to use the picture, but nothing seems to work. And since the kids in the group can't say anything, their frustration level soars. The group members look at me with pleading eyes. Soon, I see the wrong box top come flying out of the group!

Group Three is interesting. Because the kids have nothing to guide them, they do their own thing. The kids give up and just lie on the floor.

Am I a cruel teacher? No, there is a point that I make that day.

Life, marriages and families are like the pieces of the puzzle. The pieces are all there for us, but something is needed to help us bring order out of chaos.

There are a lot of competing blueprints and pictures out there vying for your commitment and mine. It only makes sense, however, to look to the God who created the family to learn a design that will work.

It's never too late to pull out your Bible and begin using the right box top.

....

Discuss:

Do you think you are building your family from the right blueprints? Do you and your spouse have the same box top? If you continue on your current path, what will your home look like?

Pray:

That God will give you discernment to recognize when you are building your marriage with the wrong box top.

AMAZING

And they were amazed at His teaching; for He was teaching them as one having authority, and not as the scribes.

MARK 1:22

Have you seen Jesus? I mean really seen Him? Not some kind of 900-foot-tall object, but rather the Jesus Christ who lives in the Bible? When I look through the book of Mark, I see a Christ who is amazing. And He obviously struck others the same when He lived on earth.

For one thing, His teachings were amazing. The people were shaken to their cores by the authority Christ had when He taught.

Second, He performed miracles that were amazing. He healed the blind, the sick, the lepers. Mark 4:35-41 gives us another little outline or a story, a brief glimpse of a miracle that Jesus performed. This is no mystical myth. This was a real event that occurred. This passage describes Jesus with His disciples and how He rebuked the wind of a storm.

On a windy day you or I could go outside and say to the wind, "Hold it." But it would just keep on blowing. A wall could be built, but that really would not stop it. The wind would flow right over it. Yet Jesus turned an angry sea into a calm surface by speaking and causing the wind to stop.

Christ healed the sick, fed the 5,000, and not only walked on water but also made it possible for Peter to do the same. I sometimes wonder what it was like to be Peter as he stepped out of that boat. He had his eyes on Christ and he stepped out and it was solid. Then he saw the wind and began to sink.

I've heard Peter criticized in sermons for seeing the wind and sinking—for his doubt and unbelief. But he still stepped out—he had the faith to get out of the boat and "onto" the water! And he's the only person in history to walk on water, other than Jesus.

What's my point? Have you ever been amazed by His teachings? Have you ever really stepped out and taken Him at His word?

....

Discuss:
How has God's teaching made a difference in your life?

Pray:
That you would see Christ as the amazing God on a daily basis.

January 6

COMMUNICATION OR ISOLATION?

*Since I have had for many years a longing to come to you whenever I go to Spain—
for I hope to see you in passing.*

ROMANS 15:23,24

*C*aptain Red McDaniel rapped on his cell walls in the "Hanoi Hilton"—
tap-tap…tap-tap-tap—practicing the special camp code prisoners used to
communicate with each other. He was risking his life since one of the
strictest rules in the celebrated Vietnamese POW camp was: *No communication
with other prisoners.*

His communist captors wanted to keep all "guests" isolated and vulnerable.
And McDaniel had already been through that; now he was in solitary confine-
ment. As the long hours and days passed, he met the real enemy—isolation.
Without human contact or conversation, he knew only the dulling, silent darkness of loneliness.

The highlight of each day was being taken to the washroom, where he managed to whisper briefly with two other Americans. They taught him the camp
code, which involved a certain number of taps or other signals that spelled out
letters of the alphabet.

McDaniel, who tells of his long years of imprisonment in his book *Scars and
Stripes*, saw nearly 50 of America's finest trained men go into isolation, never to
be heard from again. For himself, it was either communicate or die. New prisoners who did not learn the code within 30 days would gradually start to draw
inward and deteriorate. They would stop eating and slowly lose the will to live.
Eventually, isolation would suck their very lives from them.

Isolation and the failure to communicate also drain life from relationships.
Like the apostle Paul, most people long for intimacy and fellowship, but without communication, these essentials are impossible.

Communicate—your marriage depends on it!

Discuss:
Can you recall an example in your own family when the lack of communication created a problem? How could family members work together to improve
communication?

Pray:
That the lines of communication will stay open in order for your relationship
with God and your family to flourish.

DO SOMETHING OF VALUE TONIGHT

{Part One}

Therefore be careful how you walk, not as unwise men, but as wise, making the most of your time.

EPHESIANS 5:15,16

*D*riving home one night after work, I switched on the radio to catch the news. In a moment of uncharacteristic sincerity, the announcer made a statement that sliced through my fog of fatigue: "I hope you did something of value today. You wasted a whole day if you didn't."

His statement struck me abruptly. Fortunately, I felt pretty good about how I had invested my time that day, solving some of the problems of a swiftly growing organization. But in 10 minutes I would be home where one lovely lady and six pairs of little eyes would need my attention.

Would I do something of value with them tonight?

It's just one night, I thought, *and besides, I'm exhausted.* Then I pondered how one night followed by another, 365 times, adds up to a year. The nights and years seemed to be passing with increasing velocity.

Five more minutes and I'd be home.

I'll bet there are other men like me who are really tired right now. I'll bet I do better than average with my kids, I smugly concluded.

But another question came to mind and lingered: *Did God call me to be merely a better-than-average husband and father? Or to be obedient and to excel?*

But it's just one night. What would I accomplish? Would I waste it spending all evening in front of the television? Or invest it in planting the seeds of a positive legacy?

I wanted just one evening of selfishness—to do my own thing. But what if Barbara had a similar attitude? Then who would carry the baton?

One more minute and I'd be home.

Just one night, Lord. It's just one night. But then the same angel who wrestled Jacob to the ground pinned me with a half nelson as I drove into the garage.

Okay, Lord, You've got me.

....

Discuss:
Did you do something of value today? If you didn't, you just wasted
a whole day of your life.

Pray:
Ask God to help you keep your priorities straight in the midst of the pressure
and schedule you face. Ask Him to give you courage to do right.

DO SOMETHING
OF VALUE TONIGHT

{Part Two}

So then do not be foolish, but understand what the will of the Lord is.

EPHESIANS 5:17

As the kids surrounded my car like a band of whooping Indians, screaming, "Daddy, Daddy, Daddy," I was glad on this night I had made the right choice.

At supper, rather than just grazing our way through the meal, we spent a few moments on nostalgia. Each of us answered the question: What was your favorite thing we did as a family this past year?

After supper I gave the kids three choices of what we would do: Play Monopoly together, read a good book together or wrestle together on the living room floor. Which do you think they chose?

Three little sumo wrestlers grabbed my legs as they began to drag me into the living room. Dad was pinned by the kids. Mom was tickled by Dad. And kids went flying through the air (literally) for the next hour. Even our 10-month-old got into the act by pouncing on me after she had observed the other kids in action.

Will the kids remember? Maybe, but I doubt it.

Did I waste the evening? No. With the power that God supplies, I did my best to leave a legacy that counts—a legacy of love that will outlive me. I was reminded of two things. First, I thought of Paul's words in Ephesians 5, in which he reminded us to make the most of our time and to "not be foolish."

Second, I remembered my dad. He was badgered by one determined boy into playing catch over and over again. I can still remember his well-worn mitt and curve ball.

If you struggle with priorities as I do, you might want to commit to memory those verses in Ephesians. The "fool" Paul wrote about is something we never intend to become; it just happens—one day at a time.

I hope you did something of value today. And I hope you will tonight as well.

....

Discuss:

What choices do you often have to make to balance your own needs with those of your family? Do you ever resent these demands? What is one goal for family time that you want to achieve in the coming year?

Pray:

Ask God to give you favor as you invest your lives in one another and in your children.

WHERE ARE THE MEN?

Iron sharpens iron, so one man sharpens another.

PROVERBS 27:17

As he grows up, a boy needs at least one man who will pay attention to him. A man who spends time with him, teaches him, admonishes him, encourages him. If he can't find that in a father, a boy needs another man he can look up to—a mentor.

What's become of the fathers, the mentors? Well, I can tell you where they're not. They're not in the PTA meetings or the piano recitals. They're not teaching Sunday School. They're not at the pediatrician's office holding a sick child. You will see a lot of women there. A dozen grandmothers. But you won't see as many men or fathers.

Your sons and the sons in your neighborhood need godly men—men who will sharpen them to be God's best—to mentor and show them the way to righteousness. You may be the only godly man or father your neighborhood kids have. But what does a godly mentor do?

He does not bend to selfishness. He doesn't let it be his master. He's got a higher calling than just giving in to what self wants.

He says yes to the next generation of leaders. He calls his Christian brother up and says, "Come on, don't just unplug when you come home. Reject passivity. Get involved. Be the spiritual leader. Take the initiative in your home."

Boys need Christian men who will be there for them and will cover for absentee fathers—men who aren't afraid to be the Little League coaches, the Boy Scout leaders, the big brothers and the school teachers. Men who will share their love, wisdom, skills and time. Men need to give time to help with homework, baths, laundry and grocery shopping. Time to read to children, drive them to ballet and cheer at their soccer games.

What will your son or daughter remember most about you as a dad? Your gifts, toys and trinkets, or your life unashamedly connected to his or hers?

Discuss:
What do you remember most about your dad? Evaluate your involvement with your family and other kids in whose lives you have an influence. Set one goal for this week to be a better mentor.

Pray:
That God would give you the strength to make some difficult choices to make your family a priority over your work and hobbies.

MY WONDERFUL DAY

{Part One}
by Barbara Rainey

An excellent wife, who can find? For her worth is far above jewels. She looks well to the ways of her household, and does not eat the bread of idleness.

PROVERBS 31:10,27

*Y*es, just call me the "Proverbs 31 Woman." Everything runs perfectly in the Rainey household. You don't believe me? Good! Because I hate the modern stereotype of this woman described in Proverbs. She wasn't perfect; she lived in the realm of reality just like anyone else.

Let me tell you about one of those no-good, horrible, very bad days that comes along occasionally.

Dennis and I were getting ready to take our children on a trip that would combine conference speaking with some vacation. At 9:00 A.M. my washing machine sprung a massive leak and emptied its entire load of soapy water all over my kitchen floor.

Our youngest child, Laura, was sick and our eldest, Ashley, had piano and tutoring lessons. But I was able to take the laundry to a laundromat near the doctor's office and the piano teacher. It turned out Laura had an ear infection. I got her prescription, put several loads of wash through the washing machines, picked up Ashley and tore back out to the house.

The phone kept ringing, and some workmen installing an alarm system at the house kept asking questions. Laura kept fussing and banging on her ear. Suddenly it was 5:00 P.M. and I had nothing planned for dinner. Worse, I hadn't packed any suitcases and the four oldest kids had youth group meetings to attend that night at church!

I called Dennis and we decided to buy hamburgers in town. I loaded up all the kids and we met Dennis, gulped something down and dashed to church. Then I rushed back home with the two little ones, put them to bed and continued packing while Dennis stayed in town to do some last-minute work at the office and later bring the other children home.

But that wasn't the end of my wonderful day....

....

Discuss:
Describe a day in your own life similar to the one Barbara described.
Talk about what a husband *should do* on one of these days!

Pray:
That God will use the busyness of life and the many responsibilities of marriage and family to strengthen your relationship with Him.

MY WONDERFUL DAY

{Part Two}
by Barbara Rainey

*Put on a heart of compassion, kindness, humility...bearing with one another,
and forgiving each other, whoever has a complaint against anyone.*

COLOSSIANS 3:12,13

At around midnight Dennis finished his work and came upstairs to help me pack. As he pulled a suit from the closet, he made one of those classic male observations about organization: "You know, Honey, you could avoid all of this last-minute stuff if you'd just do a little planning ahead."

I felt the anger rise to the top of my scalp. But I bit my lip, knowing he was trying to be helpful.

We finally fell into bed at 2:00 A.M., only to rise again at 5:30 A.M. I was so tired I could barely function. As we drove to the airport, Dennis again tried to give me some helpful pointers:

"You try to accomplish too much before we leave on these trips. If you'd just learn to prioritize and do the essential things, this could be a lot easier on everybody, particularly you."

That did it. "Priorities! How do you prioritize a busted washer and a sick child? How am I supposed to prioritize workmen who keep the house in a state of total disaster all day before I'm leaving? Here I try to get everything right so we don't have to come home to chaos, and you talk about setting priorities!"

Dennis was stunned. His dependable, loving, normally unflappable wife had flipped! The rest of the trip was spent in near silence.

At that point we had a choice: We could resolve our conflict and save the trip, or we could let our anger simmer.

So after we had arrived and unpacked, I told Dennis I was sorry for getting angry. And he hugged me and said, "Honey, I'm sorry I said what I said. I wasn't being very sensitive. You do a great job of keeping everything straight and getting us ready. I hate it when we're at odds with each other."

....

Discuss:
Do you have any unresolved conflicts in your marriage right now? If you do, what are you going to do about them?

Pray:
That God would give you the determination to not let your anger simmer and ruin your oneness.

MOTIVES FOR MARRIAGE

It is not good for the man to be alone; I will make him a helper suitable for him.

GENESIS 2:18

Why did you get married? For sex? Romance? Companionship? Security? To have children?

There are good reasons for marriage, and there are childish ones. Years ago I read an article in *McCall's* magazine that included some humorous comments from children:

Gwen, age nine: "When I get married I want to marry someone who is tall and handsome and rich and hates spinach as much as me."

Arnold, age six: "I want to get married, but not right away yet because I can't cross the street by myself yet."

Steve, age 10: "I want to marry somebody just like my mother except I hope she don't make me clean up my room."

Bobby, age nine: "I don't have to marry someone who is rich, just someone who gets a bigger allowance than me."

Raymond, age nine: "First she has to like pizza, then she has to like cheesecake, after that she has to like fudge candy, then I know our marriage will last forever."

We chuckle at these childish impressions, yet I have counseled couples whose purposes for getting married were not much more profound. Lucius Annaeus Seneca (4 B.C.— A.D. 65) the Roman philosopher, wrote, "You must know for which harbor you are headed if you are to catch the right wind to take you there."

The book of Genesis describes how, after creating Adam, God realized it was not good for him to be alone. So He gave him a mate.

Since God created marriage, it makes sense that He has a purpose for it. God's blueprint for marriage is the plan to follow, the harbor to which we want to head. In the next few devotions I will look more closely at His plan for marriage.

....

Discuss:
Why did you marry? What did you hope to get out of marriage?

Pray:
That God will spare you and your family from drifting aimlessly through life, and that He will give your family His purpose, plan and direction.

To Mirror God's Image

And God created man in His own image, in the image of God He created him;
male and female He created them.

GENESIS 1:27

Hanging in my mother's bedroom is a photograph of the Grand Teton Mountains. I gave her that 8x10-inch enlargement after photographing the Tetons from the edge of Jenny Lake.

The morning I took that picture, Jenny Lake was like a mirror. If you take the photo and turn it upside down you can't tell which mountains are real and which are a reflection.

When I look at that picture, I think of God's first purpose for marriage: *to mirror His image*. To "mirror" God means to reflect Him; to magnify, exalt and glorify Him. A successful marriage between two committed Christians provides a tangible model of God's love to a world that desperately needs to see who He is.

Because we're created in the image of God, people who wouldn't otherwise know what God is like should be able to look at us and get a glimpse of Him. People are never more like God than when they love one another and remain committed to each other despite their flaws.

But what happens if you toss a stone into that perfect reflection? My good friend and colleague Dave Sunde told me he once visited Jenny Lake on that same kind of clear, still day. He watched a boy skip a small stone across the placid water and immediately the perfect reflection of the mountains was distorted. God's image, His reflection, is distorted when a husband or wife allows sin to enter his or her life or relationship. Your marriage represents God; protect it from the "stones"—the sin—that will distort His image.

....

Discuss:
When people look at your marriage, how do they see an example of God's love? What would people learn about God from your marriage?

Pray:
That God will help you keep your "mirror" polished and clear, so His image will be reflected in the way your family lives.

MULTIPLYING A GODLY HERITAGE

*For He established a testimony in Jacob, and appointed a law in Israel, which He
commanded our fathers, that they should teach them to their children, that the generation
to come might know, even the children yet to be born...that they should put their confidence
in God, and not forget the works of God, but keep His commandments.*

PSALM 78:5-7

One of the best ways to mirror God's image is through a line of godly descendants—our children—who will carry a reflection of His character to the next generation.

God's original plan called for the home to be a sort of greenhouse—a nurture center where children grow up to learn character, values and integrity. Psalm 78 instructs parents to teach their children to carry the message of who God is to the next generation. Through these lines of godly descendants, Satan's kingdom would be defeated.

Today, however, I observe a problem with many Christian couples regarding child bearing and child rearing: They conform more to the world's standards than to God's. First, many families comply with the popular slogan "Two and no more." And many other couples opt for no children at all, even though they are perfectly capable of conceiving.

I'm not advocating that all families be large. Nor is it wrong for a family to be small. But I do believe some Christians are becoming unduly worried about "overpopulating the world."

The world needs Christians to produce godly offspring. If Christians don't replicate a godly heritage to carry biblical values and Scriptural truths to the next generation, then other philosophies and religions will fill the vacuum.

....

Discuss:
Describe the kind of impact you want to have on our
world through your children.

Pray:
Petition your heavenly Father to help you raise children who will
grow up to love Jesus Christ with all their hearts and turn their world
upside down for Christ!

FILLING THE GAPS

It is not good for the man to be alone; I will make him a helper suitable for him.

GENESIS 2:18

God created Adam in a state of isolation in the garden; he had no human counterpart. So God fashioned a woman to meet his need for intimacy. In the original text, the Hebrew word for "suitable helper" means "one matching him." Adam needed someone who could complement him because he was inadequate by himself. And this illustrates a third purpose of marriage: *to complete one another.*

Perhaps you saw the original "Rocky" film before Sylvester Stallone started spinning off sequels left and right. Do you remember the love relationship Rocky had with Adrian in "Rocky"? She was the little wallflower who worked in the pet shop, the sister of Pauly, an insensitive goon who worked at the meat house and wanted to become a collector of debts for a loan shark.

Pauly couldn't understand why Rocky was attracted to Adrian. "I don't see it," he said. "What's the attraction?"

Do you remember Rocky's answer? I doubt that the scriptwriters had any idea what they were saying, but they perfectly exemplified the principle for a suitable helper from Genesis 2. Rocky said, "I don't know, fills gaps I guess."

"What's gaps?"

"She's got gaps, I got gaps. Together we fill gaps."

In his simple but profound way, Rocky hit upon a great truth. He was saying that he and Adrian each had empty places in their lives. But when the two of them got together, they filled those blank spots in one another. And that's exactly what God did when he fashioned a helpmate suitable for Adam. She filled his empty places, and he filled hers.

Have you given much thought to the gaps you fill in your mate's life, and vice versa? There's never been any doubt in my mind that I need Barbara, that she fills my "gaps." I need her because she tells me the truth about myself, both the good, the bad and otherwise. I need Barbara to add a different perspective to relationships and people. She also adds variety and spice to my life.

Discuss:
What gaps do you fill in each other's life?

Pray:
That God would give you a thankful heart for these differences.

LAYING BRICKS OR BUILDING CATHEDRALS?

Like arrows in the hand of a warrior, so are the children of one's youth.
How blessed is the man whose quiver is full of them.

PSALM 127:4,5

Parents today need God's perspective of children. I think many of us can relate to the story of a man who went door to door asking for donations for a new children's home. At one house he met a tired, beleaguered mother who responded, "I'll tell you what I'll do. I will give you two children."

That is how many people feel about children some days. On one hand we say, "We sure love kids." And then we turn around and complain, "They sure cost a lot, and man, you have to deny yourself to raise kids." It's as if we don't really believe that we are "blessed" when our quivers are full of children.

Children are divinely placed gifts, not accidents. They are a privilege. Barbara and I may sometimes feel that kids get in the way of life, but in reality they are part of the life that God is bringing to us every day. They are on loan with a divine purpose.

A man saw three men working with mortar and bricks. He went to the first man and said, "What are you doing?" The man replied, "I am laying bricks." He went to the second man and asked him the same question and the worker said, "I am building a wall." But the final bricklayer had a different answer: "I am building a cathedral."

In the process of raising kids, it is very easy to feel like you are just laying bricks. In reality you are building a cathedral, a child whom God has given you to train up to carry on in the next generation. There is no greater privilege in life.

....

Discuss:
Why is it easy to forget that, as we raise children, we are "building cathedrals"
and not just "laying bricks"?

Pray:
That you would develop a vision for what God wants to accomplish through
you as you build into your children.

"YOU WILL FIND REST"

Come to Me, all who are weary and heavy-laden, and I will give you rest.
MATTHEW 11:28

If there's one word I would use to describe life in these last years of the twentieth century, it is *pressure*. Everyone has demands on us and on our time.

My dentist tells me I need to floss every day and avoid using a toothpick. My doctor wants to know how much I weigh, what I'm eating and am I getting enough exercise. My CPA wants to know why I'm not keeping better records and if I'm staying within my budget.

My colleagues want me to solve problems, answer letters, return phone calls, make decisions. I have trips to plan and talks to prepare and articles to write. I am expected to meet deadlines, do it right the first time and, of course, do it with excellence—quicker, better, cheaper, faster and *always* with the right Christian attitude.

My wife, Barbara, wants me to spend time with her. She says things like, "I've missed being able to share things with you recently." She also wants me to help redecorate the house, keep things repaired and work in the yard.

I'm expected to spend time playing with the kids, impart values to them, know their friends and what their parents stand for, be involved at their schools and prepare them for adolescence.

My church wants me to be available—always willing to serve, spend time on committees, teach Sunday School. On top of that, I receive pleas for more community involvement—to help the poor, attend PTA meetings, join civic clubs. And I need to be an informed voter on all the candidates and issues.

And then there's God, who counters all these pressures with His own—calling me to love Him, obey Him, walk with Him, spend time with Him.

Oh, wait—*God is the one Whose yoke is easy and Whose burden is light.* If my busyness can be given to Him, I can find rest for my soul.

Discuss:
Are you satisfied with the way you're using your time?
What priorities are you neglecting? Decide upon two action points you can implement in the next week to begin reducing the pressure you feel, and put your burden upon the Lord.

Pray:
Ask God to teach you how to wear His yoke and find rest.

EASING THE PRESSURE

Be anxious for nothing, but in everything by prayer and supplication with thanksgiving let your requests be made known to God.

PHILIPPIANS 4:6

My guess is that most of you could come up with a list of everyday stresses quite similar to the one I gave you in the last devotion. Endless waves of everyday pressure wear us down and pull us into a predictable sequence of events.

First, *we try to accomplish too much—and end up neglecting our essential priorities.* When people try to squeeze too many activities into 24 hours, something has to give. For many, it's our relationships with God, or the time we need to put into developing quality relationships with our mates and children.

Second, *we aren't equipped to handle the communication and conflict problems we will inevitably encounter.* Many Christians have mastered the art of appearing spiritual and happy on the outside. But once they enter their homes, they let down their guards and take out their frustrations on the people who mean the most to them.

Third, since we don't know how to deal with our relationship problems, *we seek to escape from reality.* We might do this by getting a job or spending more hours at work. Men can seek to escape through their pursuit of sports. Some women can escape by volunteer work. Others shop or escape to the movies, television or books.

All this puts more tension in our relationships, and eventually this leads to the ultimate escape: what I call "fantasy love." Most people who commit adultery do so to find the love and acceptance they once received from their mates.

The irony is that so many of us avoid taking the very step that would help solve our problems—prayer. After all, we have the Spirit of God living in us, available to give us the supernatural wisdom and power and peace we need to cope with whatever pressures we face (see Phil. 4:6,7). All we need to do is ask.

....

Discuss:
What is causing pressure in your life? In what ways do you try to escape from this pressure?

Pray:
Spend time with your mate talking with God about the things that are causing pressures in your lives.

NEVER THREATEN TO LEAVE

But God demonstrates His own love toward us,
in that while we were yet sinners, Christ died for us.

ROMANS 5:8

*S*everal years ago, God gave us the wonderful privilege of helping a couple resurrect a marriage that seemed to be beyond hope. The changes were dramatic. Their commitment to Christ and to each other was real, and they grew steadily in their relationship.

But one day the wife came in, discouraged once more about their marriage. Apparently she and her husband had reached an impasse. Each time they argued about the problem, the husband threatened to leave—a tactic from the past. Unwisely, he was saturating their relationship with the fear that maybe he would follow through this time.

One of the Ten Commandments of marriage should be: Never threaten to leave. This threat creates cracks in the commitment, erodes the security of total acceptance and fuels fear.

In addition, threats rarely cause a person to change. They only communicate rejection. God gave us an example to follow. He didn't tell us only once that He loved us; He told us often and in many ways.

Your mate needs to hear words of commitment and acceptance from you, not just once but many, many times. Tell your mate often how much you love him or her.

Each time a difficulty arises in your relationship—a misunderstanding, a difference or a clash of wills—remind your mate (even in the heat of battle, if necessary) that you intend to remain loyal to him or her. Assure your mate that your commitment will not change. These infusions of truth will become the reinforcements you both need to work through difficulties in your marriage. Your marriage covenant reminds you to persevere.

Also, tell your mate occasionally that you'd choose to marry him or her again. On occasions when I've said this to Barbara she's responded with, "Really?" What she's saying to me in those times is, "I don't feel very lovable right now. In fact, I don't like myself. Are you sure you still like me?" She needs words that reinforce my love for her.

....

Discuss:
Write out a letter that tells your spouse in as many ways as possible that you would marry him or her all over again. Read it to your spouse.

Pray:
Thank God for giving you your mate, no matter what problems you face.
Reaffirm your marriage covenant with God together in prayer.

HONORING YOUR WIFE

And grant her honor as a fellow heir of the grace of life.

1 PETER 3:7

After watching as the marriages of numerous Christian leaders disintegrate, I have come to some conclusions. One is that there is no such thing as a marriage blowout—only slow, small leaks. Like a tire that gradually loses air without the driver noticing, these marriages were allowed to slowly go flat. If someone checked the air pressure in the marriages he or she certainly didn't do anything to return them to acceptable, safe levels.

Every marriage is susceptible to leaks, and ours is no exception. The world lures my wife with glittery, false promises of fulfillment and true significance. If I fail to honor her and esteem her as a woman of distinction, it's just a matter of time before she will begin to wear down and look elsewhere for worth.

Following are a few techniques to honor your wife:

Learn the art of putting her on a pedestal. Capture your wife's heart by treating her with respect, tenderness and the highest esteem.

Recognize her accomplishments. Frequently I look into Barbara's eyes and verbally express my wonder at all she does. She wears many hats and is an amazingly hard worker. At other times, I stand back in awe of the woman of character she has become. Her steady walk with God is a constant stream of ministry to me.

Speak to her with respect. Without careful attention, your tongue can become caustic, searing and accusing. I work hard to honor Barbara. I'm not always as successful as I'd like to be, but I know that honor begins with an attitude. Also, if any of the children ever talk back to Barbara or show disrespect, they know they have to deal with me when I get home. Our children are great, but they will mug her if I let them. She's outnumbered! So I encourage our children to respect her too.

Honor your wife by extending common courtesies. You may think that these little amenities were worthwhile only during courtship, but actually they are great ways to demonstrate respect and distinction over the long haul. Common courtesy is at the heart of servanthood; it says, "my life for yours." It bows before another to show esteem and dignity.

Why not increase the "air pressure" in your marriage today by honoring your wife?

....

Discuss:
Discuss the air pressure in your marriage "tire"—any leaks? A patch needed? What are two ways you can honor your wife this week?

Pray:
That you would discern slow leaks in your marriage before they cause serious problems, and your wife would feel honored in her critical role as wife and mother.

THE MACHO MYTH

by Barbara Rainey

Let the wife see to it that she respect her husband.

EPHESIANS 5:33

One day Dennis gave me a list of what he considered to be the needs most men have:

- Self-confidence in his manhood;
- To be listened to;
- Companionship;
- To be needed sexually by his wife;
- To be accepted and respected.

Counselors and pastors would give you similar lists, based on their experiences. And you know what this tells me? The "macho man"—self-contained, independent and invulnerable—is a myth.

To bolster Dennis's confidence, I try to encourage him by being his best friend. Every husband wants his wife to be on his team, to coach him when necessary, but most of all to be his cheerleader. A husband needs a wife who is behind him, believing in him, appreciating him and cheering him on as he goes out into the world every day.

The word "appreciate" means to "raise in value." When I give Dennis words of praise and encouragement, I raise his value, not only in his eyes but in mine as well, and that builds his confidence as a man.

The psychologist William James said, "The deepest principle of human nature is the craving to be appreciated."

And Charles Swindoll adds this: "We live by encouragement and die without it. Slowly, sadly and angrily."

When is the last time you told your husband you appreciated him?

....

Discuss:
As a husband, share with your wife the times you have felt most appreciated by her. Ask your husband how you can be his "cheerleader."

Pray:
As a wife, take your husband's hand and express to God your appreciation for him.

PRAYING WITH BARBARA

Behold, how good and how pleasant it is for brothers to dwell together in unity!
It is like the dew of Hermon, coming down upon the mountains of Zion;
for there the Lord commanded the blessing—life forever.

PSALM 133:1,3

As I've mentioned before, Barbara and I, early in our marriage, started the habit of praying together before we would go to sleep. If there is one simple ritual I would urge couples to begin adopting in their marriages, it is this one—the habit of praying together every day.

For us, this habit of acknowledging God's presence in our life and marriage has, I believe, saved us from many nights of isolation.

Nightly prayer keeps us from building walls between each other. And it builds bridges across chasms that have widened between us during the day.

It isn't always easy, though. I can remember one occasion where we ended up in bed facing in opposite directions. I didn't want to pray with her. But in my conscience Jesus Christ was asking me, "Are you going to pray with her tonight?"

"I don't like her tonight, Lord."

"I know you don't. But you're the one who tells people that you pray with your wife all the time."

"Yes, Lord. But you know, Lord, she's 80 percent wrong."

"But your 20 percent started the whole thing," God reminded me.

Slowly but surely, the Lord turned me over, and I said, "Sweetheart, will you forgive me?" And we talked and prayed.

I don't know about you, but we just can't seem to pray if we're out of fellowship with each other. I thank God for that little tradition He helped us build early in our marriage.

....

Discuss:
For a week, commit yourself to praying with your mate before you go to bed each night. At the end of the week, ask yourselves if your relationship has changed as a result.

Pray:
Perhaps you may need to pray this prayer first: "Lord teach me how to pray with my spouse. I'm afraid."

ARE YOU A FAKE?

And why do you call Me, "Lord, Lord," and do not do what I say?

LUKE 6:46

*S*ome people are excellent "fakes." Publicly, they may do an abundance of "Christian deeds" and use the right Christian clichés. But privately, their lives are charades. They aren't listening to God. Their lives are mockeries.

A young man who had just graduated from law school set up an office, proudly displaying his shingle out front. On his first day at work, as he sat at his desk with his door open, he was wondering how he would get his first client. Then he heard footsteps coming down the long corridor toward his office.

Not wanting this potential client to think that he would be the first, the young lawyer quickly picked up the telephone and began to talk loudly to a make-believe caller. "Oh, yes sir!" he exclaimed into the phone. "I'm very experienced in corporate law….Courtroom experience? Why, yes, I've had several cases."

The sounds of footsteps drew closer to his open door.

"I have broad experience in almost every category of legal work," he continued, loud enough for his impending visitor to hear.

Finally, with the steps right at his door, he replied, "Expensive? Oh, no sir, I'm very reasonable. I'm told my rates are among the lowest in town."

The young lawyer then excused himself from his "conversation" and covered the phone in order to respond to the prospective client who was now standing in the doorway. With his most confident voice, he said, "Yes, sir, may I help you?"

"Well, yes you can," the man said with a smirk. "I'm the telephone repairman, and I've come to hook up your phone!"

We sometimes fake the Christian life in the same way. We say we honor God, but we don't obey Him day to day. Preoccupied with self and wanting our own ways, we ignore God and pretend to be spiritual. Instead of having Christ's character imprinted on our lives, we go our own ways, and our Christianity becomes a forgery.

....

Discuss:
If someone accused you of being a "fake Christian," what evidence could you present to prove otherwise?

Pray:
That the Holy Spirit will reveal how you can walk with God moment by moment, in an authentic manner.

THREE LITTLE BIG WORDS

But I hope in the Lord Jesus to send Timothy to you shortly....I have no one else of kindred spirit who will genuinely be concerned for your welfare.

PHILIPPIANS 2:19,20

I used to think the most difficult words to utter were "I love you." I remember the first time I told my mom and dad "I love you." I was a typical unexpressive, ungrateful teenager, but on the day I left home for college I looked my parents in the eyes and said those three little words with excruciating pain.

Then there was the first time I told my wife, Barbara, I loved her. My heart jumped wildly, and my adrenaline was the only thing flowing faster than the beads of sweat on my forehead. I remember wondering how young couples in love could survive the experience!

Telling another person "I love you" represents risk and vulnerability. Yet however difficult these words of love may be, three other words are even more arduous to express: I need you.

Consider the number of people you have expressed your love to: your mate, children, parents, extended family and possibly a few select friends.

Now think of those to whom you have said, "I need you"—a much smaller number, most likely. Most of us have difficulty admitting need. But why?

Because admitting need means we are dependent upon another. It means we are less than complete by ourselves. When the apostle Paul admitted that he had no one but Timothy who could meet a particular need in Paul's life, he was making himself vulnerable, admitting his dependence on one beloved person.

It's interesting that in Genesis 2:18 Adam had to be told he had a need. God said, "It is not good for the man to be alone." And even after that divine, authoritative statement, Adam probably had to name several thousand creatures to finally get the point: he needed someone!

Today is no different—God often has to show us how we need our mates and our children. And when He does, let's not be afraid to admit it.

....

Discuss:
Focus for a few moments on each person in your family. Interact with your spouse and children on the various ways you need him or her and them.

Pray:
That you will be able to lead each family member to recognize each other's unique needs.

WHAT EVER HAPPENED TO SIMPLICITY?

And Peter got out of the boat, and walked on the water and came toward Jesus. But seeing the wind, he became afraid, and beginning to sink, he cried out, saying, "Lord, save me!"

MATTHEW 14:29,30

Rare is the family that doesn't grapple with friction caused by the complexity of life in the twentieth century. In the last 100 years a strong cultural storm has swept the family far from its moorings of commitment and stability. Consider some of these changes.

During the 1800s, life was fairly simple. The economy was basically agrarian and most people lived on farms, working 80-hour weeks to grow their own food and make most of their own clothes and furnishings.

Today, most Americans live in cities. We are urban and mobile. We turn to technology instead of agriculture to meet our needs. With more choices and more people, life becomes more complex.

Families 100 years ago learned to function as a team because survival was at stake. Their interdependence fused them together.

Today we don't have the same need to work as a team. We can seek individual careers, education, hobbies and entertainment. These interests inevitably conflict with each other at some points, causing friction. And they are a breeding ground for selfishness, which erodes the cement of commitment to each other.

All this complexity captures our attention just as the storm distracted Peter. While his eyes were focused singly and simply on Jesus, Peter was able to walk on water. When he focused on the complexities of the storm, he sank.

There is no way to go back to life as it was 100 years ago. But we can exercise some control over complexities that cause friction. We can fix our eyes on Jesus. We can eliminate options that distract our attention from Him. We can organize the smaller commitments of life around our primary commitment to Him. And we can practice the most powerful word in the English vocabulary— *No!*

....

Discuss:
On a scale of 1 to 10, how would you rate your family's ability to tolerate different interests and commitments? Should some be curtailed?

Pray:
That your family will be able to see the need to knife through the complexities of life and to organize family life around Jesus Christ.

A FORTRESS OF COMMITMENT

Above all else, guard your heart, for it is the wellspring of life.
PROVERBS 4:23 (NIV)

The day Gary Rosberg became "Doctor Rosberg" was, in his words, "the most hollow day of my entire life." For years he had studied for his degree in counseling, but he had nearly lost his wife and two children in the process.

Lying in bed one night, he asked his wife, Barbara, what, to him, was the "most frightening question" of his life: "Can I come home?"

Her response was, "Gary, we love you, we want you, we need you, but we don't know you."

From that point on, Gary resolved to become the husband and father God wanted him to be. As he and Barbara sat in our "FamilyLife Today" radio studio 12 years later and told me this story, I asked Barbara how she felt lying there at night listening to, essentially, the voice of a stranger.

"He was always home in my heart, even though he wasn't home physically," she said. "The door of my heart never closed throughout the hard times, throughout his absence."

Knowing many women in our audience face similar circumstances, I asked, "But with money being tight, with the pressures of two children, and running a household by yourself, did you ever want to quit?"

She didn't hesitate with her answer. "No, I loved him. He is everything to me. Yes, I needed him to change those patterns of lifestyle. But when I took those vows on our wedding day I meant it. I stand before God in my commitment to Gary."

Gary used Proverbs 4:23 (above) as the basis for his book for men titled *Guard Your Heart*. But listening to Barbara talk, I realized the key role she had played as a fortress of commitment during those difficult years. God had used her and her prayers to help guard Gary's heart when he wasn't protecting it himself.

....

Discuss:
Against what forces do you need to guard your heart? What tends to pull you away from your commitment to God and your family?

Pray:
That God would give you the strength to give up those thing that keep you from your priorities.

THE RICHES OF A GOOD NAME

A good name is to be more desired than great riches.

PROVERBS 22:1

*A*re you trusted by your mate, by your friends and by your children? Are you reliable? Do you fulfill your promises to your children?

My dad, "Hook" Rainey, was a man whose quiet, soft-spoken faith and rock-solid integrity won him a good name in our rural community nestled in the Ozark Mountains of southern Missouri. I learned about that reputation forcefully one year during high school when I began selling magazine subscriptions to raise money for our senior project.

Without delay I made several sales to my numerous aunts and uncles. However, my pace slowed considerably when I began soliciting subscriptions door-to-door. I was discouraged and about to head for home when I tried one more home. I was hurriedly rattling off my canned sales pitch when the old man interrupted me: "Son, what did you say your name was?"

"Dennis Rainey, sir."

"Are you Hook Rainey's son?" he asked with a slight grin.

The old man's etched face immediately brightened when I answered, "Why, yes—he's my dad."

"Well, come on in!" he beamed as he unhooked the screen door and swung it open. He proceeded to buy two magazine subscriptions.

I was no fool, so from then on I always let people know at the outset that I was Hook Rainey's son. I eventually set a record for sales!

For many years afterwards I thought Dennis Rainey had won that magazine sales contest. It wasn't until Dad's death that I realized what had really happened. It was Hook Rainey's character that had given me the victory. Without knowing it, my dad had followed Charles Spurgeon's wise counsel: "Carve your name on the hearts, and not on marble."

....

Discuss:
What does the word "integrity" mean to you? Are you a man of your word?

Pray:
That the presence of God's Spirit in your life will be so real you would never think of acting with anything but spiritual integrity.

THE NEED FOR INVOLVEMENT

{Part One}

Be on your guard; stand firm in the faith; be men of courage; be strong.

1 CORINTHIANS 16:13 (NIV)

It was 11:00 P.M., and I was "history." It had been a particularly stress-filled day. I could hear the sheets on my bed calling me, and all I wanted to do was to lie down and let them grab me.

The only problem was that our 16-year-old son, Benjamin, was sprawled across the foot of our bed. He wanted to talk.

I'm not a perfect father, but I do try to learn from my previous errors. And I have learned that when a teenager wants to talk, you'd better seize the moment—even when you're semicomatose!

I leaned forward on my side, looked Benjamin in the eye, and said, "What's up?"

Benjamin proceeded to give me an unbelievable description of a seminar he'd attended on how to counsel his peers about preventing AIDS. He had been selected by his school counselors to be one of six students to represent his high school for the seminar, sponsored by a well-known organization. This conservative organization's official position is that "abstinence" is the best prevention for AIDS. So Barbara and I had signed the parental release form.

At the seminar, five boring minutes were given to abstinence. These adult "educators" all but told the kids, "Hey, we know you don't have any character. We know you can't control yourselves. So here's how you can do it creatively and 'safely.'"

Now, they didn't use these exact words, but they might as well have. What followed was 60 scintillating, titillating and descriptive minutes devoted to creative "safe sex." It was the most graphic public description and explanation of heterosexual and homosexual sex that I have ever heard.

By the time my son had finished sharing and showing me all the material he had been given, I was fully awake. And angry.

I also was faced with a choice. There were a lot of things going on in my life at the time—a lot of responsibilities and a lot of problems to solve. This was the last thing I wanted to worry about.

But this was my child. Was I going to let it pass, or was I going to get involved? I'll tell you tomorrow...

....

Discuss:
On what occasions do you find yourself asking this same question: Am I going to get involved? What is your usual response?

Pray:
Ask God to make you sensitive to spot the "times" when your children (or spouse) want to talk. Ask Him also to help you to really listen.

THE NEED FOR INVOLVEMENT

{Part Two}

But the people who know their God will display strength and take action.

DANIEL 11:32

Benjamin's revelation was not the end of my surprise. The next day I called the school to object, and I learned no other parents had called. So I called one of the parents and asked if his daughter had said anything about the seminar. He said they hadn't talked about it at all.

I then proceeded to tell him some of what she had learned. "I can't believe they shared explicit, perverted material like that with our kids," he said. "It really is sick."

When I asked if he was interested in doing anything about it, his response stunned me: "No, I really don't want to talk to her about this. And, no, I don't want to do anything about it in our community!"

What disturbed me most was that he did not even want to talk to his own daughter about what she had heard in the seminar. In other words, he wasn't willing to get involved in one of the most crucial issues of his daughter's life.

More than anything, your children want you to be involved in their lives. They need more than your time; they need your attention.

It's not just showing up at soccer games with a cellular phone in your pocket. They need your heart knitted to theirs as they make their choices and hammer out their convictions. They need you to help them think about the clothing they wear, the types of people they date and the peer pressure they face.

In order to be a parent worthy of honor you can't just "be there" as much as possible, you have to "be all there."

That's a special challenge for us fathers. Too many of us are too consumed with our careers, preoccupied with our "toys" and hobbies.

Real men with real character act; they take responsibility head on. They may not do it perfectly, but they tackle issues and battlefronts courageously.

....

Discuss:
Think of two things you can do during the next week to get
more involved in your kids' lives.

Pray:
Ask God to help you be "all there" at home with
your spouse and children.

YOUR MATE'S MIRROR

Perfect love casts out fear.

1 JOHN 4:18

When your mate looks into your face, what does he see? Does he see acceptance or rejection?

Whether you realize it or not, you are a mirror to your mate. The amount of confidence he has as he deals with people and life is in many ways influenced by whether you accept or reject him.

Self-image, self-esteem, self-concept—these three terms are used to describe not only how your mate mentally sees himself, but how he feels about himself and what value and sense of worth he has internally.

Your mate's self-image is central to all he is and everything he does. It will either hinder or enhance his ability to learn, make decisions, take risks and resolve conflicts with you and others. Your spouse's self-image will either restrain him or refuel him.

When a person has a low self-esteem, he or she often views life through the eyes of fear. The fear of rejection is one of the most powerful forces motivating and controlling people today.

If you want to see your mate's self-image strengthened, then begin to recognize that the fear of rejection is your enemy. Fear will begin to dissolve in your mate under a steady stream of authentic love.

Love is the most powerful agent for change in the universe because love casts out fear! Perfect love—God's love—is more powerful than the fear of rejection. Perfect love that accepts and embraces another, even in his or her weaknesses, will win the power struggle against fear every time.

Discuss:
What fears help to govern how your mate reacts in different situations?
Discuss with one another how rejection and acceptance
have had an impact in your life.

Pray:
That God would use each of you to cast out fear through your love.

How Do You View God?

*[Moses replied,] "May it be according to your word that you may know that
there is no one like the Lord our God."*

EXODUS 8:10

Where do we get our concepts of God? Of who He is and how He operates this world that He created and sovereignly rules over?

Kids give us glimpses of how we used to think, or for many of us, how we still think. I ran across a little book that contained letters from children to pastors. Here are some samples:

"Dear Pastor, I know God loves everybody, but he never met my sister."

"Dear Minister, I would like to bring my dog to church on Sunday. She is only a mutt, but she is a good Christian."

Here's one that speaks of our culture: "I would like to read the Bible, but I would read it more if they would put it on TV."

And finally: "Dear Pastor, I would like to go to heaven someday because I know my big brother will not be there."

A friend of mine in Denver overheard his daughters talking during a thunderstorm one day. The older daughter said matter-of-factly, "That thunder you just heard is God moving His furniture."

The younger daughter nodded her head like she understood, and looked out the window at the pouring rain for a minute before she replied: "Yes, He just moved His waterbed, too."

Come on, admit it. You and I have some pretty silly notions about God, too. Some of us view Him as a giant policeman up there with a club, while others see Him only as a loving grandfather figure.

But God is so much more than one or the other. He's infinite. He's sovereign. He is to be feared and worshiped and loved. Honestly, how do you view God?

....

Discuss:
Make a list of word pictures or adjectives that describe
God in your honest view of Him.

Pray:
Find a concordance (the one in the back of your Bible will do).
Look under "God" and read down through the verses, jotting down what
God is and isn't. Take a moment to confess your misconceptions about Him,
and worship Him using this new list.

WHEN REALITY HITS HOME

And the seed in the good soil, these are the ones who have heard the word in an honest and good heart, and hold it fast, and bear fruit with perseverance.

LUKE 8:15

*M*any new Christians begin their new lives at an emotional high. They are overwhelmed by God's grace, by the excitement of seeing Him move in their lives, and by the love they feel from their new brothers and sisters in Christ. They involve themselves in their churches' ministries and feel the power of God working through them to minister to others.

Then, inevitably, they begin to come to grips with massive doses of reality, by making too many glossy-eyed, rose-tinted assumptions about people and life. A trusted Christian friend betrays a brother; a respected church leader commits adultery; people bicker about decisions made by the new pastor. Yes, Christians are full of faults, just like anyone else.

I will never forget Dr. Howard Hendricks's statement one day when I was attending Dallas Theological Seminary. He said, "Gentlemen, if you do not like the smell of sheep, then you'd better get out of the pasture." That statement illustrates the choice you face when reality hits and you realize just how difficult it is to work with people. You can protect yourself by withdrawing from the life of the church, or you can persevere and keep pursuing relationships.

Many Christians today choose the path of self-protection. They move from church to church, never settling down because that would require too much commitment. When you follow this path, however, it's easy to end up cynical and isolated. You miss the joy that comes when you determine not to quit and allow God to work through you, and finally, after years of struggling through relationships, see the fruit that, as Christ says, only comes through perseverance (see Luke 8:15, above).

....

*D*iscuss:
When have you been faced with the choice of self-preservation or perseverance? What did you choose?

*P*ray:
That you would be able to sink roots into a church where you have years of fruitful ministry.

PLUGGING INTO GOD

*Be strong and courageous, do not be afraid or tremble at them, for the Lord your
God is the one who goes with you. He will not fail you or forsake you.*

DEUTERONOMY 31:6

Families should be a place of security—but also a place where parents
teach their children that ultimate security is in God's hands, not ours.
One morning as I pulled out of our garage to go to the airport, my daughter Ashley, then a preteen, rushed out to give me one more hug. I could tell
something was troubling her. Reaching out through the car window to hold her
hand, I asked, "What's wrong, Princess?"

"I'm afraid your airplane is going to crash," she said, obviously a bit embarrassed by her admission. A recent airplane crash in Dallas had sent unsettling
shock waves of fear through my daughter.

"Planes are safer than driving, Ashley," I said reassuringly. "Besides, my life
is in God's hands and He knows what He's doing." By now my tender-hearted
young Ashley was clutching my hand in both of hers, and I could see that my
theological lesson had fallen short of its mark. Fear was visible on her face.

I went on to explain that fear is a normal emotion, but that she could give it
to God. "You're in the process of learning how to depend less on me and more
on Him," I said. "I won't always be here to answer your questions—but God
will. Now, it's as if there are invisible electrical cords coming from you to me and
your mom. And our responsibility is to unplug those cords from us and teach
you how to plug them into God."

I then took one of her hands and gently "unplugged" one of those "invisible
strands" from me. She frowned and then grinned as I guided her hand above her
head and helped her visualize plugging into God. "Ashley," I said as I tenderly
squeezed her hand, "I need to go, and you're going to have to take your fear to
Jesus Christ. He can give you the peace."

As I pulled out of the driveway, I waved at Ashley and she grinned back. I
thought about how the culture she is growing up in doesn't know where to "plug
in." I was glad I could point her to the Lord.

....

Discuss:
Are there any areas of your life that aren't plugged in? What can you do to
begin teaching your children how to become dependent upon God?

Pray:
Ask God to enable you to model a life that is plugged into God.

SEIZING THE MOMENT

I tell you that the "right time" is now, and the "day of salvation" is now.

2 CORINTHIANS 6:2 (NCV)

The Greek New Testament uses the word *kairos* for what Paul calls "the right time" here, in distinction to *chronos*, which just means linear time. God selected the right time to bring salvation through Christ. And He gives us *kairos* moments in the family—special times that we must seize before they pass.

That time I pulled out of my driveway and was able to share a sense of assurance and security to Ashley was such a moment. Teachable moments provide us with opportunities to imprint God's values and pass on His agenda to the next generation. Our attempts to do this are often in vain if a child simply isn't ready for the truth we want to impart. So it's important to be alert, to listen carefully, stop and respond immediately, and gently share the truth.

I could tell my little talk with Ashley took root a couple of months later when my son Benjamin, who was then 10 years old, had a similar "fear attack." It was bedtime, and I had read a few stories to the kids, tucked them into bed and prayed with them. I had told Benjamin he could read until 9:00. But at 9:05, as I was writing in my study, I felt a child's presence next to my chair. It was Benjamin.

Putting my arm around him, I said, "What's up, Buddy? You're supposed to be in bed, aren't you?"

Sheepishly, Benjamin replied, "Dad, I was reading *Huckleberry Finn* and there were these robbers...." He paused, looking at the floor, then went on, "Dad, I'm afraid robbers will come upstairs while I'm sleeping."

I pulled him close and gave him a firm hug and said, "Hey, it's all right. Let me tell you what happened with your sister Ashley the other morning." I went on to share about her fears and the process of unplugging her dependence on me and plugging it into God.

Just then Ashley appeared. She listened with a smile as I finished comforting Benjamin. As they walked up the stairs going back to bed, I heard Ashley say, "It's okay, Benjamin, I've been afraid, too."

....

Discuss:

Can you think of a time in your youth when you learned a spiritual lesson from an adult? What are the five most important truths you must teach your children? List them.

Pray:

That God will give you sensitivity to discern the right time, and the wisdom to choose the right words at your children's teachable moments.

The Mutual Admiration Society

by Barbara Rainey

How delightful is a timely word!

PROVERBS 15:23

During the early months of our marriage, Dennis and I spontaneously complimented and praised each other for newly discovered characteristics. It became almost a game to see who could find another good quality to praise. We named our exclusive "club" the "Mutual Admiration Society."

Today, with a house full of children, the situation is not quite the same. But the Mutual Admiration Society does reconvene. Some evenings at the dinner table we raise a question such as: "What do you appreciate most about Dad?" We then go around the table and answer. We've heard such classic comments as: "He goes fishing with me," "He goes on dates with me," or, from our daughter Rebecca when she was just five, "He sneaks chocolate with me." It's very difficult to be depressed when a chorus of youngsters cheers you on.

William James said, "All of us, in the glow of feeling we have pleased, want to do more to please." Thus, you can help to motivate your mate toward excellence in his or her character and his or her performance by giving generous, liberal and fervent praise. Don't forget to praise your mate for those mundane daily duties. Make a mental note of those unpleasant, difficult tasks, and give a verbal reward of encouragement the next time he or she completes one. Anytime Dennis fixes something around the house, for example, I am quick to express my appreciation. I know how inept he feels in this area and what it takes for him to crank up the courage to at least try!

Your mate also needs you to praise him or her specifically for who he or she is as a person. Sow the good seeds of praise in his or her life with statements such as:

"I appreciate you because you..."

"I admire you for your..."

"Thank you for..."

To appreciate means "to raise in value," while to depreciate means to "lower in value." You can watch your mate's encouragement "value" go up when you appreciate him or her verbally!

Discuss:

List three things your mate has done lately that are deserving of praise. Write them in a love note to him or her.

Pray:

That God will develop within you the determination to build your relationship by praising each other.

ADOPTED BY GOD

Just as He chose us in Him before the foundation of the world, that we should be holy and blameless before Him. In love He predestined us to adoption as sons through Jesus Christ.

EPHESIANS 1:4,5

I always knew, from this verse in Ephesians, that we have been "adopted" by God. We did not know Him or seek Him, but He reached down and chose us to be part of His family.

But the meaning of that passage never hit home until 1983, when God gave us our fifth child.

Barbara and I were in New York City, about to speak at a marriage conference. We received a message to call a friend back in Little Rock, and when we saw the name we looked at each other. It was the name of an obstetrician.

For three years we had prayed about the possibility of adopting a child, and we had mentioned it to this doctor. So when we called him he said, "We've got a baby for you."

We said, "You *what?*"

"We have a teenage girl who is having a baby right now and she told us some time ago, when she first came in, that she wanted the baby raised in a good Christian home. We thought that yours might be a likely one."

Soon we found ourselves conducting a family conference by speakerphone with our four kids. "Hey kids, how would you all like to have another baby?" The unanimous cheer went up, "Yeah!" They did not even need to vote on it.

So we returned home to a newly enlarged family. The little girl's name was Deborah. I believe she has been placed divinely in our home. We adopted her—making her our own. And I believe God feels the same way about you and me. We are His. We have been redeemed and placed in the family and given an inheritance. We are *in* God's family! We are His adopted sons and daughters.

....

Discuss:
What type of life did God take you from when He "adopted" you? Describe the changes in your life since you've been adopted into His family.

Pray:
Thank God for causing you to be holy and blameless before Him because of His Son, Jesus Christ.

February 6

A CLASH OF WILLS

{Part One}
by Barbara Rainey

The mind of man plans his way, but the Lord directs his steps.

PROVERBS 16:9

Cinderella—everyone knows her story. On the night of the grand ball, Cinderella was cruelly prevented from attending by two selfish stepsisters. Her heart was crushed in disappointment.

She ran to the garden in tears to be alone, only to find her fairy godmother. The wave of a wand and a few magic words transformed Cinderella into a most beautiful princess. She was whisked off to a ball where she met Prince Charming. Of course, it was love at first sight and they lived happily ever after.

Happily ever after is the stuff of which fairy tales are made. Though we wish it were so at times, life is not a fairy tale. God is not a fairy godmother with a magic wand waiting to wish our troubles away. He has plans and purposes far higher than fairy magic. The problem for me, and for other Christians as well, is the clash between two purposes and wills: God's and mine. Many times they are not the same.

In 1984, I experienced a conflict between God's will and plan and my own. We were nearing the end of an unusually busy spring, one that also contained more than its share of pressure. During those months, I was feeling particularly stretched with our five children. They were normal, active, curious children with five different personalities and five different sets of needs and problems. It was what I'd always wanted, and I was grateful to the Lord for each of these five treasures. Still, I was looking forward to graduating from nursery duty.

Then I learned I was pregnant again. I was completely caught off guard by the news. Didn't God know I had all I could handle with five children? Didn't He know I didn't want to go through all this again? I was sick physically, drained mentally, and tired just thinking about six children.

....

Discuss:

When was the last time you faced a circumstance where your will clashed with God's? Is there a clash today?

Pray:

Think through the problems you face right now, and ask God to guide your steps and keep you joyful in the process.

A CLASH OF WILLS

(Part Two)
by Barbara Rainey

"Do not fear, for I am with you; do not anxiously look about you, for I am your God."

ISAIAH 41:10

The next two months were hard ones for me. I prayed and I cried and I read Scripture—falling asleep in the middle of verses. I told God I would obey and follow Him, but it took a long time for my feelings to catch up.

Then I heard a story about Glenn Cunningham, a famous track star of the 1930s who overcame a doctor's prediction when he was nine years old that he'd never walk again. This young boy clung to a verse his father had read to him—Isaiah 40:28. I went home, turned to that passage and happened to read on to the next chapter. There my eyes fell on verse 10. I reread it several times, for it encouraged me that God said, "Do not fear, for I am with you." I knew that God had chosen to give me this new child and would also give me the strength and help I needed.

But that wasn't the end of my trials that summer. On July 3, when I was three months pregnant, my heart began racing, just as it had seven years earlier. Dennis rushed me to the hospital—my heart was beating at 200 to 300 beats a minute.

As I lay in the coronary intensive care unit, my main concern was for the child within me. Now that I was excited about the child, was I about to lose it? I prayed simply that God would protect our baby and spare its life and mine. I committed my life into God's hands as I lay there growing weaker and weaker.

The doctors finally slowed my heart by using electric shock treatment. When the nurse told me the baby's heartbeat was strong, I was so relieved I cried for joy.

Six months later, Laura Victoria Rainey was born on a cold January night. She has added joy and smiles to our family and to my life. Dennis and I concluded again that God does know what He's doing.

....

Discuss:
What situations do you fear?
Have you turned to God in those circumstances?

Pray:
That God will remind you that He is with you in every situation
you face, and He knows what He's doing.

THE BEST AND WORST OF TIMES

{Part One}

And not only this, but we also exult in our tribulations, knowing that tribulation brings about perseverance; and perseverance, proven character; and proven character, hope.

ROMANS 5:3,4

To begin his classic novel, *A Tale of Two Cities*, Charles Dickens penned the immortal words: "It was the best of times, it was the worst of times." Was Dickens indulging in an overstated contradiction? Hardly. Life is both sweet and sour…simultaneously. As someone else has said, "life is like licking honey off a thorn."

Some time ago I was tasting the "sweet savor" of a great year. It was the best of times in that our FamilyLife Conferences were growing rapidly. At the same time, I was stretched thin by the adversary. Pressure. Attacks. Seemingly insurmountable problems. The worst of times.

Then, as Barbara and I were beginning to get our strengths back, we learned she was pregnant…again…and it was not planned, at least not by us. It would mean that, in God's sovereign and loving will, we'd have six children ages 10 and under. The best of times?

Then came that day when God really got our attentions. Barbara walked into our bedroom and fell on the bed complaining that her heart was beating too fast. As we sped to the hospital, a hundred thoughts flashed through my mind. Praying for Barbara, I wondered how quickly the doctors would be able to slow her heart. Would I soon be saying good-bye to the woman I loved and be left alone to raise five children?

Are these the worst of times? *No!* Not for a Christian. For even death—the selfish, cursed enemy of man—has been "swallowed up in victory" (1 Cor. 15:54). Even tribulations, the Scriptures tell us, produce hope (see Rom. 5:3,4, above).

But I don't like this way of producing hope, I thought as our van rounded the corner to the hospital. *We don't need this right now.*

Fascinating, isn't it, how quickly our lives can be reduced to a simple faith in God. I've wondered on more than one occasion if God doesn't shake His head at how slow we are to realize we are not in control!

....

Discuss:
Have you been through some "worst of times" in which your faith grew? What situations seem to test your faith the most? Why?

Pray:
That God would strengthen your faith so that in good times or bad it will result in proven character.

THE BEST AND WORST OF TIMES

{Part Two}

The conclusion, when all has been heard, is: fear God and keep His commandments.

ECCLESIASTES 12:13

The doctors went to work on Barbara while Christians across the country prayed. Her heart beat so quickly (200-300 beats per minute) that it was not filling with blood, and her blood pressure went down. This low pressure could harm the baby if it continued.

The doctor made a quick decision. Using electric shock, he successfully reduced her heart rate to 75 beats per minute. Afterward, through tears, we gave thanks for God's intervention in saving both Barbara and the baby.

We talked quite a bit after that terrifying event. Often we *think* we are in control. We think we can plan our lives. We struggle over so many insignificant things, but we find ourselves asking, "What really matters?"

In the midst of these best and worst of times, a certain book reached us like a beacon in the darkness. It's a book that rips away the veil of idealism about life. It deals with purpose and significance. It gives meaning to life's storms, to prosperity, to our search for security.

The book? Ecclesiastes.

In its pages Solomon paints the paradoxes of life better than Charles Dickens ever dreamed. Whether we're experiencing the best or worst of times, God must be our reference point (see Eccles. 12:13, above). If not, then life is emptiness — void of meaning.

As I drove away from the hospital later that afternoon, I reflected on how different people respond to crisis situations. And I wondered, *What is their reference point for a life and death situation? Where do they find meaning? How do they make sense out of suffering?*

That night, as I put our five children to bed, we crowded together and prayed. Benjamin, then eight, prayed as only a child can: "Father, we give thanks that Mommy got sick 'cause we know You want us to give thanks in everything...and we give thanks that she's okay, too."

He prayed with childlike faith, and a mature perspective. He understood how God wants us to respond in the best *and* worst of times. Sometimes it takes a child's faith in God to remind us, doesn't it?

....

Discuss:
For what tribulations can you thank God today?

Pray:
That you would learn to fear God and that He would be your reference point in the best and worst of times.

ACCEPTING YOUR MATE UNCONDITIONALLY

There is no fear in love; but perfect love casts out fear.

1 JOHN 4:18

hy is unconditional acceptance so important? Because if you accept only in part, you can love only in part. And if you love in part, your mate's self-esteem will never be complete.

Remember, "Perfect love casts out fear." A powerful picture of how love casts out fear is found in the book *Welcome Home, Davey*. While serving aboard a gunboat in Vietnam, Dave Roever was holding a phosphorus grenade some six inches from his face when a sniper's bullet ignited the explosive. Here he describes the first time he saw his face after the explosion:

> When I looked in that mirror, I saw a monster, not a human being... My soul seemed to shrivel up and collapse in on itself, to be sucked into a black hole of despair. I was left with an indescribable and terrifying emptiness. I was alone in the way the souls in hell must feel alone.

Finally he came back to the States to meet with his young bride, Brenda. Just before she arrived, he watched a wife tell another burn victim that she wanted a divorce. Then Brenda walked in.

> Showing not the slightest tremor of horror or shock, she bent down and kissed me on what was left of my face. Then she looked me in my good eye, smiled, and said, "Welcome home, Davey! I love you." To understand what that meant to me you have to know that's what she called me when we were most intimate; she would whisper "Davey," over and over in my ear.... By using her term of endearment for me, she said, *You are my husband. You will always be my husband. You are still my man.*

That's what marriage is all about. Marriage is another person being committed enough to you to accept the real you. It means two people working together to heal their deepest wounds.

....

Discuss:
How has your self-esteem been strengthened by your mate's love?

Pray:
That you would have the ability to love your mate unconditionally and heal his or her deepest fears and wounds.

FATHERS AS SERVANT-LEADERS

For the husband is the head of the wife, as Christ also is the head of the church....Husbands, love your wives, just as Christ also loved the church and gave Himself up for her.

EPHESIANS 5:23,25

*O*ur culture has spent more than two decades redefining the roles of husband and wife. At one extreme is the Oklahoma newspaper headline that said: "State House Repeals Law Appointing Husbands as Head of Household." At the other extreme is the man who thinks being the head of the house means his wife must obey his every whim without question.

But the Scriptures clearly give us the model for being not only a man, but also a husband and father. I call that model the "servant-leader." According to this model, the husband and father is *to lead, to love* and *to serve.*

Webster's dictionary defines a leader as "someone who commands authority or influence, who shows the way, who guides or conducts, who directs and governs." God designed this position of responsibility, and the mantle of leadership comes along with it.

Flowing out of the responsibility to lead is the responsibility for husbands to *love their wives* — unconditionally. I can't help but wonder what must go through kids minds today as moms and dads have verbal slugfests. As leaders of the family, dads need, more than ever, to affirm their commitments to their wives and children.

Serving his wife rounds out the husband's and father's role. Some men cannot understand the biblical definition of a leader as a servant. Even though He was Lord, Jesus said, "the Son of Man did not come to be served, but to serve" (Matt. 20:28).

As your wife's servant, can you name her top three needs? What worries her? What circumstances quickly put her emotional gas tank on empty?

Men, let me challenge you *to lead, to love* and *to serve.*

....

Discuss:

As a father, rate yourself from one (highest) to five in all three categories: leading, loving and serving. See if you can answer the questions in the next to last paragraph.

Pray:

Men, pray that you will have the sensitivity to love and the humility to serve and lead your wives.

WHY YOU NEED ROMANCE

[Love] flashes fire, the very flame of Jehovah. Many waters cannot quench the flame of love, neither can the floods drown it.

SONG OF SOLOMON 8:6,7 (TLB)

There's a cynical one-liner that goes, "The period of engagement is like an exciting introduction to a dull book." And unfortunately, this is true for many couples.

What is it about marriage that seems to dull our romantic creativity? At some point in almost every marriage, a couple realizes that they just don't experience the same romantic feelings they once enjoyed.

Romance is not the foundation of a marriage. But it is the fire in the fireplace; the warmth and security of a relationship that says, "We may have struggles, but I love you, and everything is okay."

We need that fire in our marriages because we are emotional beings. While we cannot base marriage on romantic feelings, we also can't deny our needs for closeness and intimacy. Without these qualities in a relationship, a couple will drift into isolation.

Barbara and I have had some great romantic highlights in our years together: a fall foliage trip to New England on our tenth anniversary, a getaway at a cozy bed-and-breakfast inn, candlelight dinners at home after the kids were in bed (when they were younger)...I could go on and on.

For us, adventure has always spelled romance. And I wasn't surprised one time when I asked Barbara, "Out of all the adventures and romantic times we've had together, what has been your favorite?"

Her answer: "Our honeymoon." For us it was an all-time memory maker. I won't bore you with the details, but I took weeks to plan a two-week honeymoon in the Colorado Rockies. We went camping (and, to our surprise, got some snow) and stayed in a cabin next to a roaring river.

She loved our time together because it was an adventure with plenty of time for just the two of us to talk and share our thoughts and our dreams.

I'll wager that your marriage could use some romance.

. . . .

Discuss:
As you look back on your time together, what have been the romantic highlights? Do you think you have lost some of that romantic fire you once had? What can you do to fan the embers?

Pray:
Ask God to equip you to be the romantic partner your spouse needs you to be.

FOXES IN THE VINEYARD

Catch the foxes for us, the little foxes that are ruining the vineyards,
while our vineyards are in blossom.

SONG OF SOLOMON 2:15

In 1974, Barbara and I started having children—6 in 10 years. We discovered what Solomon calls the "little foxes": the thieves that will steal the fruit of love before it has a chance to be enjoyed. For Barbara and me, these "foxes" have included:

- Wrong priorities;
- Young kids who wear you out;
- Teenagers who won't go to bed;
- Financial pressures;

- Poor health;
- Crowded schedules;
- Unresolved conflict.

I think the most deadly fox, however, is *apathy.* If you truly are committed to making your marriage last for a lifetime, and enjoying the type of oneness God intends in a relationship, you need to make a choice to keep romance in your marriage.

If you want to put the spark of romance back into your marriage, I have two tips. First, *become a student of your mate.* Do you know that men and women view romance through different lenses? To confirm this, the next time you are in a Bible study or Sunday School class, divide the men and women into separate groups and ask them to answer the same question: What is something romantic that you would like your mate to do for you?

I'll guarantee you that the men's list will focus on physical intimacy: "Dress up in a sexy negligee" or "Meet me at the front door without any clothes on." The women, however, will say things like, "Take me to a romantic, candle-lit restaurant," "Spend time talking with me" or "Sit in front of a fire and cuddle." Men are motivated by sight and touch, while women want to develop a relationship.

Second, *take the time to plan some creative romance.* Do something different, out of the ordinary, something that will capture your mate's attention. Perhaps you need to take a weekend away, just the two of you. You'd be surprised how many couples have never done this since their honeymoons.

....

Discuss:
What is something romantic you'd like your mate to do for you?
Write down three things, then exchange lists with your mate.

Pray:
That God will give you a better understanding of what your spouse needs when it comes to romance, and the courage to act on that understanding.

"MEN OF THE TITANIC"

Let your fountain be blessed, and rejoice in the wife of your youth.

PROVERBS 5:18

Now I want you to know that for many years I've thought of myself as a pretty creative, romantic man. That was until I heard of Mark Montgomery and "The Men of the Titanic."

Mark, a pastor in Toledo, Ohio, put together a group of men who resolved to demonstrate that they love their wives sacrificially. They named themselves after the men who sacrificed their lives so their wives and children could board the lifeboats as that famous ocean liner sank back in 1912.

For six months, they planned the most incredible evening a woman could imagine:

- Made handwritten invitations, and sent limousines to pick up their wives.
- The women were escorted into a banquet hall decorated in nautical themes. A corsage was at each wife's place setting.
- The men took training on how to serve their wives the meal, which was an exact replica of the six-course meal that was served in the first-class dining room on the Titanic the night it sank.
- A ship's bell signaled the end of each course. Then men cleared the tables and sang love songs between each course.
- After the meal, one of the men stood up and announced that a letter had been found floating in the debris of the Titanic. It was now being read for the first time. Then he read a wonderful love letter of praise and affection from a man to his wife. At the end of the letter, he revealed that *he* had actually written the letter for his own wife. Then each man presented his wife with her own love letter.

When I interviewed Mark for the "FamilyLife Today" radio show, he said, "There was something sacred about the entire evening. It was a celebration that our wives were gifts from God to us."

Well now, men, how do you feel after reading that? Under the pile, like I did? Rekindling the romance in your marriage, however, doesn't require a lot of money, and it often doesn't take much time. What you do need is the commitment to do it.

Discuss:

God created romance for married couples to enjoy. How's the romance in your marriage? Share three things that communicate romance to you that your spouse could do for you.

Pray:

That you would be sensitive to your spouse's needs in developing a more intimate, romantic marriage.

WEAK ENOUGH FOR GRACE

by Barbara Rainey

My grace is sufficient for you, for power is perfected in weakness.

2 CORINTHIANS 12:9

In a previous devotion I describe the way God enabled me to accept His will when He decided to add a sixth child to our brood. Here I want to describe how I learned through that experience to be more tolerant of my humanity.

I discovered that I often want—and expect—instant maturity. I often forget that I'm only human, and that it's just that kind of human weakness that God's grace is designed for.

It's little wonder that in our humanity it can be hard to see God's will for our lives. His plan for us is much like a quilt. There is an overall pattern or design made up of hundreds of pieces. Since we lack God's overall perspective, it shouldn't surprise us to wonder what this or that dark-colored piece is doing in the quilt.

Sometimes the marriage relationship becomes one of those pieces whose place in the larger pattern is hard to see. Even the most intimate couples often find that it can take time to work out areas of disagreement. We should not expect less in our relationship with our heavenly Father. Becoming conformed to His will takes time; it's a process.

Yet, by faith I affirm that God is the Creative Designer of my life. He sees an award-winning masterpiece. With that trust, I can rely on His plan, knowing that His grace gives me time to conform to His will when the pieces I see are not of my choosing.

....

Discuss:

Talk about ways you've seen each other grow in the past five years. Then share what you think God is doing in your life today.

Pray:

For confidence in God, knowing the overall pattern of your life will give you rest to quiet the questions you have about individual pieces. Thank Him that He gives us grace that is greater than our struggles.

TUTORING YOUR MATE (WITH HIS PERMISSION)

by Barbara Rainey

It is not good for the man to be alone; I will make him a helper suitable for him.

GENESIS 2:18

As a couple, Dennis and I assist one another in many areas such as punctuality, patience with children, planning, feelings of discouragement, anger and worry. We have discovered our differences have made us more effective as a couple than we ever could have been individually.

One area in which I have assisted Dennis is in his public speaking. Early in our marriage, I noticed that he was making obvious grammatical errors as he spoke. I felt free to offer help because, on more than one occasion, I also told him honestly that he communicated well.

So, one evening after a speech, I asked Dennis if I could make a suggestion that might make him more effective as a speaker. He agreed to hear me out. Although my critique was a little threatening, he confessed that he had not done well in English in school, and he welcomed my suggestions.

Some months later, on the way home from another speaking opportunity, Dennis told me, "I still want you to help me with my speaking, but I'd like you to wait a little while before you tell me the cold, hard truth."

I realized then that my technique needed refinement. I had been too quick to tell him the "truth," and my "help" had become a discouragement because it wasn't seasoned with enough praise or separated long enough from the actual event. Had I not modified my recommendations, I would have crossed the fine line separating acceptance from rejection.

If your mate grants you permission to help him or her in an area of weakness, ask God for wisdom in *how* to help. Offer your assistance in such a way that your mate experiences your acceptance and in no way senses rejection.

Discuss:

What's the best way for your spouse to approach you when you need to be corrected or you need a little refinement? Talk about timing, location and style of communication.

Pray:

That God will give you wisdom in how to sensitively help your mate and that you will be able to hear one another.

THE PROBLEM WITH PRIDE

When pride comes, then comes dishonor, but with the humble is wisdom.

PROVERBS 11:2

Pride," said Soviet dissident Alexander Solzhenitzyn, "grows in the human heart like lard on a pig." Pride is one of the few things that can grow in the human heart without any sustenance. And although it seems to flourish more visibly in some people, all the human race suffers under its malignant grip.

Pride has many different faces. It can try to demand control: "I want it my way"; "I want to be my own god, run my own show and submit to no one."

It can be seen in the stubborn—what the Scriptures call "stiff-necked" or "hard of heart." And it is most easily detected in those who carry themselves in an arrogant manner. When I was a kid we used to call kids like this stuck-up, snooty, snobbish, conceited or cocky.

It was the well-known evangelist Dwight L. Moody who commented on how God deals with pride: "God sends no one away empty except those who are full of themselves."

Daily I attempt to put "self" to death and ask that Jesus Christ might have unhindered access to every area of my life. Then, as I am tempted to get angry because things didn't go my way, I'm reminded that to give in to pride is death.

So what is the way of humility? To know God, and to know who you are in relation to Him. Philip Brooks once said: "The true way to be humble is not to stoop until you are smaller than yourself, but to stand at your real height against some higher nature that will show you what the real smallness of your greatness is."

My pride wants to say, "I don't need God—I'm perfectly happy without Him." But what amazes me is that real happiness comes when I'm willing to humble myself and do what He wills with my life. The process may be painful, but it also brings real joy.

·····

Discuss:
In what areas of your life do you feel self-sufficient?

Pray:
That God would show you the joy that comes with humility.

GOD'S BLUEPRINTS FOR MARRIAGE

{Part One}

Unless the Lord builds the house, they labor in vain who build it.

PSALM 127:1

I was traveling in Southern California not long ago and stopped for a red light at an intersection around 6:30 A.M. There was an old restaurant at that corner and a crew was already at work, renovating and restoring it. Like little ants, the carpenters and other construction workers were moving about the building and almost every one of them had the same thing in his hand or under his arm: blueprints. It seemed that everywhere I looked somebody was referring to blueprints, holding them up and looking at what was going there and what would be going over here.

The light changed and I drove on, but that brief scene stuck in my mind. It teaches a simple truth. You don't start building or renovating without blueprints.

Many marriages today certainly need renovation. And to do it right, we need to go back to the original blueprints—the divine blueprints.

Earlier in this devotional we looked at God's purposes for marriage. Now I want to look at God's *plan* to accomplish these purposes.

I often meet Christian couples who have problems because they make a common mistake: As sincere Christians they believe they are automatically living their lives according to the correct plan. The trouble with that naive reasoning is that many different blueprints compete for their commitment.

Unfortunately, many Christian couples never stop to evaluate the blueprints they're working from. Many give into the temptation to just increase the speed at which they build. They rush through life getting married, rearing children and constructing what they believe are perfect buildings. But they find at the end that the plans they were building from were flawed. They had worked with a counterfeit instead of the real thing.

....

Discuss:

If someone asked you "What plan do you have for making your marriage work?" how would you answer? Are you both building your marriage and family from the same set of blueprints?

Pray:

That God would use the next few devotions to give you insight about His blueprints for marriage.

GOD'S BLUEPRINTS FOR MARRIAGE

{Part Two}

And the Lord God fashioned into a woman the rib which He had taken from the man, and brought her to the man.

GENESIS 2:22

To discover God's plan for marriage, let's return to Genesis 2. As we revisit the Garden of Eden, we watch the drama unfold. God makes Adam, but then says, "It isn't good for man to be alone; I will make a companion for him, a helper suited to his needs"(see v. 18). God causes a deep sleep to fall upon Adam. He takes one of his ribs and fashions it into the woman. There is a picture of completeness, and I also believe it's a picture of oneness because man and woman are made from the same material.

But now we have an all-important question: How would Adam receive Eve? The way many read the familiar Genesis account, Adam's response seems rather ho-hum: "This is now bone of my bones and flesh of my flesh; she shall be called Woman, because she was taken out of Man" (v. 23). But I like *The Living Bible* paraphrase: "This is it!" In other words, Adam was excited—he was beside himself!

Now, obviously, Eve looked pretty good to Adam. That's why he said, "This is bone of my bone and flesh of my flesh." She definitely looked better to him than all the animals he had just named, but there is a cornerstone principle for marriage here that we don't want to miss: *Adam had faith in God's integrity.*

Eve had done nothing to earn Adam's response. Adam knew only one thing about Eve—she was a gift from the God he knew intimately. Adam simply accepted her because God made her for him, and he knew that God could be trusted.

Today, God wants us to receive the spouse He has custom made for us. He can still be trusted.

To reject your mate is to reflect negatively on the character of God. It's as though you are saying, "God, You slipped up, You didn't know what You were doing when You provided this person for me." Rejection of your mate for weakness, or for any other reason, is disobedience toward God and failure to fulfill His plan and purpose for your life.

Will you receive your spouse as God's gift for you?

....

Discuss:
Is there anything about your mate that you don't accept? Are there areas in which you don't feel accepted by your mate?

Pray:
Thank God for His gift to you of your spouse.

GOD'S BLUEPRINTS FOR MARRIAGE

{Part Three}

For this cause a man shall leave his father and his mother,
and shall cleave to his wife; and they shall become one flesh. And the man and
his wife were both naked and were not ashamed.

GENESIS 2:24,25

The second part of God's plan for marriage involves construction. You may be noticing a parallel to the Christian life in these blueprints for marriage. First, you receive (accept) Christ, then you build a lifetime of obedient discipleship. After receiving your mate as God's gift (weaknesses and all), you build a lifetime of obedience as husband and wife.

Genesis 2:24 (above) presents four guidelines for building a strong and godly marriage. These are not multiple choice; all four are required for success.

1. *Leave*—that is, establish independence from parents or any others who may have reared you. It's amazing how many people have failed to do this. They may look very adult and act very mature and sophisticated, but deep down inside they've never really cut the apron strings.

There is a hidden command in this passage to parents: We should let our children leave. A manipulative parent can undermine a marriage whether it's 10 days or 10 years old. We are to let go of our children and let them go.

2. *Cleave*—that is, form a permanent bond. To cleave means commitment. When God joins two people together, it is for keeps. As the marriage vows say, "'Til death do us part."

3. *Be physically intimate*—that is, become one flesh in sexual intercourse. Notice the progression: leave, cleave and then one flesh. Physical intimacy comes after the walls of commitment have totally surrounded and secured the relationship.

4. *Become transparent*—emotionally intimate, totally open and unashamed with your mate. The Genesis account says Adam and Eve were "both naked and were not ashamed." They felt no fear or rejection. Instead they felt total acceptance by each other. Being bathed in the warmth of knowing another person accepts you is what makes marriage a true joy.

....

Discuss:

Evaluate and grade yourselves as a couple on the four components of building a marriage. Where are you winning? Where do you need to work?

Pray:

That God would give you success as a couple in each of these four areas of your relationship.

BELIEVING THE LIE

And do not be conformed to this world, but be transformed by the renewing of your mind, that you may prove what the will of God is, that which is good and acceptable and perfect.

ROMANS 12:2

I'll never forget my conversation with a friend I ran into at a fast-food restaurant. I knew he was seeing a marriage counselor, and I asked him how his marriage was going.

"Not too well," he told me. He said his wife was a constant nag. He had decided their relationship couldn't work, and he was going to get a divorce. Then he made the mistake of asking, "What do you think?"

"I think that's ridiculous," I replied. For several minutes I exhorted him to work at it, to not give up. "You can make this marriage work if you really want to," I said.

But he didn't want to be reminded of his responsibility as a Christian husband to his wife. "I just don't think that God ever intended for me to be this unhappy," he said.

To me, this was a perfect example of a person who was being conformed to the world rather than to God's perfect will. He claimed to be a Christian, but he had not allowed his mind to be transformed. As long as he cared only for his own happiness, he would move from one tragic relationship to another.

Another man, who had just seen his marriage resurrected after a divorce, heard about this conversation. He commented, "He's believing the lie. He thinks that the most important thing is to feel good. But what really feels good is working through the problems."

Discuss:

Have you found yourself believing the same lie that the most important thing in life is to be happy? Why does walking out appear to be much easier than working through problems with your spouse?

Pray:

That God would give you a joy in working through your struggles, and that He would not allow you to give up on your marriage relationship when you are not happy.

CHEMICAL REACTIONS

My son, give attention to my wisdom, incline your ear to my understanding;
that you may observe discretion.

PROVERBS 5:1,2

High school chemistry taught me a very valuable lesson: When certain substances come into close contact they can form a chemical reaction. I proved that one day during my senior year of high school when I dropped a jar full of pure sodium off a bridge into a river and nearly blew up the bridge. You'd think I would have at least had enough sense to step off the bridge!

What I've learned since then is that many people don't respect the laws of chemistry any more than I did back then. They mix volatile ingredients without giving much thought to the explosion that could occur. In particular, many married people don't understand that a chemical reaction can occur with people other than their mates. Don't misunderstand me here—I'm not just talking about sexual attraction. I'm referring to a reaction of two hearts, the chemistry of two souls.

This is emotional adultery—an intimacy with the opposite sex outside the marriage. Emotional adultery is unfaithfulness of the heart. When two people begin talking of intimate struggles, doubts or feelings, they may be sharing their souls in a way that God intended exclusively for the marriage relationship. Emotional adultery is friendship with the opposite sex that has progressed too far.

Often it begins as a casual relationship at work, school or even church. A husband talks with a female co-worker over coffee and shares some struggles he's facing with his wife or kids. She tells of similar problems, and soon the emotions ricochet so rapidly that their hearts ignite and can ultimately become fused together as one. To those who have experienced it, this catalytic "bonding" seems too real to deny.

You can take some steps to practice discretion in these matters. That's what I'll discuss in the next devotion.

....

Discuss:
In what situations can Christians find themselves committing
emotional adultery?

Pray:
That God will give you wisdom and discernment to know
when you might be risking a "chemical reaction."

AVOIDING EMOTIONAL ADULTERY

*Now to Him who is able to keep you from stumbling, and to make you
stand in the presence of His glory blameless with great joy.*

JUDE 24

It is far easier to commit emotional adultery than you may realize. You
may be converging on a chemical reaction with another person when:

- You've got a need you feel your mate isn't meeting—a need for attention,
  approval or affection, for example.
- You find it easier to unwind with someone other than your spouse by
  dissecting the day's difficulties over lunch, coffee or a ride home.
- You begin to talk about problems you are having with your spouse.
- You rationalize the propriety of this relationship with the opposite sex by
  saying that surely it must be God's will to talk so openly and honestly
  with a fellow Christian.
- You look forward to being with this person more than with your own mate.
- You hide the relationship from your mate.

When you find yourself connecting with another person as a substitute,
you've started traveling a road that ends too often in adultery and divorce. But
how do you protect yourself to keep this from occurring?

Know your boundaries. You should put fences around your heart that protect
sacred ground, reserved only for your spouse. Barbara and I are careful to share
our deepest feelings, needs and difficulties with each other, and not with friends
of the opposite sex.

Realize the power of your eyes. As has been said, your eyes are the windows to
your heart. Pull the shades down if you sense someone is pausing a little too long
in front of your windows.

Beware of isolation and concealment. One strategy of the enemy is to isolate you
from your spouse, especially by inducing you to keep secrets from your mate.

Extinguish chemical reactions that have already begun. A friendship with the opposite sex that meets the needs your mate should be meeting must be ended quickly. It may be a painful loss at first, but it isn't as painful as dealing with the
wreckage caused by a sinful relationship.

Discuss:
What barriers can you observe to avoid dangerous chemical reactions?

Pray:
Daily that God would "keep you from stumbling."

FEARING GOD

{Part One}

You shall fear the Lord your God; you shall serve Him and cling to Him, and you shall swear by His name. He is your praise and He is your God, who has done these great and awesome things for you which your eyes have seen.

DEUTERONOMY 10:20,21

One of the saddest commentaries on the state of Christianity in America is that some businessmen would prefer not to do business with a Christian. I know some of them. A friend of mine told me of a brother in Christ, a leader in an evangelical church, who, through unethical dealings, stole a deal worth about $75,000 from him. When confronted, the man registered no sense that he had breached any ethical conduct.

In another case, a nonbeliever quit his job and moved out of town because he no longer could work for an employer who worked on the edge of ethical boundaries. "And this guy says he's a born-again Christian!" he said.

Why is this? Why do so many Christians—businessmen or otherwise—slander the name of Christ by their actions? Because they have no fear of God.

The fear of God is reverential awe and respect for Him. It is a heart-felt conviction that He is not only loving and personal, but holy and just.

Proverbs 14:27 says, "The fear of the Lord is a fountain of life, turning a man from the snares of death" (*NIV*). Where there is no fear of God, there is no fear of divine punishment, of incurring divine wrath. I look at the headlines in our newspapers today and lament that our nation has lost its fear of God and divine punishment. I believe God is punishing us as a nation because we won't recognize and fear Him.

We are a people who have turned our backs on God. And change will only occur as each of us renews a holy fear of the God who gave us life. Come with me and learn the fear of God.

....

Discuss:
Do other people trust you? Do you honor the name of Christ
by the way you deal with people?

Pray:
That God would teach you to have a reverential fear of Him.

FEARING GOD

(Part Two)

And they shall be My people, and I will be their God; and I will give them one heart and one way, that they may fear Me always, for their own good, and for the good of their children after them. And I will make an everlasting covenant with them that I will not turn away from them, to do them good; and I will put the fear of Me in their hearts so that they will not turn away from Me.

JEREMIAH 32:38-40

Why do you think God wants us to fear Him? Perhaps because there are benefits to us for fearing Him.

Just look at the verse above. Here we see that God wants to do us good, and promises He will not turn away from us. But He also does not want us to turn away from Him. Let's look at a few reasons why:

First, *the fear of God is the fountain of life for the believer.* Proverbs 22:4 says the fear of God, along with humility, leads us to wealth and honor and life. And Psalm 111:10 says that it gives us skill in life and provides wisdom. A healthy respect and fear of God is the key to life.

Second, *the fear of God builds faithfulness in the believer.* That passage in Jeremiah tells me that the fear of God has been riveted into our souls by the Holy Spirit to keep us faithful. The true test of a man or woman is not what you do when everyone is looking. The real test of a man or woman is what you would do if you knew no one would find out.

Fearing God means I practice His presence in my life daily—nothing is hidden from Him. He sees everything. He knows everything. I can't hide in the darkness and sin. I can't sneak away from His all-seeing eyes or omnipotent mind. And, yes, that does keep me faithful.

Third, *God fulfills the desires of those who fear Him.* Psalm 145:19 says, "He will fulfill the desire of those who fear Him; He will also hear their cry and will save them." Fearing God doesn't just keep me from sin, it leads me out of trouble.

May God etch the fear of Him on my heart so that I may not turn away from Him.

....

Discuss:
What have you done (said or thought) recently that you knew no one else would find out about? How does it make you feel to know that the righteous God of the universe saw or heard you?

Pray:
Bow in prayer and confess any of those unseen and unheard thoughts, attitudes and actions now.

FEARING GOD

{Part Three}

The fear of the Lord leads to life, so that one may sleep satisfied, untouched by evil.

PROVERBS 19:23

The fear of God is the foundation for developing a godly character. I believe the leadership crisis we are facing today in America is really a crisis of character. There never has been a time in our history when we had perfect leaders. But the difference today is that many "leaders" deny there is anyone to whom they are accountable.

The result: Arrogance, being above the law and outright deceit all mark many of our political, civic and spiritual leaders. All of this is because men no longer fear God, and they are convinced they can get away with most anything. If we aren't accountable for our lives to God then why be accountable to our fellow man for our actions today?

Exodus 18:21 points out that fearing God *is a prerequisite for leadership*. Moses has been taking care of the children of Israel when Jethro, his father-in-law, says, "Moses, you are going to wear yourself out, and your family, too. You're going to wear the nation of Israel out" (see v. 18). From sunrise to bedtime, people were lined up to see Moses about civil disputes and leadership problems because Moses had the corner on truth. He was a candidate for dying of a heart attack.

So Jethro, in verse 21, gives Moses some advice that saves Moses' life: "Furthermore, you shall select out of all the people able men who fear God, men of truth, those who hate dishonest gain; and you shall place these over them, as leaders of thousands, of hundreds, of fifties and of tens."

Why did he prescribe leaders like that? You had to trust them. No bribes here. No compromise with darkness.

What would happen in Washington if our leaders there practiced the fear of God? What about the leaders in your church? And what about the leaders of your home?

We need to learn to fear God.

....

Discuss:
Are you being faithful in the small tasks God has appointed you over? Have you compromised lately?

Pray:
Ask God to help you and your mate be the God-fearing leaders of your home.

FEARING GOD

{Part Four}

Thou dost know when I sit down and when I rise up; Thou dost understand my thought from afar. Even before there is a word on my tongue, behold, O Lord, Thou dost know it all.

PSALM 139:2,4

*N*ow that I've told you all about the importance and benefits of fearing God, let me say a few words about how to develop that type of healthy fear. In a nutshell: Begin practicing the presence of God.

Bill Gothard says fearing God is "the conscious awareness that God is watching everything and evaluating everything I think, say and do." God sees all. He knows all. He's evaluating all.

Now that does one of two things in your heart right now. That either strikes incredible confidence: Yes, *Lord I'm a clean vessel. Thank You Lord that You, by Your grace, are making me whole. That You, by Your grace, are making me Christlike.*

Or it makes you feel very uncomfortable—guilty. You might be able to fool others, but you can't snow God. He knows what your attitude is, deep down inside you.

Have you ever noticed how people begin to obey the law when they spot a policeman driving down the freeway? Speed demons suddenly lose their heavy feet and spend a few miles driving at the speed limit—until the policeman is no longer in sight.

God is much bigger and has more authority than any policeman with a radar gun. He knows exactly what you're thinking right now, and whether Christianity for you is just a spare tire or an iron lung. He knows what your real values and attitudes are.

On one hand, God's divine authority and presence in my life is a terrifying thing. But it is also liberating. We are created, after all, for this moment-by-moment relationship with God. When you have a clean conscience, you are able to enjoy His love and freedom.

Remember, you're never alone. God is watching and waiting to spend time with you. Practice His presence moment by moment in your life.

....

Discuss:

Do you have a regular sense of being in God's presence? What would happen in your life tomorrow if you truly practiced the presence of God?

Pray:

That God would make Himself real to you and give you a divine sense that He is watching and waiting to spend time with you.

FEARING GOD

{Part Five}

I will give heed to the blameless way. When wilt Thou come to me? I will walk within my house in the integrity of my heart.

PSALM 101:2

*S*ome boys were tempting a young lad to pull a prank with them. The three young men taunted the other lad: "Come on, do this with us. Nobody will find out."

Finally, the boy mentioned his father. So they taunted him further. They said, "Oh, you're just afraid because if your father finds out he might hurt you!" And the boy looked back at the others and said, "No, I'm afraid if he finds out, it'll hurt him."

The more you fear God—the more you spend time in His presence—the more you dread displeasing Him. His presence in our lives shouldn't be a heavy yoke around our necks. But we need to have a healthy dread of displeasing or hurting or disappointing Him.

If you could stand before God today in His throne room and watch a video of your life with Him, would there be a smile on His face? Would He be nodding His head in approval, saying, "Well done, thou good and faithful servant?" Would you like to have the confidence right now that God is smiling? You can…by beginning to respect Him, to practice the presence of God daily and to make your choices on the basis of what pleases Him.

At any point of time during the day, I would like to be ready to be ushered into the presence of God and see a smile of approval on His face. I don't want Christianity to be a spare tire, fire insurance or something that is just there to bail me out of trouble. I want to walk with Jesus Christ moment by moment, yielded to the power of the Holy Spirit.

The fear of the Lord, then, should be a powerful, motivating factor in our lives. We shouldn't be legalistic about it—viewing God with a giant flyswatter in the sky, ready to crush us when we displease Him.

Let this new concept of a healthy fear of God refresh you. Let the presence of God refurbish you. Practicing Christ's presence in your life will set you free.

....

Discuss:
What will practicing the presence of God in your life liberate you to do?

Pray:
That your marriage would be characterized by the benefits of fearing God.

TESTING YOUR AUTHORITY

Foolishness is bound up in the heart of a child; the rod of discipline will remove it far from him.

PROVERBS 22:15

*M*ost people have seen the slogan in an office or on a bumper sticker: *Exactly what part of the word "no" don't you understand?*

Probably just like you, Barbara and I often get bombarded by our half-dozen banditos trying to persuade us to say yes when we've already said no. If they don't get their way the first time, they'll come back and try a second, third and even fourth pass. If they can't get us with their "superior logic" they'll just try to pester us until we're worn down emotionally.

What is there about the word "no" that they don't understand? Barbara and I have come up with a couple of answers.

First, *it's a child's nature to press issues, ignore, defy, rebel, challenge, resist or just flat out disobey.* Children will test you, and it's your responsibility to discipline him or her. Even the Minnesota Crime Commission, a secular group focusing on the reason for rising crime rates, published a startling description of a child that included these words: "Every baby starts life as a little savage. He is completely selfish and self-centered....All children...are born delinquents."

A second reason is that *we as parents have trained them that way.* It has been said that our kids are better students of us than we are of them. They can spot flaws and manipulate our weaknesses to their advantage. If they discover they can wear you down with their requests, they'll do it.

Perhaps what we need to do is to prayerfully pause and become a student of ourselves, asking whether we are strong parents or easily manipulated tools in this universal conspiracy of kids.

....

Discuss:
On what occasions do your children test your authority? What tactics do they usually employ? How do you typically respond when a child doesn't take "No" for an answer? How often do you lose your temper in the exchange?

Pray:
That God will strengthen you to say no when you need to, while communicating to your children that the word also means "I love you."

WHO IS YOUR ENEMY?

For our struggle is not against flesh and blood.

EPHESIANS 6:12

A lot of jokes picture marriage as a battlefield. *MS* magazine once advised: "Marriage is the only war where you sleep with the enemy." I would rather picture the entire world as the true battlefield and your marriage as being God's smallest battle formation for winning the war. In truth, your marriage is taking place on a spiritual battlefield, not a romantic balcony.

Every married couple needs to understand the following biblical principle:

Your mate is not your enemy.

Picture your marriage as two people joined together in a foxhole, cooperating in battle against a common enemy. Take a good look at your own foxhole. Are you fighting the enemy or each other? As a friend of ours told me, "I was so busy standing up in the foxhole duking it out with my husband that I had no time to be involved in fighting against the real enemy."

Keep in mind that whenever you declare war on your mate, ultimately you are opposing God Himself. You are rejecting the person He provided to complete you, to meet your needs.

Here's a practical test to discover if you view your mate as an enemy or as a fellow "soldier." Do you focus on the negative in your mate or on the positive? When you marry, you're so caught up in your new spouse that he or she can seem to do no wrong. But within 12,000 miles or 12 months, whichever comes first, you reverse the process. You are now so focused on what your mate does wrong that you are oblivious to what he or she does right!

I love Robert Lewis Stevenson's exhortation for us as we look at our spouses. He says, "Make the most of the best and the least of the worst."

....

Discuss:

Who is your real enemy? Think back to times when you have forgotten who your real enemy was—how did that impact your marriage and family? Do you treat your mate as a partner or as an enemy?

Pray:

That God would make you aware of the true battle and enemy you face each day, and how you need each other on that battlefield.

WHAT'S GROWING IN YOUR GARDEN?

{Part One}

Then the Lord passed by in front of him and proclaimed, "The Lord, the Lord God, compassionate and gracious, slow to anger, and abounding in lovingkindness and truth...yet He will by no means leave the guilty unpunished, visiting the iniquity of fathers on the children and on the grandchildren to the third and fourth generations."

EXODUS 34:6,7

*D*ag Hammerskjold, former Secretary-General of the United Nations, once said, "You cannot play with the animal in you without becoming wholly animal; play with falsehood without forfeiting your right to truth; play with cruelty without losing your sensitivity of mind. He who wants to keep his garden tidy doesn't reserve a plot for weeds."

Did you know that what you grow and cultivate in your garden today could spread to your offspring? Did you know that a sin you now tolerate could still be tormenting your great-grandchildren in the year 2140? That's four generations from now.

Consider the warning of Scripture at the top of this page. What does it mean? Why would God set up a system that visits one generation's sins on three or four other generations? I have a hunch that God is trying to tell us that the way we live impacts others and is of supreme importance to Him. Possibly He's using a warning of future judgment on our descendants to keep us on the straight and narrow today.

Whether you like it or not, your children are becoming just like you. Their little eyes are watching to see how you relate to your mate, how you pray, how you walk with Christ on a daily basis. They hear your words and subconsciously mimic your attitudes, actions and even your mannerisms.

And as time goes by you'll find that they've "inherited" some of the same tendencies towards sin that you learned from your own parents. That's why so many children from broken homes, for example, grow up and fail in their own marriages.

Your kids will grow up to be like you. Is that a sobering thought, or an encouraging one?

....

Discuss:
In what ways do you want your children to be like you?
In what ways do you not want them to be like you?

Pray:
Is there a sin that you've tolerated in your life that you need to go to God in prayer right now and confess? As you repent, you may want to ask God for grace to protect your children from that sin in the future.

WHAT'S GROWING IN YOUR GARDEN?

{Part Two}

*But showing lovingkindness to thousands, to those who
love Me and keep My commandments.*

DEUTERONOMY 5:10

'll be honest with you: The thought of my kids sinning in the same areas that I sin has bolstered my obedience to God. I'm reminded of the piercing statement by C. H. Spurgeon, "Sin would have fewer takers if its consequences occurred immediately."

Just think for a moment of the sins that could be visited upon your children. What do you struggle with? Lust? Selfishness? Anger? Lack of discipline? Jealousy? Pride? How about deceit? Broken promises? A gossiping tongue?

The twenty-first century could be a scary time to be alive. I wonder how the sins of adultery, divorce and addictions will affect future generations?

So what are we to do? Wallow in guilt because we are far from perfect? Are we enslaved to our ancestors' wrong choices and, thus, permanently under the punishment of God?

No, we can stop the chain reaction by our repentance and confession. God in His grace stands ready to forgive us and grant us favor. You can, by faith, stop even the most tyrannical control of a sin that has beset your family for generations.

The good news is that God also gives us a wonderful promise: Your righteousness can still be influencing others a thousand generations from now. That's encouraging!

One of our FamilyLife staff members is committed to breaking the chains from his past. When speaking to individuals considering vocational Christian ministry, he always says, "I grew up in a broken home and I don't want to end up like my father. He lived his life for himself, and at his funeral there were only 10 people in attendance. I want a packed funeral—full of people my life has impacted. I want to leave a heritage that would outlast me."

....

Discuss:
What type of faith would you like your children and grandchildren to have?

Pray:
Ask God to protect your life, marriage and family from sin. Ask Him to enable you to leave a legacy of righteousness to a thousand generations.

OPPOSITES ATTRACT —THEN REPEL

There is one who speaks rashly like the thrusts of a sword,
but the tongue of the wise brings healing.

PROVERBS 12:18

Quibbles. Quarrels. Squabbles. Conflicts in the home are as normal as breathing. Our aim shouldn't be to avoid conflict, but to handle it wisely. One reason people have conflict in marriage is that opposites attract. It's strange, but that is probably part of the reason why you married who you did. Your mate added variety, spice and difference to your life. But after being married for a while (sometimes a short while), the attractions become repellents.

A typical pairing is the peacemaker and the prizefighter. The peacemaker would rather hide than fight. The peacemaker says, "It's okay, let's forget it. It isn't worth the hassle." The prizefighter, meanwhile, says, "Let's put on the gloves and duke it out."

One husband came from a long line of prizefighters and grew up watching his whole family rolling up its sleeves and having spirited discussions. The beauty of it was that they could discuss issues, argue vehemently, and then hang up their gloves, hug and make up afterwards.

But his wife came from a long line of peacemakers who swept everything under the rug. They avoided confrontations like the plague. So what kind of a marriage did these two have? He was chasing her around trying to get her to put on the gloves, and she was searching for a place to hide.

Unfortunately, their daughter landed between them, trying desperately to bring her parents together. It took years of counseling to help her come to terms with the internal conflict she felt.

There's a lot at stake in the way you and your mate handle your conflicts. It's not just the intimacy in your marriage that's on the line, but the lives of impressionable sons and daughters as well. The African proverb is chillingly true: "When the elephants fight, it's the grass that suffers."

Discuss:
Are you aware of any opposite traits that attracted you and your mate to each other? Are the "prizefighter" and "peacemaker" (or other conflict management styles) apparent in your household?

Pray:
That the Prince of Peace will rule in your home.

"I NEVER REALLY KNEW HIM"

And fathers, do not provoke your children to anger; but bring them up in the discipline and instruction of the Lord.

EPHESIANS 6:4

D o you have any doubts about the importance of your role as a parent? Just read the following letter written by an associate of mine:

I can still picture my dad bouncing me on his knee, coaching me in Little League, showing me how to shine my shoes, helping me reel in my first fish and telling me stories about his early days as an undercover detective on the Berkeley, California, police force.

I can still hear him saying the words, "Son, I love you." I can imagine him messing my hair, wrestling with me on the living room floor and sharing a hot dog with me at a San Francisco Giants game.

I can still see him puffing up his chest when he talked about me to his friends. He was proud to be my dad. He would do anything for me. I was his son; he was my dad. I was a chip off the old block.

I can still see all of this and much more, but I don't see it in the reservoir of fond memories. Instead, I recall it from an imagination and yearning that wished then and wishes now that it were so. My dad left home when I was three. I never really knew him.

I'm 26 years old. I still miss my dad (even though that's hard to admit). I even cry sometimes when I'm honest with myself about how I feel.

Reading this poignant letter, I couldn't help reflecting on the number of children today who will replay a similar record in their minds. Not just those from broken homes, but those whose parents are absent in other ways.

....

Discuss:
How will your children remember you? Will they say you were involved in their lives—or were you physically or emotionally absent?

Pray:
That you will be able to make opportunities that create memories for your children that they don't have to manufacture.

MISSION FIELD
OR MISSIONARY?

And when I came to you, brethren, I did not come with superiority of speech or of wisdom, proclaiming to you the testimony of God. For I determined to know nothing among you except Jesus Christ, and Him crucified.

1 CORINTHIANS 2:1,2

*D*uring my first two years in college I was a mission field, and during the last two years I was a missionary. Let me explain.

Although I was a Christian during high school and early college, I believed Christ died only to save me from eternal condemnation, nothing more. As great a man as Jesus was, I had learned to treat Him simply as a spare tire. When a crisis arose, I'd pull Him out and ask for His help. Then, when it passed, He was once again relegated to the trunk.

In college I achieved almost every goal I'd set: honors and acceptance in the "in crowd," tangible achievements for all to see. Yet spiritually I felt on the bottom. My life was empty. Living had no purpose.

At the age of 20 I began to grapple with the truth about life. Then I met a Person who transformed my life from gray, dull, drab purposelessness into the Technicolor thrill of knowing, experiencing and following God.

Please note: I met a Person. I didn't learn a set of ancient precepts or a rigid collection of dogma. It wasn't law. It was love…the personified love of God manifested in the Person of Jesus Christ. That love softened a calloused, proud heart and caused it to repent. No longer did Christianity mean stale, boring rituals; instead, it was a refreshing relationship with Christ, and a knowledge of His appointed purpose for my life.

Since then I've sought daily to give my life to Jesus Christ and be used as He thinks best. That, my friend, is the greatest thrill imaginable.

John Wesley wrote: "Give me one hundred men who fear nothing but God, who hate nothing but sin, and who know nothing but Jesus Christ and Him crucified, and I will shake the world."

The world needs to be shaken. Christ the man, Christ the Savior, is Christ the revolutionary. Are you part of His revolution or are you in need of being revolutionized? Are you a mission field or a missionary?

....

Discuss:
Are you experiencing, avoiding or ignoring the love of God manifested through Christ Jesus? How does your life presently reflect your priorities?

Pray:
That the Person of Christ will take away all hesitancy and resistance to totally commit your life to Him.

HELP WANTED: COMPLEMENTARY WOMEN

by Barbara Rainey

Then the Lord God said, "It is not good for the man to be alone; I will make him a helper suitable for him."

GENESIS 2:18

ives have always found it difficult to live with what they want most: a husband. What we, as women, need perhaps more than ever, is a clear mental picture of our responsibilities as wives. The social changes brought about by the women's movement have been significant, but they have created a wake of grassroots confusion.

In the midst of our twentieth-century experience, God's design for husbands and wives still stands. And I believe that one clear scriptural part of a wife's role is *completing what is lacking in her husband*. In the words of Genesis, this involves being a helper that is "suitable" for him. Or, as the *King James Version* says, a help that is "meet" ("fit") for him. We are to *complement* or complete our husbands.

I love the story told about Pete Flaherty, mayor of Pittsburgh, and his wife, Nancy. They were standing on the sidewalk, surveying a city construction project, when one of the laborers at the site called out to them. "Nancy, remember me?" he asked. "We used to date in high school."

Later, Pete teased her. "Aren't you glad you married me? Just think, if you had married him, you would be the wife of a construction worker."

Nancy looked at him and said, "No, if I'd married him, he would be the mayor of Pittsburgh!"

God has designed women to help their husbands become all that God intends for them to be. As I fulfill my God-given purpose as helpmate to my husband, it helps build oneness between us. If I don't, it means tension, troubles and eventually, isolation.

....

Discuss:

In what ways do you feel your husband needs you?
Share 5 to 10 ways if you can.

Pray:

Ask God to weld you and your husband into partners who realistically understand one another's needs and gifts.

SIGNS OF THE TIMES

{Part One}

[Love] does not take into account a wrong suffered.

1 CORINTHIANS 13:5

*A*lthough most people get married partly to find intimacy, many couples soon begin to raise symbols of isolation. The "I do" at the wedding ceremony too often changes to "No, I won't," and the original openness toward intimacy is transformed into symbols and signs of isolation.

Here are a few signs I've observed in couples as they experience isolation:

"No Trespassing." Paul and Michelle have worked through several difficult problems during their 25-year marriage. They are considered by many to have a model marriage. But over the years they have become alienated from one another because of an unsatisfying sex life. Too proud to seek counsel, they find they can't discuss the subject anymore. They have declared that area off limits.

The ticking clock. Near retirement, Ben and Mary have raised their family and are proud of their new grandchildren. Their marriage of 35 years has withstood time, but silence has now crept into their relationship. They don't know how to talk to each other because for so many years they focused their lives on their children. Now any relationship they once had is replaced by silence, broken only by the occasional squeak of a rocking chair and the tick, tick, tick of a clock.

The crowded calendar. Steve and Angela are both aggressive professionals, actively involved in civic responsibilities and their church. But ever since they started their family, they've noticed a difference in their marriage. Gone are the walks and late-night talks they used to enjoy. They're too whipped—they now live for the weekends. Fatigue is taking its toll and neither has energy left over for romance.

....

Discuss:

How about prayerfully discussing an area that has been declared off limits with your mate? Pray first. Resist blame and defensiveness.

Pray:

Ask God to help you understand your spouse's perspective of the situation you're discussing. If you have no issues, give thanks to God that you don't!

SIGNS OF THE TIMES

{Part Two}

Be devoted to one another in brotherly love; give preference to one another in honor.

ROMANS 12:10

*A*s I said in the preceding devotion: When isolation appears in a marriage, it is symbolized by certain examples or signs. Here are a few more I've observed.

The locked door. Bill and Teresa have only been married for six months, but they have already hurt each other deeply. Their dreams and hopes of intimacy are already fading in the darkness behind locked doors where they have withdrawn. Bill was able to open up during the engagement, but now he finds it difficult to share his feelings. Teresa craves intimacy and desperately wants to be his partner in life. She can't get in, and he won't come out.

Excess baggage. Because both Bob and Jan came from broken homes, they were determined their marriage would be different. Although they have talked about their parents' divorces, neither has grasped the impact the breakups had on them. Without the model of a good marriage embedded in their minds, they are unaware of how much excess baggage they carry.

The TV dinner. Walter and Jeanne both work some distance from their suburban home, so when they arrive home they have fought rush-hour traffic after a long workday. They collapse in front of the television, eating TV dinners while watching the weekly sitcoms.

Their five-year marriage isn't in trouble, but later, after they start having children, she'll feel she's become a widow to a seasonal selection of football, baseball and basketball, not to mention his hobbies of golf, fishing and hunting. She's lonely. And he doesn't even know it.

....

Discuss:
Do any of the signs and symbols here or in the preceding devotional fit your lives? If so, how can you begin to lower these barriers? If not, talk about what you're doing right to protect your marriage from isolation.

Pray:
That you and your mate will guard and protect your relationship from isolation.

COLLECTING THE RIGHT STUFF

Instruct them to do good, to be rich in good works, to be generous and ready to share.

1 TIMOTHY 6:18

The world has seen some strange collections. Is there something innately a part of our human nature that causes us to want to collect stuff? People collect all kinds of interesting things: oil paintings, sculptures, political campaign buttons, guns, stamps, coins.

Francis Johnson of Darwin, Minnesota, has collected string since 1950. When I read about him, his ball of string measured over 10 feet in diameter and weighed five tons.

I once met a man in Dallas who had collected more than 4,000 hotel keys. (He told me of another collector who had made off with more than 10,000.)

But perhaps the prize for the most unusual collection goes to Italian dentist Giovanni Battista Orsenigo, who by 1903 had a collection of 2,000,744 teeth. How would you like to have been one of his patients? Would it be reassuring to know that your teeth would be stored up for posterity?

In Isaiah 39, the prophet speaks to unfaithful Hebrew kings who had stored up the wealth of nations they had conquered. Great storehouses of gold and silver objects, expensive garments, fine armor and objects of art were a sign of power some kings thought would last forever. Unfortunately, these collections wound up in the hands of their enemies.

In contrast, 1 Timothy 6:18 tells us to "be rich in good works." That's the only type of collection that lasts—the type you give away. Think of Dorcas, whose collection of garments she made for the poor not only became treasure in heaven, but whose story has lasted so long it's become the heritage of millions (see Acts 9:36-43).

What kind of collection are you acquiring?

....

Discuss:

Why do we typically tend to collect "things" and not deeds? Why is the collection Paul refers to more lasting? Is there a collection of deeds you need to start today in your church?

Pray:

That God will help you collect good deeds, and thank Him for His way of enabling us to store up for the future.

FAMOUS LAST WORDS

It is better to go to a house of mourning than to go to a house of feasting, because that is the end of every man, and the living takes it to heart.

Ecclesiastes 7:2

While some people collect things like baseball cards, matchbooks and menus, I have to confess I have a small and strange collection of my own: "exit lines"—the final utterances of the dying.

My collection of quotes is not as morbid as you may think. They not only tell you how a man died, but they hint at how he lived. These last words are the bookend of the legacy a person leaves.

Author Henry David Thoreau was known as an irreverent and arrogant individualist. Shortly before he died, his aunt asked him if he'd made his peace with God. Thoreau responded, "I didn't know we'd ever quarreled."

Contrast Thoreau's cynicism with the inspiring last words of the great evangelist D. L. Moody. He was reported to have turned to his sons by his bedside and said, "If God be your partner, make your plans large."

Some last lines are ominous whispers of a feared fate. Others shout the confident message: "This isn't it! Death is not the end." Ponder the contrast in these famous last words:

Bring down the curtain—the farce is over.—Francois Rabelais, sixteenth-century French philosopher and comic

Our God is the God from whom cometh salvation. God is the Lord by whom we escape death.—Martin Luther

I am abandoned by God and man! I shall go to hell! O Christ, O Jesus Christ!—Voltaire

I enjoy heaven already in my soul. My prayers are all converted into praises.—Augustus Toplady, author of the great hymn "Rock of Ages"

I am convinced that there is no hope.—Winston Churchill, whose vision and battle cry in life was to "never give up."

I have pain—but I have peace, I have peace.—Richard Baxter, seventeenth-century Puritan theologian

What will be your final words? How do you want to be remembered? How is your life today an investment in the legacy you leave?

....

Discuss:
What would you like to have engraved on your tombstone?
What would you like your last words to be?

Pray:
That your daily life will be a living testimony to the way you hope to die.

MARRIAGE IS A THREE-LEGGED RACE

Do two men walk together unless they have made an appointment?

AMOS 3:3

Among my favorite childhood memories are the picnics our family held every summer. I played all kinds of games with my cousins, including the three-legged race, which was everyone's favorite.

To make the game more interesting, partners were often tied together so one faced backward and the other forward. The starter gave the signal, and what happened next would best be described as chaos. Everyone would cheer as the forward-facing participants would half drag, half carry their backward-facing teammates toward the finish line. There were always plenty of grass-stained knees, piercing screams and roars of laughter.

The three-legged race is hard enough when everyone is facing the same direction. The teams can lock arms and step out in unison. They might stumble and fall along the way, but they always get there much faster and more efficiently.

A marriage is a lot like the three-legged race. A husband and wife can face in the same direction and try to run in step with each other, or they can run in totally different directions. I've counseled couples where the wives were headed south at 65 miles an hour and the husbands were going north at 90 miles per hour! When that happens, it means pain, difficulty and isolation.

One woman said, "My husband and I have been married for 20 years. There is nothing he wouldn't do for me and there is nothing I wouldn't do for him...and that's exactly what we do for each other—nothing."

One reason many couples face different directions in the race is they have bought into the illusion fostered by the popular culture's claim that we can live independently of each other. A healthy marriage requires two people who agree to become mutually dependent on each other.

When was the last time you and your spouse sat down and talked about the race you're running and the direction you're facing? It could explain why there's been some pain recently.

....

Discuss:
Do you sometimes feel you and your mate are not always moving in the same direction? In what ways? Be specific.

Pray:
That God will show you, as a couple, the race He wants you to run, the direction He wants you to face and the pace for the race.

THE "ONE FLESH" CHALLENGE

by Barbara Rainey

And the two shall become one flesh.

EPHESIANS 5:31

As a wife, I believe the Bible calls me to commit to my husband in a mutually fulfilling sexual relationship—to truly become "one flesh" with my husband. That means I need to understand his needs and desires in this area. My husband's sexual needs should be more important and higher on my priority list than menus, housework, projects, activities—even the children. A friend shared something with me that I think puts the sexual dimension of a man in a biblical perspective. A man can send his clothes to the laundry, eat all of his meals out, find companionship with friends, be accepted and respected at work, be listened to by a counselor and in all those things not go against the will of God. But if he meets his sexual needs with someone other than his wife, it is sin.

I believe that many wives don't really understand how important the act of "becoming one" is to our husbands. We make time for the PTA, church work and helping a child with homework. Think about it: How often do you set aside time to be together? It may be a weekend getaway or a romantic dinner in your bedroom.

Perhaps one of the most "spiritual" acts a wife might need to do is put the kids to bed and invite her husband to go to bed early.

Discuss:

At an appropriate time, ask your husband to share his needs in this area. You might want to share what would create sexual fulfillment in your marriage.

Pray:

Ask God to help you both better understand one another's needs and how you can act to meet them on a regular basis.

THE LIFELINE OF CONNECTION

*You shall rise up before the grayheaded, and honor the aged, and you shall
revere your God; I am the Lord.*

LEVITICUS 19:32

*J*ack Turpin of Dallas, Texas, is a busy man, but not too busy for his grandchildren. Several times a year he picks up some of his grandchildren who
live in the Dallas area for what he calls "Grandpa Day." Starting at 7:00
A.M., they go to a traditional spot for breakfast and then to his office. There he
has a closet filled with games and books that the grandkids enjoy. After the trip
to the office, they go to the sanctuary of their church and sit. They have lunch
and then return home.

A few years ago, when one of his daughters became ill, Jack had "Grandpa
Camp" for four days. Jack is purposely involved in his grandchildren's lives.

Let me ask you: Why are so many old people bored? Why are many of the
elderly under-challenged? What keeps them going as they approach the end of
life? Why do so many waste so much time chasing little white balls around a golf
course?

I believe one key reason is that many grandparents are not like Jack Turpin.
They are isolated from their families and are not involved in passing on a legacy.

Something tells me the problem in many cases may be their relationships
with their adult children. If you were to say to me, "I wish my parents would
start making time to be grandparents" I would ask, "How much time are you
spending with your parents?" Or, "Are you pursuing a relationship with them?"
Perhaps if we value the older generation by honoring our parents, they will
value the younger generation by getting involved in their grandchildren's lives.

Do your parents feel close to you? Do they feel loved, appreciated and needed? And if they are needed, is it for something other than just baby-sitting? If
they did, perhaps they would make the effort to be involved.

God gives grandparents a special role in a child's life. A child may learn some
character qualities more from his grandparents than from his parents. That's the
type of vision I'd like to give grandparents—helping to build another generation. And you can help make it possible by maintaining that connection.

....

Discuss:
How involved are your parents with your children? What steps can you take
to help strengthen that connection?

Pray:
For your children to experience a great relationship with their grandparents.

SLAYING THE PHANTOM

{Part One}

But godliness actually is a means of great gain, when accompanied by contentment.

1 TIMOTHY 6:6

uring World War II the American forces in France had a phantom military outfit—a group called the Twenty-third Headquarters Special Troops. With careful staging and show-business theatrics, they impersonated real troops and created an illusion of military strength to strategically fool the Germans. For example, to mask the true location of their real troops, they created fake tanks and other equipment that looked real from the air.

Many husbands and wives have such phantoms lurking in their minds—an unreal mental image that they think they need to battle. No one else can see these phantoms except the individuals who conjure them up, but they seem real nevertheless.

Phantoms are an unattainable standard by which we measure our performances, abilities, looks and characters. While there's nothing wrong with having a goal to aim for, a phantom by definition is an illusion, an apparition or a resemblance of reality.

Within your mind you have a picture of how you should act as a husband or wife, father or mother. And chances are this image is so perfect, so idyllic, that it is completely unattainable. Yet, every day you judge your performance by this phantom! And since you cannot match those standards, your self-esteem suffers.

The more distant your phantoms are from reality, the more frustrating it is to live in their shadows—and the more confusing it can be for the spouse who can't see the apparition and is left wondering why his or her mate seems always dissatisfied and unhappy. Phantoms can derail marriages.

In the next two devotions, I'll share the phantoms Barbara and I have in our minds.

Discuss:

Do you have unrealistic expectations of yourself? Are you aware of your mate having such a "phantom"? What's the difference between healthy goals for personal growth and an illusion or unattainable self-image?

Pray:

That God will enable you to be happy with the person He made you, and to find a balance between who you are and personal goals for growth.

SLAYING THE PHANTOM

(Part Two)

Charm is deceitful and beauty is vain, but a woman who fears the Lord, she shall be praised.
PROVERBS 31:30

Barbara sat down one day and described her phantom—what she felt she was expected to be as a wife and mother. Here is a portion of what she wrote:

- She is always loving, patient, understanding and kind.
- She is well organized, with a perfect balance between being disciplined and flexible.
- Her house is always neat and well decorated, and her children obey the first time, every time.
- She is serious yet lighthearted, submissive but not passive. She is energetic and never tired.
- She looks fresh and attractive at all times, whether in jeans and a sweater digging in the garden or in a silk dress and heels going to dinner.
- She never gets sick, lonely or discouraged.
- She walks with God daily, prays regularly, studies the Bible diligently, and is not fearful or inhibited about telling others about her faith.
- She "prays without ceasing." She prays over flat tires, lost keys and lost teddy bears. She "gives thanks" when her husband is late for dinner.

Remember that phantoms are illusions. Only we don't recognize them as such.

Again, having such goals may spur you to doing better and being better. But when they become illusory expectations, you become insecure and wonder if your mate accepts "the real you." You may feel like a loser when your mate may actually consider you a winner.

....

Discuss:
Sit down and write out your personal version of the "phantom." (You'll share your phantom with your spouse in the next session.)

Pray:
Close your time together by praying that God will enable you and your spouse to balance contentment with a desire to grow and change.

SLAYING THE PHANTOM

{Part Three}

My flesh and my heart may fail, but God is the strength of my heart and my portion forever.
PSALM 73:26 (NIV)

My own phantom is just as lofty and unattainable as Barbara's:

- He rises early, has a quiet time reading the Bible and praying, then jogs several seven-minute miles.
- After breakfast with his family, he presents a 15-minute devotional.
- Never forgetting to hug and kiss his wife good-bye, he arrives at work 10 minutes early.
- He is consistently patient with his coworkers, always content with his job. His desk is never cluttered, and he is confidently in control.
- He arrives home on time every day and never turns down his kids when they want to play.
- He is well read in world events, politics and important social issues.
- He never gets discouraged, never wants to quit and always has the right words for any circumstances.
- He constantly plans romantic outings for his wife and himself.
- He can quote large sections of Scripture in a single bound, has faith more powerful than a locomotive and is faster than a speeding bullet when solving family conflicts.

Ultimately these phantoms put us under a crushing pile of guilt. And here's where the marriage relationship can really help. Sit down with your mate and spend some time describing your own phantoms. Ask your mate where these expectations came from. Talk about which of these expectations are realistic and which are not.

....

Discuss:
Make up a new list of goals for yourself. Make them realistic and attainable.
Then evaluate them with your mate.

Pray:
That God will use you to encourage one another and
build into each other's lives.

THE CASE FOR TENDER MEN

And be kind to one another, tender-hearted.

EPHESIANS 4:32

wonder how many men look at this passage and think, *That doesn't apply to me.* From an early age, many men are taught not to cry, not to show feelings, not to be tender towards their wives and children.

There is a real need in our nation right now for men to be fathers who love and lead their families—who are not afraid to be tender.

I heard of a young woman whose story illustrates the point. Desperate to reach out to her unfeeling father, she got herself arrested for shoplifting. That didn't work, so she decided to stop eating. She developed anorexia and, later, a brain tumor that the doctors said was caused in part by her undernourished condition.

"I was lying in my hospital bed near death with all kinds of tubes coming out of my body when my father finally came to see me," the woman recalled. "We talked for about an hour, then he got up to leave. As he opened my hospital door, I guess I just went berserk. I began to scream, 'You just can't say it, can you?' She screamed even louder, "I'm going to die and you still can't say it!"

Her father said, "Say what?"

"I love you," she said.

He finally broke down and began to weep. He moved to her bedside and through his tears said those words the young woman needed to hear so desperately.

Fathers need to be tender. Their hearts need to be knitted to their children's souls. Real men can be gentle men.

Discuss:
When was the last time you told your children you loved them? Your wife?
Ask your spouse what tender love for a child looks like from her perspective.

Pray:
Ask God to develop your heart so you will be able to communicate the tender side of love to your wife and children.

IS THERE A MAN IN THE HOUSE?

God deals with you as with sons; for what son is there whom his father does not discipline? For they disciplined us for a short time as seemed best to them.

HEBREWS 12:7,10

Our nation's families face a desperate situation. Sixty percent of all the children born in your community today will spend at least part of the first 18 years of life without a father in their lives. And too many men who remain with their families are passive, disengaged, uninvolved.

As a result, many young men do not know what it means to be a man. They experience neither a father's discipline nor his tender care and nurture. They have no role model of what a real man does, how he acts and how he relates to the opposite sex.

Frankly, those of us in the Christian community are partly to blame. We have the truth, but we've been far too quiet. We haven't equipped men or women to understand how God designed the sexes to function and complete one another. We've not countered the feminists who have completely redefined the role of women, and emasculated men in the process.

Without being simplistic, let me recommend three things you can do. First, *pray.* As a father, pray for yourself, that you will be a real man in the biblical sense—a man who humbly and sacrificially leads and loves your family.

Second, *shape your own definition and conviction of what a real man is.* And third, *provide your sons and daughters with a clear understanding of sexual identity.* This is more than sex education. We need to train our children about the responsibilities of men and women and how they are to relate to one another.

Talk to your sons and daughters about what being a man means. Help your sons become men who honor their commitments, persevere and serve their families. Help your daughters understand what a real man is and what they should expect from him. Our youth need someone to tell them what a real man is and what he does.

Discuss:
As a man, in what areas do you need to grow?
How can your wife help you in this?

Pray:
That God will help you as husband and wife to understand manhood as God would have it, and communicate this to your children.

THE TROUBLE WITH THE "50/50 PLAN"

*But God demonstrates His own love toward us, in that while
we were yet sinners, Christ died for us.*

ROMANS 5:8

When two people get married, they have expectations of how the relationship should work. Often, the unspoken assumption is that "My spouse will meet me halfway." Sometimes it's called "The 50/50 Plan." When the husband and wife operate on this pattern, it's easy for it to spread to other members of the family.

The "50/50 Plan" says, "You do your part, and I'll do mine." This concept sounds logical, but families who use it are destined for disappointment.

Among the problems with "The 50/50 Plan" is that giving is based on merit and performance. We focus more on what the other person is giving than on what we are doing. Love is withheld until the other person meets our expectations. Since this way of measuring out our love is subjective, the motivation for our actions is based merely on how we feel.

It's impossible to ever know if a person has ever met you halfway. As Thomas Fuller said, "Each horse thinks his pack is heaviest."

Early in our marriage we tried this plan. I would give affection to Barbara only when I felt she had earned it by keeping the house running smoothly. Barbara would show me affection and praise only when I would hold up my end by getting home on time, keeping the house in a reasonable state of repair, or working in her garden.

Contrast this with the type of love God shows for us. You might say that, no matter what we do, He gives us 100 percent. As Romans 5:8 shows, He gives us love even when we don't deserve it.

I propose that couples adopt "The 100/100 Plan" in marriage. Under this plan, each person gives 100 percent no matter what the other person does.

．．．．．．．．．．．．．．．．．．．．．．．．．．．．．．

Discuss:
As you look at your marriage, do you think you've been operating according to "The 50/50 Plan"? Write down some specific ways.

Pray:
That God's spirit of unmerited giving will permeate the heart of each member of your family.

GIVE THANKS...
IN *EVERYTHING*?

In everything give thanks; for this is God's will for you in Christ Jesus.

1 THESSALONIANS 5:18

In 1993, our family was at the FamilyLife Parenting Conference in Dallas when we realized something was seriously wrong with our son's leg. Samuel, then 16, was our most athletic offspring. As a kid he never walked anywhere—he would sprint to the car, slide around corners in the house, jump to touch the top of every door facing, imitating Michael Jordan doing a slam dunk.

But there in Dallas, Samuel couldn't keep up as we raced through the airport to catch our plane. Later, the neurologist gave us the news: Samuel had muscular dystrophy (MD).

Since then, the reality of Samuel's physical limitations has descended on us in daily installments: falls down the stairs, jars of jam he couldn't open, braces on his legs, the painful time he tried without success to water-ski like his sisters and brother.

Frankly, I am still learning how to "give thanks" in all this. I know the passage doesn't mean that we must give thanks specifically for Samuel's MD, as though God sent it. But since God has all authority in heaven and in earth, He did allow it to happen. So we are trying to learn to be thankful in the situation over which God is sovereign.

Samuel himself has helped. Only a few hours after the doctor's diagnosis, we realized the disease had not robbed Samuel of his great sense of humor. He responded to the announcement with a big grin, and said, "Hey—this means I'll always get to park in the handicapped space!"

I think this is more than just cracking a joke to conceal pain. It indicates the way God is enabling our whole family to live through a family tragedy against all odds. Sometimes I find myself giving thanks merely out of obedience and faith, reminding me that faith isn't just a feeling.

And what is the Christian life about if it's not growing in faith and obedience? Giving "thanks in all things" is a test of faith.

....

Discuss:
What events in your own family have tested your faith? Did these events eventually spur certain areas of growth or other blessings for which you can now give thanks?

Pray:
That God will put a smile on your lips and joy in your heart despite circumstances that may test your faith.

A BASEMENT FULL OF FEARS

There is no fear in love; but perfect love casts out fear.

1 JOHN 4:18

I don't remember when my brother told me about "the creature," but I can recall as a little tyke standing at the top of the stairs looking down into the deep darkness of our basement. It was a dark, damp and dingy kind of place. Of course, I didn't know it but my brother pulled a trick on me when he told me about the most grisly, meanest bogeyman you've ever seen.

On occasion, my mom would send me downstairs to get some canned green beans or some potatoes she stored in our basement. You've never seen a kid run so fast. I'd set a world record going down and up those stairs. Although I never saw that bogeyman, I heard him frequently. And it scared the daylights out of me. In fact, to this day, when I stand at the top of those same stairs, I still feel a leftover trace of that same fear.

Are there any bogeymen in your life? You may couch it in terms like "I'm concerned about this," or "I've been thinking about this a lot." But anyway you slice it, most of us are fearful. We're fearful about the future, about where our lives our going. We're even fearful of God's will.

Hate is not the opposite of love, fear is. As 1 John 4:18 says, "perfect love casts out fear." To be secure in God's love and protection of us, we must have faith. And we can't manufacture spiritual fruit ourselves. Sheer effort alone does not make good fruit grow. Zechariah 4:6 says, "'Not by might nor by power, but by My Spirit,' says the Lord of hosts." As God's Spirit works in us and through us to develop this fruit, He will take away our fear and fill us with His love.

....

Discuss:
What are your top three fears in life right now? Share them with one another and talk about why you are afraid in each of these areas. When you pray, pray for your spouse to be delivered from all his or her fears.

Pray:
Ask God to begin removing fears in your life by filling you with His love and with His Spirit.

THE TOP FIVE FEARS LIST

The fear of man brings a snare, but he who trusts in the Lord will be exalted.

PROVERBS 29:25

A college professor did a survey of two thousand students and asked them what their greatest fears were. Here is the list of their top five fears:

1. Public speaking;
2. Blindness;
3. Heights;
4. Heart attack or cancer;
5. Death.

Fear is a snare. A trap. It can cause us to become paralyzed and discouraged. It intimidates us and causes us to feel inferior to others and to our circumstances. I believe fear operates like a magnifying glass, making seemingly small objects and circumstances seem giant and insurmountable.

Today, I believe too many Christians suffer from what I call the "What If Syndrome." Like a dog chasing its tail, they don't make any decisions because they continually worry "What if...?" This is exactly how the devil wants you to think.

You see, if Satan can get fear to line the interior of your soul, it becomes like a impenetrable coating that causes you to take your focus off God. Satan will do all he can to keep us from yielding our lives to God and experiencing His peace and love. First Peter 5:8 tells us, "Be of sober spirit, be on the alert. Your adversary, the devil, prowls about like a roaring lion, seeking someone to devour." He is trying to use the snare of fear to devour us!

But God's Word says, "He who trusts in the Lord will be exalted." And although Satan may win a few battles on this earth, the victory is God's in the end.

Fear is the emotional pain in the soul of unbelief. When we feel fearful, it is God's warning light to us that we need to respond with faith; fear and faith cannot exist in the same spot simultaneously.

....

Discuss:
Look at your list of fears you wrote yesterday. How are those fears causing you to take your focus off God?

Pray:
That God would fill your heart with faith so you have the ability to trust Him in fearful circumstances.

GOOD FEARS

"Do not be afraid; for God has come in order to test you, and in order that the fear of Him may remain with you, so that you may not sin."

EXODUS 20:20

ormer President Franklin D. Roosevelt was close to being right when he said, "There is nothing to fear but fear itself!" What Roosevelt didn't mention was there are actually two *good* kinds of fear.

The first good kind of fear is the fear of God or a reverential awe of God. The Bible speaks a lot about this fear in Proverbs 1:7 when it says, "The fear of the Lord is the beginning of knowledge." As we fear God, we begin to realize that not only does this fear help us honor Him and keep us from sinning, but also that God is our fortress and our stronghold and we can trust Him.

The second kind of fear is the raw fear of self-preservation. This fear can be good or it can be unhealthy, depending on whether you are facing a *real* danger or just one that you *perceive*. When confronted with real danger, this fear can save your life!

I experienced this fear while trying to unhook a fishing lure that got hung up across a stream in the Rocky Mountains. I looked down the path and spotted a rattlesnake as big as your arm in front of me. In that moment, I felt stark terror, and I turned and ran.

Perceived dangers, however, can provoke the same kind of terror. And these, unfortunately, cause fear more often than real danger. I'll never forget when my son Benjamin was about three, and he woke up screaming. Standing up in his bed, his eyes looking like half-dollars, he cried out, "Daddy, there's tigers everywhere!" So I pulled out my imaginary gun and shot all the tigers. "There, son, they're gone," I said. That calmed him down and he fell asleep again.

As adults, we can be just like my son Benjamin—we perceive something as real, when it isn't. When we live our lives as though the mythical "tigers" are real, we waste emotional energy that can be used in living life purposely and serving others sacrificially.

....

Discuss:
Talk about any real dangers or "tigers" (perceived fears) that are present in your life right now.

Pray:
Ask the Lord to help you fear Him and to recognize when you are acting fearful because of perceived danger rather than real danger.

YIELDING TO GOD

Be anxious for nothing, but in everything by prayer and supplication with thanksgiving let your requests be made known to God. And the peace of God, which surpasses all comprehension, shall guard your hearts and your minds in Christ Jesus.

PHILIPPIANS 4:6,7

*D*id you know that the Scriptures include the words "Fear not" hundreds of times. Isaiah 35:4, for example, reads, "Say to those with anxious heart, 'Take courage, fear not.'"

When we become fearful, we first feel an overwhelming need for protection. Many people build tornado shelters, install fire alarms, buy bigger locks for their doors and purchase thousands of dollars of insurance for traveling. Yet, they are still fearful and want more protection from what "could happen."

Second, we tend to procrastinate and put off decisions we know we should make. Some people actually have a hard time going shopping because they fear they'll make the wrong choices.

Third, we find ourselves erecting barriers to keep others from knowing us. Many people are so afraid of rejection in their relationships that they will risk very little.

Fourth, we become obsessed with failing. This is common with anyone who has ever been fired from a job. Still others who actually do succeed, fear they'll lose it all!

Finally, this fear drives us away from God. Some people are afraid of God and His will for their lives. Yet, the best antidote to fear is praying and yielding our lives to God. Notice what Paul says in Philippians 4:6,7 about fear and worry.

How many things are you to worry about? Nothing. Zero. Instead, you should pray about "everything."

But look at the condition "with thanksgiving let your requests be made known to God." God is not just a personal slot machine in which we inject our prayers. He wants you to approach Him with an attitude of gratefulness for what He has done and for who He is.

As we pray and yield our lives to God, He will not allow fear to control us, but He will protect our hearts.

....

Discuss:
How are your fears affecting you? How are they driving you away from God? How could you apply the truth from Philippians 4:6,7 in your life right now?

Pray:
For one another that God would guard your hearts with His peace as you yield your lives to Him.

TOUGHER THAN AN ALLIGATOR

by Barbara Rainey

Greater love has no one than this, that one lay down his life for his friends.

JOHN 15:13

Most parents will do anything they can to protect and provide for their children. A story reported of a family in Florida provides a good illustration.

Four children were swimming in a pond when a huge alligator began swimming toward them. A nearby neighbor began to scream, and three of the children escaped. But one boy was snorkeling and could not hear the warning.

The 11-foot, 400-pound alligator opened its jaws and fastened them partially on the boy's head. Miraculously, the snorkel mask became wedged in the alligator's mouth and prevented him from snapping his jaws shut. Wrenching free, the boy started swimming frantically toward shore.

Meanwhile, his mother heard the screaming and ran to the edge of the pond, urging her son on. The alligator was gaining on the boy when the mother waded out into the water and reached out to her son. She grabbed his arms just as the alligator grabbed his feet.

A grim tug-of-war began, with the mother holding her boy's arms in a death grip and pulling with superhuman strength. Finally, she literally tore her son out of the alligator's jaws and pulled him to shore and safety.

Several weeks later, the mother and her son were walking along the shore of the lake and came to the spot where that incredible tug-of-war had taken place. She looked down and noticed that the bad cut under her son's chin was almost healed. His leg, broken by the force of the animal's jaws, had mended. The only visible scars remaining were on her son's arms—the marks of a mother's love—where her fingernails had dug in and actually drawn blood.

Doubtlessly this mother would have been dragged to destruction herself before she would have let go of her son. She models a courage that should give us new resolve for our task of providing for and protecting our children.

....

Discuss:

What do you feel you are giving up to provide for your children? Do you think they feel they are your top priority?

Pray:

For the safety and security of your children, and ask God to enable you to cheerfully make any sacrifice necessary for their well-being.

AT AN EARLY AGE

But Jesus said, "Let the children alone, and do not hinder them from coming to Me; for the kingdom of heaven belongs to such as these."

MATTHEW 19:14

How old does a child have to be before he or she can place saving faith in Jesus Christ? The great English preacher, C. H. Spurgeon, said, "A child who knowingly sins can savingly believe."

Many of the great leaders of the Church became Christians when they were very young. It was said of Polycarp, a first-century church leader, that he walked with God for 86 years before he died at the age of 95. Isaac Watts, the great hymn writer, came to saving faith in Christ at nine years of age.

I was six when I began to feel my need for forgiveness. I grew up in a church with a pastor who preached about heaven and hell, a couple of places we don't hear much about these days.

I recall becoming so aware of my sin that I would lie in bed and shudder; I was afraid to go to bed at night for fear that I'd die in my sleep and spend an eternity in hell.

So one Sunday I told my mom that I felt it was time for me to give my life to Christ. She talked to me straight about my decision, and she didn't hinder me from making my commitment public.

I recall walking that church aisle with a lump in my throat; it was a public confession of wanting Jesus Christ to be my Savior and Lord. That decision marked my life. A few weeks later, my teacher asked me to draw a picture of what I wanted to do when I grew up. I will never forget that picture because God had already etched His mark on my life. I drew a picture of a stick-figure man preaching about Christ.

That was over 40 years ago. And thanks to my parents' faithful instruction, I can look back on that commitment as the most important decision in my life.

....

Discuss:
Have your children made a decision to receive Christ? What can you do to help them understand the gospel?

Pray:
Ask God to give you wisdom and clarity in teaching your children about God's forgiveness through faith in His Son, Jesus Christ.

"LOOSE LIPS SINK SHIPS"

Let no unwholesome word proceed from your mouth, but only such a
word as is good for edification.

EPHESIANS 4:29

often think of the World War II slogan that was posted as a warning in factories that manufactured ships, ammunitions and supplies: "Loose Lips Sink Ships." With the battle for the family being what it is today, perhaps we need to post a similar warning on our refrigerators: "Loose Lips Sink Partnerships."

"Unwholesome" literally means "rotten." When something is rotten, there's no mistaking it, is there? Similarly, when a rotten word is spoken, it stinks up the place. Instantly. The foulest-smelling words are negative ones, fueled with anger and aimed at another person.

Instead of smelling up the place with unwholesome talk, Paul says we should say only that which is helpful and uplifting, according to the needs of those who listen. For example, my wife, Barbara, often feels emotionally empty after orchestrating trips to the dentist, doctor, lessons and meetings, plus all the draining conflicts that take place in a family of eight. She doesn't need me to criticize her for what she hasn't done. She needs me to be on her team, cheering her on and expressing appreciation for juggling all that she does for the kids, the ministry and me.

Occasionally we'll use the dinner table to have a "Praise Mom Party." Each of us will take turns expressing appreciation and encouragement all around the table. Our teenage boys brag, "I like Mom because she cooks good food and a lot of it!" Our youngest will chirp, "I like Mom because she's pretty." Another will say, "I like Mom because she helps me with my homework." Without exception, when we've finished our praise party Barbara's countenance has brightened and her shoulders have straightened!

How about having some words with a positive aroma at your house tonight? Pick a family member and build him or her up by sharing what you most appreciate about him or her.

Discuss:
Think of areas in which your mate needs a word of encouragement and make specific plans to provide it—a letter, note, call, special praise party, etc.

Pray:
Ask God to give you sensitivity to know how to use words of edification to build up your spouse.

THE PRAYER OF THE HELPLESS PARENT

"Not by might nor by power, but by My Spirit," says the Lord of hosts.
ZECHARIAH 4:6

No one raises perfect kids. No one is the perfect parent. No one does it all. Barbara and I have discovered a secret, though, and it's the greatest one of all: *God helps parents raise their kids.* He delights when we admit our weaknesses because that's when He gives us wisdom and power through the Holy Spirit. He loves the prayer of the helpless parent.

I think that God uses our kids to get our attentions. He wants to rule in our lives, but as long as we feel we can succeed in our own power, we won't listen to His Spirit.

Psalm 127:1 says, "Unless the Lord builds the house, they labor in vain who build it." God will help you build your house. You can do it with Him as the architect and builder.

There's a gravel road in the country where I go jogging, and I like to pray for my family as I run. Often I cry out to the Lord, "Unless You build this house, it isn't going to work. You know the parents here. You know the children. Lord, you gave them to us, so help us be successful in raising them."

Pray to God for help in building your home. Pray that you might keep your marriage holy and pure. Ask Him to give you wisdom, strong and resilient commitments, pure romance and vital relationships.

Ask God to help you, the helpless parent. Ask Him to get your child's attention. Plead with Him to build convictions where you can't. Ask Him to build your home. God loves the prayer of the helpless parent.

....

Discuss:
What makes you feel helpless as a parent? What's happening in your family right now that pushes you to depend on God?

Pray:
Spend some time in prayer, asking God to give you specific wisdom and guidance for the decisions you face as a parent right now.

JIM'S STORY

For when I am weak, then I am strong.

2 CORINTHIANS 12:10

*J*im Harvey was a successful manager in a multi-billion-dollar company. He was married, had a daughter attending a top university and was deacon in his church.

But then, over a period of 10 years, God did some major surgery in Jim's life. Here's his story:

I had tremendous confidence in my own ability. I tolerated no weakness; everything was under my control.

Then I learned my daughter was on hard drugs and my wife was addicted to alcohol. A short time later my daughter left college, and my wife filed for divorce. I gained custody of my two younger children and became a single parent.

I began to understand that, when I was helpless to deal with a situation, I could turn it over to God and He would meet my needs. I also became a serious student of the Bible, finishing five years of the Bible Study Fellowship program. I met and married Carole, a committed Christian. Surely, I thought, God was through teaching me and breaking down my pride. I was wrong.

When the stock market crashed in 1987, we lost most of our savings. Carole and I saw God's mercy when she had surgery for cancer that was successfully treated.

For years I tried to talk with my daughter about Christ, but she had no interest. Finally, Carole and I decided to pray and ask God to work in her life.

Two months later I received one of the most dreaded phone calls a parent can get: "Dad, I have tested positive with the AIDS virus." With nowhere else to turn, she received Christ as her Savior and has devoted her life to ministering in a hospital for dying AIDS patients.

I feel privileged to have learned the lessons each situation has brought. I'm better able to comfort those who find themselves in similar circumstances. With each trial, God has broken down my arrogance and pride, and has shown me His sufficiency.

Honest stuff, huh? Jim learned the hard way that God is still faithful when everything is stripped away.

Discuss:
What has God done in the past to break down your pride?
What has He done recently?

Pray:
That God would show you how to depend on Him in times of trial.

OUR MOST VALUABLE RESOURCE

But a woman who fears the Lord, she shall be praised.

PROVERBS 31:30

In a recent survey by *Careers and Colleges* magazine, teenagers were asked, "Whom do you admire?" More than 7 of 10 teens chose their moms and dads over a group of celebrities.

Three percent of teenage girls selected Steffi Graf, the tennis star. Hillary Clinton received 7 percent of the votes, and Oprah Winfrey got 11 percent. But 79 percent chose their mothers.

This piece of good news really encourages me. Because often I feel there's a conspiracy in this nation to rob mothers of their dignity.

For over two decades, feminists have sought to undermine and discredit the values of the Christian family.

One recent effort is the yearly "Take Our Daughters to Work Day." Now, please hear me—I want my four daughters to learn how to support themselves. I support those who need to work. (And I realize there are millions of women who would rather be at home than working.)

But exalting careerism among women above motherhood and family is not the solution to the crisis we are facing in our nation.

Our nation finds itself groaning from the problems caused by broken families. Too many kids are abandoned—both physically and emotionally—and are growing up with no idea of what is right or wrong.

Promoting careerism for our daughters only multiplies the problem. Instead, they need to learn the importance of being a mom, of helping raise the next generation of Americans. Think for a moment: Is the most important woman in our country today the woman who "brings home the bacon" or the "hand that rocks the cradle"? The human debris of the last two decades is evidence that we can't have both.

When a mom chooses to stay home with her children, it is viewed by many as a "career-limiting move." Why can't this choice of sacrificial love be seen for what it really is: An investment in our nation's most valuable resource—our children.

Discuss:
List three ways you are having an impact on the future as you raise your children.

Pray:
Give thanks to God for your mother's impact in your life.

THE CHAIN SAW INCIDENT

In speech, conduct, love, faith and purity, show yourself an example of those who believe.

1 TIMOTHY 4:12

Every parent should be an example to their children just as Timothy was called to be an example to the believers he led. Of course no father is perfect, but we can try—even if it takes some humility as in the case of what I call "The Chain Saw Incident."

Our house is on a ridge overlooking a distant lake, but our view was obstructed by several trees. My son, Benjamin, and I were out doing a little lumberjacking to improve the view. We came upon a big oak that stood just across my property line, in a forest owned by the city. When I started up my chain saw, Benjamin asked, "Isn't that tree on city property?"

"No," I shouted over the buzz of the saw. "Property lines are never that exact." The chain saw sliced through the oak in a few seconds and down it crashed. And as it fell I saw some little orange markers, clearly showing it was a city tree!

In a few days, the Lord began to make noises like a chain saw in the back of my mind. Every time I read the Bible I saw trees. I finally realized I needed to go to the city and confess my sin.

When I finally made the call, Benjamin was standing next to me. I told the official who I was, that I had cut down the tree and wanted to make restitution. He said he appreciated my call, but restitution wasn't necessary since "The property lines out there aren't that exact anyway." I thanked him.

Benjamin didn't say much when I told him what the man said, but I could tell he was soaking it all in. I wasn't trying to be profound, just honest. I had to hope he understood his dad's willingness to do what is right.

....

Discuss:
As a parent, do you find it hard to admit to your children when you haven't modeled Christian values as you should?

Pray:
That even in your humanity you will be able to model Christian values in ways that will cause your children to grow up wanting to be good role models for their children, too.

PARENTS AS PROTECTORS

Lead me to the rock that is higher than I. For Thou has been a refuge for me,
a tower of strength against the enemy.

PSALM 61:2,3

lthough God is our ultimate security and Protector, as the psalmist said,
parents are to also serve as a "tower of strength" for their children.
Some of my most vivid childhood memories are of the hours we spent in
our family's storm cellar while severe thunderstorms rumbled overhead. As I
reflect back on the numerous visits to that musty cellar, I can't help but ponder
the need for Barbara and me to provide our children protection from the storms
that rumble through their lives.

Now it might be good for me to clarify what I mean by "protecting" children.
First, I do not mean shielding them from making decisions on their own, or so
controlling their lives that they do not grow up emotionally, mentally and spiritually. I do not mean smothering children with overprotection or insulating
them from making mistakes or taking risks.

What I do mean by protecting your children is *being proactively involved in their*
lives to prepare them for crucial decisions, problems and pressures. For example, you
protect them when:

You tell them what to do if a stranger offers a ride or candy to them.

You offer advice on how to handle a bully in their neighborhood or
school.

You help them develop good friendships, and by stepping in when a
wrong influence seems to be getting the upper hand.

You give them boundaries—like placing a limit on the types of movies
they see.

You love them enough to talk about a difficult issue like sex, or setting
rules for dating (when they can begin, what types of dates they can start
out with, etc.).

You pray for God's protection over them when you cannot be with
them (see Matt. 18:10).

Are you providing a strong tower of protection for your children?

Discuss:
A tower provides an excellent view of approaching "enemies." What
enemies/issues are your children facing now? On the horizon? How can you
prepare your children to face the "enemies"?

Pray:
Ask God for the wisdom and courage to be able to protect your children.

THE HINGE OF CHRISTIANITY

For if the dead are not raised, not even Christ has been raised; and if Christ has not been raised, your faith is worthless; you are still in your sins.

1 CORINTHIANS 15:16,17

I came across a fascinating list of questions that all have the same answer. Can you guess what it is?

- What gives a widow courage as she stands beside a fresh grave?
- What is the ultimate hope of the cripple, the amputee, the abused or the burn victim?
- How can parents of a brain-damaged or physically handicapped child keep from living their entire lives totally and completely depressed?
- Why would anyone who is blind or deaf or paralyzed be encouraged when he or she thinks of the life beyond?
- Where do the thoughts of a young couple go when they finally recover from the grief of losing their baby?
- When a family receives the tragic news that a little daughter was found dead or the dad was killed in a plane crash or the son over dosed on drugs, what single truth becomes its whole focus?
- What is the final answer to pain, mourning, senility, insanity, terminal diseases, sudden calamities and fatal accidents?

The answer to each of these questions is: *The hope God gives us because of the bodily resurrection Jesus Christ offers to all who believe in Him.*

The reality is, Christianity hinges on the Resurrection. If Christ is who He claimed to be, and He didn't come back from the dead, then as Paul said in 1 Corinthians 15:16-18, our faith is worthless and "we are of all men most to be pitied" (v. 19).

The pivotal point in all of human history is the resurrection of Christ. The one thing that separates Christianity from other religions is that God conquered death. And sin—my sin, your sin—was atoned for.

He is risen. Yes, Christ is risen indeed.

....

Discuss:

How has the resurrection of Christ affected your life? What evidence can you give for the Resurrection?

Pray:

That God will fill you with the hope of the Resurrection.

WHAT CHILDREN NEED TO KNOW

{Part One}

And they were bringing children to Him so that He might touch them; and the disciples rebuked them. But when Jesus saw this, He was indignant and said to them, "Permit the children to come to Me; do not hinder them."

MARK 10:13,14

*C*hildren and Easter. New life and new beginnings. What better time to share the gospel with your children?

But what does a child, or any person, need to know to become a Christian? The following are the basics:

First, *children need to be taught who God is and how He loves them.* They need to know what sets Him apart from humans.

God is holy; He is perfect. People, however, are not perfect.

God is just; He is always fair. We are not just in all our decisions.

God is love; He desires a relationship with us. That's why He sent His Son. We are not always motivated out of our love for another.

Second, *children need to be taught that their sins must be forgiven* (see Rom. 6:23). Many parents in this culture of tolerance feel uncomfortable talking about hell. God is patient, but He is not tolerant. His justice calls for an atonement (a payment, a penalty) for people's sins. Our children must have some understanding that their sins can keep them out of heaven. Their sins must be paid for. And that is what Jesus Christ did for us on the cross.

Finally, *children need to know that they receive God's forgiveness through faith in Jesus Christ* (see Eph. 2:8,9).

Faith involves repenting of our sins, turning to God in faith and trusting Jesus Christ to be our Savior and Lord. When we repent, we acknowledge our sins before God and express our sorrow about our sins to Him.

Those are the basics of what children need to know. The question you're probably asking is, "How can I explain concepts like these to children?"

That's what I'll cover next time.

....

*D*iscuss:

How have you done as a couple in explaining the gospel to your children?
How can you arrange your Easter activities to take time to explain the gospel to your children?

*P*ray:

That God would work in your children's hearts to bring them to Him.

WHAT CHILDREN NEED TO KNOW

{Part Two}

For all have sinned and fall short of the glory of God, being justified as a gift by His grace through the redemption which is in Christ Jesus.

ROMANS 3:23,24

I believe many parents today think their children are too young to understand the gospel. Yet, many children understand faith at an early age—our own six children all indicated they received Christ before the age of six.

Many don't realize God has given them one of the finest tools for teaching spiritual truth—the family. Kids can learn about biblical truth through their relationships with their parents and their siblings.

Even the deepest truths of a book such as Romans can be brought to life to a child. For example, kids learn of their mistakes within a family. They see their own tendency to be selfish, to disobey and to sin within a family. You can explain a verse such as Romans 3:23 to them by using their selfishness as an example of what it means to "fall short of the glory of God."

Or take the concept of forgiveness. From a very early age, Barbara and I taught our children that, when they disobey a parent or hurt a brother or sister, they need to go and ask that person for forgiveness. They learned the process of forgiveness within the family, and we referred to those experiences when we explained the gospel to them. We hurt God with our sins, and we need to come to Him and ask for forgiveness.

I am not trivializing God's forgiveness. We just need to think as a child thinks and go back to the very basic elements of the faith. Once children understand their need for forgiveness, we then explain the basis for God's forgiveness—the sacrifice of His Son, Jesus Christ.

The family is a divine incubator for teaching spiritual truths. We need to use it when teaching the fundamentals of faith to our kids.

Discuss:
Go through the previous devotion's list of concepts children need to understand to come to Christ. Then think of how you could illustrate those concepts to them through experiences within your family.

Pray:
Together that God's Spirit would speak through you to touch your children's hearts with their need for Christ.

April 7

THE THINGS KIDS WILL SAY...

*But we preach Christ crucified, to Jews a stumbling block, and to the Gentiles foolishness,
but to those who are the called, both Jews and Greeks, Christ the power of
God and the wisdom of God.*

1 CORINTHIANS 1:23,24

Easter is a great time to remember our responsibilities to tell our children, as well as others, of their need for salvation, and of how they can be forgiven through faith in Jesus Christ.

But you'd better be prepared to grin when you talk to children about spiritual matters! They'll say almost anything, as one grandfather recently learned.

As Grandpa Bob drove into the driveway he could see his four-year-old granddaughter, Julie, and a couple of her friends playing in the backyard. It was almost Easter and he wanted to know how much these children knew about the Easter story.

Approaching the three little girls he asked, "Who knows why we celebrate Easter every year?"

One friend chirped up first: "Oh, that's when you go to the mall and sit on the big bunny rabbit's lap and tell him what you want in your Easter basket."

Her second pal's answer was no better: "No, no, no! It's when you get a tree and hang eggs on it, and you wake up on Sunday and there's presents under it and..."

At this point Grandpa interrupted and gently said, "That's a good guess, but that's not quite right. Julie, do you know why we celebrate Easter?"

Julie nodded her head. "It's when Jesus was crucified. He died, and His disciples put His body in the grave. They rolled a big stone in front of the opening. And the guards went to sleep. Then, on the third day, there was an earthquake and the stone rolled away...."

Grandpa was really encouraged that Julie knew so many details. Then she continued: "And then the entire town would come out by the grave. And if Jesus came out and *saw His shadow* they knew there would be six more weeks of winter!"

Well, at least little Julie had a portion of the message right!

Discuss:
How well do your children know the Easter story? Make plans now to explain it to them.

Pray:
Thank God for sending His Son to die in our place and raising Him from the dead so that we might believe in Him and experience God's total forgiveness for our sins.

WHY WE REJOICE

"HE IS NOT HERE, BUT HE HAS RISEN."

LUKE 24:6

....

Discuss:
How has the resurrection of Jesus Christ impacted your lives,
marriage and family?

Pray:
Thank God for the victory over sin and death through His Son, Jesus Christ.

April 9

"WASTING TIME" TOGETHER

For I am mindful of the sincere faith within you, which first dwelt in your grandmother Lois, and your mother Eunice, and I am sure that it is in you as well.

2 TIMOTHY 1:5

The *Encyclopedia Britannica* gives a half page to the accomplishments of Charles Francis Adams, the son of President John Quincy Adams. The younger Adams followed the political trail of his father and became a U.S. diplomat to Great Britain. The encyclopedia makes no mention of Charles's family, but Charles's diary does. One day's entry read: "Went fishing with my son today—a day wasted."

Another diary, however, offers a different perspective: "Went fishing with my father—the most wonderful day of my life." The person who wrote those words was Charles's son Brook.

Interesting, isn't it...how a little boy's perspective can be so different from his dad's?

But it's true of me, too. I can remember a fishing trip with Dad to Canada where I caught a trophy northern pike. And another outing to a local lake where he netted my tiny catfish—a fish so small that it went through the holes in the net. He always kidded me about that fish. His laughter still echoes in my mind.

It's interesting now as an adult how my mind can play tricks on me. Looking back, those days of vacation memories are among my most cherished possessions. Yet now that I'm grown, I sometimes find myself thinking that I don't have time for playing catch and going fishing with my own kids.

Until I reflect on the value God places on a little boy or little girl.

Discuss:

Do you have special memories from your childhood of an adult taking time just to be with you? What spiritual values did you learn? Do you as a parent try to spend some time alone with each of your children every week?

Pray:

That God will give you wisdom in your schedule to see what is really important. Ask Him to give you the courage to say no to the less important so that you can say yes to spending quality time with your children.

THOSE ROVING EYES

*You shall not covet your neighbor's house; you shall not covet your
neighbor's wife or his male servant or female servant or his ox or his donkey
or anything that belongs to your neighbor.*

EXODUS 20:17

Why are so many people discontented with their mates? Perhaps one reason is they play the comparison game.

Picture a typical morning. A man gets up and starts his day. As he rolls down the freeway, he drives by two or three beautiful women who beckon seductively from billboards. One is dressed in slinky black velvet; the others aren't dressed in much at all.

Hubby walks into his office building and inhales a blend of "Obsession," "Passion" and "Giorgio Red" as he rides in an elevator full of pretty secretaries, accountants and lawyers. He greets his own attractive secretary, who is beautifully dressed, with perfect hairdo and flawless makeup.

That evening our hero arrives home and flips on the tube to relax. There it is—a rerun of his favorite James Bond movie. More beautiful women falling into bed with 007. Then up pops a commercial selling beer, cars or shampoo— with more perfectly shaped young things crowned with glistening hair, perfect white teeth and flawless skin.

Our twentieth-century warrior glances over at his harried wife. She is cooking dinner as two screaming kids with runny noses cling to her legs like small anchors. More than one hair is definitely out of place, the baby has spit food on her blouse and she smells more like broccoli than perfume. And hubby begins to think, *What's happened here? How did I end up with this?*

Of course it's easy to reverse this picture. The wife may make the same kind of comparisons.

The basic problem with comparisons is that they are based on fantasy games played from a distance. The beautiful people on TV don't look quite that good up close, particularly at 6:00 A.M. It's always easy to think the grass is greener on the other guy's lawn, until you look closely and see all the dandelions and crabgrass.

....

Discuss:
What are some ways to avoid unhealthy comparisons?

Pray:
That God will enable you to be faithful to your spouse in both
deed and attitude. Ask Him to preserve your moral fidelity in the
midst of many distractions.

THE "I-SOLUTION"

However, in the Lord, neither is woman independent of man,
nor is man independent of woman.

1 CORINTHIANS 11:11

God created man and woman to be together; it's Satan who is the father of isolation and loneliness. A veteran member of the Billy Graham Crusade team once told me that the number one need that Graham speaks on is loneliness. Even when surrounded by thousands or millions of people, we feel alone, detached. We yearn for intimacy.

Yet Satan sometimes succeeds in isolating married couples and other family members from each other. The impact of his tactics cannot be understated. Isolation makes suffering unbearable. Your heart can grow cold, indifferent to things of ultimate importance.

Isolation can make you vulnerable, bringing a loss of perspective—about self, life and others. Isolation can cause you to conjure up wild imaginations about your mate's thoughts, plans or motivations. You may even contemplate taking your life.

Isolation is particularly dangerous for a teenager. When our daughter Ashley was about 14 years old I asked her what she felt the results of isolation were. She responded, "When I'm isolated from others, I feel empty and cold—I feel alone and like I don't have value."

When our son Benjamin was a teenager, I told him, "One of the most important issues in our relationship is that we not become isolated from one another. That's what the enemy wants. He wants you to become isolated from us and think that we are your enemy, that we don't have your best interests in mind."

The solution to isolation is the "I-Solution." I must take responsibility for my part in relationships. I must ask for forgiveness when I've hurt someone and they want to hide from me.

The difficulty with applying the I-Solution, of course, is that first word, "I." The I-Solution involves dying to self, giving up my anger and pride, and the right to revenge. That's the key to defeating this enemy of intimacy.

....

Discuss:
In what ways can you implement the "I-Solution" in your
marriage to defeat isolation?

Pray:
Ask God to make you aware of any isolation that is destroying
your intimacy as a couple or as a family.

AN ENCOURAGING WORD

And let us consider how to stimulate one another to love and good deeds.
HEBREWS 10:24

I once was speaking to a group of several hundred singles, and I asked, "How many of you grew up in homes where you were told you were great?" Perhaps a dozen raised their hands. The rest of these young adults remembered words of criticism from their parents more than they remembered encouragement.

When was the last time you pondered on how to encourage those in your family? If you want your mate to live a godly life…if you would like to see your children grow up to love the Lord and walk with Him, then you need to make encouragement a part of your daily vocabulary.

I remember watching a PBS special in which Daniel Boorstein, then the Librarian of Congress, brought out a little blue box that contained the contents of Abraham Lincoln's pockets on the night he was assassinated. Among the contents were found several news clippings applauding Lincoln's leadership and great deeds. It's easy to forget that when Lincoln lived millions of people hated him, and he needed encouragement like anyone else.

All of us have an encouragement meter that is near empty at times. In fact, has anybody ever been encouraged too much? Have you ever felt too appreciated?

I've got a challenge for you. Spend some time thinking of five good things about each member of your family. Begin writing them here, and use additional paper as needed.

1.	1.	1.
2.	2.	2.
3.	3.	3.
4.	4.	4.
5.	5.	5.

Now, commit yourself to finding time to encourage each family member in these areas during the next week. Spend more time encouraging than criticizing.

Be warned though, do not wait for somebody to praise you. Someone once said, "You can sometimes catch a terrible chill waiting for someone else to cover you with glory."

Discuss:
Share your lists for each child.

Pray:
That God would cement good qualities in each family member through your encouragement.

A CHALLENGE FOR MEN

And be subject to one another in the fear of Christ.

EPHESIANS 5:21

One question I often ask men at our FamilyLife Marriage Conferences is: Do your wives have *access* to your lives?

Feminist theologians use this passage from Ephesians to oppose the concept of sex-based roles in marriages. If you read it in the context of the remainder of Ephesians 5, however, I think you will see that, while God wants the husband to be the sacrificial leader in the home, He also calls husband and wife to be accountable to one another. Husbands and wives are to be partners.

Barbara and I try to help each other make good decisions by monitoring each other's *schedule* and workload. Making good decisions in this area simply means saying yes to some things and no to others. We also talk over our children's activities because of their effect on the whole family. Monitoring everyone's schedule helps our family avoid experiencing the pain of being overextended.

Couples should also be accountable to each other in *child rearing*. Barbara and I found that we have different parenting styles because of our different backgrounds. As we draw on the parenting styles our parents modeled for us, we notice the good and the bad tendencies in each other. This enables us to complement one another and to work out what we believe is the best parenting style possible for our own children.

Of course it should go without saying that couples should be accountable to each other in the matter of *sexual fidelity*. Today, when men and women often work closely together in the business world, this becomes more vital than ever. It is even important in the context of church work.

As you and your mate face continuing pressures and stress, it's best to handle life in duet, not solo. Your mate can detect blind spots that you are missing. This type of mutual submission promotes healthy oneness as you interact and depend on each other.

....

Discuss:

Why do you, as a male, find it hard to be mutually submissive
with your wife? How can you, as a wife, help your husband be
accountable without "nagging"?

Pray:

For God to strengthen your partnership as you become
more accountable to one another.

ANSWERING JESUS' PRAYER

I do not ask in behalf of these alone, but for those also who believe in
Me through their word; that they may all be one.

JOHN 17:20,21

As I reflect on the teachings of Christ, I find that much of His instruction dealt with maintaining peace and harmony in relationships. He taught His disciples to break down barriers in relationships. He taught them to forgive each other. Love was the banner of His earthly ministry.

The prayer above is the Savior's "high priestly prayer" near the end of His life. Why did He focus on unity and oneness at this crucial point? Could it be that the strongest demonstration of the Holy Spirit's power in our lives might be imperfect Christians living with one another?

But it isn't always easy, is it? When you and your mate—or you and your children—have a conflict with each other, you probably tend to withdraw from intimacy. Then you begin to believe the worst about the other person, and eventually you lash out in anger or bitterly withdraw and let the anger fester.

Communication is vital to maintaining unity. You may have to reinvent your own "pony express" to stay close, even if it has to run through "hostile territory." Maybe you want to have one meal a day when your family sits down and eats together with the phone off the hook and the television off. Possibly you should pray together at the end of the day with your mate and with each of your children. Or maybe you'll take a walk and talk with a troubled teen who just needs you to be there.

The main thing is to take responsibility for doing your part to see that Jesus' prayer doesn't go unanswered, and that "you may be one."

....

Discuss:
In your family, how does disharmony typically start? Does fostering family harmony always mean settling kids' differences for them?

Pray:
That Christ's prayer for unity will be realized in the way your family members come together in love, acceptance and forgiveness.

THE ILLUSION OF TOMORROW

Remember also your Creator in the days of your youth.
ECCLESIASTES 12:1

My next-door neighbor was a fine man. His friends spoke highly of him. One day, after completing his rounds as an orthopedic surgeon, he went to the cleaners to pick up his laundry. As he stood at the counter, a woman walked in carrying a purse that contained a loaded gun.

She accidentally dropped the purse on the floor, the gun discharged and the bullet hit my neighbor in the head. He died eight hours later. The Lord had called my neighbor home for his day of accounting. He was 41 years old.

Why does it often take something as weighty as death to get our attention? We live daily as though we are immortal, as though we will never die.

So we put off so many important things that really should be done today. I suppose procrastination is as old as death itself. It's interesting to me how we tend to procrastinate on some of the most important decisions and actions of our lives:

- Saying words of encouragement, appreciation and love to our mates;
- Embracing our children in a hug (regardless of their ages);
- Playing with our children;
- Writing that letter of appreciation to our parents for all their hard work and labor in raising us right;
- Committing our lives fully to Christ as Lord and Savior;
- Living for eternity instead of for the moment.

Procrastination moves us steadily, slowly, methodically toward living lives of destruction. Its companions are mediocrity, compromise, laziness, lies, broken vows and promises, escapism and daydreaming.

Solomon knew about procrastination. He places priority on remembering God not on our deathbeds, nor in our middle age, but in our youth. This results in a life that honors God rather than self.

....

Discuss:
What have you been putting off today thinking you could do tomorrow?
If you or your mate tend to procrastinate, what can you do to help
each other get out of this habit?

Pray:
Ask God to teach you to number your days that you may live your life wisely.

ARE YOU COMPELLED?

*And seeing the multitudes, He felt compassion for them, because they were distressed and
downcast like sheep without a shepherd.*

MATTHEW 9:36

struggle as much as anyone with turning a conversation to spiritual things.
However, I can't escape a few truths that lead me to step out by faith:
First, *I am compelled by the realization that without Christ all men are lost and
without hope.* Sure, humans do good things, but that doesn't change the fact that
we all sin naturally. I've never taught a single one of our six children how to
steal a cookie, yet they all have done it. It's part of their natures. And it's because
of sin all men are lost.

Second, *I'm compelled to share Christ with others because of the reality of hell.*
Thinking about hell is not in vogue today. But Christ spoke of hell as a real place
of eternal judgment and torment.

Third, *I want to share the good news because it is the very reason for which Christ came
to the planet Earth.* Jesus Christ didn't go to the cross just so we could have happy
homes. He came "to seek and to save that which was lost" (Luke 19:10).

Look around you. The army of God needs fresh troops who are willing to get
into a foxhole. The hour couldn't be more urgent. And your family is an important part of the solution.

"So what do I do?" you ask. Below are a few ideas. Don't let this list overwhelm you. The important thing is to start…somewhere…with something.

- Read *Witnessing Without Fear* by Bill Bright, founder and president
  of Campus Crusade for Christ. It will show you how to share your
  faith with confidence in any type of witnessing situation.
- Have an evangelistic dinner party at your home for a few couples
  you know.
- Host a "Good News Club" for neighborhood children.
- Pick up several copies of "The Four Spiritual Laws" at your local
  Christian bookstore, and use them to explain the gospel.
- Show your children how to share their faith. Invite a neighborhood
  child to go to church with you.

Now is the time for boldness. Step out and ask people about their relationships with God.

Discuss:
Take a few minutes and identify people you know who need Christ. Make a list.

Pray:
That God will give you an opportunity to share the gospel with them.

A DAY OF REST

You shall work six days, but on the seventh day you shall rest;
even during plowing time and harvest you shall rest.

EXODUS 34:21

*S*tart by setting aside Sunday as a day of rest. Within the Ten Commandments, God has provided a long-standing truth that our modern culture is ignoring, to its detriment. The Sabbath is to be a day set apart unto God—a day of rest in which to refuel our perspectives and refresh our communion with Him.

God knows that after working hard for six days, we all need some time off. The problem is, we ignore His command and race through life. But our needs for rest can't be denied. Which word best describes our lives, our society: "rest" or "weariness"?

God knew that it's important to step out of the demands of work and the pace of everyday life. That is the purpose of the Sabbath—to give us time to rest, to reflect, to think critically about life and where our choices are taking us.

Over the last five years, Barbara and I became more aware of our need to regard the Sabbath as a day of rest. And I'd have to say that we feel like we have a long way to go on really recapturing what God had in mind. But we try to make Sunday different. A nap. Time to read. Recreation as a family that is not demanding. We usually do not work in the yard. (The kids now remind us of the Sabbath if we ask them to do something outside on Sunday!) And Barbara and I generally go out on a date to eat dinner and talk on Sunday evening.

Now, let me make one thing real clear—we don't always do a great job of observing the day of rest. Barbara would join me in saying we've failed miserably, but the standard is there and we are moving toward it in our choices about how we spend our time.

If we in the Christian community would decide to try to rest on Sundays, we would begin to reap the enriching qualities of clear minds, relaxed spirits and the knowledge that our lives are well-pleasing to God.

Discuss:
How do you spend your Sundays? What can you change in your schedule to begin to make Sunday a day of rest?

Pray:
That you will take the time God has set aside to gain the rest you need to face the pressures and responsibilities of your life.

THE BLESSING OF BURDENS

Therefore I am well content with weaknesses,...with distresses,...with difficulties, for Christ's sake; for when I am weak, then I am strong.

2 CORINTHIANS 12:10

*S*adhu Sundar Singh, a Hindu convert to Christianity, became a missionary to his people in India. Late one afternoon Sadhu was traveling on foot through the Himalayas with a Buddhist monk. It was bitterly cold and the wind felt like sharp blades slicing into their skins. Night was fast approaching when the monk warned Sadhu that they were in danger of freezing to death if they did not reach the monastery before darkness fell.

Suddenly, on a narrow path above a steep precipice, they heard a cry for help. At the foot of the cliff lay a man, fallen and badly hurt. The monk looked at Sadhu and said, "Do not stop. God has brought this man to his fate. He must work it out for himself. Let us hurry on before we, too, perish."

But Sadhu replied, "God has sent me here to help my brother. I cannot abandon him."

The monk continued trudging off through the whirling snow, while the missionary clambered down the steep embankment. The injured man's leg was broken and he could not walk, so Sadhu made a sling of his blanket and tied the man on his back. With great difficulty he climbed back up the cliff, drenched by now in perspiration.

Doggedly, Sadhu made his way through the deepening snow and darkness. It was all he could do to follow the path. But he persevered, though faint with fatigue and overheated from exertion. Finally, he saw ahead the lights of the monastery.

Then, for the first time, Sadhu stumbled and nearly fell. But not from weakness. He had stumbled over an object lying in the snow-covered road. Slowly he bent down on one knee and brushed the snow off the object. It was the body of the monk, frozen to death.

Years later a disciple of Sadhu's asked him, "What is life's most difficult task?"

Without hesitation Sadhu replied: "To have no burden to carry."

....

Discuss:

Put into your own words the lesson you get from this story. What negative pressures in your life can be turned into strength-building character qualities?

Pray:

Ask God to enable you to view life's challenges as a means of serving others and of strengthening your muscles of faith.

GREAT EXPECTATIONS

For this cause a man shall leave his father and mother, and shall cleave to his wife;
and the two shall become one flesh.

EPHESIANS 5:31

My wife and I spent the first year and a half of our marriage in Boulder, Colorado, where the winters are cold and electric blankets are standard survival equipment. We fell into a habit of snuggling under those blankets but forgetting to turn out all the lights. And every time, Barbara would say, "Sweetheart, did you remember to turn out all the lights?"

Usually I would hop out of our comfy bed and run barefoot through the 55-degree apartment, turning off light after light (that Barbara had turned on). But one time I got fed up and groaned, "Honey, why don't you turn out the lights tonight?"

Barbara replied, "I thought you would because my dad always turned out the lights."

Suddenly I was wide awake. It dawned on me why I had been suffering occasional minor frostbite for the past few months. And I shot back, "But I'm not your dad!"

We stayed up for a long time, discussing expectations—what Barbara expected of me and what I expected of her—with many of those expectations stemming from what we had imported into our marriage from our homes.

When we were married, for dinner I expected meat and mounds of mashed potatoes with butter cascading down the sides. Alas, it was not to be. Barbara leans toward exotic tuna casseroles and lots of other things I could not begin to identify.

Each partner brings a certain set of expectations into a marriage. When they are not met, the drought of disillusionment can dry up the dialogue in the streams of our conversation.

Marriage provides a relationship where two people can hammer out realistic expectations. No mate will ever fulfill all of your desires in marriage. There is only One who is capable of that.

....

Discuss:
What expectations of your mate did you bring to your marriage?
Which ones were met? Which ones were not? How reasonable are they?
If you haven't ever done so, why not consider sitting down and
communicating your expectations to your spouse?

Pray:
Ask God to help you to be realistic in your expectations of others.

DAUGHTERS NEED FATHERS, TOO

Let our...daughters [be] as corner pillars fashioned as for a palace.

PSALM 144:12

We read a lot today of the problems that occur when boys grow up without male role models. But did you know that a father is just as important in helping girls understand their sexual identities? Boys are not the only ones who lack a sense of how a man should behave. Many young girls don't know, either, because they aren't exposed to healthy male-female relationships.

How do you give your daughter a healthy perspective of male-female relationships?

The most influential way is by *how you treat her mother*. As she sees you loving your wife, giving preference to her, giving to her in a sacrificial way, she will learn how a man should treat a woman.

Second, *your daughter needs to know you love her.* She needs to be assured of your protection and your guidance. She will feel a greater sense of self-esteem if she is assured of your love. Hug her. Kiss her. Appropriately express affection for her even as she matures and goes through adolescence.

Another important way you influence your daughter is *through your spiritual guidance.* She should be shaped by Scripture and by prayer to be "corner pillars fashioned as for a palace."

Corner...like her role, designed by God to be supportive yet essential to holding a home together.

Pillars...because her inner strength is derived from a confidence and faith in God.

Fashioned...as you guide her to have a soft heart, willing to be led by God's Spirit.

For a palace...because her inner beauty attracts others to Jesus as much as it makes her willing to follow a godly man.

I pray the next generation of women will be pillars of love, faith and commitment to the husbands, families and the communities that need them. Maybe, with godly fathers involved, millions of little girls will develop into women who will, in turn, build godly families.

....

Discuss:
Evaluate together your involvement as a father in each of your daughters' lives. Prayerfully establish some goals for the upcoming year for each of these relationships.

Pray:
That God will give you the wisdom to know how to begin influencing your daughters to become "corner pillars fashioned as for a palace."

PROTECTING YOUR WIFE

You husbands likewise, live with your wives in an understanding way,
as with a weaker vessel, since she is a woman.

1 PETER 3:7

In this verse, the apostle Peter emphasizes the need for a husband to understand his wife because she is a "weaker vessel." Your wife wants a man who understands her and her needs.

Your wife needs to feel safe, secure and protected. As her husband, it's up to you to provide that security. I was reminded of this years ago when I attended a conference for couples. During the conference, a young woman was raped in her hotel room.

As the speaker told the other conferees about the incident, I noticed an interesting phenomenon. Instinctively, as though led by an orchestra conductor, nearly every husband in the audience tenderly slid his arm around his wife. Likewise, almost every wife slipped closer into his protective embrace. It was a physical gesture of a woman's need for safekeeping and a man's natural desire to protect his wife.

People use locks, burglar and fire alarms, and lighting systems to protect their most valuable possessions. When you invest in protecting your wife, you are making a statement about her value to you.

Certainly you already protect your wife physically. You wouldn't think of having it any other way. You discourage her going out at night if it is dangerous. You protect her by encouraging her to lock the car when she goes shopping. And you provide the kind of security she needs at home for the times you are away.

But are you protecting her from other muggers in her life, such as:

- Overscheduling her time?
- Her own unrealistic goals or expectations, which set her up for failure?
- Burnout at work? At home?
- The children, who would take advantage of her weaknesses that they know so well?

Obviously, you can't protect your wife from every pressure, worry, fear or loss. But you can do your best to anticipate many of these problems before they occur and to establish a solid security system for her protection.

Discuss:
Talk with your wife about how you can protect her in different areas of her life, especially those listed above.

Pray:
That God would give you wisdom and courage as you seek to protect your wife from negative outside forces.

THE GREATEST GIFT

Let marriage be held in honor among all.
HEBREWS 13:4

I will never forget the quarrel between my parents when I was in first grade. I was sitting in my pajamas, listening to them argue—I can't even remember what it was about. And I remember thinking, *Are Mom and Dad going to get a divorce?* Now, this was back in the early 1950s, when divorce was rare; it was hardly even talked about back then.

If I had that fear at that age, what must the average first grader today feel? Kids today are surrounded by divorce.

The greatest gift you can give your children is a sacred commitment to one another. You must keep your marriage relationship a priority. Your kids need your devotion to each other more than they need your devotion to them.

A woman once wrote me to tell about the changes she had seen in her marriage after attending a FamilyLife Marriage Conference. She and her husband had been divorced three years when they went. "I really did not want to go," she wrote. "As far as I was concerned, our relationship was dead. The conference changed our lives. As we listened to what the Bible said about marriage, the roles of husband and wife, we realized we had done it all wrong. As a result of the conference, we decided to start dating again. Four months later, we were remarried."

She concluded, "Our remarriage is a dream come true for our six-year-old son. He can hardly believe that the thing he wanted most has really happened. His mommy and daddy are together again."

Few things can harden the heart of a child more than the divorce of his or parents. Your kids need a mom and dad who are committed to each other.

Discuss:
How much time do you spend with your mate on a daily and weekly basis?
When was the last time you did something to cultivate your relationship?

Pray:
Ask God to preserve your legacy by protecting your marriage. Ask Him for His favor on your marriage.

FAITHFUL IN LITTLE THINGS

{Part One}

"He who is faithful in a very little thing is faithful also in much; and he who is unrighteous in a very little thing is unrighteous also in much."

LUKE 16:10

- Are you trustworthy?
- Can others count on you?
- Do you want to know how to be original in a culture of copycats?
- Do you want to be a part of a vanishing breed in today's generation?

If so, then become a person who is *faithful*. You know, a person who follows through. One whom others can count on whether things are rough or smooth. His word is good on the little stuff, as well as the mammoth, gargantuan tasks. He's the kind of person who promises to call—and does so—on time. He says he'll do it and he does—exactly like you have asked for it to be done.

Are you known as a faithful person? If you are, then here are a few of the words that can be used to describe you: Trustworthy, dependable, reliable, true-blue and responsible. All of the names are saturated with one recurring theme, *character*. Character quietly, yet convincingly, says, "You can count on me—at any cost!"

Faithfulness. Strange, isn't it, that such a simple thing would be in such short supply?

Today, our oatmeal is ready to eat in 60 seconds, our pictures can be developed in 60 minutes and our houses can be built in 60 days. We are a culture that is used to getting what we want instantly. We aren't accustomed to working patiently, or waiting on anything—even a hamburger.

I meet a lot of men who desire to have more responsibility and move up the ladder of success. Many of them, however, want to jump to the top of that ladder rather than climb it. They want you to be impressed with their talent and their skills of persuasion rather than with their faithfulness.

......

Discuss:

Are you faithful in little things or do you often seem to neglect them?

Pray:

That God would build in you a spirit of servanthood and faithfulness.

A FAITHFUL MAN

{Part Two}

"Now his master saw that the Lord was with [Joseph] and how the Lord caused all that he did to prosper in his hand. So Joseph found favor in his sight...and he made him overseer over his house, and all that he owned he put in his charge."

GENESIS 39:3,4

If you want to find a biblical example of someone who was faithful in little things, turn to the last chapters of Genesis. As you read through the story of Joseph, you see a man who was considered trustworthy:

- He was given responsibility to shepherd his father's flocks "while he was still a youth" (Gen. 37:2).
- After he was sold into slavery by his brothers, he ended up in the house of Potiphar, where he performed his duties well enough to be appointed overseer of all that Potiphar owned (see 39:5).
- He refused the amorous advances of Potiphar's wife. Unfortunately, he was thrown into prison when she lied and said he had tried to seduce her (see vv. 7-18).
- His character in prison was so strong that the chief jailer placed him in charge of all the prisoners (see vv. 21-23).
- After interpreting Pharaoh's dream, he was taken from prison and made a ruler in Egypt, second in power only to Pharaoh (see 41:38-41).

Joseph never sought to move up in responsibility. He was faithful to fulfill his responsibilities and content to allow God to give him more. Even his words to Potiphar's wife reveal his faithful character: "Behold, with me here, my master does not concern himself with anything in the house, and he has put all that he owns in my charge.... He has withheld nothing from me except you, because you are his wife. How then could I do this great evil, and sin against God?" (Gen. 39:8,9).

Many people have ambitions, but sometimes I wonder if our ambitions are in the right area. Jesus said the greatest ambition in Mark 10:35-45 was to be the slave of all—a servant.

Do you want to be a leader? Then you've got to be a servant.

....

Discuss:

Do others consider you a servant? Perhaps a better question is do people treat you like a servant?

Pray:

If you desire to have additional responsibilities, ask God to give you the desire to serve others.

WHEN LITTLE EQUALS MUCH

He who is faithful in a very little thing is faithful also in much.

LUKE 16:10

hat would happen in our homes if we saw an epidemic of husbands and wives infected with being faithful in little things? What if we really did all the little things we say we'll do?

Many people these days want the "much" without the "very little." We want the tip without the toil, the gain without the grind, the sweets without the sweat, the prize without the pain, the perks without the perseverance. Duty, diligence, hard work and attention to details are rare commodities in any endeavor—whether at home, at work or at church.

How about cheering your family members on when:

- A good deed was done for someone when no one was apparently watching;
- Your husband is honest in preparing his income tax;
- Your spouse stands up for the truth at work, regardless of consequences;
- A mother is faithfully taking the time to rear the next generation (so much of her work is unseen and unappreciated by others);
- A child tells the truth instead of lying, even when lying would be easier.

How do you view the "little things"? As picky things to be ignored or that get in your way? Or as stepping stones to receiving the "true riches" of the Kingdom?

What would happen to the next generation if we trained our children to be faithful in little as well as in what the world considers "much"—intelligence, wealth and athletic ability? If they don't learn to be faithful in the little things from you, then what kinds of leaders, workers, husbands, wives, fathers and mothers will they make?

If you don't teach them, who will?

....

Discuss:

Why is faithfulness in little things so important in a marriage? A family? How can you impart this truth to your family?

Pray:

Ask God to build your character quotient by enabling you to be faithful in little things with your spouse and your family.

TOWARD A NEW BREED OF MEN

While we look not at the things which are seen, but at the things which are not seen; for the things which are seen are temporal, but the things which are not seen are eternal.

2 CORINTHIANS 4:18

hy do Fortune 500 companies pay such huge salaries to their top executives? Because they know that leadership makes a difference. As a husband and father, your leadership will make a difference in your family. Oh, your wife and children may survive from day to day, but are they heading anywhere? Are they growing in Christlike character? Are they focusing on what is important?

There is no question why so many marriages and families are in trouble. Too many men are functioning only as material providers. We need a new breed of men who can appreciate and expend energy, time and—most importantly—focused attention on the spiritual aspect of family life.

We need a new breed of men who have the ability to focus on the unseen—the eternal—as well as the seen. Men who will say no to more bucks when it means sacrificing their families. A new breed who will ask, with every decision they make: "How will this affect the relationships within my family?"

We need a new breed of men who will recognize they need to leave something to posterity that will outlive the financial inheritances they may leave for their children: *proven character*...a new breed of men who realize that to succeed in the eyes of men but fail in the eyes of God is the ultimate failure.

One man has said, "It is better to fail in a cause that will ultimately succeed than to succeed in a cause that will ultimately fail."

Will you take upon yourself the challenge Albert Einstein gave a group of young scientists? While addressing this highly motivated group of young men, he said, "Gentlemen, try not to become men of success. But rather, try to become men of value."

....

Discuss:
What material things do you hope to leave to your children? What specific spiritual values do you hope to instill in them? Which of these "keepsakes" is more important?

Pray:
Imagine your children as grown and established in their own families. Pray for what each one will become.

THE FORGOTTEN COMMANDMENT

{Part One}

Honor your father and your mother, that your days may be prolonged in the land which the Lord your God gives you.

EXODUS 20:12

During the early 1970s, I worked with teenagers in a ministry in Boulder, Colorado. One of my favorite messages to communicate to the teens was titled "How to Raise Your Parents." Actually I camouflaged the message behind the title. The real challenge was to obey God's commandment "Honor your father and your mother."

As I spoke, I realized that I was touching a raw nerve. Many had such difficult relationships with their parents that the command to honor them presented a challenge of immense proportions, a major step in their growing faith.

Then, for several summers during the 1980s, I taught a graduate class at the International School of Theology to students preparing for vocational ministry. Of my 20 lectures, the one addressing "Honoring Your Parents" easily sparked the greatest response. It was fascinating! Every summer, dozens of young men and women would leave that particular message in tears, motivated to do a better job honoring their parents.

One young man handed me a note that affirmed the message of honoring parents:

> I appreciated your talk today. It brought back some memories I have about my dad that I would like to share with you. Every day that I can remember, my dad took me and hugged me and kissed me good night.
>
> I was with him the night he died. That night he hugged me and kissed me and told me he loved me, and I was too embarrassed to tell him that I loved him.
>
> He died of a heart attack two and one-half hours later after I went to bed. I remember standing over his body saying, "Dad, I love you." But it was a couple of hours too late.

You don't hear much these days about God's commandment to honor our parents. In fact, I call it "The Forgotten Commandment." But, as I will explain in the next devotions, it may be one of the most profound in Scripture.

....

Discuss:

What kind of relationship do you now have with your parents?

Pray:

If you struggle with the idea of honoring your parents, then ask God to make you willing to honor them.

THE FORGOTTEN COMMANDMENT

{Part Two}

Honor your father and your mother.

EXODUS 20:12

Honor, according to *Webster's* dictionary, is "a good name or public esteem. A showing of unusual merited respect." When God commands us to "Honor your father and your mother," however, He provides some additional meaning.

In the original Hebrew language, the word for "honor" meant "heavy or weight." To honor someone meant "I weigh you down with respect and prestige. I place upon you great worth and value."

It is fascinating to observe, as God originally formed Israel into a nation, that the concept of honoring parents was one of its foundational elements. Think of the setting: God had brought this nation of people, held captive for so long in Egypt, into the wilderness of Sinai. He had promised them the land of Israel, but up to this point He had never given them any written directions. They needed instructions to govern their behavior and preserve their identity as a nation.

God gave them the Ten Commandments. So you can best appreciate the significance of the command to honor parents, note that the first four commandments dealt with how man relates to God. With these mandates, God established that He is the One who should be exalted above anyone or anything else. A nation's life, and an individual's life, is defined by its relationship with God.

Then comes the fifth commandment, and I don't think that's by coincidence. Honoring parents should be a direct result of our faith in God.

Look carefully at the commandment again. Whom did God command us to honor? Only perfect parents? Only Christian parents? Parents who are spiritually mature and insightful? Only parents who never made major mistakes in rearing us?

No, God commands us to honor our parents regardless of their performances, behaviors and dysfunctions. Why? Because honoring parents demands that we walk by faith.

....

Discuss:
Would it be difficult for you to honor your parents? Why?

Pray:
That God would give you the strength to trust Him in this area and show you practical ways to honor your parents.

THE FORGOTTEN COMMANDMENT

{Part Three}

Honor your father and your mother.

EXODUS 20:12

Honoring your parents is a command for children of all ages. There is no exception clause in this command that exempts the adult child from responsibility.

I can almost sense you starting to squirm in your seat. Honoring your parents seems risky.

Let me take a few moments to tell you what honoring your parents is, and what it isn't.

Honoring your parents does not mean endorsing irresponsibility or sin. It is not a denial of what they have done wrong as parents. It does not mean you flatter them by "emotionally stuffing" the mistakes they've made or denying the emotional or even the physical pain they may have caused you.

For an adult child, honoring your parents will not place you back under their authority. It does not give them access to manipulate you. It doesn't mean crawling back into the cradle and becoming a helpless child again.

Honoring your parents means choosing to place great value on your relationship with them.

Honoring your parents means taking the initiative to improve the relationship.

Honoring your parents means obeying them until you establish yourself as an adult.

Honoring your parents means recognizing what they've done right in your life.

Honoring your parents means recognizing the sacrifices they have made for you.

Honoring your parents means praising them for the legacy they are passing on to you.

Honoring your parents means seeing them through the eyes of Christ, with understanding and compassion.

Honoring your parents means forgiving them as Christ has forgiven you.

It is an attitude accompanied by actions that say to your parents, "You are worthy. You have value. You are the person God sovereignly placed in my life."

Discuss:

What did your parents do right as they raised you? What steps can you take to improve your relationship with your parents?

Pray:

Ask God to empower you through the Holy Spirit to take one step toward honoring your parents.

THE FORGOTTEN COMMANDMENT

{Part Four}

Honor your father and mother (which is the first commandment with a promise), that it may be well with you.

EPHESIANS 6:2,3

None of the other Ten Commandments has a promise attached to it. But how will it "be well with you" when you honor your parents?

I believe one profound reason is that it helps you finish the process of growing into adulthood. A part of maturing as an adult is the growing realization and conviction that you now share with your parents the responsibility for the relationship.

For most of your first 18 to 20 years of life, your relationship with your parents could be compared to a one-way street. She nursed you and changed your diapers; he walked the floor with you at 2:00 A.M. She taught you how to walk; he taught you how to ride a bike. The "traffic" of love generally flowed in one direction: From them to you, and it probably remained that way through high school and college.

The problem with some parent-child relationships, however, is they continue looking like one-way streets even when the child is in his 30s and 40s. And then you begin hearing those famous words: "My parents don't treat me like an adult."

Diane lived in the same town as her mother, but it all seemed so strained and shallow. "She still treated me and my other siblings a lot like kids," she said, "I felt a lack of respect."

Her feelings began to change shortly after she heard the idea of writing a written document, a tribute, for her parents. She spent time remembering the good things they had done for her, and slowly her perspective changed.

To Diane's surprise, her mother immediately broke down in tears as she read the tribute. "I think part of the problem was she didn't feel any respect and appreciation from her kids."

The tribute allowed Diane and her mother to set aside their arguments and begin building their relationship. "I felt like I was more on Mom's level. I was able to relate to her more. It was sort of a rite of passage."

....

Discuss:

How have you made your relationship with your parents into a two-way street? If you feel ready, spend some time during the next few months writing a tribute for your parents.

Pray:

Ask God to begin to flood your mind with memories of what your parents did right in raising you. Write them down as He helps you recall them.

A BURDEN OR A BLESSING?

Behold, children are a gift of the Lord; the fruit of the womb is a reward.
How blessed is the man whose quiver is full of them.

PSALM 127:3,5

*M*any parents today feel like kids are a burden. That's not what the Bible calls them. It doesn't say, "Behold, children are a burden of the Lord," or "Burdened is the man whose quiver is full of them."

Our views have become distorted. What we see as a burden, God sees as a blessing. Some of us need to knock the windows out of our corrupted views and let the Spirit of God come into our homes and refresh our hearts and minds so we can see clearly again that children are a blessing.

Don't get me wrong. Barbara and I will be the first to tell you we are in process with our children. We have failed many times. And I have been so frustrated, after exhausting all rational reasoning, all reward systems and all "biblical approaches," that the only thing left for me to do was yell, throw a box of Kleenexes at the floor, slam the door and walk out—just like my kids do. Which just convinces me that one of God's greatest purposes for parents is to bring us face-to-face with our own depravity.

We want life to be easy, or at least bearable. And when children make our lives difficult, we begin to feel they are burdens. But we fail to realize what God makes clear—our children are gifts from God. God has given us our children for His glory and our good.

When I speak at our FamilyLife Marriage Conferences, I'm always struck by how surprised couples are when I explain that our mates are gifts from God. Why are they so astounded? Don't they know our God? He wants to bless us. He's out for our best interests!

In the same way, you need to receive your children as gifts from God. If you do, your whole attitude will change. No longer will you try to change your kids...no longer will you consider them burdens. Instead, you'll view them as true blessings from God entrusted to you.

....

Discuss:
How do you view your children—as burdens or blessings?

Pray:
With your mate, acknowledge your children as gifts from God.

RELATIONSHIPS REQUIRE TIME

*Let us not become weary in doing good, for at the proper time we
will reap a harvest if we do not give up.*

GALATIANS 6:9 (NIV)

What if you approached your mate after your wedding and said, "Now that we're married, please don't make me spend time with you"? Naturally your mate would say, "You're crazy! How can we build a marriage unless we spend time together?"

The same is true with your children. Barbara and I discovered that, as our kids grew older and began to spend more and more time with friends, we had to work harder to spend time with them.

Be creative as you think of things you can do that your children would enjoy. Smaller children, for example, love something as simple as a trip to a convenience store to buy a candy bar or an ice-cream cone.

We live out in the country and when we're in town with two cars, we need to decide who will drive with Mom and with Dad. Usually our two youngest girls say, "We want to go with Daddy." You know why? Because if I stop for gas at the convenience store, they figure I'm a soft touch; they try to ease me on over to the ice cream or candy section.

And you know what? I am a soft touch. I love spending time with them, and it's an opportunity to enjoy something together that they like to do. Is it always fat free and super healthy? No, but it is healthy for the relationship.

A great thing for teenagers is to go shopping with them. My girls enjoy shopping for clothes, while the boys look for sporting equipment. It's not the purchase that's important; it's the time you spend together.

Another great thing to do, which we're losing in today's culture, is reading to our kids. It is a real sacrifice of love and an easy way for both moms and dads to get involved with their kids. I read *Chronicles of Narnia* to one of my sons and he loved it!

Last night my teenage son, Samuel, and I went to town to get some groceries and "waste" some time together without any agenda. His response? "Dad, I'm glad we just spent some time together without any big goals. It was great to be with you!"

When's the last time you "wasted" an evening with one of your children for no other reason than just being with them?

Discuss:
Evaluate how you spend time with each of your children. Do you need to commit more time to your kids just doing things on their levels?

Pray:
Ask God to help you set more time aside just for your kids.

THE MOST IMPORTANT THING

{Part One}

For it is He who delivers you from the snare of the trapper.

PSALM 91:3

*S*everal years ago, Barbara and I had the opportunity to enjoy dinner with Dr. James Dobson and his wife, Shirley. Jim is president of Focus on the Family and his radio program is one of the largest of its kind. Shirley, meanwhile, is national chairperson for the National Day of Prayer. Both are very special, godly people.

There was one question I always wanted to ask them, and that night I was able to. "What is the most important thing Barbara and I could do as we raise our kids?"

Without hesitation, both Jim and Shirley looked at us and answered with one word: "Pray." And then they told us why they were so confident about their answer.

One night they had gone to bed when, at about 11:15 P.M., they began to feel uneasy about their daughter, Danae. Jim said he fought the urge to fall asleep. Instead they got out of bed, got down on their knees and prayed for Danae.

Later they learned that, at that very moment, Danae and a friend were in a pull-out curve in the mountains—looking over the lights of the cities below and eating a meal. They were just having a good time when a police car came by and shined a light on them. It made them think to lock their doors. As soon as the police car went by, a bearded man crawled out from under their car and grabbed the door handle, attempting to force his way into the car. They quickly switched on the ignition and sped off. "No one will ever convince me that our prayers did not have an impact in that situation," Jim told us.

That story reminded us how important it is to pray for our children. No matter what you do as parents, in the end it is God who is in control.

....

Discuss:
What are the greatest needs, challenges and pressures
of your children right now?

Pray:
That God would protect your children and deliver them from the snare of evil.

THE MOST IMPORTANT THING

{Part Two}

In the fear of the Lord there is strong confidence, and His children will have refuge.
PROVERBS 14:26

As a parent you know that, no matter what you do to raise your children, God is ultimately in control of their lives. You want them to walk with Him, to have "strong confidence" in Him.

The greatest power you have is to pray for your children. But how should you pray?

First, *pray that God will teach your children.* I'll never forget when two of our kids were having a conflict. We tried everything—rewards, punishments, threats, and nothing worked. Finally we said, "Okay, Lord, we'll pray."

For two nights we prayed. On the second night, one child in the conflict had a dream that the other child had died. He came to us and said, "I was sad I'd treated him so badly." The problems stopped, just like that. In one night, God changed what we couldn't change in weeks.

Also, *pray that you'll catch your kids when they do evil.* You know what it's like: One of your children is lying or stealing or manipulating others, but you can't catch him in the act. Pray, "Lord, help me catch this kid. Give me some evidence." I've knelt beside the bed of a child we couldn't catch and laid my hands on him and said, "Lord, you know the truth in this matter. If this child is lying, I pray you'll help me catch him."

Does God answer these prayers? You bet He does. I think God has compassion upon the helpless parent!

The third thing is *to pray with them.* Just get down next to their cheeks, cuddle and pray. Pray for the important things going on in their lives, and pray for their futures—that they will walk with God, marry a godly spouse, etc. They love it. And so does God.

....

Discuss:
What do you want God to teach your children?
Write down at least two items for each child.

Pray:
That God will give you wisdom as you raise your children, and that
He will teach them what they need to grow in wisdom, and help you to
catch them if they stray from what is right.

WATCH YOUR STEP!

*Keep watching and praying, that you may not enter into temptation;
the spirit is willing, but the flesh is weak.*

MATTHEW 26:41

*W*atch your step, sir." How often have you heard this courteous caution? Whether you're stepping out of an old elevator, walking through a construction area, or stepping onto a slippery sidewalk, we all appreciate someone looking out for our best interests.

I was glad I was watching my step while hiking through the woods one day with my son, Samuel. It was one of those great father-son hunting trips. Late in the afternoon we were walking along an old logging road, knee high in weeds. For some reason I looked down and instantly froze in my tracks. My next step would have placed my leg within easy striking range of a coiled two-and-a-half-foot water moccasin.

Showing how he got his name, his mouth snapped open, revealing a snowy white interior and needle-sharp fangs bared in anger. It stayed in that cocked position as if to say, "This path is mine. I double dare you to come this way."

The poisonous viper gave me no choice — it was either him or me. So I gave him a "split personality."

How many marriages have been poisoned and even slain by our frequent failures to take seriously the serpents of temptation coiled in our pathways? One trouble is that many of us don't carefully watch for them. In fact, we may flirt with them, daring them to strike, as though we didn't realize their deadliness.

I'm grateful that early in our marriage Barbara risked sharing with me a temptation she was experiencing. Almost instantly the "snake" slithered away as we talked and prayed together.

Jesus knew that temptations would always be just a step away. That's why He counseled: "Watch your step." Are you watching yours?

....

Discuss:

What recurring temptation have you faced recently that you need to tell your spouse about? What can your spouse do to help you?

Pray:

Consider yourself a "watchman on the wall" on behalf of your marriage and family, and pray that you will be personally alert in avoiding temptation.

SATAN'S SCHEMES

In order that no advantage be taken of us by Satan; for we are not ignorant of his schemes.

2 CORINTHIANS 2:11

I've noticed that many Christians are somewhat naïve about the devices Satan uses to tempt us to follow him. The "harmless" office flirtation, the casual attitude toward immorality in the media—it's as though we are unaware that such schemes can wreck our homes.

The world isn't going to issue warnings. If we are to stand the test, we will have to become more aware of Satan's tactics.

For instance, I've never seen a video rental store that placed warnings above certain movies: "Caution: This movie contains provocative material that could create an addiction to pornography, cause infidelity and violence and result in the loss of your dignity and family."

There are times when I find I can be vulnerable to the enemy's schemes.

When I am alone. Like most people, I'm tempted when no one else is looking—when I'm away on a trip, isolated from those who know me.

When I'm with someone else who is willing to be a part of Satan's scheme. If the enemy can't get me when I am alone, he throws me with people who tempt me to gossip, or to go with the crowd—to be a people pleaser.

When I am tired. When I tire physically and emotionally, I become susceptible to erroneous thoughts about God, myself and others. I've learned that temptation is easier to withstand when I'm not "living on the edge." I need to retreat periodically to allow God to replenish my strength.

When I think I can justify my actions. I am constantly amazed at my ability to rationalize wrong choices.

I think there's a mistaken tendency to think that these schemes and temptations decrease as we grow older. Biblically and practically speaking, my flesh is no better today than it was 40 years ago when I became a Christian. The mistake is made when we drop our guards to seemingly "small temptations" and give the enemy an opportunity to get a foothold in our lives. "Be on the alert!"

....

Discuss:
When do you find you should especially be on guard against the schemes of Satan? What schemes do you find him using in your own life?

Pray:
For one another that you will not drop your guard and be carried away by the deceitfulness of sin.

DEFENSES AGAINST THE LION

Be of sober spirit, be on the alert. Your adversary, the devil, prowls about
like a roaring lion, seeking someone to devour.

1 PETER 5:8

I've found a widespread misconception about Satan's efforts to devour us by presenting us with temptations. Many people think that it's a sin just to be tempted. The fact is, being tempted is normal for a Christian—especially one who is growing.

Even Christ, we recall, was tempted in that classic confrontation with the devil at the beginning of His ministry. *Giving in* to temptation is the problem.

So how can we resist the roaring lion? First, *know your weaknesses*. If temptation occurs when you are alone, build in some safeguards. Ask your spouse to keep you honest and accountable by asking the hard questions that you don't want anyone to ask you. (Example: Did you watch any provocative movies in your hotel room on your recent business trip?) Keep your mind at work; prepare for times when you are alone by setting some objectives. Or the next time you are tempted, call your mate and ask him or her to pray with you and for you.

Second, *draw upon His power to stand firm*. As Paul says, "God will not allow us to be tempted beyond what we can withstand, if we rely on His strength to deliver us" (see 1 Cor. 10:13).

Third, if you are toying with a temptation realize that *you might as well be handling a serpent*. Some people stand as close to the edge of sin as they can, thinking they are above it, when they may actually be toying with the death of their marriages, their family relationships and their ministries. In the same passage, Paul counsels, "If you think you are standing firm, be careful that you don't fall!" (see v. 12).

As I was writing this, I received a phone call from a man who was about to lose his marriage and job because he crossed the line in his job. I wish you could have listened to the agony that was in his life because of his compromise. Let me encourage and exhort you to live a holy life and resist the temptations that are set before you.

....

Discuss:
Are you crossing the line or standing anywhere near a danger point right now? If so, confess your sins so that you may be free.

Pray:
Ask God to teach you how to stand firm in the spiritual battle. Call on the Holy Spirit and His indwelling power to give you the strength to stand firm.

WIVES WERE MEANT TO SOAR

For in this way in former times the holy women also, who hoped in God, used to adorn themselves, being submissive to their own husbands.

1 PETER 3:5

There is a story about a kite that was soaring high in the sky when it saw a field of flowers some distance away. *It sure would be fun to fly over there and get a closer look at all those beautiful flowers,* the kite thought.

But there was one problem. The string holding the kite wasn't long enough to let it fly where it wanted to. So it pulled and tugged and finally broke loose. Happily, the kite soared for a few moments toward the field of flowers. But soon it came crashing down—falling far short of its goal. What had seemed to be holding the kite down was actually enabling it to fly.

The wife is the kite in this story. The string symbolizes the scriptural principles of a man's responsibility to lead and of a woman's responsibility to submit to his headship. The string was not intended to be a hindrance. Together with the wind, it is actually what is holding up the kite.

The husband's love is the wind that enables the kite to soar into the sky. Without this wind—the secure, encouraging environment the husband creates through his leadership—the wife can feel tied down, not uplifted.

A husband can help his wife soar by reminding her verbally of his love and expressing his need of her in specific ways—notes, calls and love letters. And he can show appreciation to her for all that she does for him.

Husbands need to give the kind of servant-based leadership that uplifts their wives. God means for this leadership to be liberating, not limiting. God made wives to soar.

....

Discuss:
As a wife, share with your husband ways he could enable you to "soar."
What are three things he can do to add "lift" to your life?

Pray:
As a husband, take your wife's hand and express to
God how grateful you are for her.

DUSTING EACH OTHER OFF

Death and life are in the power of the tongue, and those who love it will eat its fruit.

PROVERBS 18:21

Picture the major league baseball pitcher taking his warm-up pitches just before you. The batter steps up to the plate. The first pitch sails over the catcher's head and slams into the screen. The next one burrows wildly in the dirt and bounces up, almost hitting you in the on-deck circle 20 feet from home plate.

Nervous and uncertain, you finally step up to the plate. After three swings at the missile burning across the plate at 90 miles an hour, you're glad to trot back to the safety of the dugout.

Ryne Duren, former pitcher for the New York Yankees, liked to intimidate batters like that. He was known as the patron saint of the "psych out." He knew how to mentally harass opposing batters, "dusting them off" with an assortment of wildly launched pitches that left them terrified.

Unfortunately, words are sometimes hurled like that in the home. Instead of a baseball, we launch hurtful, intimidating words at each other, inflicting fear, pain and guilt. We learn what the wise man meant when he said death is in the power of the tongue.

Winston Churchill was a master at "dusting off" his opponents with such missiles. Once, after he had overindulged, his spiteful opponent, Lady Astor, said to him, "Mr. Prime Minister, I perceive you are drunk." Churchill smiled and replied, "Yes, Lady Astor, and you are ugly. But tomorrow I shall be sober."

Even though you may be this skillful with the quick retort, what do you gain when you fire off such verbal volleys? Scripture warns that those who love to use the power of the tongue destructively will "eat its fruits." Often, those fruits are resentment, discord and revenge. They not only hurt others; they poison relationships.

Discuss:

What is the overall tone of the conversation in your family? What influence do parents have on this issue? What can you do to decrease the inclination to attack each other with hurtful words?

Pray:

Since Jesus Christ is "the Word," pray that your speech in every aspect of home life will reflect His role as Prince of Peace and Mediator.

FAILURE AND FORGIVENESS

Forgiving each other, just as God in Christ also has forgiven you.

EPHESIANS 4:32

*F*ailures at home come in all sorts of sizes, shapes and weights. There are the small ones called mistakes, errors or goofs: breaking a piece of china, spilling catsup on a new shirt, ripping your jeans, stepping on your wife's foot (with golf shoes), failing to carry out the garbage.

There are the heavier, medium-sized packages of failure that hurt a little deeper: shouting at the kids (for the fourth time in one day), habitually promising something to your kids and then going back on your promise.

Then there are the cumbersome and heaviest of failures that leave us feeling crushed under the weight: a divorce, unfaithfulness, an estranged relationship, a rebellious teenager who thinks he is always right, physical or verbal abuse, failing to lead your wife and children spiritually.

How can families deal with big and little failures?

First, I think *we've got to be truthful about our sins.* The Bible calls this confession. When we confess a sin it means we agree with God concerning that sin and turn from it.

I need to confess my failure to God and to those I've offended and then change my mind about the sin. I just can't keep on sinning and take my sin's impact lightly.

Second, the Scriptures teach that *we've got to forgive.* Forgiveness is not optional equipment in the Christian life. We are commanded to forgive because we've been forgiven.

To forgive others means we give up the right to punish them. We no longer hold the offenses against them.

Forgiveness is at the heart of Christianity. Your marriage, and mine, must be the union of two people who are not willing for anything to come between them.

....

Discuss:
Are you usually quick to ask forgiveness, and to extend it? Why is it often hard to be quick to forgive those who fail us? Is there anything that your spouse has done that you are still punishing him or her for?

Pray:
Thank God for His willingness to forgive you, and pray for a heart willing to forgive those who fail you.

SEEING IS BELIEVING

{Part One}

Jesus said to him, "Because you have seen Me, have you believed?
Blessed are they who did not see, and yet believed."

JOHN 20:29

Have you ever noticed how some businesses creatively communicate a service or product through a catchy name or slogan?

A few years ago I noted the slogan of Johnson's Flower and Garden Center in Washington, D.C.: "Our Business Is Blooming!" Our garbage company had one of my favorites: "We guarantee satisfaction or double your garbage back!"

Another one recently grabbed my attention. A Christian optometrist named his practice "Seeing Is Believing." When I saw that, my mind raced back to when I graduated from junior college.

I was a normal 20-year-old in the midst of the tumultuous sixties. I had no purpose. My life was chock-full of compromise, doubt, perplexing questions I could not answer, and frequent despair. Everything I had touched for the past year had turned to gold—grades, girls and college athletics. You would have thought I had everything, but I had lost my faith. I had become a "practical atheist."

Just like Thomas in the book of John, I was full of doubts and had questions like: Is the Bible really God's Word? Why does God allow suffering? If Christianity is a hoax, what is the purpose of life?

Precariously balanced with one foot on the banana peel of doubt and the other foot in the world, I began to honestly seek what God had to say about my life. Throughout my quest one question haunted me: "Must I really see it to believe it?"

My slippery spiritual descent was halted in the fall of 1968 when God loved me out of my unbelief. One person He used was evangelist Tom Skinner who shared the following quote: "I spent a long time trying to come to grips with my doubts, when suddenly I realized I had better come to grips with what I believe. I have since moved from the agony of questions that I cannot answer, to the reality of answers that I cannot escape…and it's a great relief."

You see, my life was riddled with questions I couldn't answer. Ultimately, I doubted God's existence. And I realized I needed to look at the answers I couldn't escape.

....

Discuss:

What are the questions about God or Christianity that have caused you to doubt God's existence? Be honest with your spouse about your questions.

Pray:

Ask God to give you an inner conviction of the truth of Scripture, or the answers you cannot escape.

SEEING IS BELIEVING

{Part Two}

For we walk by faith, not by sight.

2 CORINTHIANS 5:7

As a young man I realized that struggling over questions that can't be answered on this side of heaven's gate was a waste of time. Why spend life questioning every minute detail of the Christian life when there are so many obvious truths that cannot be ignored?

I knew the Resurrection was true. If Christ is still in the tomb then Christianity has little more to offer me than other world religions. But it is an irrefutable fact of history—Christ is risen.

I knew the Bible to be true. We have more evidence that today's Bible is what was originally written than any other historical document of its age.

Science and archaeology continue to prove (rather than disprove) the Bible's historical accuracy. And its central theme remains clear: God loves mankind and wants to redeem men and women to Himself.

It tells us how to live. It gives us hope in the face of death. And it contains the best set of blueprints for building a home (a marriage and family) that I've ever seen.

One additional truth helped erase my doubts: I knew that the risen Lord Jesus Christ lived in me. He came to change my life. As I focused on the facts of Christianity I began to see the scales of faith tip toward belief. I began to base my life on what I knew to be true. What have been the results?

- A life that is an adventure. Walking with God is electrifying.
- A lasting sense of destiny and significance that isn't man-made or fake.
- The privilege of being used by God for eternal purposes.
- His Holy Spirit empowers me to deny my selfishness and enables me to love people.
- A sense of peace, well-being and contentment that can only come when I obey Him.

The phrase "Seeing Is Believing" may work for a Christian optometrist, but if you wait to believe until you answer all your doubts and questions, you'll be waiting until it's too late!

Discuss:

What are the truths that you cannot escape? What impact should these truths have on your life and your marriage?

Pray:

If you've never done so, give God 100 percent control of your life right now. And if you've already done that, but have taken back ownership, you may need to reestablish who is going to be Lord of your life.

A Mother's Influence

by Barbara Rainey

And do not forsake your mother's teaching.

PROVERBS 1:8

*A*s a mother, I have my days when everything is relatively easy and I wonder why I ever struggle. The children are loving to one another and circumstances seem to flow smoothly.

But there are other days when I wonder if it will ever be fun again. I struggle with guilt and discouragement. Will these children ever grow up to walk with the Lord? Am I ruining my kids for life!?

Because of my humanity, my identity is subject to attack by my emotions, by other people's perceptions and expectations, and by my abilities and failures. Learning the truth about myself and standing on that truth is a lifelong process.

I believe that if I persevere, God will give me a ministry of influence to the next generation. Most ministry activity is by adults to their own generation, but mothers can literally shape the future. President Teddy Roosevelt once said:

> When all is said, it is the mother, and the mother only, who is a better citizen than the soldier who fights for his country. The successful mother, the mother who does her part in rearing and training aright the boys and girls, who are to be the men and women of the next generation, is of greater use to the community, and occupies, if she only would realize it, a more honorable as well as more important position than any man in it. The mother is the one supreme asset of the national life. She is more important, by far, than the successful statesman, or businessman, or artist, or scientist.

To have that influence on the future through my children demands that I objectively evaluate my life as a mother in light of that goal.

Discuss:
What are the good things about being a mother?
What typically discourages you? Make a list of each.

Pray:
That God will give you a vision for the type of influence
you can have in the future through your children.

HONOR TO WHOM HONOR

Render to all what is due them: tax to whom tax is due...honor to whom honor.

ROMANS 13:7

ach May, because of Anna Jarvis, 10 million of us send flowers to our mothers and 150 million of us send Mother's Day cards. Because of Sonora Smart Dodd, greeting card companies sell 85 million Father's Day cards each year. Anna organized the first Mother's Day observances at the Andrews Methodist Church in Grafton, West Virginia. And Sonora, sitting in a church during one of the first Mother's Day celebrations in Spokane, Washington, was inspired to organize the first special observances of Father's Day.

To many, these observances have become more of an obligation and a nuisance than special occasions. I beg to differ. I think mothers and fathers are heroes, and are well deserving of their special days.

Sports heroes receive honor. If you can slam dunk a basketball, knock the breath out of a running back or throw a baseball 95 miles an hour, you can make millions in contracts and endorsements.

Entertainers receive honor. Hardly a week goes by without award presentations to musicians, TV stars and movie performers.

Soldiers and policemen earn medals for acts of courage and heroism. Employees are often honored for top performances or for years of service.

God ordained the "office" or position of parent. Our nation's greatest defense is not its military, but the family. Its greatest asset is not the national treasury, but parents…your parents.

Discuss:
Do you have some negative feelings toward your parents left over from childhood that make it difficult for you to truly honor them? What can be done to change this so that you can honor them?

Pray:
That God will heal any of your own memories that make it hard to honor your parents, and that your own parenting will be worthy of honor.

RUNNING TO WIN

{Part One}

Do you not know that those who run in a race all run, but only one receives the prize?
Run in such a way that you may win.

1 CORINTHIANS 9:24

J had lunch once with a serious runner, an ultramarathoner. Max Hooper has a unique will to win. After surgery on both knees, Max was told he would never run again. Three months later he ran a 2:47 marathon and qualified for the Boston Marathon.

But Max's ultimate race was completed years earlier in some of the most hostile environments our planet could offer a runner. The start: Badwater, California, in the oven of Death Valley, 282 feet below sea level, the lowest point in the United States. The finish: the refrigerated summit of Mount Whitney at 14,494 feet, the highest altitude in the contiguous United States. Total distance: 146 miles.

Max and a marine buddy completed the task in 63 hours, 12 minutes. Max wore out three pairs of running shoes and his feet swelled two sizes by the time he reached the summit.

You and I run in a similar race. It's a race that God has set before each of us, and it takes place on a course of extremes. Life is a race for every Christian. It is a race you and I must finish…and win.

In the Christian life, there are at least five kinds of runners:

The Casual Runner. He runs when he feels like it. For this Christian, the sacrifice demanded by the race is just too high.

The Cautious Runner. He thinks a lot about the race, but he plays it safe and seldom leaves the starting blocks.

The Compromised Runner. Unwilling to lay aside present pleasures, he has given into temptations to run outside his prescribed lane. He has few convictions and takes no costly stands in life.

The Callous Runner. This veteran runner is a cynic and is critical of people. Preoccupied with his injuries, his heart contains layers of thick, tough tissue made of bitterness, envy or apathy.

The Committed Runner. This person is determined to win and knows where the finish line is. "In training" at all times, he knows victory is never achieved by the fainthearted.

....

Discuss:
What kind of runner best describes you? Why?

Pray:
Ask God for the strength to finish the race that is set before you, and that as you run you will "feel His pleasure."

RUNNING TO WIN

{Part Two}

And everyone who competes in the games exercises self-control in all things.
They then do it to receive a perishable wreath, but we an imperishable. Therefore
I run in such a way, as not without aim; I box in such a way, as not beating the air;
but I buffet my body and make it my slave, lest possibly, after I have preached to others,
I myself should be disqualified.

1 CORINTHIANS 9:25-27

*J*f you're in the race and running, don't let anyone hinder you from running well. But has it ever occurred to you that you could be disqualified in the race? We toy with disqualification when we repeatedly reject God's leading in our lives—willful, deliberate disobedience.

Look around at the human debris of those who have been disqualified from usefulness to God. I don't condemn those who fail—I stand in ministry today because of the grace of God in my life. But those disqualified have become examples warning me that I, too, could be disqualified and declared "no longer usable" by God.

How do you run to win? Here are Paul's rules for the race:

Exercise self-control in all things. The discipline of our desires is the backbone of character. Know what tempts you and avoid it. Augustine, the great Christian philosopher, lived a licentious life before his conversion. One day, shortly after becoming a believer, Augustine encountered a young woman with whom he had sinned. Augustine turned immediately and began running away as the woman cried out, "Augustine! Augustine! It is I! It is I!" But Augustine just kept running, and yelled back over his shoulder, "It isn't I! It isn't I! It isn't I!"

Know where you are going. The finish line for the Christian is standing face-to-face with the Person of Jesus Christ in eternity. Keep your eyes on Him. Grow in your love for Him. Be pleasing to Him.

Be willing to sacrifice. The Christian life will cost you your life. You and I must deny our rights and die to ourselves.

Run to win. It's the only race that really counts!

Discuss:

Is there anything in your life right now that could disqualify you?
Share with your spouse any temptations you may be facing.

Pray:

That you and your spouse will withstand temptations and lead holy lives.

THE PARABLE
OF THE PORCUPINES

*For whoever wishes to save his life shall lose it; but whoever
loses his life for My sake shall find it.*

MATTHEW 16:25

Perhaps you've heard the story of the two porcupines freezing in the winter cold. Shivering in the frigid air, the two porcupines move closer together to share body heat and warmth. But then their sharp spines and quills prick each other painfully and they move apart, victims once more of the bitter cold around them. Soon they feel they must come together once more, or freeze to death. But their quills cause too much pain and they part again.

Family members suffer from the cold of isolation, too—and they learn of the pain of being close to someone with quills. We desperately need to learn how to live with the barbs that are part of coming together in oneness.

C. S. Lewis describes the urgency of learning this lesson:

> Love anything, and your heart will certainly be wrung, possibly be broken. If you want to make sure of keeping it intact, you must give your heart to no one, not even to an animal. Wrap it carefully around with hobbies and little luxuries; avoid all entanglements; lock it up safe in the casket or coffin of your selfishness. But in that casket—safe, dark, motionless, airless—it will change. It will not be broken; it will become unbreakable, impenetrable, irredeemable.

Intimacy extracts a price. The closer I get to Barbara, the more she becomes aware of *who I really am*. The more transparent we become, the greater the possibility that she will reject me. But if both of us are committed to each other despite our quills—if we are willing, as Jesus said, to lose our lives instead of saving them—intimacy awaits us.

....

Discuss:
On a scale of 1 to 5, how would you rate the level of
intimacy in your marriage?

Pray:
Ask God for openness and intimacy in your family that connects
one another's hearts and creates a deep sense of belonging.

"THAT'S NOT FAIR!"

{Part One}

For the Lord your God is the God of gods and the Lord of lords, the great,
the mighty, and the awesome God who does not show partiality.

DEUTERONOMY 10:17

may never buy another Hershey's chocolate candy bar for my kids to split. I'm not referring to the one with squares, but the one with almonds. There is absolutely no way to break it into equal shares.

My children's cries of injustice erupt as soon as they receive their portions: "That's not fair!" My standard and dispassionate response to them has become, "That's right, *life isn't fair!*"

But Barbara and I also devised a solution: We let one child divide the candy bar and the others get to pick their portions.

I wish fairness in all of life could be solved that easily. Most things, however, do not divide in equal portions. Life just isn't fair.

Sometimes our "portions" in life seem downright bitter. It just doesn't seem fair that:

- A divorced mother of three preschoolers should have to work two part-time jobs and raise her children alone while her irresponsible ex-husband parties and neglects the child support.
- A 34-year-old missionary and father of two little girls should die suddenly of a heart attack while on vacation with his family.
- A child has an operation on his appendix and gets AIDS through a disease-infected blood transfusion.

Left to my human reasoning, these painfully unjust circumstances don't seem to resemble even remotely our standard of "fairness." They make me angry. They cause me to question, to wonder and to shake my head.

Fortunately, most of us face unfairness on less tragic levels. But our own experiences are very real, and we, too, are left to wonder about "the fairness of it all."

It's life—in a fallen world—that isn't fair.

....

Discuss:
What does not seem "fair" in your life right now?

Pray:
With your mate that you will develop the ability to trust God in
all of life's trials and circumstances.

"THAT'S NOT FAIR!"

{Part Two}

*For the kingdom of heaven is like a landowner who went out early in
the morning to hire laborers for his vineyard.*

MATTHEW 20:1

Jesus offers a parable in Matthew 20:1-16 that could be titled "Life Isn't
Fair, but the Master Is!" It's a parable for those who tend to keep a score-
card on life, for those tempted to envy others.

I have found at least three principles here to help us face situations that seem
unfair:

First, *remember what you really deserve.* The men hired first expected a bonus (see
v. 10). They thought the landowner owed them a "little extra" even though he had
promised them no such thing. We also think we deserve more than we actually do.

I have to admit this is occasionally a struggle for me. I look at what I've done
for my Master (God), and believe that I deserve more. That's a dangerously
wrong evaluation of worth. After all, He gave me everything I have. Plus,
Scripture reminds us we ultimately deserve hell, not heaven.

Second, *envy begins when we compare ourselves with others.* The laborers' problem
was they saw too much! Their eyes betrayed them.

How's your vision? Can you look clearly at what others have and be glad
they have it? Or does the green film of envy blur your vision?

Finally, *we must ultimately trust the Master, who owns everything, and be convinced
He knows what He is doing.* God is the Sovereign Ruler of the universe. He alone
controls and rules over all. Not only does He know what He is doing, but He
also loves us.

Barbara and I want our children to grow up realizing God won't give each of
them the same share of earthly benefits. But we want them to know He will always
deal with them in perfect judgment and according to His righteous character.

Everything that occurs in their lives will either come directly from God's
hands or be gently sifted through His fingers. Circumstances, events and problems may not always appear to be fair, but they have permission to occur from
our loving Father.

Life isn't fair. But I know One who is fair. And He can be trusted. Will you
trust Him?

....

Discuss:

What can you do to exhibit your trust of God in difficult or unfair circumstances?

Pray:

For those facing unfair trials or circumstances, why not get down on your knees
and acknowledge God's sovereign rule by giving thanks for your problems.

WALK LIKE A MAN

And the king stood by the pillar and made a covenant before the Lord,
to walk after the Lord, and to keep His commandments and His testimonies and
His statutes with all his heart and all his soul.

2 KINGS 23:3

The last thing I want to do is join the "male bashing" that goes on so often in our culture. After all, I am of the same species!

But many of you men need courage. You need to walk like men.

Oh, we may try to go through life with a John Wayne swagger, but we're like milk toast, desperately in need of some courage. We need to stop whimpering and making excuses and start walking like real men.

How? By following God's Word.

In 2 Kings 22 and 23, we read that King Josiah was a man who sought after God. But his life changed when God's Word was rediscovered. He called the people to a renewed covenant before God (see 2 Kings 23:3, above). And God moved through Josiah to crush the wickedness of his country like a hurricane crumbles houses as if they were made out of toothpicks.

For years, Barbara asked me to lead our family in morning devotions. Now that wasn't something I had growing up—an excuse I used for awhile. Finally, I realized God was calling me to be the spiritual leader in our family.

You know what? I'm not batting a thousand, but I am beginning many days by praying over my kids, reading a passage of Scripture and helping them to apply it. Some days the passage concerns the fighting and screaming and the rush to the car to get to school.

The point is I've decided to stay on the job and not quit. A lot of dads just focus on their failures and never decide what they are going to do to start walking like men.

....

Discuss:
Determine today some things you can do to be the spiritual leader that God
has called you to be.

Pray:
That God would build you into a man of God and a spiritual leader.

CLEAVING AND COMMITMENT

For this cause a man shall leave his father and his mother, and shall cleave to his wife;
and they shall become one flesh.

GENESIS 2:24

A lot of people have taken romance to the classified ads these days. One that I ran across points out the need for commitment. It was from a young man who was courting a young lady and it really mirrored our times. It read:

To Mary. My love for you would climb the highest mountain. My love for you would cross the hottest desert. My love for you would cause me to swim the widest stream. My love for you would cause me to die at the stake for you. Love, Jim. P.S. I'll see you Sunday, if it doesn't rain.

That's the way a lot of people are today. Their commitments are about six miles wide and one inch deep. One reason why we have lost romance in our relationships is we don't understand commitment, and we don't practice it in everyday life.

I'll tell you when commitment is really tested—during what I call the "marriage drift." That's what takes a relationship from the balcony, when you're being swept off your feet, to the battlefield, where you turn against your mate.

When God calls a man and woman to "cleave" to one another, He means for them to make a lifelong covenant that could only be broken by death. They leave one relationship (with their parents) and establish a total dependence and commitment to a new person.

Commitment enables two people to get to know each other and to work through life's difficulties when they face them. If you don't have commitment, you're going to find a way out of that marriage relationship. Today it's easier to get out of marriage than it is to get out of a record club.

....

Discuss:
Have you seen the "marriage drift" occur in your relationship? How?

Pray:
Reaffirm your wedding vows to one another in prayer by acknowledging your absolute commitment to your spouse.

FAITH: KEY TO ONENESS

Now faith is the assurance of things hoped for, the conviction of things not seen.
HEBREWS 11:1

*F*aith makes a marriage work. It's an invisible but active ingredient in a marriage that is growing spiritually. It's the catalyst that causes you to implement biblical principles into your relationship, trusting God to use your obedience to build oneness.

Many people, however, would find it difficult to give a true biblical definition of faith. Some people use the word almost as a substitute for "belief," as in, "I am part of the Christian faith, while my neighbor is part of the Muslim faith." And cynical secularists claim that faith in Christ involves a blind belief.

I like the definition of faith provided by my friend Ney Bailey in her book, *Faith Is Not a Feeling:* "Faith is believing God's Word is more true than anything you think, see or feel." That's what the writer of Hebrews meant when he described faith as "the assurance of things hoped for, the conviction of things not seen."

A small boy in England was asked by a scientist to be lowered down on a rope over the side of a cliff to recover some important specimens. "We will pay you greatly," he said. The boy said sternly, "No."

The scientist attempted to persuade him by explaining how the mechanism would work. The boy only consented when his father agreed to hold the rope. You see faith is only as good as its object. And that boy didn't know those other people. He wanted his father holding the rope.

The object of our faith is God and His Word. You have got to place your trust in what God has said, and to do that you need to know Him. And if you don't know what He has said in His Word, how can you believe?

....

Discuss:
What is something in your life for which you must trust God?
What are you trusting God for that only He can do in your marriage?

Pray:
Ask God to increase your faith and enable you to grow
closer to Him and to one another.

TRUE FAITH REQUIRES ACTION

So faith comes from hearing, and hearing by the word of Christ.

ROMANS 10:17

When my daughter Ashley was eight I took her snow-skiing for the first time. She was a little timid athletically, and our first run down the mountain took two hours.

During our second run, she became frightened when she hit a patch of ice. She wouldn't move, so I took her little face in my hands and I said, "Ashley, does Daddy love you?"

Through the tears came, "Uh-huh."

"Are you afraid of going over the ice?"

More tears, "Uh-huh."

"Ashley, Daddy doesn't want you to crash and burn any more than you do. I love you, Ashley. I'm going to do my best to make sure we don't hit any of the ice. Now, come on and follow me."

I turned my skis downhill and moved out slowly. And guess who was right behind me, all the way down, beaming, right in my tracks?

In this case, Ashley knew that one thing was truer than her fear: Her daddy loved her and would protect her. Her faith enabled her to take action. And as a result, she was encouraged. She had hope.

In the same way, we need to know that our heavenly Father loves us if we are to trust Him with our lives. How can we trust that which we do not know? In other words, how can you exhibit faith in God if you don't know Him?

Faith is a process. To develop that "assurance of things hoped for, the conviction of things not seen" (Heb. 11:1), you need to have knowledge. Knowledge comes before conviction. And that knowledge of God primarily comes from Scripture.

Faith is not blind hope that you throw in the wind. Faith is only as good as its object. It is confidence, a conviction based on the knowledge that God and His Word are true.

....

Discuss:
How well do you think you know God?
How much time have you spent with Him lately?

Pray:
That God would give you the conviction that you cannot build a good marriage without spending time getting to know Him. Pray that you and your spouse will grow in the grace and knowledge of the Lord Jesus Christ.

THE GENTLE ART OF CONFRONTATION

But speaking the truth in love, we are to grow up in all aspects into Him, who is the head, even Christ.

EPHESIANS 4:15

No family is without conflicts, and when we let conflicts simmer without confrontation, they have a habit of boiling over and affecting our spiritual lives.

William Wordsworth said: "He who has a good friend needs no mirror." Family members can learn to be each other's best friend by learning the gentle art of confrontation. Blessed is the marriage where both spouses feel the other is a good friend—one who will listen, reflect back, understand and work through whatever needs to be dealt with. Occasionally all this requires loving confrontation.

Of course, we must face the fact that some of us don't want to be confronted. Some people would rather be comfortable than Christlike. Many of Barbara's best statements to me are the ones that hurt a bit, but I need to hear them because they keep me on the right track.

Learning loving confrontation starts with love. As 1 Corinthians 13 points out, love expects the best of others. There's no way to confront someone else productively if you expect the worst or have a chip on your shoulder.

Loving confrontation is not nagging. It states its position without dragging it out for days. Being nagged at is no fun. Someone has said it's like being nibbled to death by a duck.

Christian confrontation doesn't accuse; it focuses on "I" language, with my saying plainly how I feel. It avoids "You" language, which inevitably sounds condemning. There's a world of difference between saying, "I really don't like arriving at church late—can I do something to help?" and "You always make us late!"

Also, keep in mind that the people you love, but need to confront, are not your enemies. Your mate is never your enemy. Christian confrontation requires that you speak the truth—but always in love.

....

Discuss:
Areas of agitation you try to suppress in order to keep a smooth relationship.
Are you being honest with yourself or those you love?
When should you bring up a problem issue?

Pray:
For the courage to confront—lovingly—and also for the
wisdom to know how to speak the truth in love.

WHO ARE YOU TO JUDGE?

Do not judge lest you be judged. For in the way you judge, you will be judged;
and by your standard of measure, it will be measured to you.

MATTHEW 7:1,2

*P*erhaps the greatest roadblock to loving confrontation is the well-known "log" that seems lodged in your eyes. Such handicapped vision inevitably distorts our relationships, both with God and with each other. Here are five tips Barbara and I have found useful in keeping judgment out of confrontation:

1. *Check your motivation.* Are you bringing this up to help or to hurt? Prayer is the best way to check our motives. When we take the situation to God and He shines His light on us and the problem, then we usually see our motivation for what it is.

2. *Check your attitude.* Loving confrontation says, "I care about you." Don't hop on your bulldozer and bury your mate.

3. *Check the circumstance.* Pick a suitable time, location and setting. Don't confront your mate the moment he or she walks in the door after a hard day's work, at mealtime or in front of others.

4. *Check to see what other pressures may be present.* Be sensitive to where others are coming from. What's the context of their lives right now?

5. *Be ready to take it as well as dish it out.* Sometimes confronting someone can boomerang—he or she may have some stuff saved up for you that will spill out when you bring up an issue. If you expect others to listen, to understand, to hear you out and to accept your point of view, be ready to do the same yourself.

....

Discuss:

Think of an issue or complaint you may want to air with your mate. Ask yourself if you are "projecting"—seeing your own faults in others. Before confronting them, reflect on whether the issue might be solved by "weeding your own garden" first.

Pray:

That you can see your marriage relationship objectively, being sure you are willing to be judged by the same standards you hold for your mate.

KEEPING YOUR FOCUS CLEAR

But when Cephas came to Antioch, I opposed him to his face, because he stood condemned.
GALATIANS 2:11

This famous confrontation between Paul and Peter occurred without rupturing their relationship. Paul was able to focus on the issue at hand. He didn't use it as an opportunity to bring up other problems he may have had with Peter, and he didn't try to assassinate Peter's character.

Here are some ways to keep your focus clear in confrontations:

Stick to one issue. Don't save up a series of complaints and let your mate have them all at once. A good warning sign is finding yourself saying, "And another thing...."

Focus on behavior rather than character. Confrontation must not turn into character assassination. Let's say you need to talk about sticking to a budget. Discuss available finances and necessary expenses, instead of calling your mate a spendthrift. Avoid attacking the person, and remember to use "I" language. Say "I think we can keep from going in the hole each month by...," not "You always drain us dry before the end of the month!"

Focus on the facts rather than judging motives. Your teenager forgot to tell you what time the school function would be over. Say, "I worry about you when you aren't here when I expect you," not "You just don't care about anyone but yourself!"

Above all, *keep your focus on understanding each other,* rather than who is winning or losing. Listen carefully to what the other person says. See if some other issue is really at stake in the disagreement.

A healthy relationship with God is open to His gentle confrontation—not one that sweeps difficulties under the rug. Healthy families face conflicts openly. It is best when the focus of confrontation is clear with the overall goal of creating a family climate in which everyone is a winner. As with the difficulty between Paul and Peter, clearer focus can lead to family unity, not isolation.

Discuss:

Think of any feeling of frustration you may have right now about your family. Are a multitude of issues the cause, or is there a single root of the problem?

Pray:

That God will give you clear insight into the needs and feelings of every member of your family, as well as a sharper focus on family issues.

A CONFRONTATION REWARDED

But if you return to Me and keep My commandments and do them, though those of you who have been scattered were in the most remote part of the heavens, I will gather them from there and will bring them to the place where I have chosen to cause My name to dwell.

NEHEMIAH 1:9

The book of Nehemiah may seem like an unlikely source for advice to families, but it contains five important guidelines for confrontation. Jerusalem had been destroyed, and most of God's people were in Babylonian captivity. Nehemiah wanted to take a group back to Jerusalem to rebuild the city, but he would have to confront King Artaxerxes to gain permission. Couples facing problems can learn from Nehemiah's model.

First, *he took time to pray* (see Neh. 1:4-10; 2:4). Most problems can be solved when you get together, take the issue before the Lord and let Him simmer you down a bit before you actually begin to talk.

Second, *Nehemiah expressed loyalty, encouragement and support* before raising the issue at hand. He opened his conversation with the king by saying, "Let the king live forever!" (2:3). To apply this concept to confrontation, affirm each other and create a climate of trust so your mate can hear what you need to say.

Third, Nehemiah *was truthful*. He came right out with the problem, telling the king the walls of Jerusalem were in rubble and the few Israelites who had survived were in great danger. Be truthful with your spouse about the real problem. Glossing over sin is deceitful.

Fourth, Nehemiah *had an attitude of submission*. He let the king know that he was not only interested in the fate of Jerusalem, but in the king's interests as well. Confrontation should benefit both spouses, not just one.

Finally, Nehemiah was *specific in his request*. He asked the king for letters to take him safely on his journey and for materials for rebuilding the walls of Jerusalem (see vv. 7,8). Do you know what you need from your spouse to resolve your problem? Be specific.

Homes can be built (or rebuilt) through healthy confrontation.

....

Discuss:
Think about past confrontations. Which of the five
principles above could have helped you?

Pray:
That God will help you balance personal honesty
with sensitivity to others.

WHY YOU NEED THE SPIRIT

{Part One}

And do not get drunk with wine, for that is dissipation, but be filled with the Spirit.

EPHESIANS 5:18

Most Christians agree that the Holy Spirit is the Third Person of the Trinity. We referred to Him as the Holy Ghost when I was a little boy growing up in a church that strictly used the *King James Version* of the Bible. And for a long time I could only imagine something like the cartoon character, Casper the Ghost—floating through walls like a puff of smoke.

For years I referred to the Holy Ghost as an "it." But the Holy Ghost Jesus talks about is a Person. He was sent not only to glorify Christ, but also to be our Counselor, Advisor, Advocate, Defender, Director and Guide.

In short, if you are interested in living the abundant life Jesus promised, the Holy Spirit is vital. Just think of all the sermons you've heard on the Christian life. Think of all the books you've read about marriage.

If you try in your own power to obey God and follow all that advice, you will fail…period. It's impossible. You need God's power that He promises when we are so yielded to the Holy Spirit.

Look at Ephesians 5:18 (above). Have you ever wondered why Paul put being drunk on wine in opposition to being filled with the Spirit? Because he wanted to help his readers understand what being filled means. When you are drunk on wine, you are controlled by alcohol. The same is true in a positive sense when you are filled with the Spirit. You are allowing the Spirit to control you.

No relationship, marriage or family will ever be all that God intends unless its members are experiencing God at work in their lives through the enabling work of the Holy Spirit.

....

Discuss:

Think back over your married life and family. How has the Holy Spirit been a Counselor, Advisor, Advocate, Defender, Director and Guide?

Pray:

Together that God would help you learn how to allow the Holy Spirit to control your lives.

WHY YOU NEED THE SPIRIT

{Part Two}

And be subject to one another in the fear of Christ.

EPHESIANS 5:21

find it revealing that Paul discusses the Holy Spirit (see Eph. 5:18-21) just before moving into a practical discussion of family relationships (see 5:22–6:4). Obviously, a clear result of being "filled with the Spirit" is to have a submissive spirit. Men and women are to submit to each other and to serve each other's needs.

Each of us needs to defeat selfishness. On more than one occasion I have a desire to be angry at Barbara. Yet, at the same time, I realize that my life is a temple of God, that the Holy Spirit lives in me with the same power that raised Christ from the dead. The Spirit helps me control my temper, impatience and my desire to say things I would later regret.

In marriage, there is to be mutual submission where a woman yields to the leadership of a man who denies himself in order to love his wife as Christ loved the Church. What a mystery this is! He is still the leader, but he submits his life to his mate.

In this type of situation, the woman's responsibility of "submission" takes on an entirely new meaning. Any husband who is living out Paul's instructions here in Ephesians 5 could never treat his wife as a second-class citizen or with chauvinist disregard for her needs and feelings. That is the farthest thing from Paul's (and God's) mind.

As you and your mate ask God to empower you with the Holy Spirit, His fruit will become a growing, increasing part of your life together. And as the God of peace and harmony fills your hearts and takes up residency in your marriage, you will experience the oneness and intimacy only He can provide.

....

Discuss:

What evidence could you, as a husband, present to show that you consistently love your wife as Christ loves the Church? What evidence would you as a wife present to show that you are being submissive to your husband?

Pray:

That the Holy Spirit would give you not only an understanding of your unique roles and responsibilities in marriage, but also the ability to subject your lives to each other.

A VACATION TO REMEMBER

By wisdom a house is built, and by understanding it is established; and by knowledge the rooms are filled with all precious and pleasant riches.

PROVERBS 24:3,4

A small motel room. Strep throat. A broken windshield. And a speeding ticket in Kansas.

What do these things have in common? Answer: Our family's vacation in 1957, when I was nine years old.

It was to be a family vacation to remember! A glorious two-week caper in Colorado Springs with visits to Pikes Peak, Garden of the Gods, the Royal Gorge, trout fishing and train rides.

But the day after we arrived, I started running a temperature. My mom was a great nurse, but despite her best efforts my temperature soared. I became delirious and was rushed to the doctor.

It was the beginning of a wicked 10-day bout with strep throat that seriously disrupted our sightseeing plans. I was not a popular person!

As I began to get well and my spunk returned, my older brother, Gary, and I began to fight. I chased him outside in the parking lot, picked up a rock, wrapped my baseball cap around the rock and threw it at him.

As he artfully dodged my missile, my mouth dropped open in horror as the rock came out of my hat and smashed into the front windshield of another vacationer's car. I recall three things happening at that point: Dad was mad; Dad paid for it; then I paid for it.

Somehow we rebounded, saw a few of the sights and headed home. And I remember one other incident: After passing through a small town in Kansas, a red Ford pulled out to pass us. Gary yelled out to my mother, who was driving, "Don't let that lowly Ford pass you!" Mom, who has been known to have her fair share of spunk, smashed the accelerator to the floor. The red Ford didn't have a chance.

There was only one problem: Driving that red Ford was a sheriff. I'll never forget the total silence in our car as Mom gave the officer her autograph.

Now you might think a vacation like that as a child would cure me of ever attempting one as an adult. So you'll be surprised to know that vacation, when I was nine years old, holds some of our fondest memories. You see, *we were together as a family.*

Discuss:

What are your plans for vacation this year? What type of memories are you hoping to make for your family?

Pray:

That God will give you the wisdom to fill your home with great riches of memories made together as a family.

VACATION MEMORIES

Therefore be careful how you walk, not as unwise men, but as wise,
making the most of your time.

EPHESIANS 5:15,16

It is the wise man who recognizes that vacations can give us time to invest in the relationships that mean the most to us. Vacations can be a time where you build strong family values and make memories.

As Barbara and I look back over more than 20 years of vacations, we'd have to say this is an area where we don't have any regrets. Vacations represent adventure, discovery and shared experiences with our children.

We have made vacations a priority. Both of us work hard, but we've shared a commitment that our children would not remember us as driven workaholics.

Edith Schaeffer calls a family "a museum of memories." If that's so, then our family has racked up enough vacation memories to fill several buildings at the Smithsonian:

- We've seen traffic jams created by buffalo crossing a crystal clear stream in Yellowstone and by a herd of taxis at the Lincoln Memorial in Washington, D.C.
- We've soaked in the solitude of Yosemite Valley (in the off-season), and we've sat in Wrigley Field cheering the Cubs with 35,000 other fans.
- All eight of us have shivered through the night in a tent camping at 8,500 feet in the Sierra Nevada Mountains, and we've sweated on the beaches of northern Florida making sand castles and tossing a Frisbee.
- We've driven 4,000 miles to visit Crater Lake, Oregon, and we've vacationed at home when cash was in short supply, walking 400 yards from our back door to fish and picnic on a public lake.

I was recently in a small group of moms and dads who were discussing family vacations. After our time together, it suddenly hit me: Not a single person mentioned a theme park (Disneyland, Sea World, etc.) as one of his or her favorite vacations. Leaky tents and murky swimming holes outdistanced the computerized roller coasters, Mickey and Minnie as the favorite memory makers.

Think about it. Tonight at the dinner table share your favorite vacation memories as a child and as an adult. Then talk about what you really want to do this summer.

....

Discuss:
What can you do to emphasize relationships during your next vacation?

Pray:
Ask God to help you build relationships and make memories
this summer with your children.

NOTES FROM THE REAL WORLD

I urge Euodia and I urge Syntyche to live in harmony in the Lord.
PHILIPPIANS 4:2

Apparently contentious church members and disorderly congregations aren't modern inventions. The churches Paul worked with had their share of internal chaos and disagreements.

Homes are like that, too. In fact, I don't often look at *Better Homes and Gardens* magazine because it fouls up my sense of reality. At our house, the second law of thermodynamics—which says everything in the universe is moving from order to disorder—is fully operative.

I came home from work one day to find the garbage disposal clogged, the dishwasher broken and the house cluttered. Our 3-year-old was sick, Cheerios covered the floor, and our 12-month-old had her fist full of melting chocolate chips. Our 5-year-old was still recovering from a broken arm, and our 10- and 8-year-olds complained in unison of tummy aches.

On another day, however, these same children served Barbara and me an elegant meal—at the "Eat All You Can Eat Cafe" (our living room). The gourmet menu was handcrafted from construction paper. Smiling children waited on us with towels draped over their arms, big grins and polite thank-yous.

These contrasting stories represent reality in the life of a large but very normal family. Authentic, normal Christian families *aren't perfect*.

But we are learning. We are learning that selfish people don't last long in relationships. And we need to be authentic and admit when we're wrong. We're also trying to give generous portions of praise to one another.

We have come to realize we are not very good listeners. How can a child feel valued if no one listens to him or her? How can a couple be real if neither mate asks a question or ponders the answer?

The world today cries out for people who live in real families, who represent a God who has given them something real—something better than *Better Homes and Gardens*.

....

Discuss:
How do you deal with household chaos? Do you find that the way parents react to other family members shapes the way others respond?

Pray:
That your family members will learn and grow as they move toward God's ideal for them, and they will be real with one another.

GOD'S LANDMARKS

{Part One}

And he said to the sons of Israel, "When your children ask their fathers in time to come, saying, 'What are these stones?' then you shall inform your children, saying, 'Israel crossed this Jordan on dry ground.' For the Lord your God dried up the waters of the Jordan before you until you had crossed,...that all the peoples of the earth may know that the hand of the Lord is mighty."

JOSHUA 4:21-24

If you've traveled around the United States you've noticed historical landmarks. In Williamsburg, Virginia, they have restored a community that was very significant in the founding of our country. When you sit where our founding fathers must have sat, you feel a sense of the events that took place there. Suddenly Patrick Henry's words "Give me liberty or give me death" take on a different meaning.

Landmarks like these remind us of our heritage as Americans.

I find it significant that God gave the Israelites landmarks as well. These landmarks caused the people to remember Him and His provisions for them.

The passage I quoted above tells of a spiritual landmark that is symbolic of the provision of God. Joshua 4 tells of how one man from each tribe took a stone from the middle of the Jordan River and created a memorial. Now, why do you think God did that? I think it's because we are forgetful, and children are curious.

Children ask great questions. "How big is high?" "How far away is a star?" I can almost picture a grandfather walking along the Jordan River with his grandson, and the little boy seeing that pile of stones barely poking from the surface of the water. "Grandpa, how did those stones get out there?"

"Well, let me tell you about that...."

And when the story is over: "Aw come on, Grandpa. You've got to be kidding me. The river stopped—in flood season? It was dry ground?"

"Well, how do *you* think the stones got there?"

A spiritual landmark was designed by God to remind us of how He has provided for His people in the past and to prompt us to believe Him today.

....

Discuss:
What are some landmarks in your life? What are some ways He has worked in your life? Let me encourage you both to take a sheet of paper and list the major spiritual landmarks in your lives.

Pray:
Why not find a place where you can pile some stones together to remind you of something significant God has done in your life? Pile the stones up and celebrate God's provision by giving thanks together.

GOD'S LANDMARKS

{Part Two}

Bless the Lord, O my soul, and forget none of His benefits; who pardons all your iniquities; who heals all your diseases; who redeems your life from the pit; who crowns you with lovingkindness and compassion; who satisfies your years with good things, so that your youth is renewed like the eagle.

PSALM 103:2-5

od provides other landmarks in the Scriptures so that we will "forget none of His benefits." Perhaps one of the oldest landmarks that God gives us is the rainbow.

After Noah survived the flood, God said that the rainbow would remind people of His judgment and mercy. He judged the earth by water and destroyed it, but He never would destroy it again by water. A rainbow, set there in the sky for us to observe, is a constant reminder of who God is.

One of the greatest traditions you could begin in your family would be to record spiritual landmarks in your lives. When God does something for you, write it down so that you can always remind yourselves of God's goodness.

Many years ago, Barbara and I took a trip to a conference, and we needed to raise about $1,300 for our ministry. We visited many people who invested financially in our work, and a number wrote us checks. When we arrived at the conference, we counted up the checks, and they totaled $1,378.

This is a story we tell our children to let them know that God provides. He meets our needs. When they grow up, they may tell that story to their children—and hopefully add some similar ones of their own.

God has been faithful to you in the past. Is there any reason to doubt He will not provide for you today?

Discuss:

Record the landmarks in your family by making some plans now to begin a diary, journal or scrapbook.

Pray:

Do you have needs right now? Remember how God has worked in your life, and express your trust in Him to meet your needs once again.

THE CHARACTER
OF THE COMMITTED

Then the commissioners and satraps began trying to find a ground of accusation against Daniel in regard to government affairs; but they could find no ground of accusation or evidence of corruption, inasmuch as he was faithful, and no negligence or corruption was to be found in him.

DANIEL 6:4

If people tried to find grounds for charging you with corruption, would they succeed? Can you be trusted to do what you know is right, whether in big or little things? Are you reliable?

These traits are saturated with one recurring theme: character. Character says quietly, yet convincingly, "I do what is right. You can count on me—at any cost!"

I sense in our society a growing feeling of "I deserve a perk"; "I deserve a promotion (without the process)"; "I deserve the position, prestige and honor (without having to pay the price and take on the responsibilities)." Many are climbing the career ladder, but few seem to be on the *character* path.

Considering these questions will help you determine whether others consider you a person of character:

- Do people constantly have to remind you to get things done?
- Do you habitually forget to follow through?
- What does your word mean to you? Is it a premium seal that secures the deal, or a flimsy wrapper that can be taken off and thrown away with ease?
- Do you return phone calls?
- Do your children believe you when you promise to do something with them?
- If you promise you'll be home, do you call if you're going to be late?
- Do you speak admiringly around your children of those who are successful and faithful?

Imagine the impact Christians would have on society if we replaced compromise and unfaithfulness with dependability, consistency and obedience toward God. Perhaps our salt would become truly "salty" again.

··

Discuss:
What is at the heart of faithfulness? What's at stake in relationships when faithfulness is ignored? Is trust an issue in your life? Marriage? Family? How?

Pray:
Ask God to fill your home with relationships that are built on trust and faithfulness. Ask Him to show you ways you can be faithful and model them to your family.

WHAT'S YOUR TARGET?

Like arrows in the hand of a warrior, so are the children of one's youth.

PSALM 127:4

few years ago my oldest son, Benjamin, and I got into archery. Never fear, the deer in the woods are safe. There is no chance of us hurting anything, I promise you. When we started, we were so bad that we missed the entire bale of hay.

As I've learned more about archery, I've discovered there is much more to this sport than meets the eye. And in the process I've gained insight into Psalm 127:4, which describes children as "arrows." For example, did you know that even the best manufacturer cannot make a perfectly straight arrow? You can pay more than $15 apiece for arrows, and even they aren't perfect. In the same way, no parent can produce a perfect child. It's impossible.

Also, there are many factors that can influence an arrow after you release it—wind, trees, rain. But do these factors keep me from releasing the arrow? No, because arrows are not meant to stay in the quiver.

As we raise our children with the goal of releasing them into the world to live independently, we see the pressures and influence of a culture that is increasingly turning away from God. But children were given to us to be released.

And what is our target? Where are we aiming our children? Toward a lifetime of walking with God. No matter what factors try to influence them, they will be fine as long as we point them to the right target.

Many parents, however, have never considered where they are aiming their children. We did some research and found that more than 90 percent of parents said they had plans for raising their children, but were unable to clearly explain them. They didn't have the plans written down.

It was baseball great Yogi Berra who quipped, "If you don't know where you're going, you'll get there every time." Does that describe you as a parent?

Discuss:
What are your goals as a parent?
At what target are you aiming your children?

Pray:
Ask God to clarify your target and grant your children favor
as you release them toward it.

D-DAY FOR THE FAMILY

{Part One}

Be strong, and let your heart take courage, all you who hope in the Lord.

PSALM 31:24

*I*t was June 1994, and magazines and newspapers were awash with stories and pictures about "D-Day." Thousands of veterans revisited Normandy to recall that heroic battle and to honor their fallen comrades. These soldiers who bravely invaded enemy beaches had more than guns, bullets and provisions on their backs—they carried the outcome of World War II on their shoulders.

One picture will be forever etched in my mind. It was a German photograph of a Nazi machine gunner perched in a well-protected bunker above Omaha Beach. His advantage must have been merciless. Undoubtedly, he mowed down hundreds of our young men as they sought to make it across the beach to the protection of the hills and cliffs.

I've thought often of the fear those men faced as they lunged out of the safety of their landing craft and into the foaming tide. Bullets delivering death popped the water as they fought the surf and pushed onto the beach.

Some people think that courage means having no fear, but I disagree. Courage means moving forward in spite of your fears to face the task you've been given. And that's what those men did.

Today we're engaged in another battle—for the family. There's a big difference in this battle though. It's being fought in private—in the hearts of men and women, and in the homes where they attempt, day after day, to build loving relationships.

Every day they make choices on whether to deny themselves and follow God's plan, whether to love and serve each other or fulfill their own selfish desires. And when those battles of the heart are lost, we see the wreckage—divorce, abuse and neglect producing shattered lives and an astonishing number of young people who have entered the world without the ability to make strong and courageous moral choices.

Often we approach these choices with the same type of trepidation that those men faced on the beaches of Normandy. We forget the God who calls us to hope in Him. But the battle for the family will be won if you and I decide to conquer the battlefront that is before us.

....

Discuss:
What are some difficult battles you are facing in your family right now?

Pray:
Spend time asking God to give you courage to face the battlefronts you are facing and the ability to put your hope in Him.

D-DAY FOR THE FAMILY

{Part Two}

Just as I have been with Moses, I will be with you; I will not fail you
or forsake you. Be strong and courageous.

JOSHUA 1:5,6

*M*any of the soldiers on D-Day never made it out of the water, and many more died on the sand. But those who found a temporary place of safety faced another moment that tested their characters.

Behind them, on the few yards of beach they had crossed, the cries of death were everywhere. As they looked forward, they saw nothing but barbed wire and entrenched nests of lethal German machine gunners.

It was grim.

It was war.

At moments like these, true leaders step forward, and that's what happened at Omaha Beach. In one case, a lieutenant and a wounded sergeant exposed themselves to gunfire so they could inspect an entanglement of barbed wire.

The lieutenant slithered on his belly back to his men and asked, "Are you going to lie there and get killed or get up and do something about it?"

Nobody moved, so the lieutenant and sergeant—still under enemy fire—blew up the barbed wire themselves. This got the men moving, and eventually 300 made it through that section of the German lines.

My favorite story, though, concerns Colonel George A. Taylor, who commanded the American Sixteenth Infantry. His troops were also pinned down by the murderous gunfire, and he, too, realized they would not move unless he was willing to lead.

"Two kinds of people are staying on this beach," he yelled, "the dead and those who are going to die. Now let's get the ____ out of here!" And with that he led his men forward to attack the Germans.

History records that, on D-Day, boys became men…they stepped up to the challenge of the moment…the allied forces prevailed…and the war was ultimately won.

We're slowly losing the battle for the family because not enough leaders have stepped forward in the smoke of the battle to rally the troops.

And where are these leaders? The families of America are crying out for men to lead, love and serve their wives and children.

....

Discuss:

If you are the husband and father in your family, what is keeping you from being a courageous leader in your home?

Pray:

Ask God to grant you victory in the battle for your family.

D-DAY FOR THE FAMILY

{Part Three}

For where your treasure is, there will your heart be also.

MATTHEW 6:21

Today we need men who have the courage to do two things: First, *men need the courage to choose real family values.* They need the strength to make godly choices.

Thomas Carlisle wrote, "Conviction is worthless until it converts itself into conduct." Courage begins at home with what we impart to our children. We need to leave our children a heritage of godly values, not merely an inheritance. And it won't be achieved if we pour our lives into our careers, our pleasure and our hobbies. That heritage is secured by the priority we place upon our relationships with them.

It takes courage to live by priorities. As the verse above reminds us, your heart is where your treasure is. Have you ever thought of your children being treasures worth fighting for?

Second, *men need to step out of the safety of their homes and decide to "storm the beach"* in the same way those brave soldiers stormed the beaches of Normandy back in 1944.

The "beach" represents territory that is controlled by the enemy. As you walk with God and grow closer to Him, you will begin to see areas of your city that need to be reclaimed for Jesus Christ. Maybe it's a family in your neighborhood. Perhaps it's the school where your children go. Associates at work who are ruining their lives with ungodly choices.

I believe God has a beach for every Christian willing to follow Him. I think back to that lieutenant who asked, "Are you going to lie there and get killed or get up and do something about it?" What will be said of us when we die? Will we be remembered for courageously upholding biblical values at home and in our communities?

The next generation hangs in the balance of your choice and mine.

Most of us know what to do. We just need the courage to do it.

....

Discuss:
In what areas of your life has God revealed that you need
to make courageous choices?

Pray:
That He would press you into battle. Also, ask God for an army of "lay"
lieutenants to enlist in the battle for the family so that America's homes
might be rebuilt around Jesus Christ—one family at a time.

June 9

RESPECTING A RESPECTFUL HUSBAND

by Barbara Rainey

*Nevertheless let each individual among you also love his own wife even as himself;
and let the wife see to it that she respect her husband.*

EPHESIANS 5:33

Unfortunately, some men hear only Paul's words about women being submissive and take this as license to be domineering. It's impossible for a wife to submit to a man who doesn't respect her needs as a woman.

Every husband needs a wife who respects him. That means she notices him, regards him, honors him, prefers him and esteems him. From a negative point of view, not respecting your husband means to be insulting, critical, non-supportive or passive towards him and his needs.

One way to respect your husband is to consider and understand the weight of his responsibilities as a servant/leader in the home. It is easy to look at your husband and see what is wrong instead of right. As someone once said, "Faults are like the headlights of your car, those of others seem more glaring."

Your husband needs unconditional acceptance—faults and all. As a Kenny Rogers song puts it:

> *She believes in me.*
> *I don't know just what she sees in me,*
> *But she believes in me.*

One way to communicate respect to your husband is to accept his schedule. For example, in past years I had to learn to be content with a schedule that found us packing up and leaving for most of the summer for Dennis's teaching assignments, conferences and meetings. We also had to learn how to live a great deal of time out of a suitcase and even out of the car.

When it gets to be too much, I tell Dennis and we make adjustments. Yes, my husband's schedule is important to me. I choose to be a part of what he does, to watch and help, and to be available to him. And I know by choosing to support Dennis in these ways, I am actually showing him respect.

....

Discuss:
Ask your husband when he has most felt respected by you. Ask him why.

Pray:
As a wife, ask God to grant you a better understanding of your husband's needs so that you will be able to know how to express your respect of him.

WHAT DOES SUBMISSION REALLY MEAN?

by Barbara Rainey

In the same way, you wives, be submissive to your own husbands.

1 PETER 3:1

There is no doubt that a wife's "submission" is one of the most controversial concepts in the Bible. Just mention the word and many women immediately become angry and even hostile. This subject of submission has been highly debated and misunderstood.

The dictionary doesn't help because it defines submission in a negative way. As a noun it means "subservience and abasement." As an adjective it means "nonresisting, unassertive, docile, timid, passive and subdued."

Who wants to be described like that? I certainly don't. These negative definitions of submission often lead to abuses of the concept by husbands who fail to understand its biblical meaning and the man's role in a marriage.

Some husbands and wives actually believe submission indicates that women somehow are inferior to men. Or that women have no right to challenge something their husbands say or do. Submitting doesn't mean that you tolerate abuse or neglect.

It does mean respecting your husband and allowing him to lead in your relationship. It means interacting with your husband on a key decision, sharing your perspective as his partner and then trusting your husband. It means being supportive in what he does right.

My husband needs my *voluntary* submission in order to become the servant-leader God wants him to be. And when Dennis loves me the way he is commanded to, it is easier for me to submit to him and his leadership.

....

Discuss:
In what ways, as a woman, are you thankful for your husband's leadership?

Pray:
That submission and authority will not be a problem in your home.

YOU CAN MAKE A DIFFERENCE

You are the light of the world....Let your light shine before men in such a way that they may see your good works, and glorify your Father who is in heaven.

MATTHEW 5:14,16.

One of God's primary purposes for your family is to be a light in a world of darkness. Did you know that an ordinary family can have a tremendous impact in our world?

I'm reminded of the Battle of Dunkirk in 1940. The French army was reeling from the onslaught of Hitler's Panzer divisions. The Dutch and Belgians had surrendered and the Allied forces were trapped in the Channel port of Dunkirk with no way to escape. Hitler's tank forces, only miles away in the hills of France, were ready to smash forward.

The Royal Navy did not have enough ships to mount a rescue. But then, as William Manchester describes in his book *The Last Lion*:

> A strange fleet appeared: trawlers and tugs, scows and fishing sloops, lifeboats and pleasure craft, smacks and coasters...even the London Fire Brigade's fire-float *Massey Shaw*—all of them manned by civilian volunteers: English fathers, sailing to rescue England's exhausted, bleeding sons.

In the end, the ragtag civilian armada brought 338,682 men safe to the shores of England! Common people had made the difference.

Today there is a war being waged on the family. Our nation's marriages, specifically our children, face their own particular Dunkirk. Your family can make a difference. The nation's families hang in the balance.

The question is will there be enough common people who are willing to set sail to rescue this generation of exhausted, bleeding children of divorce and broken families? Will you let your light shine in the darkness? The value of the next generation demands it. The nation hangs in the balance of how the Church will respond to this crisis. What can you do?

Discuss:
Make a list of the families you and your children touch in the course of your everyday life. Are you aware of problems in these families that your friendship and concern might help solve?

Pray:
That God will give you a spirit of outreach and a heart of concern for other families, especially the new couples who are just starting their journeys together.

BECOME A STUDENT OF YOUR SPOUSE

Do nothing from selfishness or empty conceit, but with humility of mind let each of you regard one another as more important than himself.

PHILIPPIANS 2:3

I love what Allan Lloyd McGinnis says in his book *The Romance Factor*:

Being an artist at romance does not require so much a sentimental or emotional nature as it requires a thoughtful nature. When we think of romance, we think of gestures or events that occur because someone makes a choice to love. A man brings his wife a single rose in the evening. A girl makes the love of her life a lemon pie with just the right degree of tartness. These don't always involve the goo of sweet emotion. They are the stuff that comes from resolution and determination.

I've got a challenge for you: Become a student of your spouse. Make a list of things that communicate love to your mate and write it in something permanent that can't be easily lost or forgotten.

Then do something unpredictable that demonstrates love to your mate, not to you. For example, if you normally bring your wife flowers, do something different, like writing a love letter. Or give her a real shock and actually take her on a "creative date"—remember those?

Barbara says that one of her favorite romantic times with me was when I surprised her with a trip to New England.

I made all the arrangements—airline, car rental and even baby-sitting. Then, one week before leaving, I began to send her on a scavenger hunt. She had to put together a puzzle that, after several days, eventually formed the states of New England. I swept her away for a delightful time traveling the roads of New England, walking and talking and taking pictures together. Just like we did on our honeymoon.

You may need to start courting again. If romance is missing in your marriage, perhaps you need to begin looking at your mate's needs and think creatively about how to affirm him or her.

....

Discuss:
What communicates love to your mate? Set a date to quiz him or her and complete an inventory of love.

Pray:
Ask God to give you ideas that would communicate love to your spouse.

KEEPING A CLEAN SLATE

*Let all bitterness and wrath and anger and clamor and slander be
put away from you, along with all malice.*

EPHESIANS 4:31

*A*t one of our conferences, a man boasted to me, "You know, I've been
married for 24 years and I've never once apologized to my wife for anything I've done wrong."

"Oh, really?" I said, with a tone that urged him to tell me more.

"Yeah," he said with obvious pride. "Every time we get into a squabble or any
kind of disagreement, I just tell her, 'I'm sorry you're mad at me.' I don't admit
anything—I just tell her it's too bad she had to get so mad." Then, with a cheesy
grin, he admitted, "And all these years she's never realized that I have never
once apologized."

It's amazing how many people behave like children trying to weasel out of
punishment after getting caught with their hands in the cookie jar. Yet the
Scripture is clear: A failure to seek forgiveness and to forgive results in an angry
heart, resentment and bitterness. Left to run their unrestrained courses, these
emotions will destroy a relationship.

In Ephesians, Paul tells us to put away bitterness and wrath, but he doesn't
leave it there; he tells us how. Look at verse 32: "And be kind to one another,
tender-hearted, forgiving each other."

Forgiveness makes long-term relationships possible. It keeps our slates clean.

As difficult as it is to ask for forgiveness, it's equally hard to grant it when
you have been wronged. You can tell if you have forgiven your mate by asking
one question: "Have I given up my desire to punish my mate?" When you let
that desire go, you free your spouse and yourself from the bonds of your anger.

It's liberating to admit you're wrong, and it's even more liberating when the
other person forgives and says, "That's okay—everybody makes mistakes."

Discuss:

Why can it be so difficult to admit we're wrong? Take a moment to ask yourself if you need to apologize to your mate about a specific incident.

Pray:

For both the courage to admit when you are wrong and the grace to extend
forgiveness when you are wronged.

THE SEVENTY-TIMES-SEVEN CLUB

Then Peter came and said to Him, "Lord, how often shall my brother sin against me and I forgive him? Up to seven times?" Jesus said to him, "I do not say to you, up to seven times, but up to seventy times seven."

MATTHEW 18:21,22

With these words, Jesus Christ formed one of the most exclusive clubs in the world—the "Seventy-Times-Seven Club." He wants you to forgive each other an infinite number of times, not just when you feel like it. By an act of your will, you must put away resentment and the desire to punish the person who has wronged you.

Families can't function without forgiveness. Living together in close quarters means we inevitably have our toes stepped on. But forgiveness is hard for some people, partly because of several misconceptions about what it involves.

Here are some things forgiveness isn't:

Forgiveness isn't excusing or condoning sin. It doesn't involve changing your attitude about right and wrong.

Forgiveness doesn't require forgetting a person's sin. God has that power, but we do not. Forgiveness means that even though you remember the hurt, you give up the need to punish the other person.

Forgiveness doesn't require denying your pain, hurt or anger. It may take time for your feelings to catch up and begin to fall in line with your decision to forgive.

Similarly, *forgiveness doesn't mean stuffing your grief.* There is genuine pain due to hurt. It may take time for the wound to heal, even though you forgive the person who offended you.

Forgiveness doesn't always mean instant and full reconciliation. Even when you forgive, it can take time and effort by both parties to rebuild trust.

Now that I've discussed what forgiveness is *not*, I'll look next at what it is.

....

Discuss:
Which of these misconceptions about forgiveness have you or your mate believed? How have they hurt your relationship?

Pray:
That a spirit of willingness to forgive will be stronger in your marriage relationship than the desire to nurse hurt feelings and punish each other.

LOOKING AT GOD'S EXAMPLE

*And be kind to one another, tender-hearted, forgiving each other,
just as God in Christ also has forgiven you.*

EPHESIANS 4:32

John Wesley, founder of Methodism, was talking with General James Oglethorpe when the general remarked, "I never forgive." Wesley replied, "Then I hope, sir, that you never sin." In other words, if you can't forgive others, why should you expect God to forgive you?

Look at Paul's instruction to forgive others "just as God in Christ also has forgiven you." This raises an interesting question: What did God in Christ do to forgive you?

To answer this question I would like to take you to a pivotal moment in human history: the crucifixion of Jesus Christ as described in Luke 23. It's a story that is rich in significance.

After Christ was betrayed, tried and unfairly convicted, after He was humiliated and scourged and jeered and spit upon, He finally suffered the cruelest indignity. The only perfect man who ever lived was hung on a cross with two other criminals. Below Him, soldiers mocked Him and stripped Him of His clothing. People sneered, "He saved others; let Him save Himself if this is the Christ of God, His Chosen One."

Yet Christ's response was incredible. Even at that moment, while suffering the most terrible abuse, He said, "Father, forgive them; for they do not know what they are doing" (Luke 23:34).

This passage holds three lessons:

Forgiveness embraces the offenders. Christ offered forgiveness to the very people who hurt Him the most. And that's not all—He offered it to them while they were still hurting Him.

Forgiveness initiates. God desired your fellowship so much He took the initiative in forgiving you. He did not wait for you to earn it.

Forgiveness gives up all rights to punish. God canceled your debt against Him. You deserve to die as the penalty for your sins. But God, knowing it was absolutely impossible for you to pay that debt, had Christ pay the penalty as a substitution for you.

If you ever have trouble forgiving your mate, just remember what Christ did for you. And you didn't deserve it.

....

Discuss:

Recall how Christ has shown forgiveness to you. For what offenses do you find it hard to forgive your mate?

Pray:

Ask God to enable you through the Holy Spirit (who lives in you) to embrace your offenders, initiate love for them and give up all rights to punish.

A VISION FOR YOUR FAMILY

{Part One}

For we are His workmanship, created in Christ Jesus for good works,
which God prepared beforehand, that we should walk in them.

EPHESIANS 2:10

onathan Swift wrote in 1699, "Vision is the art of seeing the invisible." It was a vision to reach the unreached that sent Dr. John Geddie to the people of Aneityum in the New Hebrides Islands. Today a stone tablet bears testimony of Geddie's faithfulness for 24 years of service to these people who needed to hear the gospel: "When he landed in 1848, there were no Christians. When he left in 1872, there were no heathen."

Geddie had a vision, a dream, and he gave his life to fulfill it. He was just one man. But not all people look at the future with such expectancy. I came across an advertisement containing quotations that illustrate that, sometimes, people are not quite able to see into the future with imagination:

"Everything that can be invented has been invented." —Charles H. Duell, director of the U.S. Patent Office, 1899

"Who the ____ wants to hear actors talk?" —Harry M. Warner, head of Warner Brothers Pictures, 1927

"Babe Ruth made a big mistake when he gave up pitching." —Tris Speaker, baseball player, 1921

It's a good thing people didn't listen to these prophets. I have to wonder what visions and dreams lie buried, forgotten and dismissed today because those who have them are not willing to think of *what could be* rather than *what is*.

When was the last time you had a vision for the future? A dream of change, of radical departure from the norm? When was the last time you spent enough time with the Lord to glimpse how He could work through you? If we as Christians have a direct relationship with the Creator of heaven and earth (and we do), then shouldn't we be the most innovative and creative people on earth? Listen carefully to the words of Paul: "For we are His workmanship, created in Christ Jesus for good works, which God prepared beforehand, that we should walk in them" (Eph. 2:10).

....

Discuss:
What would you do if you knew you could not fail? Share an idea,
a dream, a desire that you've always dreamed of doing.

Pray:
Ask God what He wants you to do with your life.
Ask Him if you are becoming the person He wants you to be.

A VISION FOR YOUR FAMILY

{Part Two}

I will instruct you and teach you in the way which you should go;
I will counsel you with My eye upon you.

PSALM 32:8

elen Keller was once asked, "Is there anything worse than being blind?"
"Yes," she replied, "the most pathetic person in the whole world is someone who has sight but no vision."

Vision is possessing a sense of purpose in life. And mankind's purpose is found in the Scriptures. God has a plan for each believer's life, and it is our responsibility to walk by faith, totally dependent upon Him to fulfill His purpose in and through us.

God has chosen you and your mate to fulfill His customized plan in your marriage, family and world. Have you caught that vision? Has your mate?

Americans live for the moment, unmindful of the future. We want satisfaction now. We don't want to plant seeds that grow oak trees; we want to plant seeds today and harvest the trees tomorrow!

Many individuals, and most couples, are not asking enough questions about life. Caught up in the rush of living, they seldom take time to step out of the mainstream long enough to take a look at where they are going. Seneca, the Roman philosopher, said, "You must know for which harbor you are headed if you are to catch the right wind to take you there."

Do you and your mate know where you are going? Ask yourself:

What is my vision, direction, purpose and pursuit in life?
What is my mate's vision, direction and purpose?
What is God's ordained destiny for my mate? For me? For our marriage? For our family?

Can you answer these questions? Are you confident of your answers? Perhaps you and your mate are searching for your purpose, direction and vision in life. Perhaps you have never given much thought to your destiny.

Discuss:
After grappling with and discussing the above questions, talk about what should be your number one goal for the next 12 months. If you could accomplish only one thing, what would it be?

Pray:
That God would begin to give you a sense of how He wants to use you to influence your family and others.

A VISION FOR YOUR FAMILY

{Part Three}

Who is the man who fears the Lord? He will instruct him in the way he should choose.

PSALM 25:12

*I*n her book, *Gift from the Sea*, Anne Morrow Lindbergh quotes St. Exuperei: "Love does not consist in gazing at each other, but in looking outward together in the same direction." Many Christian families today lack a sense of unified purpose and, instead of turning outward, are turning inward—not toward one another, but toward self. Instead of having an impact on the world, they blend in. Instead of cutting across the grain of the culture, they go with the flow.

Conformity leads to compromise. Compromise leads to mediocrity. Mediocrity leads to sin and a wasted life. Finally, a wasted life leads to a lost legacy.

Determining your direction is like developing a sixth sense: the sense of faith. Through it you first begin to grasp the unseen. Here are two suggestions for helping you grasp God's direction for your life:

First, *look to the past*. What causes ideas to continue surfacing in your thinking and conversation? What injustice makes each of you angry? What burdens your heart about your town, your state or your world?

Barbara and I did not arrive at our present field of ministry overnight. Initially, we ministered to high school students. But during those years we often observed that a student's spiritual growth would be negatively affected by a divorced mother or father. This eventually gave us the conviction to help start what is now FamilyLife.

Second, *inventory your talents and gifts*. What unique skills and training has God provided for you? In what specific ways has God used you to influence other people for Christ?

As you think over these issues, pray that God would develop within you a conviction of how He is leading in your life.

....

Discuss:
Spend some time talking about the two issues just described:
How has God led you in the past? What are your talents and gifts?
Your burdens and passionate causes?

Pray:
That God will begin to instruct you in "the way you should choose."

BITTER LAST WORDS

One dies in his full strength, being wholly at ease and satisfied...
another dies with a bitter soul.

JOB 21:23,25

The last words of King David were spoken to his son Solomon and are recorded in 1 Kings. The dying ruler, speaking of his enemy Shimei, said, "Bring his gray hair down to Sheol with blood" (1 Kings 2:9). Shimei was the man who had thrown rocks at David and cursed him as he left Jerusalem in disgrace (see 2 Sam. 16:5-14).

Earlier, David had told his men to leave Shimei alone. Now, on his deathbed, this king who was once described as a man after God's own heart (see 1 Sam. 13:14) talks like a dying gangster putting out a contract on a guy's life. Why did he change his mind about punishing his enemy? Why were David's last words vengeful and bitter?

Do you know any people like that? Filled to the brim with resentment and enslaved to a critical attitude? Enslaved to a critical attitude about everyone and everything? How many times have you walked away from such a person and silently prayed, "Please, Lord, don't allow me to become like that person"?

Now, consider the way another Bible character, Abraham, approached his death. "Abraham breathed his last and died in a ripe old age, an old man and satisfied with life" (Gen. 25:8). It is my hope to approach the end of life like this, not as David did.

People don't become bitter overnight. Bitterness comes as a result of choices—many wrong choices. The way we live and handle our relationships today will determine our countenance and attitudes when we are in our sixties, seventies, eighties—and on our deathbeds. David allowed the seed of bitterness to sprout and flourish in the garden of his mind over many years.

Hebrews 12:15 warns us to not let a "root of bitterness" spring up in our lives. We can dig up the seeds of bitterness before they take root, or cut the young roots out now, digging them up, roots and all.

....

Discuss:
Have you ever known older persons who exemplify King David's outlook and attitude? Abraham's? What can you do to "root out" bitterness?

Pray:
That in small and everyday ways you will choose loving and forgiving attitudes, and shun all bitter thoughts and attitudes.

RX: LAUGHTER

A joyful heart is good medicine, but a broken spirit dries up the bones.

PROVERBS 17:22

*S*eriously, I like to laugh. Someone has said laughter is the sensation of feeling good all over and showing it in one place. Laughter is one of God's lubricants for life.

Spiritual giants such as C. H. Spurgeon and Martin Luther were hooked on the stuff. Luther once kidded, "If they don't allow laughter in heaven, then I don't want to go there." He went on to add, "If the earth is fit for laughter then surely heaven is filled with it. Heaven is the birthplace of laughter." When Spurgeon's elders asked him to "tone down" his humor from the pulpit, he replied, "If only you knew how much I held back, you would commend me."

Some of the most fun-loving people I know are "spiritual giants" of our age. Bill and Vonette Bright enjoy laughing with each other and teasing one another as much as anyone I know. Chuck Swindoll has people who love his laugh almost as much as his preaching! Howard Hendricks peppers his messages with hilarious stories. It doesn't take much to imagine that our Savior, Jesus Christ, had the most winsome smile and the heartiest laugh ever.

But the way some Christians live, you'd think God had neglected to create a giggle-box. They act as though enjoying a couple of laughs a week is really excessive.

We shouldn't take things so seriously that we think everything depends on us. We shouldn't get too busy to have fun. We shouldn't become so goal-oriented that we subtly begin to think that people—especially our family members—are "in the way."

When was the last time you got down on all fours and "ate" your infant's tummy? Or wrestled with your adolescent? Or did something really rowdy or goofy at the dinner table? One evening we threw marshmallows at one another and laughed so hard we cried.

Life wasn't created by God to be friction-free. Laughter doesn't level life's obstacles, but it does make the climb easier to bear.

Discuss:

Is the overall tone of your home one of laughter? Of complaining?
Of criticism? What can you do to administer the prescription of laughter?

Pray:

That God will enable you to have too much fun this year
with your spouse and family, rather than too little fun.

Is Abstinence the Goal?

For God has not called us for the purpose of impurity, but in sanctification.

1 Thessalonians 4:7

One week in my sixth-grade Sunday School class I asked the kids how "far" they intended to go physically with the opposite sex before marriage. Here's how they answered:

	Boys	Girls
Holding hands, occasional hug	1	1
Occasional light kissing	6	7
Passionate kissing, close hugging	9	15
Passionate petting, touching in private places	2	0
"All the way"	1	0

As I wrote the results on the board, I was stunned. These were kids from Christian homes who attend a solid, innovative, Bible-teaching church. If this was how far these kids intended to go *before* puberty was in full bloom, then what will their actions be when their hormones hit the bloodstream and they are alone with the opposite sex?

That classroom experience helped me realize that many parents today are not helping children maintain their innocence. Another way of saying this is: *Abstinence is not the best goal for our youths today.*

Please don't misunderstand me; abstinence is a great goal, but it's just not the *best* goal. It's just not enough to train our children to be virgins. Trust me when I say there are thousands of Christian youths who are technically virgins, but who are sexually experienced beyond one's wildest imagination. Notice, I said, "Christian youths."

Passionate kissing and hugging is a very short step away from more direct sexual behavior. How many times have you heard someone say, "I didn't want to go all the way, but I just couldn't stop myself"?

You may wonder why I would include a series on sex education in a couples devotional. My reason is simple: Sex education is much more than talking to our kids about biological functions. What it really involves is character training and the shaping of convictions. Our children must be able to handle one of the most powerful forces in life, the sex drive, and to do that they must learn how to make godly choices.

And they need us parents to help them. More in the next devotional.

....

Discuss:
How far do you want your children to go sexually before they are married?

Pray:
Ask God to give you wisdom and courage in
protecting the innocence of your children.

WHERE ARE THE PARENTS?

*Now flee from youthful lusts, and pursue righteousness, faith, love and peace,
with those who call on the Lord from a pure heart.*

2 TIMOTHY 2:22

I wish I heard more Christian parents struggling over how they will help their preteens and teenagers control these dangerous sexual desires. But I don't.

For almost three decades many Christian parents have watched as our culture has performed surgery on our children's morals—an amputation of conscience. It's no mistake that schools are full of kids who do not know right from wrong.

The bottom line is we are not challenging our youths with a high enough standard. You and I know our culture is calling them into immorality. The forces today are simply too powerful for our youths to handle their sexual urges alone. We need to help them learn how to avoid kicking their sex drives into high gear.

A lot of parents pass this responsibility on to their youth pastors. *But they are no substitute for parents who will train their kids about sex.*

Barbara and I are the God-appointed guardians of our children's purity. Will we be 100 percent successful? Sadly, no. We will fail. And our children are not robots; they will make some choices and will fall short at times. Rather than lowering biblical standards, however, we want to help our kids (and you) go for the gold: innocence.

When I hear parents talking, I sense many feel pretty helpless to protect their sons and daughters from getting involved sexually prior to marriage. Others are confused; they aren't sure what is right or which direction to go, so they say very little to their children, or nothing at all.

Yet kids want their parents to challenge them. They need parents who will help them protect their innocence. In fact, I'm starting to read surveys that show teenagers are upset at adults who assume they are going to have sex before marriage. They want to be challenged to something higher, something better.

....

Discuss:
As a parent, how do you feel about your responsibility to help
your children control their sex drives?

Pray:
For the families in your church and community. Pray for a movement
of parents who would join you in protecting their children's innocence.

HELPING YOUR CHILDREN MAINTAIN INNOCENCE

So that He may establish your hearts unblamable in holiness before our God and Father.

1 THESSALONIANS 3:13

How can you help your children stay pure in the sexual area? I have a few suggestions:

First, *remember that your relationship with your child is the bridge into his or her life.* In war, the enemy wants to isolate you and cut off your supply line. Today the enemy wants to cut you off from your teenagers, then he can isolate them and convince them of anything.

Second, *give your preteens and teens some limits that will challenge them.* Barbara and I are challenging our children to not kiss a member of the opposite sex until the wedding kiss. You may think this sounds puritanical (compared to the world, it is)—but we are praying that such a high standard will help them control their sexual urges.

In addition, we are helping them set standards that will aid them in responding to many of the temptations our culture offers. We cannot insulate them from the world, but we can encourage them to avoid viewing television shows and movies that have sexual content.

Finally, *ask your teenager to become accountable to you.* Accountability means staying involved in your teenager's life by asking some tough questions.

After church, my son went over to a young lady's home. I asked, "Her mom's there, right?" And, "What time will you be home?" I come by this training naturally because my mom used to bug me to death about where I had been, where I was going and when I would be home.

As you hold standards up for your teenager, be sure to explain some of the reasons God commanded us to abstain from sexual immorality: freedom from guilt and emotional scars, freedom from sexually transmitted diseases and unwanted pregnancies, and preservation of a gift that can only be given to one person—the gift of innocence. He has our best in mind.

And, please, after you've decided what boundaries you will draw for your children, remind them that if they fail there is grace and forgiveness—from God and from you.

....

Discuss:
Talk with your mate about the worst thing that could happen if you challenge your children not to kiss until they are married. Now discuss the worst consequence of having no standard.

Pray:
Ask God to help you get your boundaries and standards from the Scriptures and not the world.

BROKEN TO BE MENDED

The righteous cry and the Lord hears, and delivers them out of all their troubles.
The Lord is near to the brokenhearted, and saves those who are crushed in spirit.

PSALM 34:17,18

still remember driving home from work after a series of challenging days in 1983. FamilyLife was long on problems and scarce on people to help solve them.

My hands gripped the steering wheel so tightly that I can still recall the white knuckles in the twilight. "Why," I prayed, "does it seem that secular companies have no problem finding the types of leaders they need to make their millions, while we struggle to find people to join our staff? I'm losing heart—please send me some help. Please, Lord, *help!*"

And sure enough, He did. Like many answers to prayer, this one didn't come instantly or easily. But over the years God has called together an incredible team to work with the ministry here in Little Rock.

Since then, I've observed that one of God's most prized prayers is one that cries out to God in total desperation. This prayer can't be mindlessly recited from a book, because it comes from a condition of utter helplessness. It says, "Lord, I'm empty. I've come up short again. I haven't got it! Only You can provide the answer."

At one point in the mission of C. T. Studd, a British missionary in Africa, he and his family had absolutely run out of food. If the next mail didn't contain some relief, they faced starvation. They had a night of prayer, pleading for help.

The next day they received a check for 100 pounds from a man they had never heard of. In his note he said simply that God had told him to send the money.

Does God always respond to our requests as dramatically as that? No. But what He does respond to is humility that expresses utter dependence on Him.

....

Discuss:
List the most urgent needs and problems you face right now. Have you found yourself grimly relying on your own inadequate strength to overcome them?

Pray:
Express these needs to God in prayer. Confess your own helplessness in dealing with them and your total trust in God's power to render aid.

June 25

GROWING UP

*When I was a child, I used to speak as a child, think as a child, reason as a child;
when I became a man, I did away with childish things.*

1 CORINTHIANS 13:11

The apostle Paul knew that kids will be kids, and as children we behave childishly. But he also pointed out that, as we grow up, we must set aside childish behavior and become more mature.

Children are by nature petty, hurtful and faultfinding in their relationships. They speak rashly, rudely and selfishly, with little concern for how their words will affect their parents and others.

Children think life revolves around them. They're self-righteous. They think they're always right and that others are at fault, even when the evidence declares them guilty. I'll never forget the time one of our daughters came to the table with chocolate on her face—clear evidence that she'd been into the cookie jar. Evidence or not, she insisted she was not guilty! Parents often face such tests in teaching their kids to tell the truth—to grow up in their abilities to be straightforward and honest.

We tell our kids, "It's time to grow up!"

And of course some of the unhappiest husband-wife relationships are those in which one or both haven't really grown up. They are still petty, hurtful and faultfinding. They still speak rashly and rudely, with little regard for how their words may hurt each other. They still think life revolves around them, and have trouble taking responsibility for their actions and choices, and admitting it when they are wrong. They blame, ridicule and find ways to get back at their spouses.

They speak, think and reason as children.

It dawned on me one day, in the middle of an argument with Barbara, that it was time I grew up. That I stopped acting like the kids. And you know what? I realized if I was going to be a man, I couldn't act like a child. And so, just like Paul said, I put away childish things.

....

Discuss:
Think of any tense times you've had with your mate recently. Can you detect in your own attitude any of the above descriptions of childishness? What steps can you take to help your own children mature?

Pray:
"Lord God, help me be a man and put away childish words, attitudes and actions. May your Holy Spirit empower me this day. Amen."

UNDERSTANDING SEXUAL DIFFERENCES

I am my beloved's, and his desire is for me.
SONG OF SOLOMON 7:10

A TV talk show host was interviewing one of Hollywood's biggest male stars, a man known for his prowess with the opposite sex. At one point, the host asked him, "What makes a great lover?"

"Two things," he said. "First of all, it is a man who can satisfy one woman over a lifetime. *And* it is a man who can be satisfied with one woman for a lifetime." I wanted to shout "Amen!"

Husband and wife must be committed to satisfying one another's physical and emotional needs. But they also must both take it upon themselves to understand each other's differing needs and attitudes about sexuality.

A frequent problem is that husbands expect their wives to be just as interested in sex as they are. In a survey in Tallahassee, Florida, 230 married couples were given a list of 96 possible leisure activities and asked to pick the 5 they enjoyed the most. The list included watching TV, gardening, going to church, visiting friends, sex, athletic events, reading and sewing. Among the men, 45 percent picked "Engaging in sexual or affectionate activities" as their first choice. Of the women, 37 percent ranked reading first, with sex barely edging out sewing for pleasure!

Most men want physical oneness, while women desire emotional oneness. The man is stimulated by sight, smell and the body. The woman is stimulated by touch, attitudes, actions, words—the whole person.

A man needs respect and admiration, to be physically needed, and not to be put down. The woman needs understanding, love, to be emotionally needed, and time to warm up to sexual intimacy.

As you understand your mate's needs you can sacrificially act to meet them in loving, caring ways.

Discuss:

How can you communicate to your mate that he or she is important to you sexually? What differences have you discovered between the two of you in this area?

Pray:

Ask God to help you and your mate understand one another and develop an intimate knowledge of each other—emotionally, spiritually and physically.

"O MY SON ABSALOM!"

And the king was deeply moved and went up to the chamber over the gate and wept. And thus he said as he walked, "O my son Absalom, my son, my son Absalom!"

2 SAMUEL 18:33

Bill McCartney, former head football coach at the University of Colorado, tells of a greeting card company that gave away free Mother's Day cards at a penitentiary. All an inmate had to do was sign and address the card. So great was the response, the greeting card company ran out of cards and had to rush back for several additional boxes.

The leaders of the company then decided to do the same thing for Father's Day. Word was sent to the prisoners that the procedure would be the same. But this time, not a single person came to send his dad a Father's Day card.

Think about that for a moment. As you probably realize, our prisons are overflowing with men and women who never had a normal, functioning father. Most inmates grew up in homes where the father had abandoned his family responsibilities.

King David was described as a man after God's heart, but he did not pass this on to his son Absalom. In fact, there is every indication that King David had been too preoccupied with extending the kingdom of Israel to be involved in his son's life. It was only after Absalom was killed in a war against his father that the floodgate of the king's tears was opened. Then, of course, it was too late.

Leadership without relationship is emotional abandonment. Emotional abandonment leaves your kids open to premarital sex, cults, peer pressure, alcohol and drugs. As dads we need to remember: If your children's emotional gas tanks are empty, they will fill them with something or someone else.

Discuss:

Are you frequently too tired or preoccupied to be emotionally involved with your children? Do you try to overcontrol your children, causing them to feel you are too authoritarian to be a gentle and loving parent?

Pray:

Ask God to enable you to emotionally connect with each of your children so that you can pass on standards and convictions.

THE TRAINING OF THE WILL

For I know that nothing good dwells in me, that is, in my flesh.
ROMANS 7:18

*L*iving in obedience to the will of God makes supreme sense. His way isn't just the way to heaven; it's the best way to live on earth as well. Then why do we struggle with obedience to God? The apostle Paul says it's because of our sinful nature—"the flesh." When we insist on resisting the Spirit with the flesh, we get exactly what we want: our own way. Sometimes it is hard for us to learn how unpleasant this can be. While Paul was persisting in persecuting the followers of Christ, the Lord observed, "You are only hurting yourself by fighting Me" (Acts 26:14, *NCV*).

The prophet Isaiah described it like this: "All of us like sheep have gone astray, each of us has turned to his own way" (Isa. 53:6). In short, we have trouble obeying because we have a will that is contrary to God's will. We resist Him and rebel against His commandments.

Sheep are not the only creatures that resemble man's selfish plight. Dogs do, too. I can see my response to God especially mirrored in the training of that special breed of bird dogs known as retrievers. They must all be trained to fetch and return to their masters.

Each special breed of retriever, however, responds to this training differently. The Chesapeake Bay retriever is one of the most strong-willed. Trainers must use a club to teach this "hardheaded hound" to obey the commands of his master. For the black Labrador, only the sting of a freshly cut switch is needed. And the golden retriever is the most sensitive of all, the trainer needing only his voice to train him. Evidently, his "heart" is tender to the tone of the master's voice.

Like those purebred retrievers, we respond to our Master's training in different ways. Perhaps all you need to correct a bad attitude or habit is to hear a whisper of displeasure in your Master's voice. Others may need the switch or even the club. I know which one of the three is least painful.

....

Discuss:
Which retriever do you resemble the most? How has God had to use pain in
your life to get you to listen to Him?

Pray:
That your will, and that of every member of your family, will grow more and
more sensitive to the Master's commands.

June 29

SEVEN STAGES OF THE "MARRIED COLD"

*But encourage one another day after day, as long as it is still called "Today,"
lest any one of you be hardened by the deceitfulness of sin.*

HEBREWS 3:13

*S*ome clever observer has described the way family members often drift apart as "the seven stages of the married cold." The pattern can be illustrated by tracing the reaction of a husband to his wife's cold symptoms during seven years of marriage:

The first year—"Sugar Dumpling, I'm worried about my baby girl. You have a bad sniffle, and there's no telling about these things with all this strep around. I'm putting you in the hospital for a general checkup and rest."

Year two—"Listen, Darling, I don't like the sound of that cough. I'll bathe the kids and put them down. You just lie down while I get the car nice and warm."

Year three—"Feeling a little punk are you, Hon? Maybe you'd better lie down and rest. I'll bring you something to eat. Do we have any soup?"

Year four—"Look, Dear, be sensible. After you feed the kids and wash the dishes, you'd better hit the sack."

Year five—"You don't sound so good. Why don't you get yourself a couple of aspirin?"

Year six—"If you'd just gargle or something instead of sitting around barking like a seal, I'd appreciate it!"

Year seven—"For Pete's sake, stop sneezing! What are you trying to do, give me pneumonia?"

While we may smile at this imaginary degeneration of concern, it's all too real in many marriage relationships. The pattern is in sharp contrast with our text, which calls for daily encouragement that keeps relationships warm and alive, rather than steady discouragement that can only harden hearts.

It is important for you to make this atmosphere of support and encouragement a foundation of your marriage. Marriage can rob your relationship of intimacy and excitement. Why not decide today to find a fresh way to encourage your spouse.

....

Discuss:

Do the ways you and your mate express concern for each other's troubles differ now from when you were first married? Are some of these changes natural and appropriate? Do others foster isolation?

Pray:

That the "dailiness" of family life and its increasing familiarity will serve to draw your family closer instead of leading to indifference.

MAKING DIAMONDS FROM COAL

I have been...in hunger and thirst, often without food....Apart from such external things, there is the daily pressure upon me of concern for all the churches.

2 CORINTHIANS 11:27,28

*D*oes pressure ever get to you? It gets to me. Let me share a slice of our lives that I recorded in my journal several years ago:

A plumber has just informed me our house could explode any minute because of a faulty gas line. A corner of the wallpaper is peeling above the shower. On the way to work I hit every red light possible and arrived late. As I entered my office, an associate informed me of two urgent situations needing immediate decisions. A three-inch pile of unanswered letters on my desk cries out for attention—*pressure*. Barbara is on the phone needing a decision from me on refinishing our hardwood floors: "What color of stain should we use? When should the floor man come? Should we do the kids' closet?"

As if that wasn't enough, after being on the road for eight weeks, all six of us were leaving in 24 hours for a family camp in California where I was scheduled to speak.

That day, Barbara started sneezing. Ashley and Samuel chorused in, and by midnight half of the Rainey Zoo suffered from asthma. In less than eight hours we were to leave for camp. We prayed about canceling.

The next morning the lawn still needed mowing, the kids were still sick and Rebecca was crying for Cheerios. Leaving for the airport, the phone rang as we locked the door, but we had to ignore it or miss our plane. The kids chimed in unison, "Could you stop for doughnuts, Daddy?" Secretly I thought, *Who needs family camp, hardwood floors or doughnuts?*

The apostle Paul allowed God to use the pressure he faced to make him stronger, much like pressure transforms coal into diamonds.

The question is: Do we allow God to use pressure to transform us?

....

Discuss:

Can you recall a scene like that above, when all sorts of pressures seemed to pile up at once? What situations cause the most pressure for you?

Pray:

Take the time just to sit quietly and meditate on God's peace. Then pray His power will help you transform stress into strength.

PULLING WEEDS
AND PLANTING SEEDS

{Part One}

*"Behold, the sower went out to sow...And other seed fell among the thorns,
and the thorns grew up and choked it, and it yielded no crop."*

MARK 4:3,7

Maybe you've experienced the hope of planting a new garden or lawn. You had a snapshot in your mind of what it would look like—high expectations of vegetable-laden plants or of your neighbor looking enviously at your lush, green lawn. But you discovered that good gardens and thick, carpetlike lawns don't grow naturally. Weeds do.

Pulling weeds and planting seeds. It's the story of life. We are individual lots on which either weeds of selfishness or the fruit of the Holy Spirit grow and flourish. Jesus warned that the soil of our hearts is the most valuable acreage on planet earth.

In Mark 4, Jesus taught the parable of the soils to His disciples. Christ said that spiritual fruitfulness or barrenness depends upon the type of soil that receives the seed of God's Word.

Jesus warned of the choking influence of thorns—three kinds of pesky, prickly weeds that squeeze the life out of fruit-producing seedlings.

The worries of the world, the anxieties of this age, are the first weeds of which Jesus warned. Worry or anxiety means "to be drawn in different directions" or "to be distracted."

What distracts you? What pulls you in a direction you know is unfruitful? For me it can be busyness. A full schedule of good things that crowds out the best—like time in the morning spent in prayer and the Scripture. I can be distracted by urgent things which could be put off for just a few minutes.

Some people are distracted and worried about what others think about them, preoccupied with pleasing men and gaining their approval. Still others are pulled by their insecurities, trying to find significance in achieving and performing.

Good marriages and families don't grow naturally—weeds do. That's why it's so important that we listen to the words of the Master Gardener, Jesus Christ.

....

Discuss:
What things distract you from a life of fruitfulness?
What "worries of the world" influence you?

Pray:
That God would use your mate to keep you accountable
to live by God's priorities.

PULLING WEEDS
AND PLANTING SEEDS

{Part Two}

"And others are the ones on whom seed was sown among the thorns; these are the ones who have heard the word, and the worries of the world, and the deceitfulness of riches, and the desires for other things enter in and choke the word, and it becomes unfruitful."

MARK 4:18,19

The second weed Jesus spoke of in Mark 4 is the *deceitfulness of riches.* Maybe you're thinking, "Hey, I don't want to be poor. I'd rather take my chances with handling riches and whatever deceit comes with it! Wealth isn't so bad."

I remember the year we held our first Urban Family Conference in Harlem. There was no veneer of wealth in Harlem—just unveiled hopelessness. You could see it and feel it.

But when I arrived home after the Harlem conference, I couldn't help but notice the clean and prosperous suburban neighborhoods of Little Rock. Then it hit me: Many of the people here were just hiding their hopelessness beneath the veneer of their prosperity. In reality they needed the light of Jesus Christ just as much as those people in Harlem.

Wealth is a deceptive weed that takes over our lives and chokes out our responsiveness to God. The following question will help you measure the deceit of wealth in your life: Would you be willing to give up the safety of your job and salary and invest your life in full-time vocational ministry if the Lord called you? If you're not, then you may need to pull some weeds of deception.

Beware of prosperous times—they can be deadly, numbing the heart's response to God's direction for our lives. Materialism may be the number one weed that is choking out spiritual revival and awakening in America.

....

Discuss:
In what ways have you seen materialism deceive you or others into believing they do not have a need for God?

Pray:
Regardless of your income, ask God to keep you free from the deceiving clutches of wealth and materialism.

PULLING WEEDS AND PLANTING SEEDS

{Part Three}

"And the desires for other things enter in and choke the word, and it becomes unfruitful."

MARK 4:18,19

The final thorn or weed which hinders fruitfulness in our lives is *the desire for other things*. Some of these weeds are easily spotted, like sexual lust, an addiction to pornography, or perversions. But other cravings aren't so easily identifiable: food, clothing, jewelry, car, job, salary, a hobby or sport, or even the location or kind of house we live in. Any desire that drives us, controls our thinking or preoccupies our minds can be a weed that hinders growth in our lives.

One good way to spot this weed is to check your conversations: What are you most excited about? What subjects do you discuss with others? What preoccupies your thoughts daily? Is it something honorable?

I guess what scares me about all these weeds is their potential for multiplication. When I was a kid, I used to take great delight in breaking off the stem of a dandelion that proudly held a cluster of seeds. A stiff breeze or the slightest whiff of breath would instantly launch a jillion of those tiny, angel-hair parachutes. Now, as I fight the spread of these wind-borne warriors, I can't help but wonder how many dandelions there are in just one of those seed puffs?

Letting just one "weed" grow freely in your life could result in a crop failure of good fruit. Thorns and thistles reduce the yield of the harvest. A friend of mine who grows popcorn once told me that weeds left unattended can cut the harvest by as much as 40 to 60 percent. I couldn't help but think about how I need to get serious about pulling, poisoning and plowing under the weeds in my own life.

I wish I had some high-powered nuclear herbicide to help you instantly eradicate weeds from your life. The reality is that all soil has weed seeds. Lives do too. What you and I need is a personal visit from the Master Gardener and His hoe.

....

Discuss:
What desires "for other things" preoccupy your thoughts on a daily basis?

Pray:
Ask God to do some fresh cultivation in the soil of your heart.

THE SLIPPERY SLOPE

Blessed is the nation whose God is the Lord.

PSALM 33:12

Each Independence Day millions of Americans gather in parks and stadiums to watch fireworks and spend a day with their families. Yet in the midst of the pomp and pageantry, many people have no idea that our nation is sliding down a slippery slope perilously close to a cliff—a point of no return. Consider the following evidence of how grim our slide has become.

Alexander Fraser Tytler lived at the end of the eighteenth century, but his book *The Decline and Fall of the Athenian Republic* sends a chilling warning today. Tytler found that ancient democracies waned under the selfishness of human hearts. He wrote: "The average age of the world's greatest civilizations has been 200 years. These nations have progressed through the following sequence":

From bondage to spiritual faith;
from spiritual faith to great courage;
from courage to liberty;
from liberty to abundance;
from abundance to selfishness;
from selfishness to complacency;
from complacency to apathy;
from apathy to dependency;
from dependency back to bondage.

It was Abraham Lincoln who said, "The strength of a nation lies in the homes of its people." I am more convinced than ever that the homes of our nation contain the ingredients for a spiritual and moral awakening in our country. The smallest yet most powerful unit for spiritual awakening and social change is the family. *Your* family!

The real battle, the most important battle, is not in Washington, D.C.; it's in your own home.

....

Discuss:
How does the level of morality and faith in society affect the home?
Why do you think Christians are being tempted to lose heart in establishing biblical values and standards in their homes?

Pray:
For those in power, both in this country and in other nations, that they may rule in godly ways so that we may live in peace in our nation.

BEING DIFFERENT TOGETHER

Do not urge me to leave you or turn back from following you;
for where you go, I will go, and where you lodge, I will lodge.

RUTH 1:16

Early in our relationship Barbara and I struggled to be as accepting of each other's differing backgrounds as Ruth was of her mother-in-law's roots in the land of Judah. Barbara grew up in a country club setting near Chicago, while I was reared in Ozark, Missouri. She was a refined young lady; I was a hillbilly.

As our wedding day approached, Barbara chose a silverware pattern called "Old Master." I approached a distinguished, elderly clerk in a department store and asked the price of Old Master ware.

"It's $59.95," she replied.

"That's not bad for eight place settings of silver," I said.

Clearly ruffled, the clerk pushed her glasses back up the bridge of her nose, looked at me condescendingly, and said, "Son, that's for one setting."

I'm sure I could be heard throughout the entire floor of the store when I shouted, "Lady, do you realize how many plastic knives, forks and spoons that will buy? And why would I want to spend $20 on a knife? We don't even own a table!"

Barbara and I had to work through many other differences, some funny but others not so humorous. We had some lively discussions over dinner, but we always managed to reach a compromise.

Couples must learn the art of being different together. In our own family we are learning to do this by making our relationships more important than our individual preferences. We are trying to build a home on values we hammer out together.

Discuss:

What are the major differences between you and your mate? Among other members of the family? Are they usually worked out happily?

Pray:

Individually for your spouse and each member of your family, asking God that they will accept the others and be accepted in their differences.

BIG LITTLE WORDS

Death and life are in the power of the tongue, and those who love it will eat its fruit.

PROVERBS 18:21

A friend recently showed me a Hallmark card with these words beautifully scripted on the outside: *If you love something, set it free. If it returns, you haven't lost it. If it disappears and never comes back, then it wasn't truly yours to begin with.*

Inside, the words continued: *and if it just sits there watching television unaware that it's been set free, you probably already married it.*

Cute words like that bring a smile to my face. But there are other words that can bring pain, guilt and shame. As Proverbs says, your remarks, your words, can bring life or death.

As a young lad, I recall going with my dad to the ice house to get block ice for making homemade ice cream. The iceman knew exactly how to use his pick to strike the ice and break off a smaller block of just the right size.

In the family, your tongue can be like an ice pick chipping away at another's self-worth and character. I've counseled people who knew their mates' weak spots and, in a stressful moment, would use words to purposely hack, slice and cut their partners.

But the tongue can also be used as beautifully as a paintbrush. Years ago, before we started our family, Barbara amazed me with her ability to paint in ways that would cause a beautiful picture to emerge on a previously blank canvas. In a similar way, your words can encourage the image of Christ to appear in the lives of each member of your family. You can elicit the beauty in a person with words of respect and kindness.

....

Discuss:
What are some words that had a positive influence on you as you grew up?
Negative? In what areas or circumstances do you need to watch the words
you say to your mate? To your children?

Pray:
If appropriate, confess any words that you have used to tear down your
spouse or family. Ask God to empower you to use your tongue to build up
your spouse and each family member.

ENTERING THE ATTIC

{Part One}

*There is no fear in love; but perfect love casts out fear, because fear involves
punishment, and the one who fears is not perfected in love.*

1 JOHN 4:18

As a young boy growing up in a small white two-story frame home, I was terrified of the attic. An eerie stillness enveloped me as I ventured into this windowless, hot, creepy room. The scent of mothballs perfumed the air. Invisible threads of spider webs attempted to capture me if I got too near. Mysterious shapes, covered by sheets and blankets, crouched in corners, casting suspicious shadows on the plank floor.

I just knew that attic contained more than discarded junk. Something was living up there, something that would mercilessly defend its territory against pint-sized trespassers. I never saw this creature, but I knew it was there.

Everyone has an attic in their minds. It may be a room in which past mistreatment is stored. Memories of when you failed others and when others failed you may haunt and accuse you. Your self-image is shaped in your past, by whether you were praised and encouraged or criticized relentlessly when you grew up.

Although I feared going into the attic alone, with a companion I became downright courageous. That dark, scary spot in my home became little more than just another room.

You and your mate can be that kind of companion for each other. One or both of you may be extremely fearful of visiting the attics of your past. But self-confidence and reassurance will grow if you enter them together.

Have you considered that your relationship with your spouse can give him or her the courage needed to face very real fears in his or her life? Take a moment and think of ways that you can be a supportive friend who helps your mate enter attics and face down negative role models that may be lurking there.

....

Discuss:
Are the "attics" of your past fearful or inviting? If the past creates
emotional turmoil in your life, then what can your mate do to
help you "cast out all fear"?

Pray:
That you and your mate can exhibit the love of Christ to one another and help
each other conquer fear as you build a home without frightening attics.

ENTERING THE ATTIC

{Part Two}

Brethren, I do not regard myself as having laid hold of it yet; but one thing I do:
forgetting what lies behind and reaching forward to what lies ahead.

PHILIPPIANS 3:13

Did you know a husband and wife can help each other sort through the attic of the past?

Sue and Rich dated and fell in love during college. Soon they were engaged, and then married. Although Sue had shared many things openly as they dated, Rich had no idea how the lack of her father's unconditional approval had shaped her self-image and influenced her life.

When Sue was a young girl, her militaristic father inspected her bedroom every Friday evening. In preparation, she would balance one chair on another to dust the tops of the window and door facings, which her father routinely examined.

All other required work was scrutinized just as intently. Once she was grounded for two weeks for missing two sprigs of crabgrass when she weeded the lawn.

When Sue was 11, she was told to take two cases of soft drinks down the basement stairs. She could barely manage to pick them up, but she did. Halfway down, she tripped and fell head over heels to the concrete floor. She was lying in the midst of broken glass when her father jerked her up and, without inquiring about her well-being said, "You dummy, I told you not to drop them!"

Not surprisingly, Sue had an impoverished self-image. At times, during her marriage, her insecurity surfaced in the form of emotional withdrawal. Rich was often caught off guard, but he encouraged her to tell him about her experiences. He rarely said, "You shouldn't feel that way."

He remained committed to helping her resolve, and not repress, her feelings about her parents. As a result, Sue now feels loved and valued by God and Rich. She is learning to forget what lies behind, to reach what is ahead.

Discuss:

How familiar are you with your mate's relationship with his or her parents? If you haven't ever done so, take an evening and have your mate share his most memorable times with his parents.

Pray:

That you and your mate will have intimacy to share both positive and negative aspects of the "baggage" from childhood.

July 9

ENTERING THE ATTIC

{Part Three}

I press on toward the goal for the prize of the upward call of God in Christ Jesus.
PHILIPPIANS 3:14

I have five suggestions for helping your mate dig through the attic of the past and focus on the future:

First, *work with your spouse to get the problem fully on the table.* Talk about how your parents treated you and ask your mate to share his or her experiences. Be patient. Talking about these things can be very painful. Affirm and strengthen your mate by listening, and by expressing your own acceptance.

Second, *help your mate understand his or her parents.* Talk together about them and put their lives in proper perspective. Remind your mate that his or her parents probably did the best they could.

Third, *give your mate the perspective that God's grace and power is greater than his or her parents' mistakes.* No matter how bad a person's home was, God delights in resurrecting damaged self-images and restoring dignity to such people. Talk about the overwhelming power of grace, and express your confidence and belief in the greatness of God's love and acceptance.

Fourth, *encourage your mate to forgive his or her parents—completely.* You may need to first talk this out as a couple. A qualified counselor may be needed if you feel you cannot help your mate get on top of this emotionally charged area and forgive his or her parents.

Finally, *help your mate determine how he or she will respond to his or her parents.* He has no control over how he was treated as a child, but he does have control over how he will relate to them today. Bring his focus to what they did right, and how you both are the benefactors. Help him think of ways he can honor his parents.

In some cases, it may take months or years for all the hurt to be brought out in the open. But if you're patient, and if you and your mate are willing to allow Jesus Christ to be Lord of this relationship, healing is possible.

....

Discuss:
What is a tangible way to forgive your parents?

Pray:
If appropriate, tell God that you are willing to forgive and love your parents.

IT'S NEVER TOO LATE FOR GOD

With men this is impossible, but with God all things are possible.

MATTHEW 19:26

When I hear of people divorcing because of "irreconcilable differences," I think of the above verse. When a marriage looks doomed from man's perspective, that's when man needs to turn to God. If the almighty God can part the Red Sea, if He can reconcile you to Him by the sacrifice of His Son, why is it impossible for Him to heal a broken marriage?

You may be facing "irreconcilable differences" in your marriage, or perhaps in a relationship with another person at work, at church or in your neighborhood. If so, take heart from the following note given to one of our FamilyLife Marriage Conference speakers.

> Last year in March my wife, Susan, informed me she didn't love me and wanted a divorce. I wanted to work to save our marriage, but she didn't.
>
> My sister gave us a registration form to attend a FamilyLife Marriage Conference in 1992. Susan filed for divorce, so I attended the conference alone.
>
> I became aware through the conference of the reasons my marriage was failing. God was not a part of our marriage. After the conference I became involved in and eventually joined a church. I prayed for God's will in my life but especially for God to put my family and marriage back together. However, the divorce was final soon afterward.
>
> Miraculously, my new church started a single parents' support group and care group in July. I joined immediately. God supplied the support I needed to become a single parent. Afterward, Susan and I began to discuss the mistakes we had made in our lives and our marriage. We began to discuss reconciliation.
>
> Susan and I are here at the conference together, committed to rebuilding our relationship with God as a part of our family. I praise God for answering my prayer even if it's in His own way and His own time.
>
> It's never too late for God.

I love that last line. Nothing is impossible for God.

....

Discuss:
What situations are you facing that seem impossible to you?

Pray:
Ask God to help you believe that nothing is impossible with Him. Commit to praying with your mate that God would move as only He can.

PROTECTING YOUR CHILDREN'S INNOCENCE

For I am jealous for you with a godly jealousy; for I betrothed you to one husband, that to Christ I might present you as a pure virgin.

2 CORINTHIANS 11:2

When our oldest daughter, Ashley, was 16, she was allowed to date. But I made it clear I wanted to interview any boys who asked her out. I still remember that first interview. Kevin showed up at my office riding his motorcycle (?!). I bought him a soft drink to keep things as informal as possible, and then, after several minutes of small talk, I looked him in the eye.

"You know, Kevin, I was a teenage boy once," I said. "And I want you to know that I remember what the sex drive is like for an 18-year-old young man." His eyes were getting bigger—he was really listening.

"I expect you to treat my daughter just like God would have you treat His finest creation—with all respect and dignity. Whether you go out with her one time or 100 times, I want to be able to look you in the eyes and ask you if you are treating my daughter with respect and dignity—especially in the physical area. God may want her to be another man's wife, so you better be very careful to keep this relationship pure."

On my way home I wondered if I was being too intrusive. Then over dinner my doubts evaporated when I shared what had happened.

It wasn't just Ashley's response of appreciation. It was Benjamin, who was 14 at the time, who put it all in context. He said, "You know, Dad, I hope that the father of a girl I ask out wants to meet with me. I'll know I'm at the right house if that happens!"

The reason I met with Kevin is that I believe Barbara and I, as parents, have been entrusted by God to protect our children's innocence. I'm convinced that parents need to possess a godly jealousy that ruthlessly protects our children from evil.

....

Discuss:
Have you thought of how you want to protect your children in the sexual area when they become teenagers? What guidelines will you set?

Pray:
That God will give you a godly jealousy for your children, and that your children will value and respect your role as protector and nourisher.

THE COSMIC WAR
GETS PERSONAL

*For our struggle is not against flesh and blood, but against...the world forces of this darkness,
against the spiritual forces of wickedness in the heavenly places.*

EPHESIANS 6:12

We are engaged in a war of unseen spiritual forces of wickedness that want to deceive, divide and destroy families. Barbara and I once sat beside a person on a plane whose life is a snapshot of how ordinary people get caught up in this cosmic war.

Susan, in her late twenties, said she was a Christian. She was single, and three times divorced. She said her parents were in their late eighties and heartbroken about the lives of their three daughters.

Susan's first sister, whose husband was verbally and emotionally abusive, had just been institutionalized for attempted suicide. Her other sister was an "active" Christian, married for 20 years with three kids, but on the verge of divorce.

And then there was Susan, who confessed that she was sleeping with her boyfriend. Lonely and fearful, she knew her biological clock was ticking and she wanted a family. Dropping her standards, she was seriously considering marriage to a man who denied the existence of God.

It was a fascinating yet sad conversation. There sat this young woman, talking of family values. But she didn't have a clue as to what her values were. Susan's beliefs were shallow and her life reflected it.

As we said good-bye, I paused to think about the other people on that plane. Like Susan, most were dressed fashionably and looked as if they had life pretty much under control. I couldn't help but wonder how many others on that plane had similar heartbreaking stories like Susan's.

It's a struggle that occurs every day in your heart and mine. It's a life and death battle of choosing good or evil. To fight it, the Susans of the world—and all of us—need to *clarify our convictions*. Change begins with convictions. Right choices flow from right thinking.

Discuss:
What examples from your own community illustrate the battle between good and evil values? What are you and your family doing to defend godly values?

Pray:
Read Ephesians 6:10-18, and pray that you and your family will be equipped with the full armor of God in the battle against evil.

"DON'T SIN, DAD"

Pardon, I pray, the iniquity of this people according to the greatness of Thy lovingkindness.
NUMBERS 14:19

The following letter contains a sad commentary of one father's legacy. (I've changed the names and place, of course.)

Dear Dan:

Before I start this letter to you I must tell you that I love you and none of what has happened or is going to happen is in any way your fault. If I had been as good a father as you are a son there would be no need for me to write to you now.

Over the years I have been unfaithful to your mother in thoughts as well as in deeds. Because your mother had complete trust in me, I was able to cover up by lying to her. Last May I met a woman in Sacramento. Her name is Susan. I am going to leave your mother and go live with her.

What I have done is morally wrong and I hope you will not follow in my ways. When you meet the right woman make a lifelong commitment to her. I was never able to do this and it has caused much sorrow.

Please do not allow this to change your feelings about your mother and I. We love you very much and both need your love now even more than before. We will always be your family and will be here for you even though we will be living apart.

I love you, Dad.

Every time I read this letter I wonder what was going on in that man's mind. Did he really think that by telling his son to not follow his footsteps that he could reverse the damage he'd already done?

I once showed that letter to one of our children. Later I asked what he thought about it, and his response was piercing: "Don't sin, Dad."

He was too young to realize the wisdom of his words. But I do. The prayer of Moses is becoming mine: "Pardon, I pray, the iniquity of this people."

....

Discuss:

When was the last time you confessed your sins to the Lord? Spend some time now, searching and cleansing your heart.

Pray:

Confess the sins of America, a nation of divorce. Ask God to heal our land and bring about a family reformation.

MEN AND SEX

by Barbara Rainey

May he kiss me with the kisses of his mouth! For your love is better than wine.

SONG OF SOLOMON 1:2

A sphere in which we wives, for the most part, do not really understand our husbands is in how their identities as men are vitally linked to their sexuality. Sometimes we women judge our husbands' sexual needs by our own.

Many wives express that they are offended because their husbands are such sexual creatures. This attitude communicates rejection to a man. To ignore his sexual needs, to resist his initiation of sex, or merely to tolerate his advances, is to tear at the heart of his self-esteem.

In her book *To Have and To Hold*, Jill Renich states, "Sex is the most meaningful demonstration of love and self-worth. It is a part of his own deepest person." And Dr. Joyce Brothers writes, "By and large, men are far more apprehensive when it comes to sex than a woman might believe."

Those statements seem contrary to popular belief, don't they? Modern men are portrayed via the media as always being confident and assertive sexually. George Gilder said in *Men and Marriage*:

The truth is, the typical man worries a lot. He worries about his sexual performance, his wife's enjoyment, and his ability to satisfy her. A man who feels like a failure in the marriage bed will seldom have the deep, abiding self-respect for which he longs.

But, as Jill Renich writes, "To receive him with joy, and to share sexual pleasure builds into him a sense of being worthy, desirable and acceptable." To please your husband sexually is to build his sense of value as a man.

As you spend time together physically, be sure to reassure your husband verbally of your unconditional acceptance of him, especially if he is insecure in this area. Tell him that you like his body and that his imperfections and mistakes don't matter to you. His confidence will grow if you allow him the freedom to be himself and to be imperfect.

....

Discuss:

Have you understood how your husband's sexual need is linked to his identity as a man? Is he confident in this area? Discuss this together as a couple.

Pray:

That God would give you the ability and the desire to meet your husband's needs while also experiencing fulfillment in this area.

NARCISSISM AND SELFISHNESS

Do not merely look out for your own personal interests, but also for the interests of others.
PHILIPPIANS 2:4

Obviously, Paul couldn't have been reading my heart early in my marriage, but it certainly sounds like it. I wanted to look to my own interests, and to do my own thing.

On Saturdays I would get Cokes and chips, crawl into my chair and settle down to watch hours of baseball, football, tennis and golf. Unfortunately, these actions produced an unhappy wife who had other ideas for how to spend the weekend!

According to Greek legend, Narcissus was enamored with his reflection in a still, clear pool. He sat admiring himself so long that he became rooted to the spot, giving his name to the bright yellow flowers of springtime.

Like the Greek figure Narcissus, we Americans have by and large become so mesmerized by our own reflections, our own needs and interests, that we are indifferent to the needs of others. We no longer know much about self-sacrifice and self-denial. As Christopher Lasch wrote in his book, *The Culture of Narcissism,* many people believe that "satisfaction depends on taking what you want instead of waiting for what is rightfully yours to receive."

Lasch also wrote that the very institutions that might have been thought to counter selfishness—the school, the church and the family—have let us down. He adds, "To live for the moment is the prevailing passion—to live for yourself, not for your predecessors or posterity."

The authors of our commercials know us very well. They shout: We do it all for you....Don't you really deserve a Buick?...You deserve the best today at McDonald's....L'Oreal: because you're worth it!

I once met a pastor who frequented Christian bookstores and libraries for the sole purpose of avoiding his wife. And I have counseled women who spend countless hours shopping, not for their families but to gratify themselves.

Is Narcissus, or the selfless Christ the ideal in your family?

....

Discuss:
What are your spouse's top three needs right now? What could you do to meet them? What happens in your marriage when one of you becomes too preoccupied with your own desires? Give some specific examples.

Pray:
That the selflessness of Christ will characterize you and your family.

THE INSULT-FOR-INSULT CLUB

*To sum up, let all be harmonious...and humble in spirit, not returning evil for evil,
or insult for insult, but giving a blessing instead.*

1 PETER 3:8,9

*Y*ou may have heard of the husband who asked his wife, "Why did God make you so beautiful but so dumb?"

She answered, "He made me beautiful so you would marry me, and dumb so that I could love you!"

While the insult-for-insult relationship may be funny on paper, it is deadly for a relationship. How much better to be like Linda who was married to Lou, a fourth-year seminary student. They had four children, and you can imagine their hectic schedules.

They decided to take a break and enjoy a pleasant, romantic evening. Lou was due home at 6:00 P.M. and Linda got all the kids ready for bed, picked up the baby-sitter and at 6:30 P.M. was beautifully dressed and waiting. But Lou, at the seminary library, became so involved in studying Hebrew that he forgot the time and arrived home at 8:45 P.M. By that time Linda had taken the baby-sitter home.

Lou offered nothing more than a lame "I'm sorry." As they prepared for bed, Linda began to pour out her heart, telling Lou how she had been looking forward to some time together. Then she looked over and saw Lou...fast asleep.

How did Linda respond? This was a godly woman who knew how to live according to Scripture. The next morning she arose early, put on a favorite negligee and made breakfast, which she served him in bed. Then, to cap it off, she initiated making love!

How did Lou react to Linda's effort to pay back insult with blessing? For the next month, he couldn't do enough to serve her. Her actions had heaped coals of fire on his head and he realized how wrong he had been. It was something of a turning point toward intimacy in their marriage.

....

Discuss:

Whose rights and feelings are you focusing on when you feel it necessary to insult someone? What is usually gained by an insult?

Pray:

That the Spirit of Jesus Christ, who endured such unjust suffering, will help you overcome the natural spirit to avenge yourself and to give insult for insult in your marriage and family.

"WRONG WAY RIEGELS"

And let us not lose heart in doing good

GALATIANS 6:9

It is surprising to learn how many parents feel inadequate and helpless. I can relate to this because Barbara and I struggle as much as anyone else with these feelings. We are not raising little robots that dutifully go about perfectly obeying us. We moan over our failures and wonder if our kids will ever turn out right.

Have you heard of "Wrong Way Riegels"? Roy Riegels played in the 1929 Rose Bowl for the University of California and made one of the most famous mistakes in the history of football. He picked up a fumble, looked up and saw nothing but green grass ahead of him. He ran more than 60 yards—in the wrong direction! Finally he was tackled by his teammate inside their own 10-yard line. California was forced to punt, and Georgia Tech blocked the kick and scored.

At halftime, the California coach gave a rousing call to his dispirited team. At the end he declared, "Same team that started the first half, will start the second half." This meant Roy was going to start the second half.

All the players ran out to the field except Roy. "Coach, I cannot go out there," Roy said. "I'm humiliated."

The coach looked Roy in the face and said, "Roy, the game is only half over. Now get out there and play the rest of it."

The words of that coach are worth remembering today if you're a parent. You may have a nine-year-old, and you're thinking, *The game is half over—in nine years he will be going to college.* Or your oldest may be 12 or 15 or 25. You look back with regret at your mistakes in parenting, and you think you've already lost the game.

It is at this point where we need the encouragement of Charles Spurgeon who said, "It was by perseverance that the snail reached the ark."

You cannot change what happened in the past, neither can I. What you can change is what you do in the future.

....

Discuss:
Do you feel like a failure as a parent? Why?

Pray:
Ask God to encourage you to not grow weary in doing good as a parent. Ask Him to show you how you can encourage your spouse in the battle.

THE LOST ART OF THINKING

For wisdom is protection just as money is protection. But the advantage of knowledge is that wisdom preserves the lives of its possessors.

ECCLESIASTES 7:12

*S*ince wisdom requires thinking, it's an endangered species in this culture. It's too hard. It's much easier to just go along with the herd. Even King Solomon sought happiness in mere knowledge, hobbies, possessions and status before concluding that wisdom is of greater value than them all.

In a word, Solomon stopped pursuing and started thinking. Eventually he saw the value of thinking seriously about life, and viewing it through God's eyes.

When we become too fuzzy in our thinking to ask any profound questions, we search for happiness and significance in all the wrong places. But, as someone has said, we can live for a few minutes without air, for a few days without water, for a couple of months without food—but for a lifetime without an original thought.

I'm starting to relearn the lost art of thinking right about life. I've decided to deliberately reflect on questions like these:

- What do I really believe?
- Why am I doing what I'm doing?
- What really has brought satisfaction to my life?
- What creates pressure for me? And what does God want me to do about it?
- How does my schedule reflect my ultimate values?
- How will my present lifestyle affect my family in 20 years?
- What does God want me to do with my life, my family and my possessions?

I'm learning that thinking can be gritty, lonesome work. God is still in the business of creating new original thoughts...life-changing ideas...innovations that will redirect our families and shape the destiny of our homes. I'm learning that real thinking is a pioneering work.

I'd like to encourage you to become an original thinker. Turn off the TV, the car radio, put down this book or your newspaper, and ponder your life. If you're like me, you'll find it's hard work. But like a lot of hard work, thinking and seeking wisdom has its rewards.

....

Discuss:
How does the pace of your life allow time for reflection and thinking? What answers would you give to some of the questions above?

Pray:
That God will inspire you to think His thoughts and reflect on His ways, daring to approach life with creativity and original thinking.

THE CURSE OF COMPARISON

Friend, I am doing you no wrong; did you not agree with me for a denarius?

MATTHEW 20:13

Do you ever struggle with envy? Envy can germinate in our souls when we decide to plant the seeds of comparison. It all starts with a prolonged look at what someone else has achieved or received. We compare what we know we have with what others appear to have. Generally, we can find a way to compare ourselves unfavorably with others. Envy has now taken root.

Jesus taught a parable about envy in Matthew 20:1-16. A landowner hired laborers for his vineyard early in the morning for a fair day's wage. Throughout the morning and even into the afternoon he hired more workers, promising to pay them "whatever is right" (v. 4). They agreed to his terms and went to work.

Later that evening he paid each laborer the same wage, regardless of how long they had worked. Predictably, those who had worked diligently in the scorching heat all day compared and grumbled, "That's not fair!" But the vineyard owner reminded them that they had agreed to work for what he had stipulated, and the money was his to do with as he pleased.

We become just like the "grumblers" when our limited perspective leads us to compare what we think we deserve with what others appear to get. The invariable result is *envy*.

We live in the "culture of comparison." Everyone has their rights—their entitlements. A Christian should avoid comparison at all costs. Don't plant the seed. Instead we must learn what the employees did on that hot day. Our heavenly Master is just and good in all His judgments. And because He can be trusted, we can learn to be content in circumstances that by all outward appearances seem downright unfair.

Ultimately the choice for each of us is whether or not we truly believe that God is in control.

....

Discuss:

How do you struggle with comparison and envy? Is there a way that Jesus' parable applies to you today?

Pray:

Ask God to help you realize when you are being tempted to compare and become envious. Pray for your spouse and yourself that you will learn to be content in all circumstances.

HOW DEEP ARE YOUR ROOTS?

Abide in Me, and I in you. As the branch cannot bear fruit of itself, unless it abides in the vine, so neither can you, unless you abide in Me. I am the vine, you are the branches; he who abides in Me, and I in him, he bears much fruit; for apart from Me you can do nothing.

JOHN 15:4,5

few years ago I was working in my office when the sky suddenly became dark. The trees began to bend, rain started coming down horizontally and a tornado siren went off. We got word that a tornado was coming right up the street.

I dashed out and joined all our office staff who were already underneath the concrete stairwell, and prayed. We stayed there for about five minutes, and then we got the all clear and came out. Well, that tornado "bounced" right over our office, touched down 50 feet away and uprooted several massive pine trees.

Looking at those trees, I noticed something fascinating. One pine tree lying across the road must have been over a hundred years old. But about 50 feet away was an oak tree still standing tall, with only a few limbs broken off.

I learned afterward that pine trees have a terribly shallow root system, leaving them susceptible to damaging strong winds. But the root systems of oak trees go deep into the soil, and they can withstand storms much better.

In the same way, there are going to be storms of adversity in your life. To the degree that you obey God, you dig your roots down deep, giving you the strength of character to withstand storms. Or to use the metaphor Christ used in John 15, you need to abide in Him, as a branch abides in the vine.

I think the reason some Christians lose heart during times of trial is that their roots are terribly shallow. They are not abiding in Christ—drawing their lives from Him on a daily basis. You and I cannot prepare ourselves on the day the storm hits, we must practice obedience to Christ today. The storms will come. Will you be obedient today?

Discuss:

How deep are your roots of faith? Is there something in your life right now that God has been speaking to you about that requires your obedience?

Pray:

For one another that you will practice "abiding in Christ" today so that when the storm hits you'll stand strong as a couple.

NOBODY'S FAULT

And the man said, "The woman whom Thou gavest to be with me,
she gave me from the tree, and I ate."

GENESIS 3:12

*A*lthough we technically have six children in our family, occasionally we are visited by a seventh child called "Nobody." Nobody spills apple juice, jelly and peanut butter on the floor and then walks off and leaves it—presumably to let it grow. Nobody leaves doors wide open during the fiercest heat wave in the summer and when the wintry winds are whistling.

The interesting thing about Nobody is that he never gets credit for beds made and rooms that are picked up. But when games, toys and dishes are strewn all over the living room floor, Nobody gets the blame, receiving full accusations by six kids. "Nobody did it." Barbara and I would probably discipline Nobody if we could ever catch him.

In Genesis, Adam tries to avoid his responsibility by blaming Eve for eating from the forbidden tree. In fact, He even seems to insinuate that perhaps God is at fault for giving him Eve as a mate!

Adam and our invisible child, Nobody, are reflections of the irresponsibility of people in our society. They want to clarify their "rights," but when accountability and responsibility come knocking, they flee for the back door.

The kids of this culture aren't being told there are consequences for their wrong choices. Undoubtedly some of them eventually find themselves in a jail cell, puzzled that we still have some laws that do hold us accountable for our actions.

Let me suggest that you and your mate model a different message. When you have a conflict, quarrel or disagreement, take responsibility for resolving it. When you make a mistake, admit it—even if it isn't all your fault. Instead of finding a flaw in your spouse's argument and blaming him or her, take responsibility and say you're sorry. I am confident that you don't want to be married to "Nobody."

Discuss:

Does anyone called "Nobody" live at your home? How have you noticed a tendency, in your own life, to deny you're at fault? How can you encourage your children to take responsibility for their own actions?

Pray:

Ask God to help you resist the tendency to blame others, and be responsible and accountable to God and your mate for your life.

No Fault, No Responsibility

Confess your faults one to another, and pray one for another, that ye may be healed.
JAMES 5:16 (KJV)

Hundreds of thousands of marriages are dissolved each year in the courtrooms of our land under relatively recent laws called "no-fault divorce." This is the thoroughly modern and practical way for two people to wash their hands of a marriage and terminate all responsibility to one another.

It's cleaner, faster and easier than in the old days, when the courts attempted to establish responsibility for the breakup of the marriage. Now, if no one is at fault, no one can be blamed. If neither party was wrong or wronged and both want out of the relationship, then shouldn't two people be allowed to dissolve their relationship?

It all sounds perfectly rational, but it should raise questions for Christians. Marriage was established by God for our good and His glory. Marriage occurs because of a covenant between a man, a woman and God. If (in man's mind) accountability is removed, then marriage vows are reduced to meaningless words. Commitments become conditional, temporal bargains.

Furthermore, if it's no one's fault that the marriage failed, are we also saying it is no one's responsibility to make the marriage work? The permanence of my marriage vows to Barbara motivates me to be responsible for the health of our relationship. It's for life. No excuses.

A society that allows for no-fault divorce cannot escape the long-term consequences of its no-responsibility marriages. Most people will say they "believe in marriage." The facts suggest that our society believes in marriage like Zsa Zsa Gabor, who said, when she married and divorced for the eighth time, "I really do believe in marriage."

Someone is "at fault" here. The cure for our nation's divorce epidemic is a vaccine of biblical accountability and godly responsibility to keep our covenants, vows and commitments.

....

Discuss:
Tell your spouse today that you'd marry her or him all over again. Reaffirm your love and commitment by telling him or her: It's still 'til death do us part!

Pray:
That you can model the kind of commitment and responsibility that will communicate to your children the permanence of marriage and its vows.

BUILDING BLOCKS FOR A HOME

By wisdom a house is built, and by understanding it is established; and by knowledge the rooms are filled with all precious and pleasant riches.

PROVERBS 24:3,4

The wise man Solomon describes three fundamentals not only for building a house, but also a home.

By wisdom a house is built. I define wisdom as "skill in everyday living." Solomon also said, "The fear of the Lord is the beginning of wisdom" (Prov. 9:10). When homes are built on godly wisdom, family members respond to circumstance according to God's design, not their own.

A wise home builder recognizes God as the Architect and Builder of the family. As you search the Scriptures and ask God for wisdom, He supplies the skill to build your home.

Through understanding it is established. Understanding means responding to life's circumstances with insight—having a perspective that looks at life through God's eyes. When you have God's perspective of your mate and children, you accept each other's differences and learn how different personalities can complement each other.

A couple once shared with me how they finally understood this. At one time the husband had said, "My wife is a prosecuting attorney. I felt like she prosecuted from eight to five and persecuted from five to eight." After a year and a half of trying to change her, he finally understood that he didn't have to compete with her strong personality. "I can let her be who she is, and not feel insecure about who I am," he said.

Through knowledge its rooms are filled. Our culture virtually worships information. But information without application is an empty deity. Every Sunday morning thousands of preachers present polished gems—outstanding biblical knowledge. But what do we, the parishioners, usually do? At 11:55 A.M. the preacher finishes, we sing a song, there's a prayer and we leave at 12:00 P.M. The knowledge Solomon speaks of is more than information. It is knowledge that results in conviction, application and family values.

....

Discuss:

Which of these three building blocks are most evident in your home? Which need the most work?

Pray:

That God will deepen your wisdom, sharpen your understanding and enrich your knowledge of what He wants you, your marriage and your family to be.

THE PEOPLE ON GOD'S HEART

*This is pure and undefiled religion in the sight of our God and Father,
to visit orphans and widows in their distress.*

JAMES 1:27

Throughout the Scriptures, God demonstrates a special compassion for the poor, the needy, the helpless. He often mentions our need to care for the widow and the orphan because He knew the types of hardship families face without husbands and fathers.

I suppose that, if you narrowly define "widow," you would not include divorced mothers. But if you look at our society today and the terrible hardships faced by most single moms, scratching out a living while trying to raise their children, you can't help but feel a special compassion. So when I pray about widows and orphans, I think about divorce and how it creates widows and orphans—people who have to be close to God's heart.

But we can do more. We can pray for families who have not yet been torn apart by divorce. Sometimes I walk downstairs in the FamilyLife office and look at a board where we keep track of registrations for each of our FamilyLife Marriage Conferences. I praise God for those who have come, and I pray for those who are deciding whether to attend. I know these numbers represent families who will be strengthened and healed—husbands who will stay committed, wives and children who will not become widows and orphans.

One couple wrote on their conference evaluation just three words: "Saved our marriage." Only God knows the impact of these three words.

When I was recently speaking at one of our conferences in Orlando, a couple came up to me to say this was the eleventh time they had attended! I kidded them and asked, "You mean you still haven't got it right yet?" But they were excited because of how the conference has kept them together, and now they were bringing other couples with them each year.

Each day, all around you, a fierce battle goes on in the marriages of your friends, your neighbors and your fellow church members. These people are on God's heart. Are they on your heart as well?

....

Discuss:
Who are some couples you know who need help in their marriages?
Make a list.

Pray:
Ask God to give these couples the strength and commitment to build solid families according to His blueprints.

AN OLYMPIC DAD

Be on the alert, stand firm in the faith, act like men, be strong.
1 CORINTHIANS 16:13

As much as children need love from a dad, they also need a dad who is a warrior, involved in the battles they face every day. I was enjoying the Barcelona Olympics when I observed a father-son scene I will never forget.

Derek Redmond of Great Britain had trained for the Olympic 400-meter run for years. After the Seoul Olympics, he had five operations on both Achilles' tendons, but he bounced back. Now he was running well, and competing in the Olympic semifinals.

Halfway around the track, however, Derek's right hamstring gave way. He fell to the track, sprawled across the fifth lane. The television cameras focused on defending Olympic champion Steve Lewis as he won the race and headed toward the tunnel.

Then, suddenly, Derek got to his feet and began hobbling around the track. He was determined to finish the race.

Derek's dad, Jim Redmond, sitting high in the stands at Olympic Stadium, saw his son collapse. The 49-year-old machine shop owner from Northampton, England, ran down the steps and onto the track. All he knew was his son needed help.

The crowd realized that Derek Redmond was running the race of his life. Around the stands, and around the world, fans stood and honored him with cheers. At the final turn, Jim Redmond caught up to his son and put his arm around him. When Derek saw who it was, he leaned on his dad's right shoulder and sobbed. An usher attempted to intercede and escort Jim Redmond off the track, but his efforts were futile.

They crossed the finish line, father and son, arm in arm.

If you and I as dads will become involved that heroically in the lives of our children, we will be successful as men.

·······························

Discuss:
In what areas do your children need your help and encouragement?

Pray:
Ask God to show you specific ways you can be involved
in the battles your children face.

"THREE DOLLARS WORTH OF GOD"

And then I will declare to them, "I never knew you."
MATTHEW 7:23

How well do you think you know God? Have you settled for knowing less about God than He wants you to know? Do the following words penned by Wilbur Reese describe you?

I would like to buy three dollars worth of God, please. Not enough to explode my soul or disturb my sleep, but just enough of Him to equal a cup of warm milk or a snooze in the sunshine. I don't want enough of Him to make me love a black man or pick beets with a migrant. I want ecstasy, not transformation. I want the warmth of the womb, not a new birth. I want a pound of the Eternal in a paper sack, please. I would like to buy three dollars worth of God, please.

The Church, the body of believers, is only as great as its concept of God. If you sense that your Christian experience is not what it should be, chances are that your problem is that you are not taking time to cultivate your relationship with the God who gave you life.

After Elvis Presley died, newspapers told of people who had almost made him god of their lives. One young man in Florida actually had plastic surgery to alter his face to look like Elvis. "Presley has been my idol since I was five years old," he said. "I have every record he has cut twice over, pictures by the thousands, even two leaves from a tree from the mansion in Memphis...." But the tragic words of his interview fell flat as he confessed at the end, "I never got close to him. I never saw him. I never knew him."

I wonder if you and I will stand before God on the Day of Judgment and confess: "I represented You, but I never got close to You. I never knew You deeply. I was busy about the work of Christianity, without getting to know the Father of it all."

....

Discuss:
How intimately do you know God? What does John 14:21 tell you about what you can do to experience God daily?

Pray:
Ask God to help you to see Him at work around you in everyday life. Ask Him to help you be spiritually responsive to His work in your life.

July 27

BEHOLD HIS GLORY

In My Father's house are many dwelling places...for I go to prepare a place for you.

JOHN 14:2

One of the greatest ways to learn about God is to spend some time looking at His creation. His power, His majesty, His beauty and His incredible creativity all come out in the world He made.

But that's not all you'll learn. I'll never forget going up on a ski lift with a friend. On our left was a range of 13,000-foot peaks. To our right was a beautiful lake surrounded by a host of mountains on that frosty February morning.

I shook my head and said, "Isn't it amazing to see what God made?" And my friend replied, "Yeah, and God made this in a day. And 2,000 years ago Christ said He would be preparing a place for us. And He's been gone 2,000 years preparing that place for us. Heaven is going to be a magnificent place!"

As a child I used to think heaven would be boring. What would I do for all eternity—sit around and strum a harp? But my friend's statement helped me realize that, although I have no idea what heaven will be like, it will be much, much, much greater than I can even imagine.

Dr. Charles Ryrie once said, "God must be highly puzzled at us as humans to reach down out of heaven to redeem us, to take us to heaven and have us fight against dying so hard." Isn't that interesting? Because if you went to the doctor this afternoon and learned you had an incurable form of cancer, you wouldn't be smiling initially. You would be depressed, fearful, worried about your family and loved ones.

But we're all going to die eventually, and I think God has given us a beautiful world so that we can behold just a glimpse of what is in store for us. I love what one person said: "Nature is God's Braille for a blind humanity." Nature is God's way to help us see Him even though we don't have the eyes to really behold His glory.

....

Discuss:
Take a walk in the woods or in the country and take some time to behold God's creation. What do you learn about His character—and about heaven—through what you see?

Pray:
Take an after-dinner drive to a beautiful park or overlook.
Worship the God of all creation who died for you!

July 28

THE NUMBER ONE
THREAT TO FAMILIES

*I will set no worthless thing before my eyes; I hate the work of those who fall away;
it shall not fasten its grip on me.*

PSALM 101:3

We once retained a research firm to ask our FamilyLife Conference guests what societal problem posed the greatest threat to their families. Was it alcohol and drug addiction? Materialism? Pornography? The breakup of families?

Nearly 36 percent answered: *television.*

I shouldn't have been surprised. After all, surveys show that the average American adult watches TV a whopping 30 hours a week. And preschoolers are watching the "plug-in drug" an average of 27 hours per week. I guess that's what we should expect from a society that boasts of more homes with TVs (98 percent) than those with indoor toilets (97 percent).

I believe Christian families rightly consider TV to be a threat to the family for three primary reasons.

First, *TV replaces real relationships.* Communication ceases when the TV is turned on. Who can compete with such a vast menu of images, $500,000 commercials and programs that parade slinky, sexy bodies in front of us? I agree with the great theologian Erma Bombeck, who said that if a woman has a husband who watches three consecutive TV football games on a given Saturday, she should have him declared legally dead and have his estate probated!

Second, *TV often undermines the commitments and moral integrity that bind a family together.* "Leave It to Beaver" has been replaced with adultery, premarital sex and perverted behavior.

Third, *TV robs families of both quality and quantity time.* After attending a FamilyLife Marriage Conference, one dad went home, unplugged the TV and lugged it to the garage. In its place he hung a picture of the family. Their five-year-old son sat down on the floor, stared at the portrait, looked up at his dad and asked, "Does this mean we're going to become a family now?"

Discuss:
How many hours of television (or movies on video) do you think you watch each week? Your spouse? Your children? Keep track of your viewing habits for seven days, then evaluate television's grip on you and your most important relationships.

Pray:
Ask God for discernment. Then make some choices that reflect your Christian beliefs.

MANAGING A MONSTER

*For the grace of God has appeared,...instructing us to deny ungodliness and worldly
desires and to live sensibly, righteously and godly in the present age.*

TITUS 2:11,12

*I*f, as the previous devotion maintained, much of what comes into our homes via television does not contribute to a sound Christian home, then what can be done to manage this monster?

Why not start a "Just Say No" campaign against TV? I am not advocating total abstinence, although for some families that may be a good solution. But I suggest taking TV in moderation—say, six to eight hours a week.

Here are some tips we try to follow in our family:

- Instruct the kids to ask you for permission to watch TV. Don't let them treat it as a "given," but a privilege. Don't let them watch it randomly, but determine what you want them to watch.
- Make TV off-limits in at least these two rooms: The room where you eat your meals, and your bedroom.
- Agree on the number of hours and the programs that can be watched during the week and on weekends. Let the kids choose from a list you approve.
- Don't let your children watch a video movie unless you know what's in it. Read the reviews of movies when they first appear at the theater to get clues about the level of bad language, sex and violence.
- Don't just "watch TV"; watch specific programs for a specific purpose. Once, when I had plopped down to watch nothing in particular Barbara said, "There's nothing on worth watching. There are other things more valuable to do, like spending time with me!" And she was right.

Yes, all this will take a great deal of self-control and discipline. But think of how "the tube" undermines the family, and you will realize it will be worth it. In the early '80s, a Michigan State University study reported that one-third of four- and five-year-olds in the U.S. *would give up their relationships with their dads in favor of TV.*

That's scary evidence of television's power. I believe God wants us to rule over this twenty-first-century monster.

....

Discuss:

Do you have rules about watching TV in your home? If not, talk
about implementing some of the tips discussed above.

Pray:

That God's Spirit will enable each family member to identify
and resist unhealthy influences.

MID-FAITH CRISIS

Let us run with endurance the race that is set before us, fixing our eyes on Jesus....
For consider Him who has endured such hostility by sinners against Himself,
so that you may not grow weary and lose heart.

HEBREWS 12:1-3

*A*ny runner will tell you that the toughest part of a race is not the end—it's *just before* the end. Most milers, for example, find that the third lap (of four) is usually their slowest. That's when you feel dog tired and wonder why you ever started running in the first place.

That's how faith is. At some point, after they've been Christians for several years, many believers encounter what I call the "mid-faith crisis." It's characterized by restlessness; a desire to return to the days of youth; a questioning of commitments, identity and personal values; and a loss of enthusiasm for work, marriage, family.

Have you lost your zest for life? Lost your love for people? Kind of bored with God and with church? Can't be impressed anymore? Do you have joy?

Is your job a chore or are you doing it as unto the Lord? Are you wondering why your circumstance seems so unfair?

Do you find you can't remember when you last confessed a sin to God? Are temptations becoming more alluring? Are you in a valley?

There are no simple answers for a time like this. Life is difficult. It isn't ever going to be easy. As Mick Yoder, a good friend who lost his six-year-old son in a plane crash four days before Christmas, said, "Life wouldn't be so hard if we didn't expect it to be so easy."

Some of us expect the Christian life to be one of endless prosperity, when we will feel little pain. This is called the "Prosperity Gospel." Well, Christ didn't enjoy this type of prosperity when He lived, did He? Whenever you are weary of the race, follow the advice of Hebrews 12: Keep your eyes on Him and keep on running to win.

....

Discuss:
Have you ever experienced a mid-faith crisis? Share, if appropriate, a time when you were tempted to drop out of the race.

Pray:
That God would give you an "endurance mentality" for the Christian life. Ask Him to enable you to come alongside your spouse as he or she runs, and encourage him or her to finish the race and win the crown.

SETTING YOURSELF FREE

If we confess our sins, He is faithful and righteous to forgive us our sins and to cleanse us from all unrighteousness.

1 JOHN 1:9

Is your daily life free from the mistakes and sins of the past? Do you have difficulty letting go of your feelings about people who have hurt you? If so, consider completing a project we gave a woman a number of years ago.

Mary was bitter. She was angry at her parents for the neglect she felt as a child and at her husband for his inconsistencies. To help Mary put aside her bitterness, we told her to begin by writing a detailed explanation of how her parents had wronged her and how that had made her feel. She also listed disappointment after disappointment in her relationship with her husband.

When she finished her list of grievances, she read it aloud. Seeing her anger on paper and hearing it in her own words gripped her, and she began to cry.

Through her tears, Mary bowed her head and prayed, "Forgive me, God. What I've written here is sin. You've commanded me to honor my parents; I haven't. Instead, I've harbored anger against them for 25 years.

"Forgive me, too," she went on, "for my unloving spirit and critical attitude toward my husband."

When she finished, a great relief swept over her. Mary then took a large red pen and printed across each of the three pages in bold letters the words of 1 John 1:9 (above).

She smiled as she crumpled up those sheets of paper. Then she walked outside, dug a shallow hole and dropped the sheets into it. She lit a match and set the pages on fire. Mary then covered the ashes with dirt until the hole was filled and piled seven rocks on top.

Today, when the old bitterness attempts to burst through the soil of her life and she is tempted to look back, she looks at her rock pile. It reminds her that her sins are forgiven and buried.

....

Discuss:
What things from your past need to be buried and remembered no more?

Pray:
Privately, confess any sin to God and thank Him for cleansing you and forgiving all your iniquities.

WHAT VALUES ARE YOU COMMUNICATING?

by Barbara Rainey

Let your speech always be with grace, seasoned, as it were, with salt.

COLOSSIANS 4:6

As a wife and mother, I often ask myself, "What values are being communicated by what Barbara Rainey says?"

I heard the crashing sound of the Hummell figurine, and my mind raced back to my grandmother. She had purchased the "Little Apple Girl" back in the early 1930s when she was in Germany. I had received it after her death, and of course it was very valuable to me.

I'll never forget the day I saw an ad in the newspaper saying that "Little Apple Girl" was worth $15,000. I put ours up high in our bedroom—supposedly in a safe spot. (Later, we found out that our figurine was much smaller—worth only $150!) But as I heard it break that day, I knew that "Little Apple Girl" had developed a split personality. I felt like wringing the boys' necks—I had just reminded them they couldn't play ball in the house.

When I arrived at the scene of the crime I found the guilty party, Samuel (then age four), sheepishly awaiting his sentencing. I told him to go sit on his bed because he was going to get a spanking. I picked up the pieces of my Apple Girl. Holding them in my hand, I went to Samuel's room, took his precious blue-eyed, blond-haired face in my other hand and said, "Samuel, do you see this?" His eyes became little blue saucers, probably wondering whether his fate would be electrocution or hanging.

He nodded. His eyes met mine and I made my point: "I want you to know, Samuel Rainey, that I love you more than this." Glancing down at the remnants I cradled in my hand, I went on: "And I love you enough to spank you for disobeying me."

Dennis said he was really proud of me for the values that scene represented. It would have been so easy for me to have overreacted! I don't know if Samuel will remember that day or not. But I do thank God for His power that enabled me to model for Samuel values worth imitating.

Discuss:

What values do you think young Samuel learned from this event? What values do you want to communicate to your children?

Pray:

Ask God, the Source of all true values, to help you model His standards and to instill them in your children.

"HE WAS A GOOD MAN"

Then when he had come and witnessed the grace of God, he rejoiced and began to encourage them all with resolute heart to remain true to the Lord; for he was a good man.

ACTS 11:23,24

What memories do you have of your father? What legacy did he leave with you?

One way to learn more about yourself is to think back on your father's character. I enjoy doing this because my dad had such an influence on the type of man I am today.

My dad was a unique blend of no-nonsense and discipline with a subtle sense of humor. He was a quiet and private man. He didn't seem to need many words to get the job done.

His countenance commanded respect. In fact, several boys had personality transformations when they graduated from the third-grade Sunday School class to my dad's fourth-grade class. Paper airplanes were grounded and eight boys sat up straight, listening dutifully to the lesson.

I recall the easy chair that used to carry the shape of his exhausted form. It was as he read the evening paper that I usually planned my assault on him. I'm sure I nearly pestered my weary dad to death while asking him to play catch.

"Hook" Rainey, they used to call him. The tall lefty got his nickname from his curve ball—a pitch so crooked it mystified batters. When he threw that patented knuckler, the entire front yard was filled with laughter—his and mine. I always loved to hear him laugh. Somehow it told me that everything was secure.

When I was three or so, he went hunting in Colorado and "bagged" a fierce teddy bear. He staged the "action" on film and brought the "slain" beast back to me. My kids now play with that well-worn, 45-year-old black-and-white bear.

I watched Dad look after the needs of his mother—he used to visit her three or four times a week. He modeled what it meant to honor one's parents. Most important, he taught me about character. He did what was right, even when no one was looking. I never heard him lie, and his eyes always demanded the same truth in return. The mental image of his character still fuels and energizes my life today.

....

Discuss:
In what specific ways do you hope to influence your children? How does your life match up to the ideals and values of Scripture?

Pray:
That God will give you the strength and wisdom to be a godly parent.

FORWARD, BACKWARD OR STILL UNFOLDING?

More than that, I count all things to be loss in view of the surpassing value of knowing Christ Jesus my Lord, for whom I have suffered the loss of all things, and count them but rubbish in order that I may gain Christ.

PHILLIPIANS 3:8

In one of Charles Shultz's "Peanuts" cartoons, Charlie Brown was sitting in a deck chair near the front of a large boat when Lucy walked up. "Some people go through life with their deck chair facing forward, gazing out where they are going," Lucy said philosophically. "Others go through life with their deck chair facing backwards, looking at where they've been." Then, looking directly into Charlie Brown's sunglasses, she asked him, "Charlie Brown, which way is *your* deck chair facing?"

Charlie Brown shrugged his shoulders, "I really don't know—I've never been able to get my deck chair unfolded!"

In these days when family issues have become not only a major issue for private citizens but also in political campaigns, Christians need to get their deck chairs unfolded. Unfortunately, many people have not taken a thoughtful look at what they believe in as family values and, even more important, the *basis* for those beliefs.

But with our culture in crisis over the issue, this is not a time to be struggling with our deck chairs. We need to be speaking up in the political arena and the marketplace about what matters.

A few years ago, when our whole family was in the car, I asked the kids what they thought our family values were. The words started popping furiously like premium popcorn. Here's what they said: "God, limited TV, responsibilities, chores, friendship, kindness, respectful speaking, education, church, encouragement, servanthood, obedience, discipline, sharing, giving, boundaries, keeping your word, home life, prayer, perseverance, doing what you're supposed to do, love, dignity of kids, food and shelter, spending time with each other, resolving conflicts, forgiveness, physical affection, our siblings, laughter, having fun together, memorizing verses, wholesome speaking, reading, wise counsel."

Barbara and I were pleasantly surprised by what our kids had to say. Perhaps we were getting through to these kids after all!

Discuss:
If you have kids, ask them the same question:
What do you think our family's values are?

Pray:
Ask God to help you clarify your values as a person and as a family. Ask Him for His favor in building those values into one another's lives.

THE GREAT COVER-UP

{Part One}

And the man and his wife were both naked and were not ashamed.

GENESIS 2:25

Nothing is as easy as talking; nothing is as difficult as communicating. Good communication is a longed-for luxury in all kinds of relationships, but it is especially essential in families. And one of the most basic requirements for good communication — *transparency* — is hinted at in the Scripture above.

Before the Fall, Adam and Eve were the picture of true transparency. Not only were they uncovered physically; they had nothing to hide emotionally. But after the Fall, "The eyes of both of them were opened, and they knew that they were naked; and they sewed fig leaves together and made themselves loin coverings" (Gen. 3:7).

This is the beginning of "The Great Cover-Up." Many people diligently continue the practice to this day. They spend a great deal of time and energy acquiring façades and veneers in order to hide their insecurities and fears.

Transparency can be very threatening, especially for men. For example, many men believe that to be so vulnerable that they shed tears openly is a sign of weakness. They have been taught that men are to be strong, self-contained and invincible. Fortunately, this pattern has been changing in recent years.

Paul modeled transparency when he wrote to the Corinthians, "For out of much affliction and anguish of heart I wrote to you with many tears; not that you should be made sorrowful, but that you might know the love which I have especially for you" (2 Cor. 2:4). Jesus wept over the death of His friend Lazarus (see John 11:35), and lamented His rejection by hard-hearted Jerusalem (see Luke 13:34).

Reversing "The Great Cover-Up" and becoming open and dropping your guard with others can be risky. It requires a high level of trust, and the willingness to accept the other person no matter what his or her transparency reveals. But the rewards of transparency make it worth the risk. True intimacy is enjoyed only by those who are willing to be seen as they really are.

....

Discuss:

Why does being transparent involve risks? On a scale of one to five, with one at the top, how would you rate the level of transparency in your family? When have you been the most transparent in your marriage?

Pray:

Ask God to enable you to be transparent with Him. Pray that a deeper level of this openness can be incorporated in your marriage and family.

THE GREAT COVER-UP

{Part Two}

For now we see in a mirror dimly, but then face to face; now I know in part,
but then I shall know fully just as I also have been fully known.

1 CORINTHIANS 13:12

This passage shows that the ultimate level of communication, in which we know fully as we are known, is reserved for heaven. But by God's grace, we can begin to reverse "The Great Cover-Up" even in this life—by growing in our ability to be vulnerable, open and transparent with those we love.

Like most skills, you have to start at the bottom and work up to transparency. Author John Powell described this process in his excellent book *Why Am I Afraid to Tell You Who I Am?* He observed five stages or levels of communication.

Most people start at level five—sharing mere *clichés*. We might call this "elevator talk," in which you speak, but share nothing: "Hello, how are you?" and "Have a nice day."

Moving up to the fourth level involves sharing *facts*. You are willing to report what you know, or what so-and-so said, but you share nothing of yourself.

At level three, people reveal *opinions*—their ideas, judgments and viewpoints. At this level you finally start to come out of your shell and reveal a little of who you are. You risk disagreement or even rejection, so you are very careful at this stage, ready to retreat.

You begin to share *emotions* at level two. Now you are definitely coming out of the closet and letting the other person know just what you are feeling. Again, this is risky business and you must be careful not to hurt each other, but it is an essential step if families are to live beyond superficiality.

Level one is *transparency*—being completely open with each other, sharing the real you, from the heart. Of course this level of communication requires a large amount of trust and commitment. When you reach the transparency level, you can begin to know even as you are known.

....

Discuss:

Compare how you rated your family's level of communication in yesterday's devotional with the five stages described here. Discuss how you can move toward deeper, more meaningful communication.

Pray:

As you pray, think of how intimately God knows you. Ask Him to help your family members grow in their abilities to really know and accept each other.

Is There a Minister in the House?

If any man be above reproach, the husband of one wife, having children who believe, not accused of dissipation or rebellion.

TITUS 1:6

Is there a minister at your house? The apostle Paul wanted elders in the church who could also minister the gospel to their own households.

When I suggest to fathers that they are to be ministers to their families, they tend to shy away, thinking I mean they have to be accomplished theologians and do a lot of eloquent praying before meals. But that's not what being a family minister is all about.

By being there and making your family a priority, you'll find plenty of opportunities to minister to your children by showing them what's really important in life. I'm learning to take advantage of the "teachable moments" when my kids are open to spiritual truth.

Years ago I was cuddled up next to our daughter Ashley on the lower bunk at bedtime. Somehow we found ourselves discussing the second coming of Christ. I told her, "Yes, Jesus is coming back, and He's going to take all those with Jesus in their hearts with Him, and it's going to be fantastic."

Ashley had received Christ, but she wondered about her brother Benjamin. "When it comes time for him to invite Jesus into his heart, he'll do that," I said.

Benjamin was lying in the upper bunk, and he popped his head over the edge. "Dad, tomorrow would you tell me how to invite Jesus into my heart?" he asked.

So the next day he, too, made a profession of faith. And his very next words were, "Daddy, could we play ball?"

I couldn't know at that time whether Benjamin had made a true, life-changing commitment to Christ. But the fact was that when he was interested, I was there.

Discuss:

As a father, do you find it difficult to discuss spiritual matters with your family? In what other ways can you "minister" to your family? Have you found a good time, such as bedtime, for having heart-to-heart conversations?

Pray:

Pray that you will be able to embody the essentials of being a minister, especially "being there," in your family life.

LIVING FEARLESSLY

There is no fear in love; but perfect love casts out fear.

1 JOHN 4:18

Husbands and wives sometimes discover it takes years of living together to create an atmosphere that is safe for total openness with each other. Part of the passage above is inscribed inside Barbara's wedding band: "There is no fear in love. But perfect love drives out fear."

I work at making this message reassuring to Barbara. For example, I'm more outgoing in groups than Barbara. When we're at a party, I'll pick up a lagging conversation by asking questions. But I frequently err by not allowing time for Barbara, who is not as aggressive, to enter into the conversation.

Early in our marriage, we would drive home after an evening like this and I would say, "Goodness, Sweetheart, we were with those people for several hours and you didn't say two or three words all evening!"

Barbara would reply, "Well, you didn't give me a chance!" We would usually drive a few blocks in silence and I would apologize for not including her. Later I would ask what she thought of one of the people at the party, and she would begin to make profound observations about what had taken place that evening and what had been said. She has keen insights and perceptions about people. I've learned to rely on her insights.

Instead of getting irritated or resentful when Barbara is sometimes reluctant to share her feelings, I see that my behavior can be intimidating to her, and that's a form of fear.

We both know that we are totally committed to each other, and I want to be more sensitive to her disposition. I've also sought ways to gently encourage Barbara to open up—and she's learning to take more risks as well.

Although we've been married since 1972, we are still learning how to love one another perfectly so that fear never has a grip in our lives.

....

Discuss:
How are you different from your mate? How can these differences
be handled in a way that makes your relationship a totally safe
"environment" for each other?

Pray:
That just as you want your faith and trust in God to grow, you can grow as a
couple to trust each other completely and feel safe with each other.

GUILTY AS CHARGED

The joy of the Lord is your strength.

NEHEMIAH 8:10

*S*ometimes Christians look like they have been drinking pickle juice. They appear as though they're not having any fun at all—as if life is just one serious endeavor. They look like their faces might crack open if they tried to smile!

Yes, life is difficult. But a family needs to be a free place, a place of enjoyment and laughter. Barbara and I want our kids to remember us laughing, having a good time.

I remember one day that had been hard and heavy for Barbara. I decided we needed to laugh a little, so we organized a "refrigerator trial" for her. We convened the entire Rainey clan, and I appointed our oldest son, Benjamin, as judge and the rest of the kids as jury.

"This woman, Barbara Rainey, is charged with neglect of the refrigerator," I declared. We began pulling out food, "Exhibit A," "B," etc. And I want you to know that it was a sorry sight. We found some objects that had been in there so long they had shrunk away from the sides of the plastic bowl and kind of looked like hockey pucks.

We found green things. Living things. We would take off the lid of something and let the "jury" smell it, and they would nearly get sick. Even our dog ran for cover.

Finally, we had all the exhibits out on the table, and the jury declared, "Guilty as charged—neglect of the refrigerator." With a pound of the gavel, the judge declared, "Guilty as charged!" And then we all piled in and cleaned the refrigerator for Mom.

I have a suggestion: Clean out your own refrigerator tonight (and hold a trial if needed). Then put up a card on the refrigerator door that says, "I want to be guilty of having too much fun in life!"

....

Discuss:
When was the last time you had some fun with your mate, or with your family? Plan a creative time of fun for tonight.

Pray:
Ask God to help you make memories of laughter with your family.

To Spank or Not to Spank?

*Foolishness is bound up in the heart of a child; the rod of discipline
will remove it far from him.*

PROVERBS 22:15

What can make a child cry and a group of parents tense up like they are about to receive a shot at the doctor's office? It's the *S* word— *spanking*.

Most of us know that the book of Proverbs affirms using "the rod of discipline." Because some parents have physically abused their children, an increasing number of people consider spanking to be synonymous with child abuse.

However, I believe properly administered spanking is a positive, biblical approach to raising children. Here are two simple guidelines:

First, *clarify the boundaries and the punishment for the offense.* Decide what behavior is "worth" a spanking, and be sure your child understands it. We have six children, and we only have half a dozen issues warranting a spanking. We have used spanking sparingly, as a last resort in the training of our children. But we have used it.

Second, *it should not be administered in anger but out of love, and in the context of a relationship with the child.* The purpose is to help the child understand that his or her wrong choices have consequences. We always showed love to our children before and after they'd been disciplined. I didn't get that many spankings as a child, but I can tell you this—I always felt loved, and I definitely needed the correction!

As parents, we are in the process of producing a harvest of character, helping our children learn to be responsive to God and themselves for their lives. As parents, we can't gloss over flagrant disobedience and pretend it didn't occur. If we do, we allow foolishness, rather than wisdom, to have a foothold in our children's hearts.

....

Discuss:

Are you and your spouse in agreement when it comes to disciplining your child? What are your boundaries and the penalties for crossing them?

Pray:

Ask God to give you the courage to follow the Scriptures in your family. Ask Him to help you achieve that blend of authority and love that tells your children that you really care about them.

SOWING WORDS OF PRAISE

A soothing tongue is a tree of life.

PROVERBS 15:4

Everyone loves to be praised, and your mate is no exception. William James wrote: "The deepest principle in human nature is the craving to be appreciated." And Mark Twain said, "I can live for two months on a good compliment."

Praise is valuable because it is a virtue seldom practiced! We seldom praise our employees; we seldom praise our kids, and we seldom praise our mates. Yet, our homes ought to be a haven where praise is liberally applied.

Carefully read this definition of praise: to give value, to lift up, to extol, to magnify, to honor, to commend, to applaud. If you give some creative thought to this definition, you can come up with hundreds of ways to praise your mate. The more you verbally express your appreciation (praise), the more secure your mate will become in his or her self-esteem.

Have you ever asked someone to repeat a compliment? I have. "Oh, you really liked our FamilyLife Marriage Conference? Tell me what meant the most to you." Inwardly, I am saying, "Yes, I need to hear this! Would you tell me one more time so I can relish your comments for a few seconds longer?" Life can seem intolerably heavy at times, and a good, encouraging word can help to lighten the load and lift your mate's spirits.

Arnold Glascow has said, "Praise does wonders for our sense of hearing." It also does wonders for our sense of sight. When you praise another person, you take your eyes off yourself and focus on someone else for a few, brief moments. This positive focus on another person not only helps to put his or her life in perspective, but yours as well.

....

Discuss:
When was the last time you made an effort to praise your mate? Praise your mate three times before you go to sleep tonight.

Pray:
That God would give you creative ideas on how to praise your mate. And if you haven't ever done it, take a few minutes in prayer and praise God for who He is and what He has done in your lives.

COMPLACENCY VS. COMMITMENT

Therefore let him who thinks he stands take heed lest he fall.

1 CORINTHIANS 10:12

We need to make certain our marriages are divorce proof. Pastor/author Chuck Swindoll asks a great question: "Are there any termites in your troth?" One of those termites could be complacency.

First Corinthians 10:12 offers a formidable warning to the one who thinks this infestation of termites can't reach into his marriage. How many ministers, missionaries and laymen have fallen into affairs and divorce after allowing romantic complacency to settle into their marriages?

We need to resurrect the true meaning of commitment. In this age of lite beer, lite syrup and lite salad dressing, it's no wonder we exhibit lite commitment, too. But for a Christian, commitment is a sacred vow and promise to God. It's two people who hang in there during the best and worst of times and who won't quit. It's a husband and wife who find working through problems much more rewarding than walking out.

We need to pass on to our children the real definition of commitment while continually exposing the lies that their peers and the media propagate. A person who does not understand his or her ultimate accountability to God has little reason to fulfill a vow or commitment to another human being.

There's another type of complacency we need to address: We need to fight for other marriages besides our own. A growing number of Christians, upon hearing of the hurt and anguish of their friends, do not reach for their Bibles, but, instead, hastily offer a parachute and say, "Bail out!" Or they simply sit by, saying and doing nothing. They just let it happen. Hey, I understand. When there's only a slim thread of hope, what are you going to do?

You and I have got to go to the guy who just left his family and tell him it just isn't going to be that easy. He can't just walk out on them. And that woman in our Sunday School class? She can't leave her husband for this other guy and think things will be business as usual. Plead, beg and pray with them. And get them some help.

....

Discuss:
Do you know any couples who are struggling in their marriages?
What can you do to encourage them?

Pray:
Form a "'til death do us part" bond with your mate.
And keep praying with me that God will purge our land of divorce.

ENTERING LION'S COUNTRY

{Part One}

Be of sober spirit, be on the alert. Your adversary, the devil,
prowls about like a roaring lion, seeking someone to devour.

1 PETER 5:8

$\mathcal{I}$'ve been smelling lion's breath recently, and have nearly gagged at its odious smell. Where have I been? On a lion country safari? In Kenya? Sudan? At the zoo? No. None of these.

Let's just say I've been in lion country.

Pastor and author A.W. Tozer made numerous visits there. In fact, he may have lived in lion country. After a particularly difficult time, Tozer noted the following: "But I will tell you something—it is a delightful thing when you know that you are close enough to the adversary that you can hear him roar! Too many Christians never get into 'lion country' at all!"

After pondering Tozer's observation, I've concluded that we should charge headlong into lion country. You see, "lion country" is territory controlled by the devil. It is the daily domain of the ruler of this world.

Lions in Africa prey on weak, unsuspecting animals and those straggling behind the protection of the head of the pack. Likewise, the devil prowls about trying to deceive (devour) those with weak convictions and naive beliefs. For example, if a Christian refuses to submit to the accountability of other believers in the local church, he will find himself isolated, delicious prey for the crafty deceiver. He may not be able to defend himself when he's faced with temptation.

How does a lion devour its prey? One bite at a time. I wonder at times if twentieth-century Christians have been anesthetized by prosperity and busy schedules while the enemy chews off three-quarters of their legs!

Far too many Christians are being fooled by the enemy. They have been deceived into thinking that run-of-the-mill Christianity is all there is. Jesus Christ may be a part of their lives, but He isn't Lord of their lives.

I know, because for more than 14 years I was the prey of the enemy. I thought I knew what was best for me. I wanted God only as my emergency Savior, when I was in a crisis and needed Him. And if you're like I was, the lion has you in his jaws.

Discuss:
When was the last time you took a spiritual safari into lion country? What areas of your life would you say are controlled by God, and what areas are controlled by the devil?

Pray:
Ask God to help you be of sober spirit and be on the alert to schemes of the adversary.

ENTERING LION'S COUNTRY

{Part Two}

We know that we are of God, and the whole world lies in the power of the evil one.

1 JOHN 5:19

Instead of falling prey to the devil, Christians must be aggressive soldiers recapturing the land for Christ. One goal of our spiritual battle is to prevent our adversary from having any sphere of influence in our lives. Successful invaders are risk takers. Men and women of faith and action. The victory will go to those who move their faith the 18-inch distance from their heads to their hearts. Many Christians, however, seem to prefer comfort to conflict.

Winston Churchill believed the battlefield is the place where great issues are resolved. And I believe the great issues of our day will only be decided when well-equipped Christians invade lion country. Just as Churchill refused to negotiate until the adversary had capitulated, neither can we afford to give in to temptation or compromise.

As you encroach on the enemy's territory, remember these admonitions from Scripture:

Stand firm and let God's Word be your guide. We have God's assurance that we won't lose the war.(see Eph. 6:14-17).

Pray always and give thanks (see 1 Thess. 5:17,18).

Don't take temptation lightly; flee immorality (see 2 Tim. 2:22).

Walk by faith, not by what you feel and see. God's Word and His promises are either 100 percent true or they are not. Since His Word is true, your faith is the difference. Grab hold of His Word and step out (see 2 Cor. 5:7).

C.T. Studd, a missionary to China, understood the challenge well. He wrote, "Some people want to live within the sound of chapel bells, but I want to run a mission a yard from the gate of hell."

The battle has been tough recently, but I wouldn't trade being in lion country for any of the peace and comfort that depended on compromise.

What about you?

....

Discuss:
Talk with your mate about enemy territory you want to reclaim
as a couple. Spend some time in prayer asking for God to show you where
He wants you to invade.

Pray:
Ask Him for wisdom, guidance and power to stand firm in the battle.

AN AGONIZING DECISION

If any of you lacks wisdom, let him ask of God, who gives to all men generously and without reproach, and it will be given to him.

JAMES 1:5

Our daughter Rebecca was involved in gymnastics, and she was doing well. As her level of skill increased, she was expected to spend more time at the gym. She would train from 4-8:30 P.M., three days a week.

Barbara and I were concerned about the direction this was taking. We realized that, if Rebecca kept moving into higher levels in gymnastics, it would take her away from her family. She was spending more time with her coach than she was with us. And she was fast approaching the turbulent years of adolescence.

While we appreciated gymnastics for the discipline it gave Rebecca, we had other priorities. Ultimately, we felt God was leading us to fortify our relationship with Rebecca before she became a teenager.

The more we prayed the more we realized that, if Rebecca continued in gymnastics, we would not have the time to work with her in areas we considered more important. In a year she would turn 13, and we consider the time just before teen years to be crucial for building character and preparing for the pressures and choices.

After months of agonizing prayer, we decided to pull Rebecca out of gymnastics. While we would not argue with a parent who made an opposite decision, the point I want to make is that we had a vision for the type of woman Rebecca could become—a woman who would walk with God and make an impact for Christ. And we believed that the best place for her to learn and grow and mature was not in a gymnasium but in our home.

As parents, we need to be clear about the character qualities and relationships we are building in our children. Children are a high and holy calling. They are the legacy we leave to the next generation. Neil Postman said, "Our children are the living messages we send to a time we will not see." What kind of message are you sending?

....

Discuss:
What is your vision for the type of people your children will become? Why not consider listing the qualities you want to see in your children.

Pray:
Ask God for His favor as you seek to raise children that will be "living" messages of hope to the next generation.

REALITY CHECKS FOR CONFRONTATIONS

*And why do you look at the speck that is in your brother's eye,
but do not notice the log that is in your own eye?*

MATTHEW 7:3

As important as it is to be able to lovingly confront your mate when you have a conflict, it's also important not to be judgmental. It's essential that you don't just see your spouse's flaws while ignoring your own. Here are some reality checks Barbara and I have found useful:

1. *Check your motivation.* Do you want to help or hurt by what you say? Will bringing this up lead to healing and oneness? Prayer is a good barometer of motivation. When you take your situation to God you can usually see your motivation for what it is.

2. *Check your attitude.* Loving confrontation says: "I care about you. I respect you and I want you to respect me. I want you to know how I feel, but I want to know how you feel, too." Don't hop on your bulldozer and run your partner down. Don't pull up in your dump truck and unload all your garbage. Approach your partner lovingly.

3. *Check the circumstances.* This includes timing, location and setting. The time for Barbara to confront me is not just as I walk in from a hard day's work. I need to confront her sometime when she isn't settling a squabble among the kids.

4. *Check to see what other pressures may be present.* Be sensitive to where your mate is coming from. What's the context of his or her life right now?

5. *Be ready to take it as well as to dish it out.* Sometimes confronting your mate can boomerang on you. Beware of what psychologists call "projecting"—seeing your own faults in others. You may start to give your spouse some "friendly advice" only to learn that the problem you are describing is actually your fault!

....

Discuss:

Think back to a confrontation that didn't go especially well. Can you determine whether more attention to one or more of the above suggestions may have made a more fruitful discussion?

Pray:

For the courage to confront and the love and self-awareness to keep such episodes as positive contributors to intimacy in your home.

STAYING IN FOCUS

See that no one repays another with evil for evil, but always seek after that which is good for one another and for all men.

1 THESSALONIANS 5:15

If you've read this far, then it's time we shook things up a bit for this day's devotional with a "Pop Quiz on Marital Conflict!" C'mon, be honest and discuss your answers with your spouse.

1. Do you stick to one issue during a conflict or do you focus on many issues? Don't save up a series of complaints and let your mate have them all at once. Deal with one thing at a time.

2. Do you focus on your spouse's behavior rather than attack his or her character? Don't try to make your mate feel like an enemy or the bad guy. And avoid sweeping statements like "You are so forgetful" or "This is just like you!"

3. Do you focus on the facts rather than judging the motives? If your partner forgets to make an important call, deal with the consequences of what you both have to do next, rather than saying, "You don't really care about this, do you?"

4. Do you focus on understanding your mate rather than on who wins or loses? When your mate confronts you, listen carefully to what is said and what isn't said.

It may be, for example, that your spouse is upset about something else that happened during the day and you're just getting the brunt of that pressure. In other words, you may not be the problem. Your mate may just need to vent some pent-up frustrations and feelings. While that may not always be fair, part of being a loving partner is willingness to listen and to help.

5. When you're confronted, do you listen with a teachable spirit or do you justify your behavior? Be willing to hear and receive the truth when you are confronted. The natural thing to do is to employ a defense lawyer's tactics. Fire the lawyer; hire the teachable student.

6. Do you use phrases like, "You always do ..." or "You never do ...", or do you usually give your spouse the benefit of the doubt? Generalizations are seldom true—avoid using them in your marriage.

....

Discuss:
Recall an argument when you probably wanted to win more than just solve the problem. Why can staying focused in a confrontation be so difficult?

Pray:
Each of you pick one of the six questions that you struggle with and pray with your spouse that God will enable you to do what He wants in your next conflict.

THE LAW OF GIVING

*Give, and it will be given to you; good measure, pressed down, shaken together,
running over, they will pour into your lap. For by your standard of measure
it will be measured to you in return.*

LUKE 6:38

Christianity is full of apparent paradoxes, including one that Jesus teaches us: If we give, we will receive. Somehow a transfer takes place so that, when we give, we are enriched. We are not depleted, even if we do not see it or feel it at the time.

This "Law of Giving" applies to many areas of life, but is especially relevant to self-esteem. As one woman wrote in a letter to Barbara and me, "I have realized that in giving of myself, I am actually getting in return a spouse who feels good about himself, which then makes me feel good about myself."

The world whispers to us, "You can give away only what you have. Wait until your own needs are met. Then you will be able to reach out to others and really give." But is that what Jesus meant when He said "give"?

We think not. Why? Perhaps Jesus knew that nobody ever reaches that point where all needs are met.

Perhaps you get tired of giving. You may be thinking, *You don't know my mate. I don't want to give this time.* I can understand a little bit—what spouse hasn't had his or her moments. But when truth is not ruling in your life, feelings are. Acting on negative feelings will not build your mate's self-image or your marriage—it will only tear down what you've already built.

Even if you feel you've given and given and given for years, please don't give up. Your mate needs you more than you realize. God sees, and He will reward you.

Theologian F. B. Meyer has said, "He is the richest man in the esteem of the world who has gotten most. He is the richest man in the esteem of heaven who has given most."

Where do you want to be the richest?

....

Discuss:
How can you begin applying the "Law of Giving" in your marriage this week?
Write down two or three ways.

Pray:
That God would help you make daily choices to put aside your own selfish
desires and have a giving heart.

RUNNING IN THE RUTS

So I hated life, for the work which had been done under the sun was grievous to me;
because everything is futility and striving after wind.

ECCLESIASTES 2:17

Have you thought lately about where you're going in life?
A sign on the rugged Alaskan Highway reads: Choose your rut carefully. You'll be in it for the next 200 miles.

Too many of us like ruts. Predictable and familiar, ruts offer us security. Like a numbing narcotic, however, they cause us to waste a lot of our lives. It has been said that a rut is nothing more than a grave with both ends knocked out. This must have been part of the futility Solomon experienced when he wrote those words in Ecclesiastes.

Children naturally resist ruts. As Barbara and I attempt to raise six, we're challenged by their probing questions. We're told a child asks at least 250,000 questions growing up. No wonder they learn so rapidly…and stay out of ruts.

Maybe one reason we adults feel that we're stuck in a 200-mile rut is we don't ask enough questions. Daily we climb on the merry-go-round of life, getting up and going to work. Then we come home and ritualistically collapse in front of the TV set.

Occasionally we wonder about getting out of our ruts, but we usually give in to our insecurities, and decide to stay where we are. At least we know the boundaries. Some people try to escape the sense of meaninglessness simply by accelerating the pace of their lives. But their direction doesn't change; the rut still determines where they're going.

Where is your rut going? As one man put it, "Most of us live a lifetime looking for the pot at the end of the rainbow, only to find a pot of salty liver soup."

Solomon's sense of futility stemmed from the fact that all his ruts were "under the sun"—devoid of the transcendent presence of God. Only when he decided to "fear God and keep His commandments" (Eccles. 12:13) was he able to escape the futile sameness of life's ruts.

....

Discuss:
What element in your life and work helps you escape a sense of futility?
How does God lift us out of our "ruts"?

Pray:
Ask God to keep you out of the ruts of a boring "Christian" life and to enable you to see Him at work in your life and family.

THE THUMP TEST

The good man out of the good treasure of his heart brings forth what is good;
and the evil man out of the evil treasure brings forth what is evil;
for his mouth speaks from that which fills his heart.

LUKE 6:45

ax Lucado once wrote about the way a potter checks his work. When he pulls a pot out of the oven, he "thumps" it. If there's a good, ringing sound—if the pot "sings"—it's ready. But if there's just a "thud," the pot is put back into the oven. As Max wrote, a person's character is also checked by thumping:

Late-night phone calls. Grouchy teacher. Grumpy moms. Burnt meals. Flat tires. "You've-got-to-be-kidding" deadlines. These are all thumps. Thumps are irritating inconveniences that trigger the worst in us. They catch us off guard. Flat-footed. They aren't big enough to be crises, but if you get enough of them, watch out!

Jesus said that out of the nature of the heart a man speaks (see Luke 6:45). There's nothing like a good thump to reveal the nature of a heart. The true character of a person is seen not in momentary heroics, but in the thump-packed humdrum of day-to-day living.

How do you respond to "thumping"—to the knocks and blows and trials of life? Do you sing? Or do you thud? Your answer depends to a large degree on what your "pot" is made of—what's in your heart, as Jesus said.

But even if you have a tendency to thud more than sing, take heart. There is hope. We can learn from the thumps. We can be aware of "thump-slump" times, like "blue Mondays," after a holiday and such. No thump is a disaster. All thumps work for good if we are loving and obeying God.

....

Discuss:

What kind of "thumps" tend to discourage you most? What are the
"thump slump" times in your spouse's life? Ask your spouse how you
can be sensitive during such times.

Pray:

Is your mate or a child in a "thump slump" right now? Go and pray with him
or her that God's grace and love will be real. Then hug him, tell him that you
love him and go get an ice-cream cone together.

"Me First!"—Crowding In

Be devoted to one another in brotherly love; give preference to one another in honor.

ROMANS 12:10

Few of us over the age of 35 will forget those long gasoline lines that occurred during the "oil crisis" in 1973-74. Naturally, some greedy people wanted to cut in line to get ahead of others. Newspapers carried stories about everything from profanity and lawsuits to stabbings and shootings, as people fought for their places in line to get gas.

One woman cut in front of a motorbike. The cyclist slowly got off his bike, took off his helmet and glasses, and proceeded to let the air out of all four of her tires while she sat helplessly caught in the line!

But the most creative stunt I read about was the young man who got cut off and retaliated by unscrewing the gas cap from the offending car, replacing it with his own locking gas cap, and driving off—with the gas cap key in his pocket!

All too many of us get caught up in the rush to the shallow well of "me-first-ism." "We're Number One!" becomes not just a yell at a football game but a personal motto. But selfishness is possibly the most dangerous threat to oneness that any marriage can face.

The apostle Paul's counsel therefore becomes a prescription for marital oneness: "Give preference to one another in honor." Marriage provides the opportunity to live life for someone besides yourself and to avoid the terrible judgment: "All I've got is me. I can't depend on anyone else."

....

Discuss:
How can you show preference to your spouse?
Think of 10 ways and do one of them!

Pray:
For God to give all members of your family the desire to serve one another
and that they would feel no compulsion to compete to be "first in line."

A FELLOW HEIR

And grant her honor as a fellow heir of the grace of life.

1 PETER 3:7

oday the business world has all kinds of partnerships: silent partners, financial partners, equal partners, controlling partners, minority partners, and more. But in marriage, God intended for us to have only one kind: a fully participating partnership.

The apostle Peter sets forth the concept of mutual partnership as he instructs a man to treat his wife as "a fellow heir of the grace of life." Although her function and role as a woman differs from yours as a man, she has an equal inheritance as a child of God.

You will make your wife a participating partner in your life when you tenderly look her in the eyes and say, "I need you." Why not make this an experiential reality in your marriage by frequently saying:

- "I need you to listen as I talk about what's troubling me. And I need your perspective on my problems and your belief in me as a person."
- "I need you to help me become the man God created me to be."
- "I want you to have total access into my life. I need you to keep me honest in areas of my life in which I could stray from Christ. You may question me or confront me on any issue."
- "You are the person I most trust with my life."
- "I need you for your advice, judgments and wise counsel on decisions I face, especially at work."
- "I need your prayers for a temptation I am facing."

When I become the sole proprietor in our marriage and treat Barbara as a silent partner, we both lose. She loses the opportunities I can give to include her, develop her and make her feel important. And I lose because I tend to make poor decisions when I am isolated from her.

Most wives beam with joy when their husbands let them into the interior of their lives. Wives long to be trusted with their husbands' challenges, emotions and self-doubts.

Discuss:
Discuss this concept of partnership. Does your wife feel she is part of your life? What adjustments can you make to make her your partner?

Pray:
That God would give you the courage as a man to give your wife even greater access to your life, and that He would use you as a team to be more effective than you would be individually.

TEND TO YOUR RICHES

Know well the condition of your flocks, and pay attention to your herds;
for riches are not forever.

PROVERBS 27:23,24

*I*n most marriage studies I've seen, couples say their finances cause the most frequent disagreements and arguments. Often the problem is the simple but addictive habit of overspending. Just as a sheep owner must know the condition of his flocks, so many of us do not keep track of the condition of our budgets.

In our society we are surrounded by advertisements trying to convince us that we need a product to be fulfilled or happy—as though mere *things* are the real source of contentment.

One credit card company wants you to believe you can't leave home without it because you need the privilege of being one of its members. Another credit card commercial suggests that it can bring you the whole world at the flick of a piece of plastic. Analyze these commercials and you soon see they are ploys tempting people to escape from reality through the fantasy of getting whatever they want *right now*.

Ask the average person if he (or she) believes he is a materialist and he will say, "Of course not." He doesn't purchase things from want but because of need. "The kids needed new shoes, I needed the sport coat, and my wife needed a new dress. Last Christmas we definitely needed the new color TV, and now it's pretty obvious we need a new car."

As we pursue what we think we need, the real needs of our families often go unmet. Much of what we think we need we don't need at all. I've heard Bill Bright exhort staff, "I must warn you, wear the cloak of materialism loosely."

Discuss:

Are budgeting and spending issues a common source of disharmony in your family? Think about materialism—to what degree does it have a grip on you and your family?

Pray:

That God will give you a heart to appreciate the material means He has given you, and the discipline to manage your resources responsibly.

LAUNCHING OUR ARROWS

{Part One}

Like arrows in the hand of a warrior, so are the children of one's youth.

PSALM 127:4

I find it interesting that the Scripture describes children as "arrows" because arrows are meant to be released. As we raise our children, Barbara and I know we are responsible to prepare them to live independently.

All of our efforts as parents are made with the knowledge that, eventually, these "arrows" will be flying on their own. We make a conscious effort to give them skills in living and in making godly choices.

There's an important characteristic of an arrow: it is an offensive weapon. God wants every Christian to make an impact in our world for Christ, and He wants us parents to emphasize this vision as we raise our children.

When I drive our kids to school, I pray for them: "Lord, I pray that they will never forget that they are Your representatives at school today. I pray that they will be lights in the midst of the darkness."

Knowing we will release our kids, however, doesn't make it any easier when the time actually comes. The "twang" of our bowstring was first heard in August of 1993 when we took our oldest child, Ashley, to college. I remember the scene well: Barbara, Ashley and I stood in the dorm parking lot, huddled-up, arms entwined, sobbing. I was crying so hard that I couldn't pray; my own daughter had to pray for herself!

As we drove away from the dorm, my "little girl" stood on the sidewalk, waving good-bye. I turned to Barbara and said, "One down and five to go! Can you believe that in a year we've got to do this again with Benjamin?"

I paused for a moment. The tears were drying on my face, but the pain of the loss was fresh. "This hurts too much," I said. "I'm not doing it next year. I'm going to rent a dad for a day to do it for me!"

....

Discuss:
Are you preparing to launch your arrows as offensive weapons?
What can you begin doing now to give your children a mind-set
of helping reach people for Christ?

Pray:
Thank God for the privilege of having influence on the direction your arrow
flies. Ask Him to always keep His target in front of you.

LAUNCHING OUR ARROWS

{Part Two}

Prove yourselves to be blameless and innocent, children of God above reproach in the midst of a crooked and perverse generation, among whom you appear as lights in the world.

PHILIPPIANS 2:15

During the next year, Barbara and I notched the bowstring with another arrow, Benjamin, and prepared for our second release. We spent a lot of time talking to him about the temptations he would encounter at the university. Over breakfast Bible studies we discussed drinking, peer pressure, dating, girls and sex.

Some of these talks began when Benjamin was in fifth and sixth grade. Any good archer will tell you that you don't prepare for hunting season by practicing for a couple of weeks right before it begins.

In August, just days before Benjamin was to leave for college, I set up a surprise breakfast for him. We were joined by three godly men whom Benjamin respected. It was powerful! They encouraged Benjamin to grow in his love for Jesus Christ, to guard his heart and to be faithful to God.

Finally the day came. Arriving on campus, we spent most of the afternoon cleaning our son's room so he could move in.

It was nearly dusk when the first poignant moment came. Benjamin and I went outside the student housing for some fresh air and sat on the tailgate of a truck parked near the door. There we watched a steady stream of young men pass by, most of them drinking.

At this point I was becoming fearful for my son. I wanted to protect my arrow and put it back in the quiver, not release it into this "crooked and perverse generation." I turned to Benjamin and looked him in the eye. "Son, I've got to tell you that watching all these young men get wasted on booze really causes me to question the wisdom of sending you into the midst of all this."

There was only a brief silence and then he returned my gaze. "Dad, this is my mission field," he replied. "It's going to be tough, but if it were easy these guys wouldn't need Jesus Christ. This is what you and Mom have trained me for. God has led me here and He will protect me."

There I sat, rebuked by my 18-year-old son. He was a young man of faith.

....

Discuss:

How many years do you have before you release your "arrows"? How are you preparing them for spiritual battle?

Pray:

That your children will desire to have an impact on their peers for Jesus Christ.

HOW MANY CAPS DO YOU WEAR?

*Therefore be careful how you walk, not as unwise men, but as wise,
making the most of your time, because the days are evil.*

EPHESIANS 5:15,16

I'm addicted to baseball caps. I have caps from several baseball teams including the Chicago Cubs, Detroit Tigers and Cantrell Lawn and Turf, my boys' Little League team that went 1-14 two years in a row. My other caps advertise a variety of vacation spots, deer and duck hunts, float trips and a couple of lesser-known corporations.

These caps serve as reminders of the different roles and responsibilities I have as a man. Recently my schedule was getting the upper hand, so I decided to take a year-end inventory of the "caps" I was wearing to see if I could reorganize them or shed some. A few from my list, in no particular order, were: employee, Sunday School teacher, friend, speaker, counselor, recruiter, writer, broadcaster, citizen, manager, motivator, hunter, housepainter, fisherman, taxpayer, financial planner, husband, father of six children.

Many of the "caps" I wear represent people I am responsible for. As I contemplated all these responsibilities, something I frequently ask myself came to mind: The question is not *will I succeed*, but *where must I succeed*. What caps must I be successful in wearing?

When I read in Ephesians that I should walk wisely, "making the most of your time" I realized I needed to weed out unessential responsibilities in my life so I would have room for the essentials. When we recently reorganized our closet, Barbara said I had too many caps and that I had to get rid of "a few." Painful as it was, I filled a small garbage can with half my original stock. My shoes fit neatly on the shelves again, I still have my emotional favorites in my possession, and I saved my marriage in the process!

I saw a T-shirt the other day that said, "I want it all." That just isn't realistic, is it? You and I can't have it all—something, or someone, *will* suffer.

Discuss:
In addition to your responsibility to God, what other "hats" do you wear?
Help one another by regularly tossing "hats" that are keeping you from being
the best at your essential responsibilities.

Pray:
That God will make you equal to the variety of tasks you shoulder and give
you discernment regarding priorities.

CHRIST IN EVERY ROOM

Love the Lord your God with all your heart, and with all your soul,
and with all your strength and with all your mind.

LUKE 10:27

For several years as a young man I compartmentalized my life, allowing God access to only small portions of it. Then I came across a simple booklet by Robert Boyd Munger called *My Heart, Christ's Home* that had a profound impact on me. I was challenged to give Jesus Christ full access and authority over every "room" in my heart. Let me challenge you to reflect on His presence in the rooms of your own heart and home.

Allow Christ to rule the room where you keep your ego. This room has a small door, but we all know how large an ego can lurk inside. When Jesus isn't allowed into this room, husbands and wives bicker, we may become too proud to bury the hatchet with offending parents, children are too competitive and selfish, and everyone is too proud to confess sins. Let Jesus replace your ego and be Lord of this room of your life.

Open to Christ the room of expectations. In this room, we keep our expectations of others' behavior. With Christ excluded, this room can become filled with longings and unmet hopes—some of which are unrealistic and perfectionistic, some of which we've never even expressed to our loved ones.

Let Christ into the room of relationships with your parents. Too many adult children have closed off this room from Christ's presence. They have not fully obeyed the Scripture when they married to "leave and cleave"; they're still too dependent. Or they have ignored their parents and been too distant from them. The Scriptures command those who get married to leave their parents (see Gen. 2:24,25), but to love and honor them as well. Closing off this room from Christ results in inappropriate relationships between adult children and their parents.

Is Christ welcome in every room of your heart and home? Is there one of these three rooms that is off limits to Him?

....

Discuss:

Have you ever given Jesus Christ access to every room in your heart? Does He still have that unhindered access today? Focus on one of the "rooms" above and suggest practical ways Christ can be invited in, and clean it up.

Pray:

For the kind of openness, vulnerability and commitment it takes to truly invite Jesus to be Lord over every aspect of your daily life.

THE AFFAIR WITH CAREERISM

But seek first His kingdom and His righteousness;
and all these things shall be added to you.

MATTHEW 6:33

The stereotype of the executive in the three-piece pinstriped suit working long hours to make it to the top has been around for decades, but his female counterpart is a more recent development. Today, a growing number of men and women are more devoted to their careers than they are to their families. The siren call of careerism lures us away from intimacy and oneness.

Magazines carry articles on husbands and wives who pursue careers with brilliance, energy and drive. Somewhere in the article the wife mentions that she would like to have a child, but her career has been her all-consuming passion. Or she will lament the fact that she has to leave a small baby in some kind of day care situation while she zooms off to catch a jet to the next sales conference. These articles make these couples sound content, chic, sophisticated and totally fulfilled. In a word, they seem to have it all.

We seldom think of careerism as an "affair." But it is. What is an affair? It is breaking your marriage vows and giving yourself to someone or something else–a person, a career or material possessions.

Ironically, careers can be cruel lovers. In the end this kind of love affair is very unfulfilling. There is always another mountain to climb, another business victory to pursue; it's a life void of meaningful relationships. Those who put career above family are rarely satisfied. They are tragically addicted to riding the corporate escalator, and with no way to get off. They must ride it all the way to the top—only to find that at the top it's lonely.

Meanwhile, back at home the fires are slowly going out…

....

Discuss:
Based upon your calendar, what are you giving your life to?
What are your stated values? Your real values? What does God
want you to do about any contradictions?

Pray:
That God will help you remain true to the priority of the family, and that you
will experience satisfaction there and not seek it elsewhere.

HELLFIRE AND BRIMSTONE

{Part One}

Righteous art Thou, O Lord, and upright are Thy judgments.

PSALM 119:137

*I*n Scripture we see two sides to God: One is His loving, compassionate, caring side. He is the God who created us and made the supreme sacrifice to offer us eternal life.

Then there is the God of holiness, the God of wrath; the God who judges sin.

I'm afraid the Church today has lost the balance on the teeter-totter between these two sides to God's nature. Too often we emphasize His love and forget that He is just and righteous; He will not tolerate sin.

I don't think we talk enough today about sin and its consequences. The Bible tells us the penalty for sin is hell. These are not popular concepts in our culture of tolerance.

Hell isn't in style today because it represents a couple of things that are repugnant. It represents accountability to someone in authority, and we want to avoid authority. And it represents absolute eternal judgment. We have a difficult time believing that such a place could exist, and we don't want to really believe that everlasting punishment and torment is a reality. And when we no longer see the eternal retribution of our sins, we lose any urgency for repenting of those sins.

So we don't talk much about hell to our children, extended family or our friends.

But hell is real.

To the Greeks, the distance between the bull's-eye and where the arrow hit was known as "the sin." It meant to fall short of the ideal. To sin means to "miss the mark."

God is patient, but He is not tolerant. He is holy. His justice calls for an atonement (a payment, a penalty) for man's sins. Our children must have some understanding that their sins can keep them out of heaven. Their sins must be paid for. And that is what Jesus Christ did for us on the cross.

....

Discuss:
Think back to your life before you became a Christian. What was it like?
What sins did Jesus die for?

Pray:
That God will give you a holy fear of Him.

HELLFIRE AND BRIMSTONE

{Part Two}

The fear of the Lord is to hate evil; pride and arrogance and the evil way,
and the perverted mouth, I hate.

PROVERBS 8:13

*C*harles Spurgeon, the famous evangelist and theologian, was teaching young men in seminary how to preach. He told them, "Gentlemen, when you speak of heaven, let your face be all aglow and smiling and lifted up and brilliant and let it be unashamed when you speak of heaven. But when you speak of hell, any old face will do."

He was on target. It's too bad we don't have one of the great, old Puritan preachers to come visit our churches more often to present some fiery sermons about hell.

Here's what one of them wrote about hell:

There is no way to describe hell. Nothing on earth can compare to it. No living person has any real idea of it. No mad man in the wildest flights of insanity ever beheld its horror. No man in delirium ever pictured a place so utterly terrible as this. No nightmare racing across a fevered mind ever produced a terror to match that of the mildest hell. Let the most gifted writer exhaust his skill in describing the roaring caverns of unending flame and he would not even come close to the nearest edge of hell. Hell was originally created for the devil and his demons, not for...man. Little wonder there is great joy in heaven over one sinner who repents. He is saved, redeemed, rescued. It makes the hearts of heaven glad.

I wonder what would happen if we could visit hell for just 10 seconds? I think it would change our perceptions of life, sin and evil. And I think it might just motivate us to share the good news about Jesus Christ's redeeming work on the cross with anyone who would listen.

Discuss:
Together as a couple, talk about your burden (or lack of burden)
for reaching your family and neighborhood for Christ.
What is one action point you can make?

Pray:
Thank God that He has rescued you from spending an eternity in hell.
Ask Him to give you boldness in proclaiming that good news to others.

TRUST IN A SOVEREIGN GOD

On the contrary, who are you, O man, who answers back to God? The thing molded will not say to the molder, "Why did you make me like this," will it?

ROMANS 9:20

I once heard a pastor say that, on any given day, 90 percent of the families in his congregation are facing some challenge or crisis. As I have previously shared, such a crisis struck our own family when our 16-year-old son Samuel came down with muscular dystrophy.

Let me confess that I've come close to "talking back to God" over this and many other questions. After 26 years of trying to yield to Christ's rule, experiences of my own and others often leave me with many thorny questions that remain unanswered.

Why would God allow some children to be sexually molested?

Why do so many couples who want children find themselves infertile?

Why do some spouses who have every reason to remain faithful suddenly abandon their families?

I don't believe Scripture provides simple answers to these questions. But I do believe the passage above gives a strong overall answer that invites me to embrace the deepest hope and the strongest faith.

When the Bible asserts that God, the divine Potter, is in control, it raises for some the question of why He allows this or that to happen. But it also invites supreme confidence that, however tragic its effects, evil does not have the last word.

A loving God, who can assume sovereign control over the world, can also be trusted to overwhelm present evils.

In our own situation, a hint of how God's power can empower us to overcome tragedy came one evening when Samuel and I were driving home from the grocery store. We had been talking about his limitations due to MD. Samuel turned from gazing out the window, looked at me and said resolutely: "Well, Dad, I guess you don't need legs to serve God."

Discuss:
For what situations are you asking God, "Why?" Has He given you a reply?

Pray:
That God will give you the ability to trust Him in any situation.

PARENTAL DISCOURAGEMENT

by Barbara Rainey

In this you greatly rejoice,....that the proof of your faith, being more precious than gold,... even though tested by fire, may be found to result in praise and glory and honor at the revelation of Jesus Christ.

1 PETER 1:6,7

o you want to know what the chief of all emotions for mothers is today? It's not anger, worry, fear, loneliness, lack of confidence or feelings of failure. It's discouragement. It begins as exasperation and can become feelings of being out of control.

At times raising six kids has a way of getting you discouraged. I remember going to a pancake house and the kids were really at each other's throats. Dennis and I were thinking, *We're failures. We're raising juvenile delinquents. Here we are speaking at conferences and on the radio every day, and we're failures!*

But that is just part of raising kids. If there is anyone who is doing it perfectly, then he or she better peel back the cover on the kid and find out if he or she is a robot. We don't raise robots, we raise kids with wills of their own. They are going to disappoint us and we will be discouraged.

I think Christians are more susceptible to discouragement because our standard is holiness. Nothing less than 100 percent perfection. Somehow we start believing that our faith will eliminate failure. In reality, our faith will help us battle the discouragement that comes after failure.

We need to hold on to our faith. "Being more precious than gold," our faith combined with a lot of perseverance will result in an imperishable reward—and a generation of children who are raised up in Him.

....

Discuss:
Discouragement and raising a family. How does it impact you? How can you come alongside your spouse?

Pray:
Ask the Lord to help you and your mate to allow yourselves the freedom to fail as parents, and to teach you how to handle those times when you feel like failures.

TAKING A STAND

For I am not ashamed of the gospel, for it is the power of
God for salvation to everyone who believes.

ROMANS 1:16

One fall day I felt a big lump in my throat as our kids left early for school. Ashley, age 17; Benjamin, 15; and Samuel, 13, were going to participate in "See You at the Pole," a nationwide movement of Christian junior and senior high school students gathering around flagpoles to pray for their schools.

The previous evening our family had seen a video promoting "See You at the Pole." We had been thrilled to watch as 250 teenagers prayed around their flagpole. We applauded the courage of a group of only five students who dared to pray around their school's flagpole while the rest of the student body went their ways. But I got a catch in my throat when the video showed one lone girl at another school standing by the pole—praying.

Ashley and Benjamin knew of at least a dozen students who were planning to pray with them at their high school. But Samuel knew of only two other students who might pray with him—and even that wasn't a sure thing. *What if he's the only one?* I thought.

I looked down at my son through watery eyes. Everything within me wanted to spare him the pain of what he might face. But I realized this was a time for Samuel to count the cost of what it means to be a follower of Christ.

Well, as it turned out, nearly 50 kids out of a student body of 425 showed up with Samuel. God used that event to teach all of us some important lessons. Barbara and I realized our kids need the opportunity to hammer out their own faith in the midst of their doubts, *just like we did.* And it reminded me to take courageous and public stands for Christ, and not be ashamed!

....

Discuss:
How have you and your children had the opportunity to take a public stand for Christ? Share a recent time where you've been ashamed to stand up for Jesus Christ.

Pray:
That you and each member of your family will never be intimidated or ashamed to affirm Christian values in a non-Christian world.

DECISION MAKING IN MARRIAGE

But I want you to understand that Christ is the head of every man, and the man is the head of a woman, and God is the head of Christ. However, in the Lord, neither is woman independent of man, nor is man independent of woman.

1 CORINTHIANS 11:3,11

Barbara and I made a commitment early in our marriage that we would make all decisions together. Only if we come to an honest yet unshakable disagreement do I make the decision as head of the house.

I mention this because many men use their "headship" as a sort of club to force their wives to "submit." I don't think it's a mistake that Paul writes, "Neither is woman independent of man, nor is man independent of woman." We need each other in marriage, and in the decisions we make as a couple.

One lesson I've learned with decision making in our marriage is just because Barbara says something once doesn't mean that she's felt like I have heard her. Sometimes I need to hear her again and again and understand the emotional power behind her words. This is especially important when she disagrees with a decision I make because only if she knows I understand her will she be ready to follow that decision.

In the decision we made about our daughter Rebecca's gymnastics involvement, I maintained that we should move her out of gymnastics. As Barbara recalls, "I knew intuitively Dennis was probably right, but I wasn't ready to make that decision yet. I loved watching Rebecca perform. She was built for gymnastics and she loved it.

"I also was concerned because I didn't want her to grow up and resent us for forcing her to quit. I needed to share with Dennis how I felt. It just took me time to come to where I felt like I had adequately expressed that."

The reality was, there was truth in what Barbara said. Her cautions against Rebecca resenting that decision were sound. As husbands we err in decision making when we don't really take our wife's opinion into account. It is the wise man who does!

....

Discuss:
What do you like most about the way you and your mate make decisions? Least?

Pray:
Is there a decision you need to make? Why not stop and pray together about that decision right now?

THE WEIGHT OF EXPECTATIONS

*And, fathers, do not provoke your children to anger; but bring them
up in the discipline and instruction of the Lord.*

EPHESIANS 6:4

A doctor, on his way to visit a new baby in the hospital, found a small
piece of paper on the floor. On the crumpled sheet a new father had
scribbled: *John Peter Jones…John P. Jones…Governor John Jones…Pastor
John Jones…President John P. Jones…J. P. Jones all the way.*

This young fellow may be fortunate to have a father with vision, ambition
and a healthy degree of flexibility. However, he also may have some problems if
these same expectations become unreasonable demands.

Parental expectations have a great effect on developing your child's self-
esteem. The God-given influence you have over your children's formative years
is crucial to your child's view of him- or herself. In her book *Your Child's Self-
Esteem,* Dorothy Corkille Briggs writes, "Children rarely question our expectations; instead they question their personal inadequacy to achieve those expectations."

Today, many Christians carry excess and unnecessary baggage in their walks
with Christ due to poor self-esteem developed while they were children. As parents, it is imperative that we raise our children to know Christ and to have
healthy, balanced perspectives of who they are: sinful, but also highly valued
and loved by God.

I will never forget one of my first counseling appointments when we started
this ministry to families. A mom sat in my office and told the story of her 11-
year-old son's relationship with his dad.

The father constantly criticized the boy: "You dummy—you left the door
open!" "Look at these grades—that's pitiful!" "You struck out at the game—I
can't believe you did that!" "Look at your room, it's a mess and *so are you!*"

That boy is a man today. And I wouldn't be surprised if, each day, he hears
a loud inner voice of self-doubt. His own father, in his zeal to make his son a success, programmed him for failure instead.

Discuss:

Talk with your spouse about your expectations for yourself and your children.
Are they realistic?

Pray:

That God's acceptance of you will cause you to be so secure that you willingly
extend acceptance and realistic expectations to your children.

KIDS AND THE IMAGE OF GOD

And God created man in His own image, in the image of
God He created him; male and female He created them.
GENESIS 1:27

How do you communicate to your children that they are cherished and accepted both by you and by God, while still holding up realistic standards for them?

The world places a premium upon performance. As a result, three false values have arisen: intellect, beauty and athletic ability. You must respect your children's uniquenesses above the imposing pressures of the world's value system, showing that they are made in God's image regardless of performance.

It's also difficult to build self-esteem when parents have differing expectations. Consider the boy who grows up with a father who wants him to be aggressive, competitive and outgoing. Add a mother who desires a quiet, calm, "mommy's boy." The result is a son caught in a vice, unable to please either of his parents.

Your own upbringing influences your ability to communicate reasonable expectations. If your parents held unachievable standards over you, you will tend to do the same thing to your children, even though you fight fiercely to avoid it.

What can you do to correct unreal expectations? First, *know your child*. Know his or her true abilities and interests. Each child should be uniquely considered, apart from siblings.

Second, *clearly verbalize your expectations*. Unfortunately, many standards are never spoken until they are violated. One suggestion: Write down all the major expectations you hold for your child and post them on a personalized bulletin board.

Third, *praise your children for genuine effort*. Warm praise and respect will encourage the growth of positive self-esteem. You might ask yourself, "How many times do I positively reinforce my child for his or her efforts each day?" Don't be guilty of withholding your approval from your children. Lavishly grant approval of a "job well done."

....

Discuss:
On a scale of 1-10 (1 = low), rank your parents' expectations of you
as a child. Discuss with your mate how those expectations affect
you and your parenting style today.

Pray:
That you can experience God's acceptance in order to communicate
acceptance and self-esteem to your children.

WITH OPEN ARMS

Create in me a clean heart, O God, and renew a steadfast spirit within me.
Do not cast me away from Thy presence....Restore to me the joy of Thy salvation.

PSALM 51:10-12

The devil is called "the father of lies" (John 8:44), and for good reason. He will try to lead you to believe anything that will keep you from turning to God.

One of his greatest lies, I believe, is that God will reject us when we confess our sins to Him and seek to repent. Somehow we start thinking that our sins are too terrible for Him to forgive.

The truth, of course, is that God loves a contrite heart, welcomes the repentant sinner back and restores "the joy of Thy salvation." Recently, I received a letter that underscores the power of God's forgiveness:

My wife and I have been married for six years, and together for eight. Recently I was having a lot of problems. I was unfaithful to my wife. I had fallen far from the path. She found out about the adultery and consulted a lawyer and filed for divorce.

My life was over. I didn't know what to do or where to turn. Suddenly I realized what I must do. I went to church, fell to my knees and asked God to forgive me and take over my life, set me straight. I gave it all up to Him.

Much to my surprise, He welcomed me back with open arms. I relearned how to pray and started reading the Bible. God took it from there.

This man asked his wife to attend a FamilyLife Marriage Conference with him. Reluctant at first, she finally agreed.

The Lord not only answered my prayers (by restoring my marriage) but 10 times what I had asked for! We not only did away with the lawyers and divorce papers, but we recommitted to God and each other.

Just like King David, who wrote those wonderful words in Psalm 51, this man learned that life can start anew when you are willing to approach God with a repentant heart.

....

Discuss:
Talk about your understanding of God's forgiveness—is it absolute, total? Do you harbor any fears that God will reject you? What for?

Pray:
If you need to confess any sins, do so now and thank God for His forgiveness.

DISCOVERING SOMETHING BEAUTIFUL

Whatever is true, whatever is honorable, whatever is right, whatever is pure,
whatever is lovely,...let your mind dwell on these things.

PHILIPPIANS 4:8

*A*ccording to legend, a Chinese emperor once said to his wife, "I notice that our mulberry trees are being damaged. I'd like you to find out what's wrong."

The empress discovered that a small, drab-colored moth was laying eggs on the leaves. The tiny eggs would hatch into little worms that, after a few days, would spin cocoons and damage the leaves.

Wondering if she could destroy the little cocoons, she dropped one of them into a pot of boiling water. To her surprise, the cocoon began to slowly unwind into a silvery thread. Upon further inspection, the thread proved to be a half-mile long!

Thus, through the process of solving a problem, she discovered something beautiful — silk.

To me, this story illustrates the importance of attitude when you deal with differences between you and your mate. Like flies at a summer picnic, differences buzz in the ears of many couples, threatening to rob their relationships of their peaceful, accepting love. As humorist Sam Levenson once said, "Love at first sight is easy to understand; it's when two people have been looking at each other for a lifetime that it becomes a miracle!"

Ironically, these differences may have attracted you to each other in the first place. He was outgoing; she was shy. He was a big spender, which made her feel special because she was a tightwad. He was a hard worker; she was impulsive and fun loving. At some point after marriage, when you discover that these differences begin to annoy you, it's time to make a critical choice. Are you going to reject your mate, or accept him or her?

One practical way to demonstrate acceptance is to train your mind to focus on the positive qualities of your mate. As Paul writes in Philippians 4:8 (above), let your mind dwell on what is honorable and lovely in your mate.

These differences are what make you strong as a couple. A friend of mine summarized this principle, "My wife and I had both accepted Christ, but we were shocked to discover that we had never accepted one another."

....

Discuss:

Make a list of all your differences and how you complement one another. Then make a list of all the positive qualities in your mate. Write out a love letter that is a statement of your acceptance of your mate.

Pray:

That you will develop the ability to accept the gift God gave you in your mate.

SATAN'S LIES TO FAMILIES

{Part One}

He [the devil] was a murderer from the beginning, and does not stand in the truth, because there is no truth in him.

JOHN 8:44

The "Desert Storm" conflict that Saddam Hussein fueled a few years ago caused me to reflect on the spiritual battle that daily swirls around your family and ours.

Families don't seem to talk about spiritual battle much. Our enemy is unseen. The theater for operations and battles—our souls (our minds, emotions and will)—does not appear on any map. Maybe it sounds a little too mystical for us to think of life being more than what is seen, but the Bible says spiritual battle is real. And what is at stake is of the utmost importance.

Joe Louis, one of the greatest heavyweight boxers of all time, was once asked about the secret of his success. Lewis responded by saying that he and his manager always studied each opponent thoroughly. As a result, Louis said, he was seldom *surprised* and was able to stay on the *offensive* throughout the entire fight.

I feel that too many Christians are uninformed about Satan and his tactics. As a result, many are living defensive, shell-shocked lifestyles. I want to help you stay on the offensive and win your family's encounters with the adversary by learning one of his primary strategies.

A good friend, Ney Bailey, made a profound statement about our spiritual adversary, Satan, and his daily tactics on our spiritual lives: *"The only power that Satan has is in his lies and getting us to believe them."*

It was interesting to watch how Saddam Hussein used lies to intimidate, create fear and keep us off balance in battle. In the first 24 hours of the ground war offensive, Baghdad radio reported that, "Allied troops were dying like flies." I felt afraid. I just knew he had killed thousands of our troops with chemical and biological weapons. I felt that perhaps this ground war is not such a good idea after all; maybe we should pull out and go home.

But I was believing a lie. It was only as the truth became clear, that my fears were relieved: Our forces were achieving overwhelming victory. Satan knows better than Saddam Hussein that his real power in your life is through his lies.

....

Discuss:
How frequently do you doubt God's Word?
What lies undermine your faith in God and His Word?

Pray:
In prayer resist the devil—the promise is he will flee from you. Ask God to help you recognize your real enemy, spot the lies and grow in faith.

SATAN'S LIES TO FAMILIES

{Part Two}

*Whenever he [the devil] speaks a lie, he speaks from his own nature;
for he is a liar, and the father of lies.*

JOHN 8:44

I can think of at least four lies Satan tells families:

1. "You're a failure. You'll never make it." The lie of self-condemnation is one of Satan's chief weapons. You may struggle with feelings of guilt, failure or inferiority. Satan would have us believe that our faults are much too damaging to be covered by the grace of God. If you believe this lie, it renders you powerless, passive and paralyzed without any hope of progress as a parent.

2. "You don't deserve to be unhappy." Of course God does want us to be happy, but the way Satan puts the statement is a lie because he means, "All you need to do is get out from under this relationship or these family pressures and you'll be happy." It's a "feel-good lie" because what really feels good is working through problems together.

3. "Nobody will find out." Have you ever heard a little voice tempting you to do something illegal or immoral that would bring instant satisfaction or pleasure? You may think nobody will discover what you do, but that's a lie. The truth will come out.

4. "If I had what Sam has, I'd be happier." Satan wants you to think that what you have is inferior to what someone else has. The lie is exposed when we realize that such comparisons are always made from a distance. If we had what Sam had, we would probably experience Sam-type problems, and they may be worse than ours.

Remember that Satan is a counterfeiter. If we refuse to believe his lies, he is rendered powerless. Resist him by remembering the truth of God's Word.

....

Discuss:
Which of these lies do you see Satan using with you? Be specific.

Pray:
That a sense of God's own power will fill your heart, and that His voice through the Word will drown out each of Satan's lies.

MOTHERHOOD AS A CAREER

by Barbara Rainey

That they may encourage the young women to love their husbands, to love their children,
to be sensible, pure, workers at home, kind, being subject to their own husbands,
that the word of God may not be dishonored.

TITUS 2:4,5

Our society often sends the wrong signals to mothers. It tells moms they are dispensable. It tells us that all mothers need to do is provide maid service, shuttle service and offer purchasing advice; that real mothering can be done by trained caretakers.

I believe Christian mothers need to think critically about these cultural messages and challenge them. More moms need to make a career of busying themselves at home, and investing in their husbands and the next generation.

I realize there are many reasons for mothers to have full-time or part-time jobs. But I also know some couples need to look critically at whether this is for survival, for personal fulfillment or simply to maintain a higher standard of living. If a couple feels it's necessary for Mom to work outside the home, some crucial questions should be addressed.

A Christian mother should ask whether her husband is in total agreement with this decision. The two-career marriage may solve financial difficulties, but it creates others because many needs of the family will not receive full attention.

Another good question is: If extra income is essential, can it be earned on a flexible time frame, or by working at home? A woman in my church was able to develop a part-time photography business out of her home. She was always sure that whenever she had appointments she could leave her little boy with her husband or a friend.

A career speaks of total commitment and full-time focus. No commitment or focus is more worthy of being a career than mothering the children you bring into the world.

Discuss:
What are some prices children sometimes pay for both
parents working outside the home?

Pray:
That God will guide you to make decisions about career and family that reflect
the priority that rearing children should have in a Christian home.

WORTHY OF PRAISE

Her children rise up and bless her; her husband also, and he praises her, saying:
"Many daughters have done nobly, but you excel them all."

PROVERBS 31:28,29

The crowning glory of the woman in Proverbs 31 is that her children and husband praise her. I think one thing we're not emphasizing today is praising moms for being the keepers of our greatest national treasure — our children.

I think Debbie Haley really sums up what a mom is all about. Here is a portion of Debbie's tribute to her mother, Jane:

Mom was born in a small town in Kentucky. She was married in the middle of her senior year in high school. Two years after I was born, Mom didn't go to college and pursue a glamorous career. She did something much greater. She raised four children who now rise up and call her blessed.

Mom showed me what it was to have a faith in God. Mom showed me what generosity and sacrificial giving were all about. She taught me about being honest. She taught me about manners. Mom showed me what it was to love your husband. She has now loved him in marriage for some 38 years.

Mom took care of herself. She was so beautiful and I always was proud of her. I wanted to grow up and be a mother just like her. Mom showed me that the most important thing a woman can do is to serve her family by staying at home with her children.

Mom is now reaping the rewards of being a grandmother. My children are blessed to have her for one. I know that God has called me to be a mother. I am proud to be one and proud to have a mother like the one I have. I pray that I can take what she has given me and pass it down to my daughters.

Thank you, Mom. I love you.

These are words more mothers need to hear from their children.

....

Discuss:
For what qualities can you praise your mother?

Pray:
That God would give you the opportunity soon to thank your mother for the good things she has done in your life.

ACCOUNTABILITY: YOUR PERSONAL ALARM SYSTEM

And be subject to one another in the fear of Christ.

EPHESIANS 5:21

One of the tallest skyscrapers in New England is the John Hancock Building in Boston. When this structure of over 40 floors was built, there were all kinds of problems with the windows. During the stress of the freezing and thawing of the New England winter, the windows actually popped out of their frames and shattered. People walking on the sidewalk below were showered with glass. Businessmen working at their desks suddenly found themselves seated a few inches from nothing, staring straight down at the street.

The architects and contractors got together and finally decided to install a small alarm system in each window. When the windows began to bulge and contract, the alarm system would let maintenance people know so they could make adjustments that would take tension off the glass before it blew out and shattered.

I believe every person needs an alarm system that can help him or her relieve the tension before something shatters. One of the best alarm systems I know of is to become accountable to each other.

Accountability is a scriptural principle that tells us to "be subject to one another in the fear of Christ." This means I choose to submit my life to the scrutiny of another person to gain spiritual strength, growth and balance.

Accountability means asking the other person for advice. It means giving the other person the freedom to make honest observations and evaluations about you. It means we're teachable and approachable.

For me as a husband, father and leader of a growing ministry, accountability has not been an option. It has been a crucial ingredient in my Christian growth.

Some people challenge me on this subject, saying that becoming accountable to one another would be like playing policeman. But the opposite is true. And I'd like to explain why during the next few devotions.

....

Discuss:
Do you find the concept of being accountable to another person uncomfortable? Why?

Pray:
For humility and vulnerability, and that your life will be an open book before the Lord, before your family and before some selected Christians who you trust.

CHARACTERISTICS OF THE UNACCOUNTABLE

Reprove a wise man, and he will love you.
Give instruction to a wise man, and he will be still wiser.

PROVERBS 9:8,9

I believe if there is anything that can ensure and incorporate character, godly character in your life and in mine, it is through accountability. You don't have to go long before you learn of some Christian pastor, singer, evangelist or ministry leader who has lost his or her ministry, usually because of adultery. And because of my position I hear many more stories that never made it into the media.

I once sat down and wrote a list of characteristics of people who have fallen to temptation. Over and over, this is how other people described them:

- A loose spirit with few boundaries;
- Rationalizes and justifies behavior;
- Detached, reclusive, insulated from people;
- Makes decisions without consulting others;
- A lack of authenticity and realness about his or her life;
- Defensive, proud, unwilling to admit mistakes and failure;
- Hides major areas of life from others;
- Intimidating, unapproachable, secretive.

It's amazing to see how these descriptions pop up again and again. They are isolated, keeping people at arm's length, and not willing to submit themselves to the scrutiny of others.

When you are isolated, you are much more susceptible to temptation. Years ago I attended a Christian writers' conference in Minneapolis. I was walking down the stairwell in the hotel when I looked down and saw a pornographic magazine lying there. I walked on, but later in the day I saw it in the same spot.

Here I was, alone in Minneapolis. I could pick up that magazine, carry it a few feet to my door and read it in the privacy of my room, and nobody would ever know.

Fortunately, I made the correct decision and left the magazine alone. But I could understand the power of temptation to a person who is alone. Isolation is one of the most powerful weapons the enemy uses to trap Christians.

....

Discuss:
In what situations do you find yourself most open to temptation?

Pray:
That you would have the strength and wisdom to avoid situations where you are isolated from others.

THE BENEFITS OF ACCOUNTABILITY

And be subject to one another in the fear of Christ.

EPHESIANS 5:21

Back in the 1800s, a husband in a village of Pennsylvania Quakers was beating his wife. The other men in the village decided to take action. One man wrote, "...a bunch of us men went over there and took all of his clothes off and drug him through a field of thistles backwards. Then we told him, if he continued to deal unkindly with his wife, we were not going to take to it very lightly. We were going to get upset next time."

I'm not advocating such extreme measures when I encourage you to be accountable to other people. But I do think there are many benefits to it.

Look again at Ephesians 5:21 (above). People don't like the phrase "be subject to one another" these days. The independent "give me my rights" spirit in America conflicts with the thought of being subject to other people.

But accountability helps you in so many ways. For one thing, it helps protect you—from isolation, from pride, from sin, from giving in to temptation and weakness. One of the best ways I know to protect you from those weaknesses is to let someone know about them and ask that person to keep you accountable.

My friends Stu and Linda Weber shared how they were driving in a blizzard on a dangerous, narrow road in the mountains when their car spun out of control. Just as they were about to slide over the edge and to their deaths, the car smashed into a guardrail. That guardrail is just like a friend who can protect us from disaster and even death.

Accountability also helps you avoid extremes. Without someone who can give you an objective evaluation of who you are and what you do, you will have a difficult time keeping balance in your life. For example, if you are accountable to someone for your goals, that person can help you decide if your goals are realistic and how you should spend your time attempting to meet them.

A final benefit is that it can help you stay focused on your dreams. Are you getting so caught up in the minutia of life that you are not accomplishing what you feel like God called you to do? Nothing may help you more than to define your goals and stay accountable to someone for reaching them.

Accountability is absolutely essential if we are to experience all that God has created us to be and to do.

....

Discuss:
How would you personally benefit from accountability?

Pray:
That God will lead you to some people who will love you enough to protect you and help you stay focused on what God wants to do through you.

ACCOUNTABILITY IN MARRIAGE

Two are better than one because they have a good return for their labor.
For if either of them falls, the one will lift up his companion.

ECCLESIASTES 4:9,10

More than anyone else, I have determined that I will be accountable to my wife, Barbara.

Marriage is a perfect arena for accountability. As you and your mate face continuing pressures and stress, it's best to handle life in duet, not solo. Two can always see more clearly than one. Your mate can detect blind spots that you may not be able to see.

Here are some areas where Barbara and I practice accountability in our marriage:

Schedules: We try to help each other make good decisions by monitoring each other's workload and schedule. When somebody invites me to speak somewhere, I say, "I can't give you an answer now. My wife and I have agreed that I don't take any speaking engagements without talking with her." And so we do talk about it, and Barbara helps me say no.

Money and values: We constantly check our personal values. What is really important to each of us? Why are we doing what we are doing? Where do we dare not lose?

Fidelity: Some years ago I led a Bible study that included several new Christians. During those studies, Barbara began to sense that one of the men was increasingly friendly toward her. At first she thought she was imagining things, so she kept it to herself. When she finally told me what was happening, I could see unmistakable relief spread across her face. What had been her personal secret quickly evaporated as we discussed her feelings together.

Fortunately, Barbara's admirer never tried going beyond being friendly. But looking back on that incident, we see that it was a test for both of us. It reaffirmed our commitment to each other as we stood together against a potential threat to our marriage.

Your spouse should be your number one accountability partner.

Discuss:
Do you feel free to be accountable to your mate? Why? Why not? If appropriate, discuss accountability with your spouse.

Pray:
That God would use accountability to your mate to help you and your spouse grow closer to Christ and preserve your marriage.

THREE STEPS TO BECOMING ACCOUNTABLE

Iron sharpens iron, so one man sharpens another.

PROVERBS 27:17

While your mate should be your primary accountability partner, there also is great benefit in getting "sharpened" by other godly Christians. If you want to see some significant growth in your spiritual maturity this may be the most important step you could take.

I have three suggestions:

First, *determine your needs*. What are the two or three things that seem to entangle you more than anything else? Is it finances? Lustful thoughts? Overeating? Not spending enough time with the Lord?

Second, *select a mature Christian—of the same sex—who would have the courage to speak the truth and ask you tough questions*. This should not be someone who would fear your rejection, or someone who has a weakness in the same area, or someone you feel you can manipulate or control. This is especially important if you are strong-willed or have a powerful personality.

Third, *approach this person and ask him to keep you accountable*. Here is what you might say: "Bill, I have a problem and I really need your help in an area of my life. I need for you to love me through this and hold my feet to the fire, but not be judgmental. Because, Bill, I really need to get victory over this."

Finally, *meet with this person on a regular basis to set measurable goals and to allow him to ask you how you're doing*. Agree to a list of questions he will ask you. "Frank, have you written out a budget yet?" "Why not?" "When will you do it?" And here's a powerful one: "Have you lied to me at all today?"

If you're trying to mature in Christ and gain victory over sin by yourself, you're missing it! Praise God that He has given us the Body of Christ...to strengthen us, encourage us and keep us accountable!

....

Discuss:

What are your greatest needs that would lead you to find an accountability partner? Who are potential accountability partners you could approach?

Pray:

That God would lead you to people who He can use to sharpen you.

OF FIRST IMPORTANCE

*For what I received I passed on to you as of first importance: that Christ
died for our sins according to the Scriptures, that he was buried, that he was
raised on the third day according to the Scriptures.*

1 CORINTHIANS 15:3,4 (NIV)

The Bible is a large book—or a collection of many books. We are blessed that in this passage the apostle Paul singles out the core of it all. Of course nothing in Scripture is unimportant, but nothing else is "of first importance" like the death, burial and resurrection of Jesus.

In the same way, you and your mate would benefit from spending some time singling out what is most important to you. Barbara and I have pondered and struggled with this issue for years. Among the core values we have listed are: compassion, discipline, courage, integrity and the fear of the Lord.

At one session, as we prayerfully interacted over our individual core values, we made a profound discovery: Our priorities were different! One of Barbara's top 5 values was "teaching our children the work ethic." I didn't even list that in my top 10! Nor did she have one of my top 5 core values down on her sheet— "relationships."

Suddenly it became clear why our weekend schedule sometimes felt like a battlefield. It was a battle over values—work vs. relationships. Barbara wanted to use our Saturdays to work on the house or in the yard. My preference was to slide away (from the work) and go build memories and relationships in a boat on the lake.

Neither value was wrong—just different.

That day we learned a lesson I will never forget: Each of us spends our time on those things we feel are most important. And because most of us never get around to defining our core values as individuals and as a family, we end up living scattered and hectic lives, driven by unreal expectations.

....

Discuss:

Write a "mission statement" for your family, listing the core values you would like to see emphasized. Does the way you spend most of your time and money reflect these values?

Pray:

That God will help you choose the most important values for your family, and to spend your time and finances in ways that honor Him.

LIVING WITH DIFFERENCES

by Barbara Rainey

Make my joy complete by being of the same mind, maintaining the same love,
united in spirit, intent on one purpose.

PHILIPPIANS 2:2

It's one thing to acknowledge that differences make you strong as a couple, but it's another to figure out how to live with those differences! Here are a few suggestions:

Pray for yourself. Ask God to examine your attitudes and motives and to give you a greater capacity to understand, accept and even appreciate your mate's differences.

When we were first married, Dennis's free spirit and impulsiveness tended to drive my disciplined nature crazy. I felt that we had no schedule, no budget and no regular devotions.

I remember praying diligently for God to change all the things in Dennis I didn't like. Then I realized my attitude needed to be changed. In time I began to see how much I needed his spontaneity to balance my more rigid control.

Talk about differences with your mate. Tell him you are not rejecting him and that you remain committed. If you find that your mate is not emotionally prepared to discuss a touchy issue, leave the subject alone.

If your mate is willing to talk about a difference that is bothering you, *share your feelings without accusing him and pointing the finger of blame.* Let him know you realize you're not perfect and that you understand him, or want to understand him, in this area.

If your mate considers a difference to be a weakness, *ask if you can help.* Then, at the end of your discussion, remind your mate again of your commitment and acceptance. We call this the "bookend principle." Just as bookends are used to prop up books that contain truth, so your reminders of love and complete acceptance at both ends of the discussion will support the truth of what you have said. And it makes the truth a whole lot *easier* to hear!

·····

Discuss:
How do your differences make you stronger as a couple?
Your spouse's?

Pray:
For the ability to discuss differences openly without being defensive or feeling threatened.

THE GREENHOUSE

For He established a testimony in Jacob.

PSALM 78:5

We all know the last words of Christ before He ascended to heaven—the Great Commission of Matthew 28:18-20, where He commands us to "make disciples of all the nations."

I'd like to point you to another passage in which God lays out an important part of His plan to fulfill that commission. Psalm 78:5-7 reads:

> For He established a testimony in Jacob, and appointed a law in Israel, which He commanded our fathers, that they should teach them to their children, that the generation to come might know, even the children yet to be born, that they may arise and tell them to their children, that they should put their confidence in God, and not forget the works of God, but keep His commandments.

As I read Scripture, I see that God formed two institutions to pass His Word from one generation to the next. One, of course, is His Church. The other is the *family.* God's original plan called for the home to be a sort of greenhouse—a nurture center—where children grow up to learn godly character and biblical values.

As a parent, it's so easy to get caught up in the pressures of daily living—of changing diapers and settling sibling disputes and ferrying kids to piano lessons and scout meetings. From time to time you must look above that and remember that the most important work during your years on earth will be to teach your children how to know and love the Lord God. Through your words and your actions, *your very life*, you have the power to shape the future of our nation by shaping a few of the people who live in it.

I love what Charles Swindoll says about the importance of a family and a home in this process:

> Whatever else may be said about the home, it is the bottom line of life. The anvil upon which attitudes and convictions are hammered out. The single most influential force in our earthly existence. It is at home, among family members, that we come to terms with circumstances. It is here that life makes up its mind.

....

Discuss:
What convictions and values do you want to pass on to your children?

Pray:
Ask God to give you wisdom in raising the next generation and
imparting biblical values.

DARE TO RISK

{Part One}

He makes my feet like hinds' feet, and sets me upon my high places.
Thou dost enlarge my steps under me, and my feet have not slipped.

PSALM 18:33,36

I am a daredevil, a risk taker. No, I don't go hang gliding, skydiving or bungee jumping. But I like adventure—trying something new with enough risk to make it exciting.

One summer I did something that causes me to tremble and tighten my muscles even now. My boss put together a two-day camping adventure for several leaders of Campus Crusade for Christ.

Our first day's challenge was mountain climbing. Words and phrases like "rope up," "rappelling" and "sewing-machine leg" gained new meaning. To keep climbing, we had to mentally decide to take a risk. I found in most cases physical limitations were not my enemy. My mind caused me the real trouble because I wanted to play it safe.

But it was going down on the second day that brought the most fear. As we thought of sliding down a rope from the edge of a cliff to a ledge 175 feet below, there was a lot of nervous laughter among these men.

I was number 12 out of 14, which meant I had a lot of time to think about it. Sometimes thinking is dangerous.

Finally, it was my turn. With cold, sweaty palms, I stood to fasten my rope on my belt. At the edge of the cliff I had to lean back almost horizontally. *This is it,* I thought. *This is the way I'm going to die.*

In a few seconds I found myself dangling with the valley floor 1,500 feet below to my left. I glided safely down the rope for about 30 seconds to the ledge below. The risk had been worth it. Unhooking my ropes, I looked up at the mountain and thought, *I really can't believe I did that.*

I learned that day that risk is inevitable if we are to climb mountains and accomplish great things for the kingdom of God. Your mind may say, "Play it safe," but the Scriptures command us to lean on God.

....

Discuss:
Are you a risk taker, or do you play it safe in your walk with God?

Pray:
At the end of your life will it be said of you, "He believed God for too much rather than too little?" Ask God to help you be more of a spiritual risk taker.

DARE TO RISK

{Part Two}

*Thou hast also given me the shield of Thy salvation, and Thy right hand
upholds me; and Thy gentleness makes me great.*

PSALM 18:35

What is the real need among Christians today? It's not safety, security or a fat savings account. It is not better facilities, better programs, flashier television shows, a celebrity's testimony, more people in the ministry or an open door for the gospel in a closed country. These are all needs. But what is the real need?

Dawson Trotman, founder of the Navigators, was asked about the need of the hour. He replied:

> The need of the hour is an army of soldiers dedicated to Jesus Christ who believe that He is God, that He can fulfill every promise He ever made, and that nothing is too hard for Him. This is the only way we can accomplish what is on God's heart, getting the gospel to every creature.

The real need is for risk takers—those who dare to lean out over the cliff's edge on the promises of His Word. Jesus called them disciples.

I can assure you I'm a novice, but if I keep going out over the edge, sooner or later I'm going to become a veteran in the faith.

Stepping out in faith doesn't have to be knee jarring, heart pounding or spectacular. For some it may mean volunteering to teach Sunday School, or additional giving. But for others the hazards may be more costly, such as witnessing to a boss or a neighbor. The risk includes the exposure that comes from attempting something that can be pulled off only in and through Jesus Christ.

Venture out! Don't play it safe. Life is too short. Remember Helen Keller's words: "Life is either a daring adventure or nothing." Find your true safety in Christ and go for it!

One thing I learned while mountain climbing is that Jesus is my Rock. Those ropes were bolted in six places to that immovable granite mountain before we dangled over the edge. Likewise, Christ, our Rock, is immovable. He is our refuge, our strength, our safety.

....

Discuss:
What would you do if you knew you could not fail?

Pray:
If you don't have a vision for your life and marriage, why not get on your knees tonight as a couple and ask God to help you see what He wants you to do?

NO PAIN, NO GAIN

All discipline for the moment seems not to be joyful, but sorrowful; yet to those who have trained by it, afterwards it yields the peaceful fruit of righteousness.

HEBREWS 12:11

*H*ave you seen the advertisement of the young man with the washboard stomach, with glistening muscles rippling as he pumps his exercise machine—and its haunting reminder: *"No pain, no gain"*?

The same is true spiritually speaking isn't it? Of course we want the faith of Moses, but we'd rather avoid the 40-year visit to the wilderness where God made him strong in faith through humility.

We want David's heart for God, but we don't want blisters from shoveling smelly sheep manure. We want the glory of the spotlight, the prestige of the position, but we are reluctant to pay the price of preparation.

And who wouldn't want to have the spiritual impact of Paul? He shaped the first-century church. He journeyed to other countries, preached to massive crowds, entrusted his life to men like Timothy—we're talking gain, real gain.

But we're also talking pain—major league pain. Paul did time in prison. He was beaten near death "many times"—five times the Jews gave him 39 lashes. He was stoned and beaten with rods. He spent a night and a day in the sea. Often he was without food, water and clothing (see 2 Cor. 11:23-27). No discipline, no growth. No pain, no gain.

In spiritual terms, your stomach is the residence where courage resides. Courage makes tough decisions—hard choices. It is said of a courageous person, "He has guts." But our society is flabby at the waistline. We don't want to go against the flow; we want comfort.

Paul promised that God has the power to give us guts: to endure pain for spiritual gain. Paul wrote to Timothy, "God did not give us a spirit of timidity, but a spirit of power, of love and of self-discipline" (2 Tim. 1:7, *NIV*).

Do you really want the gain?

....

Discuss:

What attitudes of mind are required to accept pain as gain? In what areas do you and your family need to be better disciplined?

Pray:

Ask God for the courage, faith and perspective that embraces pain in your life. Ask Him to make you more fruitful, knowing that fruit bearing is always preceded by pruning.

THE TREADMILL

Therefore we do not lose heart, but though our outer man is decaying,
yet our inner man is being renewed day by day.

2 CORINTHIANS 4:16

D o you ever get the feeling that life is like a treadmill?
I try to run three miles at least three times each week. But when I started out several years ago—on my fortieth birthday—I could barely run downhill for one mile. I had to build up quite a bit of stamina to reach three miles a day.

The older you get, the steeper the incline of the treadmill seems to become. Sound like bad news? It really isn't. As Paul said, a law of "inverse proportion" works in our favor. While our outer man is growing old, our inner man is being renewed.

But if I understand the Scripture, the longer we live, the more we have to die. The more you want to grow, the more you and I must say no to self and yes to Christ.

God gives our legs hills so that we can grow stronger. The prophet Isaiah gives us the secret of where strong legs come from: "Yet those who wait for the Lord will gain new strength; they will mount up with wings like eagles, they will run and not get tired, they will walk and not become weary" (Isa. 40:31).

Now *there's* an encouraging word. As you persevere on the treadmill of life, you can count on God's grace empowering those tired muscles. And remember that if you are following the Lord your walk is really taking you somewhere. You're not just a sweating sufferer on a treadmill; you're a pilgrim on a journey. And you have the promise of God: "Blessed is the man who perseveres under trial, because when he has stood the test, he will receive the crown of life" (Jas. 1:12).

....

Discuss:

How has your faith grown stronger as the road grows longer? As our bodies deteriorate, why is it important to grow in our "inner man" every day? Ask your spouse: What can I do to help you grow spiritually?

Pray:

Ask God to enable you to be the kind of spouse that will encourage every member of your family to grow spiritually into a man or woman of faith.

THE FINISHED WORK OF PATIENCE

Consider it all joy, my brethren, when you encounter various trials, knowing that the testing of your faith produces endurance. And let endurance have its perfect result, that you may be perfect and complete, lacking in nothing.

JAMES 1:2-4

Dr. Mavis Heatherington works in an organization on the East Coast that helps parents through traumatic experiences in marriages where a child died or was born deformed. According to her studies, 70 percent of such couples separate or divorce within five years.

Why does this happen? Many couples simply have no strategy for living beyond romance. They don't have a plan that will hold their relationships together during that desperate period of suffering and pain.

Death and suffering are part of life. Part of the strategy for facing troubles is to realize that God allows difficulties in our lives for many reasons. British writer Malcolm Muggeridge once wrote:

> Contrary to what might be expected, I look back on experiences that at the time seemed especially desolating and painful with particular satisfaction. Indeed, I can say with complete truthfulness that everything that I have learned in my 75 years in this world, everything that has truly enhanced and enlightened my experience, has been through affliction and not through happiness.

In other words, if it were ever to be possible to eliminate affliction from our earthly existence by the means of some drug, or some other medical mumble jumble, the result would not be to make life delectable, but to make it too banal and trivial to be endurable.

Many families can echo this experience. Yet despite all this valuable testimony, many couples seek to deal with trials by turning against one another rather than turning to God together in prayer.

When trials come to you and your family, do you process the pain together or fall apart? Will you be able to consider them as "joy"?

....

Discuss:
Do you feel prepared to handle suffering in your marriage relationship? Why?

Pray:
Together pray through (not around) a problem, trial or other issue, asking God to give you patience to allow time to learn from the experience. Ask God to increase your oneness as a couple.

PLEASING YOUR MATE

{Part One}

Now we who are strong ought to bear the weaknesses of those without strength and not just please ourselves. Let each of us please his neighbor for his good, to his edification. For even Christ did not please Himself.

ROMANS 15:1-3

I am convinced that great marriages and great families are rooted in self-denial. In a truly biblical, Christian marriage, both people are willing to give up their lives for one another in order to love their mate properly.

During the early years of our marriage, I remember looking in the rearview mirror of the car as I pulled out to go fishing with several of our children one Saturday. Barbara was standing on the porch, left with a couple of kids in diapers while I went off to the lake with the older kids to have a good time.

While I was sitting in that boat, not catching anything, I continued to think about Barbara. I thought, *You know, I am pleasing myself, but I have not done a good job of pleasing her.* I realized I needed to give up some of my hobbies for awhile in order to please her and reduce her burden.

In our nation's economy, one usually determines the value of a piece of merchandise or a service by how much one has to give up, or sacrifice, to gain it. If my son wishes to buy a new basketball, it will cost him a couple of weekends of freedom in order to complete enough chores to earn the money to pay for it.

In a similar fashion, your mate often interprets how much you love or value him or her by how much you are willing to sacrifice for him or her.

For the woman trying to please her husband, it has often been said that the way to a man's heart is through his stomach. Why not cook the foods he enjoys? Be careful not to become his mother, feeding him only what is "good for him." Spoil him a little.

A husband can please his wife by finding out what her number one need is, and then helping to meet that need if he can. It may be as simple as a walk and time to talk with her. Or as complex as a child that has her under his or her control.

The main concern here is to do the right thing: Please your spouse.

....

Discuss:

How Romans 15:1-3 can be applied to your marriage? Take the pulse of your heart to please one another. Write down, then discuss the three things your spouse could do that would truly please you.

Pray:

For the ability to focus on pleasing your mate rather than yourself.

PLEASING YOUR MATE

{Part Two}
by Barbara Rainey

So teach us to number our days.

PSALM 90:12

One of the greatest forms of sacrifice you can make to please your mate is to give your time. You can make more money, and you can buy more flowers, but you can't make or buy more time. Each day is made up of 24 hours—nothing will change that.

We're all short of time. Psalm 90:12 admonishes us to "number our days." How many days do you have left? How will you use them?

I have always had an interest in art, and I enjoy looking at paintings in art galleries and museums. When we married, Dennis thought art museums were great places in which to get bored quickly. But to please me, he has spent time with me to visit quite a few museums.

In contrast, although Dennis has always loved fishing, I had no appreciation for the sport when we married. I tended to agree with the person who said, "A fisherman is a jerk on one end of a line waiting for a jerk on the other end."

But to please Dennis, I did a lot of fishing during the early years of our marriage. Later, when our expanding population of children made it impossible for me to go with him, I encouraged him to go alone or with other men, and later, as our children grew up, to take them along.

In the process of pleasing one another, we have become richer. Our horizons have expanded. I have learned that there is skill, patience, perseverance and reward in fishing. I no longer consider it to be a waste of time. Fishing has become important to me because it's part of what makes Dennis who he is. We have great vacation memories of fishing at night while our children were asleep.

To give of your time requires the greatest sacrifice. Take time for a quiet walk or a scenic drive. Above all else, simply take time for each other. If blood is the gift of life, then time is the gift of love.

Discuss:
What arrangements can you make to spend more time together during the next week? Each of you share one thing that you like to do that would give you some time together.

Pray:
That you will build your marriage around Jesus Christ and that you will develop some common interests that both of you can enjoy.

MAKING ADJUSTMENTS IN MARRIAGE

Good understanding produces favor, but the way of the treacherous is hard.

PROVERBS 13:15

*M*any couples are surprised by the adjustments they need to make to each other once they are married. Usually the intense feelings of romance and love last for 6 to 18 months after the wedding. And then there is a period where you begin to realize that this relationship will not be as easy to build as you once thought. You begin experiencing problems because of differing backgrounds, varying expectations, job pressures, personality differences, etc.

To continue building oneness, you need to pinpoint problems and make adjustments in how you relate to each other. Even little problems are important. If you don't talk about where to leave dirty socks or whether the toilet seat should be left up or down, isolation will begin to work its way into your marriage.

I remember some of the adjustments Barbara and I made. Take yard work. Barbara believes grass and flowers are meant to be tamed and made to grow beautifully in front of white picket fences. My dad, however, discipled me in the fine art of avoiding yard work. He would let the yard die a slow death each summer from the heat so he wouldn't have to mow it in July and August.

For many men the issue is learning how to lead as a husband. If a wife can show empathy and compassion to her husband, especially when he is a young man, it helps him as he learns to lead her. Many times a woman tends to come into marriage unfairly comparing her new husband with her father. One young man told me, "My wife had to give me grace and flexibility so I could learn how to lead her."

You'll never get beyond adjustments until you subject your values to the overall good of the relationship. Which means that at points you're going to give in and flex. A marriage between two people who each demand to have their own way is tantamount to the Civil War—it's a divided union.

Like me, you're going to have to decide how you take off your undershirts and where you toss them! The Union is at stake!

································

Discuss:
Where have you had to make adjustments in your marriage,
individually and as a couple?

Pray:
That your hearts may not become hardened to one another and that you'll
never lose your desire to please one another.

LOVE CAN FIND A WAY

Love is patient, love is kind...does not take into account a wrong suffered.

1 CORINTHIANS 13:4,5

Do you have a family member who resists love, or even the Lord? Nina Cameron, who assisted me one year with my sixth-grade Sunday School class, told the class a story I'd like to share with you.

She and her daughter met a woman in a nursing home who was known as hard to get along with. Most of the time she spent complaining about the nurses, food, roommates, just about anything she could think of.

"She didn't like anything about us," Nina said, "right down to my name. For some reason she decided to call me Luke." Trying to find some way to reach her, Nina finally asked, "Isn't there anything you like?"

The lady looked up briefly and mumbled, "I like butterscotch candy and I like to draw." And sure enough the old lady had quite a talent, although her eyesight was so poor she could rarely finish a drawing.

Nina asked her if she would like for her to bring the Bible and read to her. But she replied, "Luke, I don't like that religious stuff, and I don't want to hear anything about it again."

Eventually the woman contracted cancer, and Nina could see she was dying. She hadn't spoken with her son in years, so Nina called him. Nina breathed a prayer for the Holy Spirit to penetrate through all past pain, and he finally broke down. "Lady," he said, "I don't know who you are, but I love my mother."

He didn't have the money to come to see her, so Nina purchased a plane ticket. Over the next few days, she had the pleasure of seeing a mother reconcile with her son. And the next time Nina came to the nursing home, the woman had a peaceful look on her face. She looked up and said, "Luke, I love you. I want you to bring that Bible when you come back, and read it to me."

....

Discuss:

Do you know someone who resists love? Are there relationships in your life that need to experience healing? What steps have you taken to bring this about?

Pray:

That the love of God that penetrates people's hearts will also characterize your own ability to love the unlovable with perseverance.

AS THE YEARS GO BY

We love, because He first loved us.

1 JOHN 4:19

*J*have never hesitated to tell Barbara I love her. But I remember one time when I was especially surprised by her reply.

We had been married a number of years, and perhaps on that day she wanted actions to back up my words. Because she said, "Well, I know you love me. But you're supposed to. You're my husband."

At the time, I was puzzled. But she went on to explain that many things test commitment in marriage—and perhaps nothing tests it more than the passage of years. As we mature and go through various seasons of our lives, it's easy to begin wondering if your husband is really just going through the motions by declaring love for you.

Barbara concluded by saying, "When you first marry, you declare your commitment and trust to a person you hardly know."

Isn't that amazing? You *think* you know all about this new life partner, but in reality you probably just see the tip of the iceberg.

As years go by, you see each other in a variety of situations. You see the achievements and the failures. You raise a family, you experience ups and downs in your career, and you struggle through problems with relatives. You develop godly disciplines and, perhaps at the same time, some bad habits. You encounter health problems; you gain weight; your hair turns gray.

And through all that, as your mate grows to know you more than any other person on earth (and vice versa), it's easy to begin thinking, *I know you say you're committed to me, but are you glad you are committed to me? Would you do this again? You say you love me, but do you really?*

Many marriages fail because both partners lose their commitment and trust over the years. No matter what struggles you work through, no matter how many heated discussions you have until 2:00 A.M., each of you should know without a shadow of a doubt that you have no escape clause in your marriage vows.

And in the end, your commitment needs to be based on one thing—your faith in the God who brought you together. That bedrock should be like a granite foundation—rock solid and immovable.

....

Discuss:
What has tested your marriage commitment over the years?

Pray:
That God would deepen your relationship with Him and, therefore, deepen your commitment to each other.

NO PRUNING, NO FRUIT

And we know that God causes all things to work together for good to those who love God,
to those who are called according to His purpose.

ROMANS 8:28

*D*o you really believe God works for good in all things?

Being able to make that statement begins with acknowledging that God knows what He is doing. He is not only all-powerful, or sovereign, but also all-knowing. Even when pain and tragedy strike, we can trust God to know what is best for our good.

The problem is we don't know His plan. We would like to know the reason for our trials, but God doesn't always reveal it to us. We wonder how He could possibly cause this or that problem to work for good.

But through Scripture and the natural order, God gives us a hint *that* it can happen, even when we can't see *how*. Jesus said:

I AM the true vine, and My Father is the vinedresser. Every branch in Me
that does not bear fruit, He takes away; and every branch that bears fruit,
He prunes it, that it may bear more fruit (John 15:1,2).

During the last several years, our own family has endured several such prunings. Barbara has weathered major heart surgery, the removal of a benign lump in her breast, five debilitating sinus infections, sinus surgery and Lyme's disease. And I have previously told of our son Samuel's bout with muscular dystrophy.

I don't know about you, but sometimes I grow a little weary from so many snips from pruning shears in my life.

But I really love the fruit bearing. While I wish it could happen without the pruning, life just doesn't work that way. Our family has experienced growth from the pruning. It has enriched my ministry to other families who hurt.

Scientists don't fully understand the pruning/fruit-bearing connection in the plant world. Why should I insist on understanding it in human lives? It's more important to bear fruit than to understand the pruning process.

....

Discuss:
How has God pruned you in the past in order to make you bear more fruit?

Pray:
For the faith to believe that God can enable you to become "more than conquerors" over any hardship or tragedy in your life.

PRIMING THE POSITIVE PUMP

Grace and peace to you from God our Father and the Lord Jesus Christ.
I thank my God every time I remember you.
PHILIPPIANS 1:2,3 (NIV)

I wonder how many of us thank God every time we remember our parents? Almost everyone has negative memories of their childhoods. But there seems to be an epidemic of parent blaming these days, and I want to suggest a way to balance this with positive memories of your home.

In case it's hard to get these positive thoughts flowing, here are some pump primers. (You might want to answer several of these on a date with your spouse.)

- Where did your parents take you on vacation, and what did you do?
- What did you enjoy doing with your dad most? Your mom?
- What smells today remind you of Dad and Mom?
- What was your favorite room in your house?
- What was your favorite family tradition?
- What were the family jokes?
- What special phrases or nicknames did your family invent?
- What was your favorite Christmas? Your favorite birthday?
- What problems did your parents help you through as a teenager?
- What did other people think about your parents?
- What values from your childhood home are you trying to pass along to your children?

As you think about these questions, thank God for the positive memories and the power they have to give your own home strength and stability. You may want to write some of your thoughts down and, if possible, send them in a letter—or perhaps a more formal tribute—to your parents. It's a practical and tangible way to let them know you wish them "grace and peace."

Discuss:
Spend some time answering the above questions.

Pray:
That you will be able to extract the strongest positive memories from your childhood home and implant them into your own family life.

A Woman's Emotions

{Part One}
by Barbara Rainey

Do not let the sun go down while you are still angry.

EPHESIANS 4:26 (NIV)

We know we are created in the image of God, but many don't realize our *emotions* are a part of God's image imprinted within us. Women need to grow in their understanding of their emotions. And this isn't easy, because many women aren't prepared to handle the different emotions they feel at different stages of their lives.

As a woman experiences various emotions, she needs to feel loved and accepted so she can face these times positively. This is not only critical for her emotional health, but also for impacting her children with positive emotional identities so they will grow up to be mature adults. These emotions are a part of the image of God, and we should grow and mature when we experience them.

When we got married, Dennis and I were completely caught off guard by my emotions as we moved into a marriage relationship. I remember the first time I was angry with Dennis. I had never felt angry with him the entire time we dated, during our engagement or in the early days of our marriage. I honestly didn't know what to do about my anger.

I remember thinking, *What do I do? Where do I go?* Dennis was pursuing me to solve our conflict, and I was so confused that I went into the bathroom, shut the door and thought, *I can't get out of here. I'm stuck.* My emotions were telling me something was very wrong in this relationship.

I held the future of my marriage and my family in my hands. I decided my relationship, which was a covenant I'd made to God, was too important not to work it out. So after stewing for awhile, I got up out of that bathroom and Dennis and I, after some real communication, resolved the problem.

Dennis and I have found that God designed marriage as a covenant relationship where a man and woman can work through their emotions and glorify God in the process.

....

Discuss:
How are you in controlling your emotions when it comes to dealing with your mate or your children?

Pray:
Ask the Holy Spirit to fill you, guide you and direct you in how you are to handle your emotions in your marriage and family relationships.

A WOMAN'S EMOTIONS

{Part Two}

You husbands likewise, live with your wives in an understanding way.

1 PETER 3:7

There is this maddening part of being a man. When Barbara comes to me with a problem, my mind immediately shifts into a "fix it" mode. I wanted to solve the problem, you know, get to the bottom line! But often, the most important thing our wives need is to know we hear them and we care.

The other day Barbara came to me discouraged because our lives had been incredibly busy, and she hadn't been at home as much as she wanted. She was so busy going to ministry, church, school activities and driving kids to different functions that she hadn't been able to clean the house.

And guess how I handled it? First I took it personally. I said, "Well, I help around the house a lot." But she wasn't accusing me of not helping—she was just sharing a burden she felt.

Then, typically, I came up with a solution. That night, I declared, the entire family would participate in a "Clean Up the House" campaign. And once again I missed the real issue—how she felt. It took a few moments for me to understand that what she needed was for me to just listen and understand her.

So I dug myself out of the hole I'd fallen into and told Barbara I was sorry I had missed her clues, that I didn't hear what she needed. I began to move toward her with the understanding and compassion she needed in the first place.

Want some advice? When your wife approaches you with a problem, repeat back to her what you think she said and ask her to confirm it. For example, I could have said to Barbara, "It sounds to me like you're discouraged because you feel like you've been busy. And the kids and I have allowed the house to get to where it looks like a small volcano has gone off. Is that right?"

Believe it or not, men, often that's all a wife needs—an understanding husband. Resist the urge to fix it immediately.

....

Discuss:
Ask your wife if this is what she generally needs in the above situation.

Pray:
That God will give you the ability to live with your wife in an "understanding way." Ask Him to help you communicate this to your wife.

A WOMAN'S EMOTIONS

{Part Three}

Husbands love your wives just as Christ also loved the church and gave Himself up for her.
EPHESIANS 5:25

I like what Erma Bombeck says, that "marriage is life's last chance for adults to grow up." That's what many men need to do when dealing with the emotions their wives naturally face during different seasons of their lives. We need to understand those emotions and not belittle them.

The first thing I had to do to help Barbara grow emotionally was put aside my own agenda and selflessly reach out to her. You can't simultaneously be understanding and defending yourself. One gives way to the other.

Have I always known what to do when Barbara was working through her emotions? No. Did I take it personally? Absolutely. I remember taking all of Barbara's emotions like I was a failure. I had to choose to "give myself up for her," to help her with her emotions.

The second thing I needed to do was verbalize my commitment to her frequently. I was caught off guard by Barbara's insecurity regarding my love for her early in our marriage. Barbara's trust in me had to be built one brick at a time. You don't just walk down the aisle and all of a sudden have a trustworthy relationship. You have to constantly reaffirm that love and trust.

The third thing I had to do was to give her space for her identity, to reflect who God is in her life that makes her a woman. My assignment, as a man, is to take her emotions and to value them, never saying, "You shouldn't feel that way." I need to let her express what she's feeling. And respond by saying, "I'm glad you shared with me because I'm interested in how you feel."

Finally, you can gently point your wife to find her confidence in God by leading her in prayer together. Read through Psalm 31:1, which declares "In Thee, O Lord, I have taken refuge; let me never be ashamed; in Thy righteousness deliver me." In Him, I have nothing to fear.

....

Discuss:

Are you encouraging or discouraging your wife in sharing her emotions? What can you do to start encouraging her and stop discouraging her?

Pray:

Ask the Lord to help you both grow in your understanding of one another's emotions and to learn to be sensitive, to lovingly listen and affirm your mate.

PERFECTLY CLEAN

Whoever speaks, let him speak, as it were, the utterances of God; whoever serves, let him do so as by the strength which God supplies; so that in all things God may be glorified through Jesus Christ, to whom belongs the glory and dominion forever and ever. Amen.

1 PETER 4:11

*S*ometimes Barbara and I laugh at the image people have of our family. They hear us speak or read our books, and they think we do everything perfectly. They know in their minds that this cannot be true, yet they still form some type of fuzzy, golden mental picture of life being "perfect" in the Rainey household. They think that our kids always obey us, that our marriage is in a state of perpetual romance, and that we keep an immaculate, well-ordered house in which everything is always in its place.

So let me tell you about the census I took of our floors one day. I took these notes a few years ago, but it could have been last week because little has changed.

There were enough children's books on the floor to load a good-sized library truck. Enough dolls to populate Toy City. And Legos! Ten zillion pieces specially designed to disappear forever down heating vents.

In the dining room, where we had just finished dinner, there was enough spilled food to feed a small African nation. On the floor lay an empty Coke can, two ribbons from some frazzled doll's hair and one coat (our six-year-old threw it there, I guess, hoping it would grow and multiply in the fertile debris of the floor).

We have one child who is a pack rat and another whose profession is a miner who digs into everything the other is attempting to pack away. The result is their rooms can be described in one word: debris.

Some husbands may read these words and think I'm criticizing Barbara because the house sometimes looks like a mess. Far from it. One thing Barbara and I realized long ago is that we can't do it all—we can't always maintain a clean household and emphasize relationships at the same time.

We chuckle at a sign we once saw: "A Clean House Is a Sign of a Life Misspent!"

....

Discuss:
How much emphasis do you put on orderliness in your household? How are you tempted to sacrifice relationships for a clean house?

Pray:
Ask God to enable you to glorify Him by keeping the proper tension in your home between orderliness and relationships.

"I BELIEVE IN YOU!"

Love...believes all things.

1 CORINTHIANS 13:4,7

*W*hat's the one thing every teenager needs as he or she navigates adolescence? What is needed by every young mother as she assumes a responsibility she's never had before—being a mom? By every athlete to achieve his or her ultimate performance? By every husband to become the man God made him to be?

To be believed in.

All of us need someone to express *positive expectancy* about our lives.

Two boyhood friends, Johnny and Marty, loved baseball and each other so much that they made a pact to play together always—regardless of what happened. As time went on, Johnny became a baseball star, and his coach called him aside and told him about the upcoming tryouts for the minor leagues. Johnny said, "That's great. Marty and I will sign up right away."

But the coach responded, "Don't worry about Marty. He's just an ugly duckling—too skinny, too slow, can't field and can't hit."

But Johnny's response was, "I know he can make it if he has a chance. He's got determination. He can learn to field and hit."

Sure enough, training camp resulted in a contract for Johnny—but Marty was cut. Johnny, however, wouldn't sign without Marty, so the club gave in and awarded both a contract.

Motivated by his friend's actions, Marty slowly began to improve. During their third year in the minor leagues Johnny washed out and quit. Marty became the rising star. Eventually he was called up to the majors for the St. Louis Cardinals as a shortstop. He played in four World Series and seven All-Star games, and in 1944 was named Most Valuable Player in the National League.

Years earlier Marty's mom had asked Johnny, "Why are you so determined to keep this pact?"

Johnny replied, "Belief is a kind of love. I believe in Marty. We're friends. Believing in someone is the best kind of love."

....

Discuss:

What communicates affirmative belief to you? In what one area would it most encourage you if someone believed in you more? List an area in which you can show positive belief in your mate and in your children.

Pray:

That as a parent you will be able to inspire every member of your household by expressing positive expectations.

SPINNING PLATES, BROKEN PEOPLE

Unless the Lord builds the house, they labor in vain who build it.

PSALM 127:1

Do you remember the man who spun the plates on the "Ed Sullivan Show" years ago? I've never forgotten him.

He would start at one end of a long table, place a stick perpendicular to the table, then spin a plate on the stick. Working on down the table, he would place other plates and set them to spinning on their own sticks. As the first plate began to wobble, the man would rush back and expertly spin it again as the audience breathed a sigh of relief.

On he would go...seven, eight, nine plates. By this time, plates two, three and four were now beginning to wobble. But just before you knew everything would come crashing down, he would quickly scoop up all of the plates in his professional hands and bow to the applause of the audience.

Similarly, the roles we assume in life as husband, wife, father, mother, businessman, civic leader, church leader, Sunday School teacher...all represent different plates in our lives. We begin spinning them early in our married lives, with plate number one being our marriages. Through the years we add other plates—career, children, church responsibilities—and our efforts to focus become more difficult.

The real problems come when we begin to make wrong choices. We mistakenly choose to meet more material "needs" by applying our efforts primarily to our work. This isn't about keeping our families from starving, but more about status, significance and the accumulation of "more."

The result is that our focus is lost. We add even more plates. Important plates begin to wobble—even fall and shatter. Like my friend Robert Lewis says, "Kids don't bounce—they break."

How are your essential plates spinning? Any wobbling? Are you giving your energy to the right "ones" according to God's value system?

....

Discuss:
What are the different plates that you spin? How do they affect your family time? How would your family benefit if you dropped some?

Pray:
Ask God to show you any plates that are getting too much of your energy, being neglected or need a spin.

THE RISK OF RESPONSIBILITY

And we urge you, brethren, admonish the unruly, encourage the fainthearted, help the weak, be patient with all men.

1 THESSALONIANS 5:14

In his best-seller, *The Third Wave*, Alvin Toffler writes that much teenage rebellion today occurs because teenagers no longer feel needed by the family unit nor economically productive during the prolonged adolescent years. Children need to be given jobs to do in the home, partly because of their need to be needed.

This can be difficult for perfectionistic parents. But, for example, if you want to train your children to clean the kitchen, you've got to lower your expectations of what a clean kitchen looks like—at least initially. If you want to teach your child to help with the laundry, you've got to expect clumsy folding jobs. And if you dare to help your child learn how to cook, be ready to put up with spills, splatters and splashes.

None of our children is a "neat freak." Ashley, our oldest, is a pack rat. She wants a souvenir from every exciting moment of her life. Benjamin is the champion of expediency. He wants to put off his cleaning chores because "If I vacuum now, it'll be dirty again by tonight." (Unfortunately, he's right.) Deborah is our resident artist. She starts picking up the playroom, but before long she's decorating the room—or herself.

Yet we want our children to come to maturity. If we expect them to learn dependability, we have to depend on them. If we want our children to learn responsibility, we have to risk this gap between our expectations and their performances.

....

Discuss:
How does your family divide household chores? Do any of your children complain that their part is unfair? What jobs do you sometimes think you had rather do yourself than risk children doing them inadequately?

Pray:
For the courage to risk allowing your children to be children, as well as for their continued growth toward maturity and increasing dependability.

THE IMPORTANCE OF EXPRESSING LOVE

Love...does not seek its own.

1 CORINTHIANS 13:4,5

I'll never forget at the end of a FamilyLife Marriage Conference in Washington, D.C., when a couple came up who had been married 31 years. I knew of this couple because of a friend who had encouraged them to attend. He had told me how much of a drought had surrounded their marriage in terms of true intimacy and sharing with one another.

As this man came up, I was curious to hear what he had gained from the weekend. So I asked, "What's the most important thing you've received from this conference?" I'll always remember his answer.

He said, "Dennis, I realized that I need to tell my wife I love her." He added, "I told her I loved her 31 years ago, and I haven't told her since."

I looked over his shoulder at his wife. She was seated on the edge of the platform and tears were streaming down her face. Tears of joy that she had heard the words, but undoubtedly tears of sadness, too, for those years of pain from a man who was thinking of himself more than his mate.

Far too many men have trouble expressing their most intimate feelings—being open and verbal is hard work. But because we are called to meet our wives' needs, we really don't have any option.

Many times all I need is a reminder that Barbara needs to know that I love her. How about thinking of a creative way to reaffirm your commitment by expressing your love—either verbally or in writing?

One year I gave Barbara a coupon book filled with 31 ways that said how I love her. And they were things she could cash in on. Each was a tangible statement telling her I cared for her and loved her. She still has that coupon book. In fact, it was really an ingenious idea because she doesn't want to tear the coupons out and cash them in!

....

Discuss:
What tangible way will you say "I love you" to your mate today?

Pray:
Ask God to show you five ways you can communicate love to your spouse so that he or she feels loved.

REAPING WHAT YOU SOW

A gray head is a crown of glory; it is found in the way of righteousness.
PROVERBS 16:31

Do you want your children to regard you as wise when you are older? Do you want them to listen to you when you're as old as your parents are now?

Your children are watching you, and will follow your model. If you aren't honoring your own parents, then you run the risk of having your children do the same to you.

In the same way, if you casually dishonor your parents, your kids may dishonor you.

The story is told of a wealthy widower who left his property to his only son and daughter-in-law on one condition—he would be allowed to live in the country with them for the rest of his life:

> After a few years, when the inheritance had been spent, the daughter-in-law got tired of having the elderly gentleman around and told her husband he would have to leave. The son agreed and broke the news to his father.
>
> A short time later he and the feeble old man walked down the dusty road to a state-supported home for senior citizens. Being very unsteady on his feet, the father finally asked if he could rest for a few moments on a sawed-off stump to regain his strength for the last mile of the journey.
>
> As he sat there, he suddenly put his head in his hands and began to sob. The son, pricked in his conscience, tried to make excuses. Finally, the father controlled himself enough to say, "I'm not crying so much because I'm going to this lonely home for the poor and unfortunate. I'm weeping because of my own sins. Forty years ago I walked down this road with my father and brought him to the very same place. I am now seeing the results of the evil deeds I have sown!"

The saying goes, "The apple doesn't fall far from the tree." The example you set for your children in honoring your parents will actually help determine your own future.

....

Discuss:
How would your children complete this statement: My parents honor my grandparents by _____.

Pray:
That God would give you creative ways to involve your parents in your family.

WHATEVER HAPPENED TO THE FAMILY TREE?

"For I hate divorce," says the Lord, the God of Israel.

MALACHI 2:16

*A*n ax has fallen on the family tree. For nearly 30 years the ax has chopped at the tree's trunk, leaving only the stump and a few roots showing. The branches and fruit lay withered, spoiled on the ground.

What is this destructive ax? Divorce. Far too many people use this deadly tool to sever human problems from their lives.

Many who read this have been the unwanted recipients of heart-splitting divorce decrees. I do not relish piercing your old wounds. Nor do I want to sound pious just because our marriage has worked when others haven't. Nor do I intend to place a heavy yoke of guilt on your neck.

There is no question that divorce brings deep humiliation and hurt. It can be seen on the faces of those who endure it. Newspapers print wedding pictures of smiling brides, but the divorce section contains only names. You can feel one man's anguish in a local classified advertisement:

> I want it known to the public that I made mistakes all through my marriage to Linda. I said things that weren't right. I battered and abused her both physically and verbally. I was unfair in the property settlement. I acted like a fool. I am lower than the ground I walk on. I have to live the rest of my life now without the person I truly love and who used to love me with no chance to undo the wrong I've committed. I lost the best thing that ever happened to me—my best friend. People, don't take your marriages for granted like I did. Divorce is not just a seven-letter word. I ask to be forgiven by all those concerned.

Over one million tragedies like this take place every year. We can no longer be spectators in this battle for the family. There is more at stake than just two isolated people when a couple chooses divorce. Our nation's future is literally on the line. How can our nation survive when a field full of stumps replaces its rich heritage of thriving family trees? The erosion of our most precious resource—our children—will have a devastating effect on our nation's future.

Discuss:
Why do you think God hates divorce? (See 1 John 4:17.)

Pray:
That God will cement your family together and that you can realize His purpose for your home. Join me in asking God to heal our nation from divorce and the devastation it is bringing to millions of children's lives.

AFFAIR PROOFING
YOUR MARRIAGE

*Let marriage be held in honor among all, and let the marriage bed be undefiled;
for fornicators and adulterers God will judge.*

HEBREWS 13:4

*T*wo tragic days stand out in my memory. One was the day of President Kennedy's assassination. Hearing the news of his death was like being struck with an emotional sledgehammer that pounded spikes of grief, fear and confusion into this 14-year-old boy's heart. I'll never forget that day.

Twenty-five years later another day brought news that pierced my heart. No visible bullet was fired. There was no assassin at whom I could vent my anger. There was only the word that a hero of mine had fallen. His spiritual influence had been tarnished by adultery. I was nauseated when the news came, for I had drunk deeply from the well of his writings, his preaching and his life.

I've pondered over the growing number of Christians who have lost their marriages, families and ministries due to sexual infidelity. How many more will fall before we make an effort to "affair proof" our marriages?

Here are a few suggestions:

1. *Make your marriage bed your priority.* Don't let your daily work lead you to bedtime exhaustion, the great zapper of passion.

2. *Talk together about what pleases one another, and what doesn't.*

3. *Add the element of surprise to your marriage bed.* Caution: It might be good to "ask permission" before cooking up something that may be offensive to your spouse (see Rom. 15:1-7).

4. *Be patient with your mate.* This area of married love and commitment demands that we continually grow and learn about one another (see 1 Thess. 5:14,15).

5. *Beware of bitterness.* Keep short accounts and ask forgiveness when you fail or if you have become bitter (see Eph. 4:26,27).

Vonette Bright, wife of the president and founder of Campus Crusade for Christ, says this about sex: "It's just as important to be filled with the Holy Spirit in bed as it is in witnessing to another about Jesus Christ."

You probably have not been asked this question in a devotional recently: Why not turn out the lights early tonight?

Discuss:
Pick a time and set the scene for sharing with your mate exactly how you feel about physical intimacy in your marriage.

Pray:
Ask God to bless your physical relationship with your spouse.

MEN AND WORK

by Barbara Rainey

Let them rule over the fish of the sea and over the birds of the sky and over the cattle and over all the earth.

GENESIS 1:26

The past three decades of new ideologies about women's rights have left Christian women swimming in a wake of confusion. Consequently, many Christian wives have lost sight of their husbands' needs and have focused intently on their own. Even though more than 50 percent of you reading this book work outside the home, I'd like to explain briefly the importance of work in your husbands' lives.

Man was given the responsibility by God to toil, sweat and gain from the labor of his hands. A man's work is part of the ruling and managing purpose that God spoke of in Genesis 1:26 (above). Your husband needs work in order to realize the satisfaction inherent in executing God's stated purpose for his life. His work gives him a sense of significance and importance in the world as he sees his efforts affecting life for good in the present and the future.

But this drive for significance sometimes pushes a man to extremes. In his effort to gain a sense of well-being and significance, he often becomes enslaved to his job. Attempting to gain importance through wealth or position, he makes his work his god. For hundreds of years men have confused their net worth with their self-worth.

On the other hand, a man who is out of work lacks true self-respect. In this age of workaholism, losing a job is a traumatic blow to a man's esteem. It strikes at the core of his dignity. A man who doesn't work can't enjoy the satisfaction of a solid day's productivity.

Your husband needs you to help him keep these two extremes in balance. He needs you to praise him for his work, but not to push him to gain too much too quickly. When a man loses or quits his job, his self-esteem can sink. During these times, he needs you to stand beside him and encourage his efforts at finding employment. Men need to work.

Discuss:
How can you help your husband keep a balanced perspective about work?
What are your husband's needs right now when it comes to work?

Pray:
That you can help your husband live by his priorities, balancing his need for work with his need to focus on his family.

THE VALUE OF A
LISTENING EAR

But let everyone be quick to hear, slow to speak and slow to anger.

JAMES 1:19

aul Tournier, the Swiss psychiatrist, advised husbands and wives to be preoccupied with listening in their marriages. Unfortunately, unlike our text, we are usually slow to listen, quick to speak and even quicker to become angry. Most of us don't need hearing aids; we just need aid in hearing.

The first step to really hear each other is to *focus on the person speaking.* Sometimes my kids are waiting for me when I come home after a hard day's work, and they try in vain to get my attention. Finally, Barbara will say, "Children, it would be better to talk to your dad in a few minutes, but not right now. He isn't home yet."

"Yes, he is," they'll exclaim. "He's right here."

"Yes, *we* know he's right here, but he doesn't know it yet. Be a little patient with him."

And sure enough, she's right. After I have a few minutes to relax, I can usually give focused attention.

Active listening helps to focus. To practice active listening, try sending back messages of empathy that let your spouse know you are trying to put yourself in his or her shoes. Don't try to evaluate or offer a lot of advice. Just reflect what you hear being communicated, showing that you're interested in what your spouse is feeling.

Once you establish communication with your mate through focused attention and active listening, you can seek clarification by *asking questions.* Questions are like crowbars that dislodge thoughts and emotions from another person's heart. But you have to use those crowbars deftly and gently.

Asking the right questions is particularly valuable if you're married to a person who is reserved and has a hard time opening up. And when you're disagreeing at even the mildest level, use questions to focus on clarifying valid points rather than defending yourself against what you feel are incorrect accusations.

Focus on finding the truth rather than gaining indictments. Ask questions to gain understanding, not to make judgments.

....

Discuss:

Pick a topic that's begging for discussion, and spend 5 or 10 minutes talking about it while practicing the listening skills outlined above. Then evaluate how you think the discussion might have been improved.

Pray:

That you and your family can maintain a healthy balance between speaking openly and focused listening.

TOO HEAVY TO CARRY

And be kind to one another, tender-hearted, forgiving each other,
just as God in Christ also has forgiven you.

EPHESISANS 4:32

*S*omeone once asked, "Did you know the longer you carry a grudge the heavier it gets?" Refusing to forgive those who wrong us can be a wearying weight on the soul.

On the other hand, when we choose to forgive, we shed a huge burden we simply don't need to carry through life. It can make us absolutely "lighthearted" to put down the burden of a grudge.

What can you do to keep from carrying grudges and an unforgiving spirit through life?

For one thing, clarify your "inner occupation." Do you want to make judging others your spiritual career path? Jesus said, "Do not judge lest you be judged" (Matt. 7:1), indicating that pursuing the occupation of judge will boomerang on you.

Judging, just like taking vengeance, belongs to God, not to people: "Vengeance is mine; I will repay, saith the Lord" (Rom. 12:19, *KJV*). Even after David had committed adultery with Bathsheba and had her husband killed, he said to God, "Against Thee, Thee only, I have sinned" (Ps. 51:4).

Since God makes the rules, He is the only true Judge. People who wrong others really wrong God more than others. Relieve yourself of the responsibility that actually belongs only to God.

Giving up the judgeship means you also relieve yourself of the responsibility of punishment. Forgiving someone doesn't necessarily mean we forget immediately or even completely, but it does mean we no longer hold a private grudge that desires to punish, or to see them punished.

We can also avoid carrying grudges by resolving conflicts as they occur. "Do not let the sun go down on your anger" (Eph. 4:26). Which would you rather face—the short-term, emotional pain of asking another to forgive you for your anger, or carrying the cancerous feelings of bitterness for a lifetime? It's your choice.

....

Discuss:

How would people who know you best describe you? Do you tend to carry grudges? Evaluate if you are carrying any grudges at home, at work or at church.

Pray:

That the forgiving grace of God you've experienced in your own life will characterize also your attitude toward those who wrong you.

GRIPES, GRUMBLES AND GROUCHES

{Part One}

Do all things without grumbling or disputing.

PHILIPPIANS 2:14

Do you ever get annoyed with the complaining around your house? I do. Over the years the rooms of the Rainey household have resounded with gripes about:

- Who gets to sit where at the dinner table;
- Who gets to sit in the front seat on the way to school or church;
- Tubs littered with dolls, boats, bottles and melting bars of soap;
- Who has to clean up the dishes;
- Whether the food for (pick your meal) looks, feels or tastes appetizing.

It became so bad one year that we all memorized Philippians 2:14: "Do all things without grumbling or disputing." That helped. Like sulfuric acid, complaining can eat away at whatever it splashes on. Complaining corrodes joy and dissolves good attitudes. Spiritually, it's dangerous and deadly.

If you have a problem with grumbling, you're not alone. The Old Testament book of Numbers could easily be renamed "The Grumbler Chronicles." The children of Israel grumbled against Moses, Aaron and God. They didn't like manna, so they complained: "Manna for breakfast, lunch and dinner! Is this all we get, this manna?" So God gave them quail instead. They had quail boiled and broiled until they were sick of it. Can you empathize with them? A little complaining is understandable, isn't it?

But the complaining by the children of Israel wasn't a trivial matter, and God didn't view it lightly. He had delivered them from Egypt and was providing for them daily. They were just plain ungrateful.

I wonder what we would find if we performed open-heart surgery on a complainer. Exploratory surgery would reveal that grumbling can be a form of heart disease, rebellion against authority. It also shows a loss of perspective, a failure to remember Who is in control. It's an attitude that questions, "Does God really know what's best for me?"

....

Discuss:

What are you trying to do when you grumble and complain? What are your children trying to do when they gripe?

Pray:

If appropriate, have each family member specifically confess the sin of grumbling, and in prayer give thanks to God for at least three things.

GRIPES, GRUMBLES AND GROUCHES

{Part Two}

*These are grumblers, finding fault, following after their own lusts; they speak arrogantly,
flattering people for the sake of gaining an advantage.*

JUDE 16

Griping and complaining are vocal amplifiers of one's heart attitude. What's the solution for us gripers?

First, *realize that complaining is dangerous*. While many Christian leaders have fallen into immorality, I wonder how many more Christians have been declared "unusable" by God because of their complaining? For many of us, that snare is the temptation to gripe, grumble and complain against God (see 1 Cor. 9:24—10:13).

Second, *remember God knows what He is doing*. Joseph puts me under the pile. He was tossed into a pit by his brothers, sold into slavery, unjustly accused of fooling around with Potiphar's wife, thrown into prison and forgotten by a friend he had helped. Yet Scripture doesn't record a single complaint from his lips.

What was the secret of his complaint-free life? The answer is in Genesis 45:5-8, where we find Joseph, now the governor of Egypt, addressing his starving brothers. Three times in four verses Joseph says, "God sent me here." His perspective came as a result of an uncommon faith in an omnipotent God. Joseph grasped the truth that God is in control and knows what He is doing.

Third, *put away past complaints that may become bitterness*. If you have a complaint against a brother, go to him in private and clear the slate.

Fourth, *"in everything give thanks"* (1 Thess. 5:18). Jesus gave the disciples a "test" of their faith by putting them in a little boat, on a big sea, in an even bigger raging storm. The disciples complained that they were perishing, instead of acknowledging God's sovereignty and trusting Him.

God wants you to see Him in the midst of your circumstances, to trust Him even when you do not see the outcome clearly presented in front of you. That is true faith; knowing His Word is truer than anything you can think, see or feel.

....

Discuss:

Are you satisfied with what God has provided for you today (your mate, your children, your circumstances)? Does God know what He is doing in your life?

Pray:

Give thanks, right now, for where God has you as individuals and as a family. Be specific as you thank Him for your circumstances.

NEEDED: SPIRITUAL WORKOUTS

{Part One}

On the other hand, discipline yourself for the purpose of godliness; for bodily discipline is only of little profit, but godliness is profitable for all things.

1 TIMOTHY 4:7,8

The fat-farm advertisements finally reached me one Christmas season. After seeing all the television ads showing how to shed those holiday pounds, and after looking in a mirror one morning, guilt got me. So with my bag of sweats and jogging shoes in tow, I dutifully followed those pied pipers of unwanted pounds to the local health club to shed some cellulite (that sounds better than "fat," which just lacks dignity).

There I stood in the doorway of this workout room, looking at all these slim and trim, toned and tuned hard bodies. My greatest fear was that they would all look up at me simultaneously and fall to the floor, laughing hysterically.

After enduring the humiliation of walking to the dressing room and getting into my sweatsuit (I wish I had arrived already dressed), I couldn't help but notice the *mirrors*. They were everywhere. I felt like I was in some sort of narcissistic cathedral. People throughout the room were staring at their bodies. For my part, I carefully ignored the mirrors—I already knew what I looked like.

Then the Scripture above from 1 Timothy hit me. As I began to perspire while working on my "perishing" muscles, I thought about my spiritual muscles and the truth of that Scripture.

Here I was, moving from machine to machine, an out-of-shape, plump glob of midlife molecules, surrounded by the "saints of Muscledonia." But I couldn't help pondering Paul's admonition to train ourselves in godliness, and asking whether as a people we are equally concerned about our spiritual conditioning.

That isn't just "of little profit." It's of eternal importance.

....

Discuss:

Do you have regular times of jogging or other physical workout? Do you have regular times of spiritual discipline—prayer, Bible study, ministry to others? How can you give more importance to these disciplines?

Pray:

As a couple, set aside a 24-hour period to pray and fast together. Consider using this time to pray together about a problem you're facing as a couple or in your family.

NEEDED: SPIRITUAL WORKOUTS

{Part Two}

Therefore I run in such a way, as not without aim...I buffet my body and make it my slave.
1 CORINTHIANS 9:26,27

I'd like to invent a spiritual workout system with machines similar to those in health spas that can zero in on specific muscles you want to develop. My spiritual spa would be a place with individual stations where muscles of the faith would be purposely developed, a place where we could be *intentional* about cultivating spiritual stamina.

My first station would help bridle the tongue when it is tempted to say harsh words, and toughen it up when it needs to speak out boldly for the Lord. It would build control of our gossip muscle, and teach us to clean up our language.

I'd have a station that addresses the faith muscles of the eyes. Above this machine would be pictures of biblical heroes whose lives were ruined when they lost control of their eye muscles—Samson and David, who were deceived when they allowed their eyes to gaze too long upon the opposite sex.

I would also have a machine that works on the spiritual muscles of the neck. It would increase flexibility in those who have become "stiff-necked"—especially those who are too proud to admit mistakes, too stubborn to ask for forgiveness or too arrogant to admit they need to depend upon God.

I'd have an exercise that would require a person to be on his knees, with neck bent downward in prayer. Prayer loosens muscles that are tied in knots by worry, pressure or long hours of hard work.

Sweating yet? Any increase in your heart-for-God rate? Out of breath? Sore? Like any good workout, it wouldn't be good to overdo it the first time out...or can it be overdone?

....

Discuss:
What areas of spirituality in your own life need strengthening?
What pressures keep you from devoting more time each day to
spiritual disciplines or "workouts"?

Pray:
Ask God for the courage to exercise your faith daily and grow
stronger in Jesus Christ.

DEAD WOOD

Blessed is a man who perseveres under trial; for once he has been approved,
he will receive the crown of life.

JAMES 1:12

Lloyd Shadrach is a good friend, a leader in our ministry to families and sensitive to lessons God has for him to learn. He once told me about walking down a road after a thunderstorm and stepping over dead limbs that had blown off a row of mature trees. "It was as though God was giving me a personal object lesson of what 'storms' can do in our lives," he said.

"In the middle of the storm when the wind is gusting, the lightning is popping and the storm clouds are getting darker, it's difficult to believe that our troubles are purposeful. But God may allow a storm in our lives to clear out the deadwood so that new growth can occur. And isn't it interesting how fresh the air feels after a storm is over?"

As Lloyd shared his parable with me, I couldn't help but think back and reflect on the deadwood, several cords of it, that has been blown from my life over the years. One of the most important things Barbara and I have learned from these storms is that God is interested in our growth. He wants us to trust Him in the midst of the storms and to grow together as a couple and not fall apart.

Lord Kelvin was lecturing his students on an experiment that failed to come off as planned. He said, "Gentlemen, when you are face-to-face with a difficulty, you are up against a discovery." How much better for family members to allow life's storms to enable them to depend on each other and discover new strength.

....

Discuss:

How have you reacted to the storms in your life? Have they drawn you closer as a couple, or have you allowed them to drive you apart?

Pray:

That your family will be able to persevere in all trials. Pray about a specific problem, and for your family to discover strength in Jesus Christ through it.

DISCOVERIES
FROM DIFFICULTIES

And the rain descended, and the floods came, and the winds blew, and burst against that house; and yet it did not fall, for it had been founded upon the rock.

MATTHEW 7:25

I see two major ways in which families fail to respond properly to adversity. First, and most typically, *they fail to anticipate the trials and problems that will come.* When Jesus spoke of building our lives on a sure foundation, He seemed to *assume* that the rains will come and the winds will blow.

To the well-known saying that only death and taxes are certain, we can add that troubles are certain, too. As I read recently, "The man whose problems are all behind him is probably a school bus driver."

Second, when troubles do hit, *many couples simply don't know how to respond.* They have no foundation in Christ, no plan for dealing with the pain—so they turn against one another.

I was just ending a FamilyLife Conference in Dallas when a trim, well-muscled gentleman came up to greet me. He was a Green Beret. I had touched a nerve when I talked about having a plan to face problems because he said, "Dennis, in the Green Berets we train over and over, and then over and over again. We repeat some exercises until we are sick of them, but our instructors know what they are doing. They want us so prepared and finely trained that when trials and difficulties come on the battlefield, we will be able to fall back upon that which has become second nature to us. We literally learn to respond by reflex action."

Families—especially parents—should be so well grounded in God's plan that their reactions to crises and difficulties will be an automatic reflex, not a panic. If you wait until a crisis hits and then turn to the Scriptures, you won't be as prepared—and you'll be more vulnerable to the enemy.

....

Discuss:
If a life-altering crisis hit your family tomorrow, do you feel you'd be ready?

Pray:
That you will be able to call on your long-standing faith in Christ, and the life of trust you have built on Him, when crises strike.

GRANT HER HONOR

You husbands likewise, live with your wives in an understanding way...and grant her honor as a fellow heir of the grace of life, so that your prayers may not be hindered.

1 PETER 3:7

We all realize that well-known pastors and Christian leaders are as human as anyone else. Yet something within us always remains surprised when we hear them tell stories that demonstrate just how fallible they are!

That was the case recently when I interviewed pastor and author Chuck Swindoll for "FamilyLife Today." Chuck was talking about a key event in his relationship with his wife, Cynthia: The day he realized how selfish he was.

They had been married for 10 years and were sitting in their kitchen in Boston. Cynthia began crying and said, "Honey, I don't want you to tell people that we are partners in ministry any more. Because we're not."

Chuck was stunned. "What do you mean?" he asked.

"You don't really want me as a partner," she replied. "You just kind of need me at certain times...I'm not the Holy Spirit in your life, and I'm not giving you an agenda. I can just tell you I am one unhappy woman. I feel distant from the ministry. When I hear you preach, I'm watching one man. When I live with you, I'm with another."

As Chuck looks back on that day, he sees it as a turning point in his marriage. "I really was living a single life as a married man," he recalls. "When I saw it, I was ashamed. That's the only word I know to use.

"I began to see little things I had done for 10 years, such as not bothering to introduce Cynthia to others. When she served the meat, I'd take the biggest piece. I'd tell jokes about her. If we had a busy weekend, I'd take care of my agenda. She'd take up the slack.

"I realized I am a selfish man."

Since then Chuck and Cynthia began forging a true partnership in their ministry; in fact, he says his best ideas come from her. Their marriage stands as a testimony to the grace of God because Chuck is living out the truth of 1 Peter 3:7: granting honor to his wife as a "fellow heir of the grace of life."

....

Discuss:

How do you treat your wife? Is she a true partner in your life? Would she say you are unselfish?

Pray:

Ask God to help you be the servant-leader your wife needs you to be.

ARE YOU LISTENING?

Be gracious to me, O God, according to Thy lovingkindness; according to the greatness of Thy compassion blot out my transgressions. Wash me thoroughly from my iniquity, and cleanse me from my sin.

PSALM 51:1, 2

King David had sent a man to his death so he could take that man's wife for his own. But when the prophet Nathan rebuked him for this terrible sin, David had a choice: He could turn from God (perhaps even finding a way to blame others for what he had done), or he could admit his offense and repent.

As we all know, David recognized that God was speaking to him through Nathan, and he decided to repent. The beautiful words of Psalm 51 speak of his broken heart.

I wonder how many people hear God speaking through another person yet make the wrong choice? What if Chuck Swindoll, in that defining moment in his kitchen during his tenth year of marriage, had refused to listen to his wife's cry of pain? What if he had continued in his selfish ways?

One of two things probably would have occurred. First, he might have continued to progress and achieve fame and notoriety—only to have his life and ministry fall apart at a later date. Second, God might have clamped shut the working of the Holy Spirit in and through him, and today he'd be ministering somewhere with very little impact.

Sooner or later, a man who continues on the path of selfishness and rebellion will end up empty and defeated. If he is fortunate, he will listen to the voice of the Holy Spirit, often speaking through his mate, early on and save himself years of misery.

When Cynthia Swindoll told Chuck that she didn't feel part of his ministry, "It was like a light clicked on in the room." He told himself, "Swindoll wake up. This is the best thing you could be hearing. This could be the making of your marriage."

You can thrive in a marriage when you commit to create a partnership under the guidance of the Holy Spirit—and when you're willing to listen to Him speaking.

....

Discuss:
What has God taught you through your mate? In what situations has the Holy Spirit used your mate to help you become more Christlike?

Pray:
Take your wife's hand and genuinely thank God for her.

THE FEAR OF FAILURE

Love covers a multitude of sins.

1 PETER 4:8

In an address to a nation divided by the Civil War, Abraham Lincoln underscored the need to persevere in spite of failure. He said, "I am not concerned that you have failed. I am concerned that you arise." The following excerpt, which appeared in an advertisement in the *Wall Street Journal*, also emphasizes this point:

> You've failed many times although you may not remember. You fell the first time you tried to walk, didn't you? You almost drowned the first time you tried to swim. Did you hit the ball the first time you swung the bat? Heavy hitters, the ones who hit the most home runs, also struck out a lot. R. H. Macy failed seven times before his store in New York caught on. English novelist John Cracey got 753 rejection slips before he published 564 books. Babe Ruth struck out 1330 times, but he also hit 714 home runs. Don't worry about failure. Worry about the chances you miss when you don't even try.

In a performance-oriented culture such as ours, failure belts us like a punch in the stomach. Repeated failure often results in a knockout blow, and many people give up altogether. As Comedian W. C. Fields once quipped, "If at first you don't succeed, then quit. There's no use in being a fool about it."

The problem is that a life with little failure is a life of little risk. This type of life may appear to offer safety and security, but it actually leads to guilt, boredom, further apathy and even lower feelings of self-esteem. God designed and commissioned us to be productive—many times that demands faith and risk.

Does your mate have the freedom to fail? Is he or she assured of your love—no matter what mistakes he or she makes? By slowly forging in your mate the freedom to fail, you'll help him or her become more open to change, more willing to take risks and more confident in decision making.

....

Discuss:

Evaluate your own fear of failure. Are you a risk taker? Are decisions difficult? How would you evaluate your mate? What can you do to encourage him or her to move past fears?

Pray:

That God will give you enough faith to move beyond your fears and trust Him even in the midst of failure.

THE FREEDOM TO FAIL

*Be strong and courageous! Do not tremble or be dismayed, for the Lord your
God is with you wherever you go.*

JOSHUA 1:9

*A*t our house we have experienced plenty of failures, both great and
small. For years, a meal without a spill was nothing short of miraculous.
The milk may have gone shooting across the supper table or formed a
lazy river that cascaded over the edge, splattering onto the floor. We've seen
some classic spills: two simultaneously, four at one sitting, and one glass of
chilled apple juice that spilled perfectly into Dennis's shoe (while he was wearing it). Our favorite phrase for the children became, "It's okay. Everybody
makes mistakes."

One evening, I spilled my drink during dinner. A little hand patted my arm,
and Rebecca (then a five-year-old) reassuringly said, "It's okay, Dad.
Everybody makes mistakes."

When you give your mate the freedom to fail, you begin to remove the pressure to perform for acceptance. You free your mate to set aside his or her fear,
to trust God. Failure then becomes a tutor, not a judge. In the presence of freedom, we learn from failures instead of being condemned by them.

For years, we talked about moving to the country. The thought of the children having room to roam sounded inviting, but moving a large family is a
chore. More importantly, it was a risk. What if we didn't like driving back and
forth to town? What if we didn't like being isolated from friends? So we put off
the decision.

Then one day Barbara said, "So what if we decide we don't like it? We can
sell and move back to town!" Her statement clicked; it gave me the freedom to
make a decision—even a wrong one! We decided to try it, and we love it. It's
important to note that the freedom to risk making a decision came only after we
had given each other the freedom to fail.

Discuss:

Share what you would consider to be your greatest failure. How has that
impacted your decision-making process today? Discuss a decision you are facing and how the fear of failure is influencing that decision.

Pray:

That God will increase your faith to match the challenges you face, and that
He will teach you how failures have helped you mature in Christ.

AN ANATOMY OF FAILURE

*But Moses said to God, "Who am I, that I should go to Pharaoh, and that
I should bring the sons of Israel out of Egypt?"*

EXODUS 3:11

Have you ever thought about how Moses felt after he murdered an Egyptian and, fearing for his life, fled into the wilderness? For 40 years Moses lived in the desert, undoubtedly hounded by a host of condemning voices.

So when God appeared to him in the burning bush, Moses was struggling with an identity problem—the result of failure and rejection. Just look at how Moses responds to God in Exodus 3 and 4. God told Moses that He was going to send him to free the Israelites, but Moses replied, "Who am I?" God simply said, "I will be with you." Above all, Moses needed God's reassuring presence. Without Him, Moses could never stand before Pharaoh; left alone, he would certainly fail.

But Moses continued to question God, even after repeated assurances and demonstrations that God would work miracles to free His people. Finally he said, in essence, "I can't do what you've asked. Please choose someone else" (see Exod. 4:14). Rather than focusing on God, Moses focused on himself. He was like the little boy in the school play whose one line was, "It is I, be not afraid." But on the night of the play, the boy came out on stage and exclaimed, "It's me, and I'm scared!"

Only when Moses saw that there was no way out did he submit to God's call. He was so convinced of his own worthlessness that it took time for God to convince him otherwise.

Likewise, your mate also may have a difficult time believing God and you. Note that in this chapter of Moses' life, part of God's solution to Moses' crisis of confidence was a companion—Aaron. The two brothers became a team. Undoubtedly, Aaron frequently reminded Moses of the truth: He was God's man for the assignment, and God would be faithful to His promises. Just as Moses needed Aaron, your mate needs you.

Discuss:
Have you ever questioned God's ability to use you in the same way Moses questioned God? Talk about how you need to "stand with one another" and have the courage to do what is right.

Pray:
That you will be sensitive to find ways to encourage your mate to be assured of God's power and faithfulness.

A DATE WITH ASHLEY

*But we proved to be gentle among you, as a nursing mother
tenderly cares for her own children.*

1 THESSALONIANS 2:7

Unlike some stereotypes of macho men, it's important for dads to be as gentle as Paul was with the Thessalonians, his children in the faith.

I'll never forget the rewards I've received for trying to be tender and loving with my children. My first "date" with our daughter Ashley was when she was three. I called her from the office and said, "Hi, this is Dad. I would really like to have a special date with you tonight, Princess."

She giggled and I heard her tiny voice saying, "Daddy wants to take me out on a date!" Barbara already knew my plan, so Ashley was all dressed up by the time I pulled up in front of the house. I knocked on the door and when Barbara opened it I said, "Hello, Ma'am, is your daughter home?"

Ashley came out, and we held hands as we walked down the steps of the front porch out to the car. I walked around to her door and opened it and she got in.

As we drove down the road, she slipped her little arm around my neck. We went to a restaurant and got chocolate pie, chocolate milk and chocolate ice cream. Then we went to a movie. Ashley had a great time crawling all over the seats and occasionally watching *Bambi*. We ate popcorn. We spilled popcorn. We got soft drinks, and we spilled soft drinks. We did it all, and we did it right.

After the movie we drove home, the faint green light from the Rambler dashboard shining in our faces. I turned and asked, "Ashley, what was your favorite thing about tonight?"

Her little hand came over to pat me on the arm and she said, "Just being with you, Dad, just being with you." It's too bad we didn't have a little more popcorn. I became a pool of melted butter right there.

....

Discuss:
As a man, do you find it hard to be tender and intimate with your children?
Describe some times when your attempts to be tender with them really
"worked."

Pray:
As a father, pray that your need to be a strong leader will not conflict with
being gentle and tender with every member of your family.

THE AUTHORITY OF CHRIST

{Part One}

And He put all things in subjection under His feet, and gave Him as head over all things to the church.

EPHESIANS 1:22

*J*once found a fascinating quote by A.W. Tozer that went like this:

The present position of Christ in the gospel churches may be likened to that of a king in a limited monarchy. He is lauded, supported. But his real authority is small. Nominally that king is head over all, but in every crisis someone else makes the decisions. On formal occasions he appears in his royal attire to deliver tame, colorless speeches put into his mouth by some real rulers of the country. The whole thing may be no more than good-natured make-believe....

Then he draws the parallel to Christ and the Church. Read carefully:

Among the gospel churches, Christ is now in fact little more than a beloved symbol. All hail the power of Jesus' name is the church's national anthem and the cross is her official flag. But in the week by week services of the church and the day by day conduct of the members, someone else, not Christ, makes the decisions.

I believe Jesus Christ has been robbed of His authority in the home today. To have authority means to have the right to rule, to take the rightful responsibility, power and ownership of ruling, and to give it to another person who has authority to rule you 100 percent. We haven't rejected Christ; we've just cordially reduced Him and robbed Him of the ownership He deserves within our individual lives.

No, we haven't rejected Christ outright. Instead we have simply modified Him. When God's Word gets too hard, we begin to modify and reinterpret those things as they best fit us.

But He wants much more. In the next two devotions I'll continue discussing Christ's authority.

....

Discuss:
How do you think your life and marriage would be different if you gave Christ authority in your life?

Pray:
Honestly go to Jesus Christ in prayer right now. Pray about His authority in your life and home.

THE AUTHORITY OF CHRIST

{Part Two}

And Jesus said to them, "Follow Me, and I will make you become fishers of men."

MARK 1:17

In Mark we find Christ meeting Simon and Andrew as they were casting fishing nets into the sea. He challenges them to follow Him, and they spend a couple of weeks making their decisions—figuring if it would cost them financially, determining if it would damage their reputations.

Wrong. Simon and Andrew *immediately* left the nets and followed Him. They instantly recognized Christ's authority in their lives.

I believe that one of the reasons why we don't see more people leaving their nets and following Christ is because we in the Church have not presented the authentic, real, living Lord Jesus in all of His splendor, majesty and glory. When we see Him for who He is, no possession, no worldly honor or success can compare with the King of kings.

Not all who see Jesus continue following Him. John 6 records that, after Christ made some difficult and challenging statements, "Many of His disciples withdrew, and were not walking with Him anymore" (v. 66). Then Jesus says to the remaining 12, "You do not want to go away also, do you?" (v. 67).

And Peter makes a profound statement: "Lord, to whom shall we go? You have words of eternal life" (v. 68). He had come to the conclusion that there was no other to follow.

The longer I am in the Christian life, the more I see there is nothing else that matters other than Jesus Christ and His Word. In recent days I've asked Him to infuse my life with the conviction that He alone is worth following.

....

Discuss:

Do you know of someone who has withdrawn and no longer follows Jesus? How has that decision affected his or her life? And those around him or her? Have you left your nets to follow Jesus?

Pray:

That you will grow in your hunger and thirst for knowing the One who has the words of eternal life.

THE AUTHORITY OF CHRIST

{Part Three}

The Spirit of the Lord is upon Me, because He anointed Me to preach the gospel to the poor.
He has sent Me to proclaim release to the captives, and recovery of sight to the blind, to set
free those who are downtrodden, to proclaim the favorable year of the Lord.

LUKE 4:18,19

When we give Christ authority in our lives, we also discover that He has the authority to make our lives so much better than they would be without Him. Just look at the verse from Luke, for example.

Are you brokenhearted over a child, a relationship with a family member or something happening between you and another person? These heartbreaks and sorrows are a part of life. I have faced too many of them and found myself without any word for them. But Jesus said to give Him our hurts and sorrows.

Will you take your broken heart with you to the grave and end up hopeless? Or will you take your broken heart to Christ and let the Great Physician heal you on His authority? Jesus said He can heal the brokenhearted.

In addition, Jesus has authority over sin. Nothing gives us freedom and heals our sorrows more than forgiveness of sins. Look at Mark 2:5, where Jesus says to the paralytic, "My son, your sins are forgiven." And then, to squash grumbling among the scribes who said only God has such authority, He proved who He was by healing the same man!

Finally, He has authority over death. We see this in the raising of Lazarus in John 11 and then, of course, through His own resurrection.

Knowing you have eternal life because of Christ gives new meaning and hope to your years on earth. As Jesus said, "O death, where is your victory?" (1 Cor. 15:55).

....

Discuss:

What is causing heartbreak and sorrow in your life right now? Have you spent time talking with God about it?

Pray:

That God will give you hope and joy in the midst of troubled times.

THE PRIVILEGE OF BEING CALLED MOMMY AND DADDY

How blessed is everyone who fears the Lord, who walks in His ways. When you shall eat of the fruit of your hands, you will be happy and it will be well with you.

PSALM 128:1,2

Teddy Roosevelt was unashamedly "bullish" on children:

It is exceedingly interesting and attractive to be a successful business man or railroad man or farmer, or a successful lawyer or doctor or writer, or even a president; but, for unflagging interest and enjoyment, a household of children...certainly makes all other forms of success and achievement lose their importance by comparison.

When you make your children your top priority, you will receive many blessings from the fruit of your labor. Barbara and I saw this during a FamilyLife staff banquet in the summer of 1992. We were brought up front for a question-and-answer session, only to be told that the real purpose of the evening was to honor us for our upcoming twentieth wedding anniversary.

Several good friends who had been hiding at the back of the room were brought up to say a few words. But the real highlight came when all six of our children showed up to read tributes to us.

Laura, seven at the time, went first, standing on a chair: "Thank you, Mom, for all the dresses you made me. For hugs and kisses. For being a great mom. Dad, thanks for being my ice-cream buddy, for the stories you tell at bedtime, and for wrestling with me."

One down, five to go. I looked at Barbara—we both were choking back tears.

Deborah was next. In her quiet, soft voice she thanked her mom for helping her with homework and cutting her hair short. She thanked me for taking her on fishing dates. Then she said: "And I want to thank both of you for adopting me when I was a baby."

That did it! Barbara and I were basket cases for the rest of the evening.

That evening will go down as one of the greatest memories we've ever experienced. Barbara and I count it as our greatest privilege and accomplishment to be called "Mommy" and "Daddy."

Discuss:

Prayerfully reflect on the high and holy calling of being a mom and dad. Share why it is such a privilege.

Pray:

That you will never forget that children are a blessing.

GOOD AND STRESSFUL

*Apart from such external things, there is the daily pressure upon
me of concern for all the churches.*

2 CORINTHIANS 11:28

We refer on more than one occasion in this book to the stressful nature of modern life. Or is it just a modern issue? It's obvious from this Scripture that Paul faced pressure, too. How was he able to bear it so well?

I've found that pressures come from two directions: What others expect of us and what we expect of ourselves. It is so easy to let yourself be driven by the agendas of other people. Externally, their voices form a deafening chorus, incessantly telling us what we ought to do. But Paul had an inner settledness that enabled him to affirm, "I can do all things through Him who strengthens me" (Phil. 4:13).

Dr. Hans Selye, a leading pioneer in the study and treatment of stress, described something called "eustress." This pressure is actually good for you. Then there is "distress"—pressures that overload your system and prey on your weakness and vulnerability.

There is no such thing as a pressure-free life. Perhaps in heaven we'll feel no pressure—only total peace and contentment. But here and now we have responsibilities, and responsibilities create pressure and stress.

We can, however, allow that pressure to point us to Jesus Christ and draw upon His strength. J. Hudson Taylor, the veteran missionary to China, said this: "It matters not how great the pressure is, only where the pressure lies. As long as the pressure does not come between me and my Savior, but presses me to Him, then the greater the pressure, the greater my dependence upon Him."

Spiritually, what is pressure doing to you? If you and God are not as close as you used to be, then don't be deceived about who moved!

....

Discuss:
Evaluate with your spouse how you handle pressure.
Discuss how you'd like to handle it.

Pray:
That the Lord as "God Almighty" will strengthen your ability to eliminate unnecessary stress and empower you to turn remaining stress into positive forces that press you against Him.

LEAVE SOME FOR HOME

An overseer...must be one who manages his own household well,
keeping his children under control with all dignity.

1 TIMOTHY 3:2,4

The apostle Paul required that an overseer in the early church be a man who was a good manager of his household. My dad was that kind of man. I remember him as a man of quiet authority, who had time for us.

What kind of memories will your children have of you as a father? Will they remember a father who spent time with them, played with them, laughed with them? Or will they think of you as someone who was preoccupied with work, unfinished projects or a hobby?

And now let's really get personal: What would happen if you switched the energy you give to your job with the energy you give to your home and family? What would happen to work? What would happen to your home?

I realize this may be an unfair question because by necessity many men work long hours away from home. But too many fathers give almost all their energy to their jobs and leave none for their families.

I have a friend who has a 3x5-inch card on his desk that reads: *Leave some for home*.

He realized that, without this reminder shouting at him daily, he'd go home with no energy most of the time. His job was that draining.

We need to balance things out if the next generation is to get the kind of leadership it needs. Today we need fathers who are determined to save the energy to succeed at home, regardless of the cost.

As leaders and managers of our homes, we can't lead from afar. We've got to be there. And be all there!

....

Discuss:

As a father, what areas of home life do you find the most challenging to manage? How about time management? Do you make time to be present and available for each member of your family?

Pray:

Ask God to give you, as a father, the spirit of a servant and the strength of an overseer who manages his household well.

RAISING KIDS WITH A SENSE OF MISSION

Go therefore and make disciples of all the nations, baptizing them in the name of the Father and the Son and the Holy Spirit, teaching them to observe all that I commanded you; and lo, I am with you always, even to the end of the age.

MATTHEW 28:19,20

The other day my pastor, Bill Parkinson, exhorted me with a thought-provoking question: "What if you reach the end of your life and the Great Commission was accomplished, and you had no part in it?"

In Matthew 28:19,20 (above), Christ commands us to "make disciples of all nations." Do you realize that your most important disciples are your own children? I especially wish more mothers had this vision. The enemy is trying to get moms to devalue their positions so they won't raise the next generation to go to the world and have an impact for Christ.

If you want to raise your children with a sense of mission, begin when they are young by talking to them of God's plan. Then help them reach out to their peers.

Is one of your children a strong-willed child? She is the kind who will storm a country for Christ. He will be the one who never quits until he impacts his sphere of influence.

Pray for their mates with them. Why do I put mate in with mission? Because the mate will determine a great deal of what is accomplished in that mission.

Next, teach them they are pilgrims in this world, not wanderers. A wanderer is aimless. A pilgrim must travel lightly if he is to get where he needs to go. I believe a sense of mission will emerge if you shape their convictions.

Finally, give them the freedom to allow God to work in their lives. Affirm their decisions and direction as they get older. Do you know what the biggest deterrent is to missions today? It's parents who want their kids to make money and be successful!

When Jesus Christ washed the disciples' feet and went to the cross, He gave them the torch of the Great Commission that has been passed down throughout all of history. Our responsibility is to lead our own children to Christ and to give them a sense of mission to reach the next generation.

....

Discuss:
How are you helping build the Great Commission right where you are?

Pray:
Ask God to send laborers into the harvest. The harvest is plentiful but the workers are few.

NEITHER DEATH, NOR LIFE...

by Barbara Rainey

There is therefore now no condemnation for those who are in Christ Jesus.

ROMANS 8:1

Early in our marriage, I experienced some difficulty with depression and low self-esteem. There were days when I would feel like such a failure and would think to myself, *I'm just not a good wife. I'm not a good mother. I'm not worthy.*

Then Dennis would come to me and say, "It's okay. I love you, and God loves you."

But that seemed too good to be true. I'd look back at him skeptically and say, "You can't love me. I'm just not good enough for you to love me." I'd argue with him, allowing my feelings to overrule the truth.

One day Dennis finally said, "Barbara, I want you to know that I love you and God loves you, and it's the truth. Now, you have a choice as to whether or not you will believe it."

The light came on in my mind, and I thought, *You know, he's right. I'm calling him a liar by saying that he doesn't love me because he does, and God loves me as well.* That was a real turning point for me in acknowledging the truth, regardless of how I felt about myself.

Poet Edwin Markham has said, "Choices are the hinges of destiny." For me, the choices I began to make that day have influenced my whole life and our relationship. As I slowly began to choose to believe in Dennis's love for me, my poor self-esteem began to lose its grip on my life.

Some people never stop condemning themselves, forgetting that Christ took the punishment we all deserve. You have such a privilege of being able to remind your mate of this truth that "neither death, nor life...nor height, nor depth, nor any other created thing, shall be able to separate us from the love of God" (Rom. 8:38,39).

....

Discuss:

In what areas do you condemn yourself? In what ways do you find your spouse's love for you difficult to fathom?

Pray:

Read Romans 8 together and pray that God will give you the eyes of faith to believe that He will never stop loving you.

A RECIPE FOR MEMORIES

So these days were to be remembered and celebrated throughout
every generation, every family.

ESTHER 9:28

Esther's kinsman Mordecai had just succeeded in sparing the Jews from the genocide that had been planned by the Medo-Persians. No wonder every family was called on to remember it!

Families today need memories, too. They have the power to spare us from the feeling of rootlessness that pervades much of our culture.

Our home nestles in a spectacular setting, complete with woods, hills and a lake. But it's the memories we make together—not the setting—that make our house a home.

I recall one of the kids' business ventures—"Kids Kookies Inkorporated." Move over, Mrs. Fields. These freshly baked diet-busters—95 cents a dozen—were made from the finest ingredients. The children even washed their hands before making them! They set up their portable business safely near a busy fork in the road about a mile from our home.

We also created great memories with a blue-ribbon fishing vacation one summer. For eight days we parked our car beside a cabin and didn't move it—a record. The trout in the lake smashed our lures. And Ashley, our oldest daughter, won first prize in a local fishing contest with her four-pound, four-ounce German brown trout. We made that old trout a permanent memory—on her wall!

Another special memory is the day the last disposable diaper was thrown away in the Rainey household—after 12 years of being a faithful consumer of Pampers. No, we didn't have the diaper bronzed.

It has been said that God gave us memories so we could smell roses in December. I'll never forget the smell of a newborn or the feel of a baby's soft cheeks and tummy. I'll miss it a little, but maybe someday a grandbaby will prompt my recall of those coos and grins forever stored in my memory.

If you haven't done something wild and crazy recently to make a memory with your kids, do it tonight.

Oh yes—don't forget to take a picture of it!

Discuss:

Name a significant memory or two from your own family activities. What can you do today to plant more seeds for special family memories?

Pray:

That what the members of your family remember most about family life will serve to root and establish them firmly in happy homes of their own.

BE STILL!

by Barbara Rainey

Be still, and know that I am God.
PSALM 46:10 (NIV)

*J*wonder if you share one of my concerns for my children: the pressure to be busy. Do you find it as difficult to "be still" as our family does?

There is a strong current in our country to involve our children in a myriad of activities at younger and younger ages. Parents naturally want to produce the brightest, best-dressed and most-talented children. They fear that, if they don't provide Tommy with music lessons at age three, gymnastics at four, art and nature studies two afternoons a week in the summer, and T-ball by the time he is five, that he will grow up handicapped.

And what do the children feel? Do they really want all this activity? Or have their parents persuaded them to want it?

It is my opinion that children who grow up with an abundance of activity and busyness become adults who can't live without it—sort of "activity junkies." They don't know how to contemplate, to rest, to think, to "be still, and know that I am God" (Ps. 46:10).

And many parents are not much better. Why, really, are we hurrying so? We need to ask, "Why am I involved in Junior League, PTA or the midweek women's Bible study? Or working full-time?" I've had to ask just how essential it was for me to do the watercolor painting, sewing, quilting and handiwork I used to do. Gently over the years, He has guided me in setting aside (perhaps just temporarily) most of these activities in order to have time to be more focused as a mother.

It isn't always easy to give up such busyness, or to assert authority over your schedule. But I wouldn't trade the opportunity to instill a calm heart in my children for all the busyness in the world.

....

Discuss:

Do you feel that you and your family are too busy? What activities do you and your children participate in primarily because of social pressure? Have you taken a recent inventory of family activities in order to rank their importance?

Pray:

Pray that God will increase your ability to claim your time schedule for Him, and to experience His presence even in the midst of necessary busyness.

PARENTS UNDER THE INFLUENCE OF CHILDREN

In the fear of the Lord there is strong confidence, and His children will have refuge.

PROVERBS 14:26

erhaps you can identify with a bumper sticker on a school bus that read: "Approach with caution. Driver under the influence of children." That's the way parents feel at times. We feel the effects of being under the influence of our children.

I recently traveled to Seattle to observe two focus groups composed of young Christian parents raising kids under 10 years of age. The five feelings these parents expressed reveal tremendous insight into the impact that raising children has on parents:

Fear. Fathers and mothers talked of their fears of adolescence, of not being able to communicate with their children going through these turbulent years. They were fearful their kids would turn out to be just like them in ways they didn't like. They feared failing as parents.

Guilt. They felt guilty over their mistakes and failures. They wondered if they were ruining their kids. They regretted things they had said and had done to their kids.

Frustration. They were frustrated and even angry when their kids didn't obey them. They felt they had to explain everything too many times to their kids.

Self-doubt. Were they doing it all wrong? Were their expectations too high or too low? Should they just let the underwear lie on the floor? How long should they let a child throw a tantrum? And if they disciplined a child, how could they know they did what was right?

Discouragement. They felt like they failed too often. They saw their own weaknesses—and their parents' weaknesses—emerging in their children. They felt they lacked skills to raise their kids right.

These feelings, I believe, are like the worm that eats away at the apple, and they lead us to hopelessness and despair. It's no wonder that today's parents feel like they are "under the influence of children."

Yet God promises you in His Word that He is your confidence. He is the Master Encourager. As you seek Him, He will be faithful to cause His will to come to pass…in your life and in your children.

....

Discuss:
Which of the emotions listed above can you identify with?

Pray:
With your mate that God will give you the confidence, wisdom and strength to be an effective parent who doesn't give up.

CONSIDER THYSELF

You who boast in the Law through your breaking the Law, do you dishonor God? "For the name of God is blasphemed among the Gentiles because of you," just as it is written.

ROMANS 2:23,24

I still recall those sad days in 1987, when the storm of media attention focused on the downfall of a well-known television evangelist. As I saw the dirty laundry of another believer's life strung out on television and draped over the printed page, I couldn't help but wonder why God let such a man's ministry continue to flourish for so long.

Questions ricocheted around in my head. Who really lives the Christian life, beyond the glossy, air-brushed and choreographed public performances? Will unbelievers judge Christianity on the performance of these few? Should we be embarrassed and silent? Should we question God and His work? Is there too much hype and not enough substance surrounding Christians in media? Should we stop giving financially to such ministries? Should those of us in the ministry quit? Should we become skeptical and cynical about everyone in the ministry? Should we grieve for God and with God?

As important as such questions may be, there is another question more basic. Such events should probe each one of us to ask: Is there any area in my own life that is not under the authority of Christ?

In Romans 2, Paul was concerned that God's Old Testament people had shamed God's name before the very people whose religion they claimed was inferior. The personal integrity of the individual heart—not the performance of high-visibility believers—was the place Paul began with his questions.

Scandals are bad news. They sadden us. We wonder about the reaction of unbelievers and new Christians who have recently cut their spiritual molars and are now doubting what they have committed themselves to. But the place to begin dealing with the issue is "considering thyself, lest thou also be tempted" (Gal. 6:1, *KJV*).

Discuss:
How would you rate your character? Is there any area of your life not under the authority of Jesus Christ?

Pray:
For the integrity of your heart and the heart of your mate.

MARRIAGE CEMENT

I want them to be strengthened and joined together with love. I want them to be rich in the strong belief that comes from understanding.

COLOSSIANS 2:2 (NCV)

True partnerships are cemented—"joined together" in Paul's terms—as couples frequently and specifically verbalize their needs for each other. But at some point in time, between the walk down the wedding aisle and the fifth anniversary, a thief often makes off with our mutual admission of interdependence. Isn't it ironic that marriage, the ultimate declaration of one person's dependence on another, so often winds up being an accomplice to the thief?

Think back to those early days of romance and intrigue. You needed each other then, and you still do. You need her for a balanced and truthful view of yourself. You need him for a full-color view of life since he looks at life through a different set of lenses.

Often during marriage you begin looking at your differences as hindrances rather than benefits. You are a broader person because of these differences. Why try to change your mate when you *need* these differences?

You need her to believe in you when others don't and you can't. She is your mirror of positive acceptance, expectancy, praise and the belief that you are as significant as ever, though perhaps in different ways. You need him to multiply your laughter, share your tears and add his experience with God to yours.

You need each other to raise healthy and balanced children. Two people tempering one another's weaknesses complement each other's blind spots and help accentuate one another's strong points as they raise children together.

Beware of living independently of one another. Sometimes busy people build their lives around activities only to find, years later, that they are alone. Imprisoned by selfishness and a failure to take risks, they live independently of the person God has sovereignly given them to share life with. You really do need your mate.

Discuss:
Make a list of 5 to 10 specific ways you need your mate. Use your list to compose a letter to him or her, expressing your needs. Or take a long walk and talk over the list together.

Pray:
That God's Spirit will keep the two of you cemented together, expressing and fulfilling mutual needs.

A CONSPIRACY OF SILENCE

{Part One}

Hear, O sons, the instruction of a father, and give attention that you may gain understanding.
PROVERBS 4:1

A number of years ago a friend told me how his dad talked to him about sex. Evidently his mom wanted his father to have a "birds and bees" talk with him. So his dad came home from work one evening and said, "Tomorrow, Son, after school I want you to put on your Sunday clothes. We're going to town."

The next afternoon they drove two hours to the "big" city of West Helena, Arkansas. The father took his son into a bar and ordered dinner. Above them on a stage, a woman came out and proceeded to strip. The young man and his father sat there throughout the entire meal, not saying a word.

They drove home for two hours in darkness. When they arrived, the father walked in the front door, turned to the mother and declared, "There, I've done it. Now, I'm going to bed."

That was this young man's sex education.

How did you find out about sex? Was it through parents or peers? A book? School? A brother or sister giving you the scoop?

If there ever has been an era when parents need to have a game plan for educating kids in human sexuality, it is today. In a recent survey, 16- and 17-year-olds were asked, "Where have you learned about sex?"

- 22 percent: Parents
- 37 percent: Friends
- 15 percent: School
- 18 percent: Entertainment

I hope you caught that: Only 22 percent learned from their parents. The problem today with parents in the Christian community is there has been a conspiracy of silence on this subject.

We, of all people as Christians, ought to have a good, firm grip on the truth because our God created human sexuality in the first place. As my mentor and friend from Dallas Theological Seminary, Dr. Howard Hendricks, reminds us, "We should not be ashamed to discuss that which God was not ashamed to create."

....

Discuss:
How did you learn about sex?
What was good and bad about your sex education?

Pray:
For God's favor as you talk to your children about human sexuality.

A CONSPIRACY OF SILENCE

{Part Two}

For at the window of my house I looked out through my lattice, and I saw among the naive,
I discerned among the youths, a young man lacking sense.

PROVERBS 7:6,7

In a culture saturated with conflicting and damaging views about sexuality, we need to aggressively seize the opportunity to shape our children's views. May I suggest three barriers every parent must dismantle if children are to receive training necessary to traverse a landscape that is infested with traps, temptations and tests?

Barrier One: Our own ambivalent feelings about sex. Many parents never received solid sex education as children, so they don't know how to teach their own kids.

And many others have baggage to deal with—their past mistakes. Growing up in an era where sex was said to be "free love," they learned that it was neither free nor was it love. Many have told me they fear their children asking, "Were you a virgin when you married?"

Barrier Two: A shallow relationship with your child. Good relationships demand intimacy, risk and courage. Some parents instinctively sense that they have not built strong relationships with their children. When the time comes to broach this subject, they are uncomfortable because they know that the foundation isn't there.

But I believe God wants us to have these discussions with our children not merely to educate them about sex, but also to move our relationship to a deeper, more intimate level.

Barrier Three: Fear. I've heard parents make statements like, "Well, I could never talk to my kid about that." What I want to say to you as a parent is you don't have to be an expert to talk to your kids. Just walk in there empowered by God, representing His perspective of this sacred area of life. It's a great privilege. And it's your responsibility.

Parents are standing by while their children are being robbed of their innocence. It is time for us to seize our children back from a culture that has held them as hostages.

....

Discuss:
Which of the barriers to teaching your kids about sex apply to you?
How would you describe your current plan for sex education?
Do you feel it's adequate? Why, or why not?

Pray:
For one another that you will tackle the barriers that would keep you from training your children, and practice your Christianity where it really counts—
at home with your teens.

SOLVING OUR NATION'S PROBLEMS

I urge you therefore, brethren, by the mercies of God, to present your bodies a living and holy sacrifice, acceptable to God, which is your spiritual service of worship.

ROMANS 12:1

Early every week, you can pick up a newspaper or magazine, or watch a television show, focusing on the distressing social problems we face in our nation. CBS devotes an entire evening of prime-time television to a look at violence in America...*Newsweek* magazine runs a cover story on battered wives...*Time* reports that nearly half of Americans are worried "a lot" about our economy, and 89 percent think the crime problem is getting worse.

But let me ask you this: How often do you hear about workable solutions to these problems?

I think the apostle Paul hints at the most practical solution of all in Romans 12:1 when he urges us to "present your bodies a living and holy sacrifice, acceptable to God."

Large social problems will end when they are solved, not in the halls of government, but in the hallways of homes across America. In short, change will occur when Christians get serious about their relationship with God and live out their values and priorities in the family.

Change will come when dads get down on their knees and ask their wives and children to forgive them when they make an error. It will come when men take responsibility for their families and don't expect the Church to do it for them. It will come when men say, "I will lead my home."

Change will come when more women decide to make motherhood a greater priority than careers. It will come when more children are raised with godly character by parents who are involved in their lives.

We have been called to proclaim Christ, to obey Him as we make an imprint on our society. To give ourselves as a "living and holy sacrifice" to God means we will allow nothing to come between us and Him—that we will live in obedience to His will no matter what the cost.

And if enough families begin living holy lives, making right choices, loving one another—America will experience a family reformation.

....

Discuss:
As you look back at the last year, would you say that you have lived your life in complete, sacrificial obedience to God? If not, why?

Pray:
How would it affect your family if you began to get serious about living for Christ?

WANTED: A MASS MOVEMENT OF WOMEN "MENTORS"

Older women likewise are to be reverent in their behavior...that they may encourage the young women to love their husbands, to love their children.

TITUS 2:3,4

I remember when, early in our marriage, Barbara went through periods of doubt as to how she was doing as a new wife. I would encourage her, saying, "You're doing fine, you're doing great." But I felt powerless to really affirm her.

After we moved to Dallas, Barbara began attending a Bible study for young wives led by an older woman. This seasoned mother was on a mission—she loved coaching and encouraging these young moms. Under this woman's mentoring, Barbara's confidence soared as she saw that her struggles were not unique.

There's no doubt that the early years of marriage are really important. Roles are hammered out. Adjustments made. Expectations clarified. It's no wonder the divorce rate is the highest during the first five years of marriage.

I believe we could dramatically reduce divorce if more wives and mothers experienced what Barbara did—a mentor. A mentor is a women who has been there, who has lived it, who has loved her husband faithfully (not perfectly) and has biblical values to pass on.

As Barbara says, "A husband's encouragement means a lot, but sometimes it doesn't mean as much as another woman who has been there, who has done it, who comes alongside."

A number of years ago I watched with fascination as a dozen young wives and mothers answered the question: What would you like to see your church provide for you as a wife and mother? They were very clear in their responses—they didn't want a video, a tape, a conference, another book or a radio program. They wanted a real live mom to talk to and cry with—someone they could relate to and ask questions.

So I started challenging older wives and moms to become mentors. Their response? "We don't have all the answers. We've made too many mistakes." You know what? That's exactly the qualification you need to be a mentor.

....

Discuss:
In what areas do you need encouragement in your role as a wife and mother?

Pray:
Ask God to give you the faith to live your life as
a "living and holy sacrifice" to Him.

TIME OUT FOR YOUR MATE

*I must arise now and go about the city; in the streets and in the
squares I must seek him whom my soul loves.*

SONG OF SOLOMON 3:2

An important step to building a strong marriage is to consistently set aside time with your mate. Unfortunately, we allow ourselves to become so busy that we don't make it a priority to spend uninterrupted time with our mates.

Want some advice? Get alone. Find some time to get away together on a weekly basis.

Barbara and I have kept a Sunday night date for years. If someone invites us to do something else that night, we politely tell them no. We need this time to look at our schedules for the coming week or month, to talk about values, hassles, kids and how we can succeed in our marriage and family. It's also a time to enjoy each other's company.

Also, set aside daily time to get alone and talk. I'll never forget a couple of friends telling us, "Just wait until you have teenagers. You'll see." Boy have we seen! They come trooping into your bedroom at 11:00 or 11:30 at night and they want to *talk*! And they don't think anything about it.

You've got to shut the door and train your kids to leave it shut. Otherwise you will never have any private conversation for a husband and wife, let alone romance. This is download time—to talk, discuss and reconnect.

A third thing Barbara and I do a couple of times a year is get away for two nights—away from the children, away from TV, away from the hustle and bustle of life. This is a time to refresh and review our values.

One of the most important gifts you can give your kids is the gift of being committed to your spouse. And believe me, it is awfully hard to be committed to one another when you don't make the time to have a relationship.

....

Discuss:
Figure out, as accurately as possible, how much time you have spent with each other—just the two of you—during the last week. What changes could you make in your schedule to make more time for each other? Pull out your calendars and pencil in your first date night and a two-day overnight getaway.

Pray:
That you would begin making your relationship a higher priority.

WHEN THE HEART GROWS FAINT

*Hear my cry, O God; give heed to my prayer. From the end of the earth
I call to Thee, when my heart is faint.*

PSALM 61:1,2

Discouragement. Who hasn't felt its chilling grip on the heart? Discouragement neutralizes optimism, assassinates hope and vaporizes courage. For many, a frequent source of discouragement is when it seems that God doesn't answer a crucial prayer.

Close friends of ours once went through the heart-ripping experience of a divorce. Their five-year-old, freckle-faced daughter was jerked north, then south as the marriage unraveled. For nearly three years Barbara and I had prayed. We counseled. We called. We wrote letters. We got them to attend two FamilyLife Marriage Conferences. We pleaded, reasoned and wept. We gave it our best shot. We kept praying.

The day the divorce was finalized, a piece of our heart was crushed as the judge's gavel came smashing down. We were bewildered. Confused. Didn't God say He hated divorce? We were left with a living mosaic of deceit, betrayal and broken promises. We were tempted to lose heart.

In the midst of such times I like to remember the British missionary Elizabeth Aleward. Miss Aleward had two great sorrows as a young girl: Her hair was black and straight (when all of the popular girls had a head full of golden curls), and while all her friends kept growing, she ended up short.

Years later, God called her to the mission field in China. As she stood looking at the people to whom God had called her to minister, she said two very apparent observations occurred to her. "First, each and every one of them had long, straight black hair. And, secondly, each and every one of them had stopped growing at exactly the same moment that I did. And I bowed my head and prayed, 'Jehovah God, You know what You are doing!'"

You and I will never lose heart as long as we know that God is in control. He knows what He's doing, even though we don't comprehend many times what His purposes are. He wants us to keep the faith, not lose it.

....

Discuss:
Can you cite a heartfelt prayer of your own that apparently went unanswered? Have other events tempted you to lose heart?

Pray:
Thank God that He is in control and ask Him to help you when you go through periods of discouragement that rob you of your faith.

DEALING WITH DISCOURAGEMENT

*And let us not lose heart in doing good, for in due time
we shall reap if we do not grow weary.*

GALATIANS 6:9

A story is told about a public auction that the devil had. As the prospective buyers assembled, they noticed Satan was selling his tools of worry, fear, lust, greed and selfishness. But off to one side, standing alone, was one well-worn tool labeled "Not for sale."

Asked to explain, the devil replied, "I can spare my other tools, but this is the most useful implement that I have. With it I can work my way deep into hearts otherwise inaccessible. It is the tool of discouragement."

What tools do we need to overcome discouragement? First, *truthfulness.* I've found that God is not fooled by my lofty prayers for the missionaries in Africa, when deep inside I'm hurting. God is able to handle your emotions. Be honest with yourself and God about your disappointment.

Second, *pray about it.* Are you discouraged about a child who rarely reaches your expectations? Tell God. Disheartened about your mate and an unresolved conflict? God knows already, but pour it out.

Third, *find the source of your discouragement.* Sometimes it's a goal that was not attained…again. Or the problem may be a friend's cutting remark, or the feeling that you're carrying a particularly heavy burden alone, or the lack of approval by an important person in your life.

By isolating the source of my discouragement, I often find my hope was in the wrong person or in the wrong place. Or I find my response was normal—and, because I can't quit, I've just got to work through my feelings of wanting to toss in the towel.

Fourth, with a heart of faith *look beyond your circumstances* and your emotions to a God who will renew you day by day. Realize that God uses hardship to perfect our faith (see Rom. 5:1-10). God promises that we'll one day reap if we don't grow weary.

Discuss:
What is causing discouragement for you right now?
Which of the tools do you need to use to combat discouragement?

Pray:
Get on your knees and pray that neither of
you would grow weary and lose heart.

AIR-BRUSH CHRISTIANS

*Therefore, confess your sins to one another, and pray for one another,
so that you may be healed.*

JAMES 5:16

Oliver Cromwell, the British statesman and leader of the British Isles, war hero and leader, was posing one day for a portrait. He got up from his seat after the artist had done a great deal of work, and examined it. Then he turned to the young woman and rebuked her, "When you paint me, you paint me warts and all!"

The artist had done a beautiful job of painting Sir Oliver, but it was too good. And I think that little story typifies the kind of the air-brush society we live in. Today you can take an unflattering photograph of yourself and have all the "warts" removed. They will fix your lumpy nose, change the color of your eyes, improve your smile and remove any unsightly blemishes—all with either an air-brush or what we call today "computer enhancement"!

We are a culture of fake people: air brushing our lives, creating illusions, never willing to admit our faults to others. And this is often just as true of Christians. Once you know how to talk and relate to other Christians, it's often easy to give them the impression that you are much more mature in Christ than you really are.

The irony is that true maturity begins to occur when you are willing to confess your sins to others. We're often afraid to be so vulnerable, and yet people always seem to respond with warmth and understanding.

As James 5:16 says, healing occurs when you come to the point in your walk with God that you know you won't get rid of sin by concealing it; you need to become accountable within the Body of Christ. When we confess our sins to God and to others, then little by little we become like Jesus Christ.

Perhaps there is no better relationship than marriage for two people to begin to experience authenticity. There's no air brushing faults and removing blemishes here; it's life, up close and personal. Just like God intended it.

....

Discuss:
Are you concealing any sins that you need to confess,
first to God and then to others?

Pray:
That God will conform you to His image as you make yourself more accountable to others in the Body of Christ.

LEAVE IT TO HEAVEN

Never take your own revenge, beloved, but leave room for the wrath of God,
for it is written, "Vengeance is mine, I will repay," says the Lord.

ROMANS 12:19

This classified ad actually appeared in a San Francisco area newspaper: For sale: 1984 Mercedes, 240 SL. Loaded. First $50 takes it. 868-5737.

Not believing his eyes, a man called the number to see if the "$50" was a misprint. A woman assured him it wasn't. So the man rushed to her home and gave her $50 in cash. As she handed him the title to the luxurious automobile he asked the obvious question: "Why are you selling a Mercedes for $50?"

"Well," she explained, "my husband just phoned me from Las Vegas. He's there with his secretary, and he said he's leaving me. He went broke gambling, and he asked me to sell the Mercedes and send him half of what I get for it."

This woman got what she thought was "sweet revenge." Unfortunately, it's a pattern of behavior that often creeps into families that aren't breaking up, as well as those struck by the tragedy of divorce. We justify getting back at people when they take advantage of us. Accounts need to be "evened up."

Why does the Bible challenge such thinking and behavior? Why are we to leave vengeance to God? Because He, not us, is the source of right and wrong. When your mate hurts you, it ultimately wounds God more than you. Furthermore, God is the One who can dispense forgiving grace to you when you hurt your mate.

To take on the right of getting back at others is basically a sign of pride. The apostle Paul's counsel, "Bless those who persecute you" (Rom. 12:14) is followed closely by the command, "Do not be proud" (v. 16, *NIV*). We dare not clutch for ourselves that which belongs to God.

Punishment belongs to Him. Marriages work better when we leave such lofty matters to heaven.

Discuss:
What types of offenses typically lead you to seek revenge?
How has your mate sought revenge against you?

Pray:
That you and your mate can develop the humility to be more forgiving
toward each other, leaving revenge in the hands of God.

PEBBLES IN MY SHOES

{Part One}

Rejoice always; pray without ceasing; in everything give thanks;
for this is God's will for you in Christ Jesus.

1 THESSALONIANS 5:16–18

Do you mind if I camp on a verse for a couple of days? First Thessalonians 5:18 demands our attention.

Do you ever feel as though the "little" circumstances of life are about to overwhelm you? It is said we are worn down less by the mountains we climb than by the grain of sand in our shoes. I agree.

Would you like to know what pebbles seem to frequent my sneakers?

- People who try to make me feel guilty;
- My unbalanced checkbook;
- My garage (It continually proves the second law of thermodynamics—the universe is moving from order to disorder.);
- The incessant ringing of the telephone;
- Sibling rivalry;
- A drippy faucet, a smoking fireplace, a leaky pipe in the ceiling;
- Car problems that always occur at the most inopportune times;
- A whining child;
- Things that aren't where I left them, or forgetting where I left them;
- More sibling rivalry;
- An unresolved conflict with a family member;
- Tripping over all the stuff that six children can drag out!

Little things get to us—frequently. Honestly, big problems are difficult, and there are more serious problems that do confound us, but today, right now, this is where I live—in the midst of the little things.

It's called reality. It reminds me of a bumper sticker I saw on a pickup truck some time ago: REALITY IS FOR THOSE WHO CAN'T COPE WITH DRUGS. I really do understand why we have a culture of "cop-outs."

Is God involved in the details of life? Could God possibly want to teach us something in a flat tire? Does He really want to invade every moment of our days, or would He prefer to reserve the 9:30 until 12:00 time slot on Sunday mornings?

Give thanks—in everything.

....

Discuss:
What little circumstances often cause frustration for you?

Pray:
Why not bow in prayer right now and by faith give thanks in everything?

PEBBLES IN MY SHOES

{Part Two}

In everything give thanks; for this is God's will for you in Christ Jesus.
1 THESSALONIANS 5:18

For many years I didn't react well to those nagging little problems—the "pebbles in my shoe." I was used to either calling things "bad luck," getting ticked off, or just shrugging my shoulders while muttering "What's the use?"

Then I discovered 1 Thessalonians 5:18, and I began to measure my walk with God by those four simple words: "In everything give thanks." To my amazement, I started to notice a change in my attitude about life in general. I began to realize that God wants to invade every area of my life.

Let me suggest three reasons God commanded us to give thanks in all things:

First, *giving thanks in all things expresses faith*—faith in the God who knows what He's doing; faith in the God who sovereignly rules in all that happens to us. Isn't that what He wants from us?

Second, *He knew we wouldn't do it naturally.* Giving thanks in all things means I am no longer walking as a mere man, grumbling and griping, but walking as a spiritual man (see 1 Cor. 2:14,15)—a man who sees God at work...even in the grains of sand that tend to fill my shoes.

Isn't that a little bit of what's wrong with twentieth-century Christianity? Don't we divorce God from the details of daily experience? Don't we ultimately dislike those things that we can't seem to control? Let's be honest, we'd rather gripe, complain and be miserable about circumstances than give thanks.

Finally, God wants to teach us how to deal with the irritating grains of sand *so we can get on with climbing the mountains He has for us.* All we see are the pebbles, and we think if we could just remove all those pebbles then we could get on with real life. But the pebbles are the real life that God brings us day by day. He wants to use those irritants to instruct us and to see us mature in Christ.

....

Discuss:

Do you have some grit and gravel in your shoe that feel like a herd of boulders? Before you try to empty them out, why don't you stop right now and give thanks for that rock pile and ask Him to teach you what you need to learn.

Pray:

Tell God you want to submit to Him to learn the lessons He has for you in the midst of daily life. Ask Him to teach you through these pebbles that are in your shoes.

PUTTING THE "THANKS" BACK INTO THANKSGIVING

Oh give thanks to the Lord, call upon His name; make known His deeds among the peoples.

1 CHRONICLES 16:8

We often hear about the need to put Christ back into Christmas. But in our culture, when the Christmas shopping season is in full swing by mid-November, many families find that Thanksgiving is little more than a nice meal to kick off a whirlwind of Yuletide activities.

When we think of Thanksgiving, we think of a family feast. It's "Turkey Day." In fact, some school textbooks say that the Pilgrims' original celebration was organized to thank the Indians for helping them! Even historians are forgetting that the Pilgrims originally feasted to thank God who had given them the courage and perseverance to overcome tremendous hardships.

Thanksgiving can be one of the most meaningful holidays of the year…if you give it the right focus.

Barbara does a great job of helping our family celebrate Thanksgiving — the Rainey Thanksgiving Brunch.

Everyone wears their Sunday "dress up" clothes for the meal. The children make up place cards, decorate the table and set it with fine plates and glasses. The brunch always includes a special French toast that requires 45 minutes to bake. While this meal is in the oven, we gather around the table and begin the brunch by reading selections from *The Light and the Glory* by Peter Marshall and David Manuel. This book tells of the strong Christian faith of many original settlers in America, and includes two chapters on the Pilgrims.

On each plate are five kernels of corn. The family passes a basket around the table, and each person places one kernel of corn at a time into the basket and tells of one thing he or she is thankful for. The basket goes around the table five times.

After we are finished, we have each person write on his or her place card what he or she said. These cards are kept to look over in future years.

While we do this for brunch, you can see that these ideas can easily be adapted for the regular Thanksgiving meal. Kids love the tradition, and it helps them focus on putting true "thanks" into "Thanksgiving."

Discuss:

What can you do to give this holiday a stronger spiritual emphasis?

Pray:

Tonight at dinner ask God to help you to remember His goodness and to be grateful. Then have each family member give thanks for something God has done.

CATCHING A GLIMPSE

I have no greater joy than this, to hear of my children walking in the truth.

3 JOHN 4

I've already described the Rainey Thanksgiving Brunch, in which we emphasize thanking God for how He has worked in our lives. It's been interesting—and gratifying—to hear what our kids have expressed.

A couple of years ago, our daughter Rebecca wrote, "I'm thankful for being able to have a family. I'm thankful to have a big sister. I'm thankful for being able to be a part of God's family. I'm thankful for being able to learn. I'm thankful for Dad's sixth-grade Sunday School class."

Here's what Benjamin, then a senior in high school, wrote:

"1. I'm thankful for God in my life and the things He has given me to be thankful for. 2. Samuel's friendship. 3. Mom and Dad and the example they set of how to live a godly life. 4. My ministry at my high school and my sisters and all they've taught me about relationships."

And Samuel, then 15, had this to say: "1. I'm thankful that Ashley can come home." [This was her first year away at college and we were all thrilled that she was home.] 2. My family. 3. My muscular dystrophy and my trip to Mayo Clinic. 4. *I got to shoot a deer.* 5. A great brother."

It was special to hear our kids thank God for each other as well as hardships in their lives—Samuel had only learned the previous summer that he had MD. After all the conflicts the kids have had over the years, Barbara and I could now see them starting to come together.

Parenting is a long and relentless task. You often wonder whether you are succeeding or failing, and you may not know the results of your efforts for many years. So when you catch just a glimpse that your kids are starting to walk in the truth, you can't help but rejoice.

....

Discuss:

Have your kids done something recently to show that God is working in their lives? If so, write it down so you won't forget it.

Pray:

Thank God for a right choice your spouse or child has recently made.

FOCUS ON RELATIONSHIPS

I thank my God in all my remembrance of you.
PHILIPPIANS 1:3

I once read of a survey in which people were asked if they would be willing to take $1,000 to give up celebrating Thanksgiving with their families. Most said they would decline the money; they wanted to be together as a family. Isn't it ironic, then, that so often we get lost in the trappings of the turkey and gravy and mashed potatoes, and we forget that we should be focusing on relationships?

One way to make this Thanksgiving meaningful is to spend time expressing appreciation for the members of your family. I realize this will be uncomfortable for some; in fact, it may be impossible. But sometimes we need to stretch ourselves and say those things that need to be said.

For "FamilyLife Today" we taped a number of people around the country who expressed thanks for their families. Here's a sampling:

Greg Fast, Colorado Springs: "I'm thankful for three gorgeous miracle babies we were not supposed to be able to have. Just last night I went into the kids' room while they were sleeping, and I remember the feeling of thankfulness for being able to pray over these children."

Charlie Boyd, Little Rock: "I am thankful for my dad. He is a man of integrity, and he loved my mother. I remember him coming home from work every day, walking into the kitchen, putting his arms around my mother and giving her a big kiss and telling her he loved her. I can still see it as if it were yesterday."

Linda Allaback, Tulsa: "I am truly thankful for my husband. We celebrate 12 years of marriage this Sunday, and I am thankful because he accepts me for who I am."

Darcy Kimmell, Scottsdale, Arizona: "I'm very thankful for my mother. She raised six children. I look back at her example of how she loved us so much and took such good care of us. Whenever I had someone spend the night, my mother would tuck in both my girlfriend and me and then she would give us both a kiss. My girlfriends always appreciated that."

Can you imagine how meaningful it would be to hear words like that on Thanksgiving?

Discuss:
Spend a few minutes writing down what you are thankful for.

Pray:
Ask family members to write out prayers of thanksgiving to God. Read them at Thanksgiving or at a similar mealtime celebration.

BARBARA'S SURGERY

{Part One}

The steadfast of mind Thou wilt keep in perfect peace, because he trusts in Thee.

ISAIAH 26:3

*A*t 6:45 A.M. I walked into Barbara's hospital room and found her peacefully asleep. At least she was resting—I sure couldn't.

The IV hooked up to her arm told me this was for real. The doctor told me the surgery my wife would face that day would be a lengthy procedure—I hoped it would be about five hours, but I had a hunch it would be much longer.

Barbara and I had traveled to Oklahoma City to correct a problem that, on four occasions, had caused her heart to race at over 300 beats per minute. When she suffered two such episodes in 1990, we decided to seek treatment from a doctor who had developed a new surgical procedure for people with Barbara's problem.

As I sat there that morning, waiting for her to wake up, a horde of fears went through my mind.

As I went to the waiting room with Barbara's parents and friends, I had no idea of what lessons God had waiting for me. *What if they damage her heart further, rather than repair it?* I thought. *Am I about to say good-bye to my wife, friend and partner?* I felt so helpless, knowing that there was nothing I could do. Except pray.

At 1:00 P.M. a partially informed receptionist in the waiting area told me that everything was going according to the plan, even though Barbara's heart had taken off racing a few times. "But they got it under control," she said. A combination of things—the look on her face as she talked to the nurse, and the way she reported back to me—told me that more was going on than she was telling me!

Finding peace in the midst of such fear was elusive, but it finally came in getting alone, reading the Psalms and praying. Isaiah 26:3 became a reality because I knew I could trust in God. I learned that it is really tough during suspense-filled times to keep the mind steadfast and full of faith.

....

*D*iscuss:
When have you felt most helpless and dependent on God?

*P*ray:
For assurance that, no matter what your situation, God is in control.

BARBARA'S SURGERY

{Part Two}

I know that Thou canst do all things, and that no purpose of Thine can be thwarted.

JOB 42:2

We knew that people all over the nation were praying for Barbara. Just that knowledge brought incredible comfort and strength. But somewhere along the way I began to think that, because of all these prayers, God was obligated to bring the operation to a quick end. That kind of thinking set me up for disappointment.

At 5:30 P.M., nine and one-half hours into the surgery, the doctor informed us, "Barbara is testing us…. You might as well go get dinner. It's going to be awhile!"

Not only was I now in a wrestling match with fear, but disappointment had also jumped into the ring. I questioned God: "Why do Barbara and I have to go through this? What about all those prayers for her? Why can't this be easy?"

Four hours later, though, the suspense was finally over. When they rolled Barbara out, she was so sleepy she didn't feel my kiss or see the relief on my face. The doctor said the operation was successful, but was one of the most difficult he had performed.

I'm thrilled that Barbara apparently will never experience a racing heartbeat again. And the experience has moved our friendship and partnership to some new levels of intimacy and oneness.

That day was the most challenging of my life. As I laid down to sleep at the foot of Barbara's hospital bed, tears of relief that had been withheld earlier came in abundance. My emotionally turbulent day of suspense, fear, discouragement and doubt had finally come to an end. Through the tears I thanked God that He loved me throughout the day and that He had given me my wife back again.

Discuss:

In what situations have you expressed anger at God when things didn't go your way? Why do we struggle so when we find out we are not in control, but Someone else is in control?

Pray:

Thank God for His power to do all things according to His purpose, and ask Him to give you the faith to accept His control over every aspect of your life.

WILD AND CRAZY

*You have made my heart beat faster, my sister, my bride; you have made
my heart beat faster with a single glance of your eyes.*

SONG OF SOLOMON 4:9

What was the craziest, silliest thing you did when you courted your mate? Recently I asked some coworkers about crazy things they did when they first dated. Here are some of their answers:

Brent Nelson: "I organized a treasure hunt on Catalina Island in California. For six hours we ran around Catalina Island dressed up like pirates. And that was the day I gave her the ring and asked her to marry me. Later we had a romantic dinner."

Kim Spyridon: "On our one-year dating anniversary, my dad called out, 'Kimberly, I think there's something in the front yard that belongs to you.' And in my parents' front yard were helium balloons and a four-foot red heart that said, 'Happy anniversary, darling.' We still have the heart in our garage."

Bob Lepine: "One year I got the pizza guy to make a heart-shaped pizza and deliver it to Mary Ann at work. So she got a heart-shaped pizza. Another year I bought a box of kid valentines, and I addressed each one using a different variation of her new name as my wife. 'The future Mrs. Bob Lepine.' 'The future Mrs. B. Lepine.' And mailed each of them individually so she had 28 kid valentines in her mailbox on Valentine's Day."

Lee Walti: "To propose to Jeannette, I arranged for a friend at a radio station to play our favorite song at a specific time. And in the middle of the song I dubbed in my voice, asking her to marry me. I rented a limousine, we had a nice meal, and then we pulled off the side of the road to listen to the radio. She couldn't understand what I was doing, but when she heard the song and then my voice, she burst into tears."

When was the last time you did anything creative like this during your marriage?

....

Discuss:
Now that you have some ideas, what silly thing are you
going to do with your mate? Don't tell—it's a secret.

Pray:
Ask God to help you keep the romantic fires burning in your marriage.

A TEST OF COMMITMENT

What therefore God has joined together, let no man separate.
MATTHEW 19:6

*W*hen we enter into marriage, we should do it with such total commitment that we don't consider the possibility of bailing out. There should be no escape clauses in a marriage relationship.

I think, however, that we sometimes don't realize how often we do and say things that undermine the marriage commitment. I have a series of questions I'd like you to answer—a test, if you will, of your commitment:

- Do you ever threaten to leave your mate?
- Is your mate secure in your commitment to your marriage?
- Are you more committed to your mate than to your career?
- Are you more committed to your mate than to your children?
- Are you more committed to your mate than to your hobbies and favorite activities?
- Do you emotionally leave your mate by withdrawing for an extended period of time because of conflict?
- Do you mentally leave your mate by staying preoccupied with other things?
- Are you interested in meeting your mate's needs and actively doing what you can to meet them?
- Finally, how do you think your mate would answer each of these questions?

Questions like these can surface some important marital issues such as resolving conflict, making your spouse a priority over children or hobbies, or meeting your mate's needs. Why not take a quick commitment inventory by really answering those questions!

....

Discuss:
After going through the questions, rank the top two or three issues that need to be addressed. Then write out how you're going to practically demonstrate commitment to your mate.

Pray:
Ask God to give you the courage to fulfill your commitment,
even when your spouse doesn't respond.

DIVINE SUFFICIENCY

And such confidence we have through Christ toward God. Not that we are adequate in our-selves to consider anything as coming from ourselves, but our adequacy is from God.

2 CORINTHIANS 3:4,5

It's so easy to feel overwhelmed by life. When we consider our respon-sibilities in marriage, family, work, church and extended family, feelings of inadequacy and hopelessness can rise suddenly and envelop you like a thick fog.

Yet you can keep from being overwhelmed by focusing on the sufficiency of Christ. He is alive today, and He stands ready to guide you along the way.

There's a great poem that says:

Lord, I crawled across the barrenness to You with my empty cup
Uncertain of asking for any small drop of refreshment
If only I would have known You better,
I would have come running with a bucket.

God wants us to know Him and to receive His blessings and to live a life of peace, purpose and pardon. The Bible contains many wonderful principles and truths, but these principles will be only stale dogma and doctrine to you unless you allow the person of Jesus Christ to be at the center of your life. As A. W. Tozer states, "The most important thing about you is what you think about God."

No matter how inadequate you feel in helping your mate, God is completely able to do what appears impossible. His power is most evident when we are weakest. As Paul says in Philippians 4:13, "I can do all things through Him who strengthens me."

Why not submit to Him today and ask Him to be your sufficiency and your strength?

....

Discuss:
In what areas do you feel inadequate?
How has God proven His sufficiency to you in the past?

Pray:
That you would be able to trust in God's sufficiency even when you feel
you are unable to do anything worthy on your own.

TALKING WITH TEENAGERS

{Part One}

That they may arise and tell them to their children, that they should put their confidence in God, and not forget the works of God, but keep His commandments.

PSALM 78:6,7

My son Benjamin was standing in the kitchen, nibbling on some barbecue potato chips. We hadn't really had any substantive, meaningful conversations in a week or more, so I'm certain I stunned him with a question I asked for no other reason than staying "connected" with a 14-year-old boy going through puberty. I asked, "You been keeping your mind clean at school, Son?"

I paused for emphasis, not that the question needed any help. Then I added, "You know, pornography—the kind of sleazy stuff boys pass around and look at?"

He looked me straight in the eye with a half-grin, like I'd been reading his mail, and said, "Funny you should ask. Today at school a friend brought a *Penthouse* magazine into the locker room. But I didn't look at it. I just turned and walked out."

"Good for you! Good for you!" I said twice, to let my affirming words soak into this growing boy's heart. The big grin that made its way across his face told me he was proud he had done what was right.

The sad truth is that many parents just don't have the nerve to ask teenagers such an intrusive question. It's as if something happens to parents when their kids become teenagers and they don't know how to talk to them.

Adolescence is the age when kids should be learning how to bring their Christian faith into the realities of everyday life. It's one thing to teach your kids about God, as Psalm 78 says, but it's quite another thing to teach them how to walk with God and avoid temptations such as pornography.

I'll let you in on another secret: Your teenagers probably want you to talk to them. And if you doubt that, I've got some proof…in the next devotion.

....

Discuss:
Why is it so threatening to talk to teenagers about such critical issues? As a couple, discuss your level of comfort.

Pray:
For one another that your faith would be marked by the same courage that the Old Testament saints used to battle their enemies.

TALKING WITH TEENAGERS

{Part Two}

These commandments that I give you today are to be upon your hearts. Impress them on your children. Talk about them when you sit at home and when you walk along the road, when you lie down and when you get up.

DEUTERONOMY 6:6,7 (NIV)

Yes, I know all about teenagers—their bravado, their "I know it all" attitude. I know they often think their parents are stupid. But regardless of how they act, they still desire to have meaningful conversations with you. If you doubt that, here's some evidence. A few years ago my church's youth pastors gave the youth group a two-question survey. Here's a sampling of their answers to question one: What subject do you wish you could have someone else ask your parents to discuss with you?

- Petting
- Marriage
- Sex
- Grades
- Allowance
- Dating
- Marijuana
- Drugs
- Using the car
- Curfew
- God

- Drinking
- Guys
- Friends
- Making my own decisions
- Their divorce
- Dating relationships
- Big responsibilities
- Bathing suits
- Peer pressure
- Love

- Beliefs of my own
- Me
- My faults
- Boyfriend problems
- Girls
- Money
- College
- Overcoming failures in my Christian walk

And you're wondering what you can talk to your teenagers about? What an opportunity to help them learn how to make choices that honor God in the problems they face on a daily basis.

Discuss:

If you have a teenager, give him or her an assignment to answer this question: What are things you would like to talk about with us? Give him the above list and have him circle his top three.

Pray:

Ask God for His favor upon you, as parents, as you raise teens during these dangerous days.

TALKING WITH TEENAGERS

{Part Three}

Nathan then said to David, "You are the man!"

2 SAMUEL 12:7

King David was on the hot seat. He had slept with Bathsheba, then sent her husband off to be killed at war. When the prophet Nathan approached him with a hypothetical case of a man who committed the same sin, David responded by saying the man deserved to die. Imagine his shock when Nathan cried, "You are the man!"

I think of that verse because parents should be prepared to be on the hot seat when they talk with teenagers.

The youth at our church were asked, "What questions would you like to ask your parents if someone else could ask them for you?" Here were some answers:

- Why do parents have more trouble talking to kids than kids have talking to parents?
- Were you a virgin when you got married? Was it worth it?
- Have you ever done something horrible that you regretted?
- Why do you avoid tough issues?
- How would you feel if your child didn't go to college?
- Are you willing to admit to your children the mistakes you have made and then ask forgiveness?
- If you had to give up me or your business, which would it be?
- Do you love or even care about me? Do you think I am worthy or can do anything? Why won't you ever listen to me?
- Why is it so important to be a "success"? Is that going to get you to heaven?

Do you know what these kids were saying? They wanted to ask their parents these questions, but they didn't feel the freedom. Your kids need your example and involvement. And they need to have the freedom to put you on the hot seat. It is better to be embarrassed by a question you don't want to answer than to raise a child who will become a fool and humiliate you later.

....

Discuss:

For only the courageous: Take this list of questions and show them to your teenager. Have him or her mark off which ones he or she would like you to answer someday.

Pray:

Thank God for His grace and forgiveness through faith in Jesus Christ.

GOD'S PLUMB LINE

The Lord was standing by a vertical wall, with a plumb line in His hand. And the Lord said to me, "What do you see, Amos?"...Then the Lord said, "Behold I am about to put a plumb line in the midst of My people Israel."

AMOS 7:7,8

The strength of a nation," said Abraham Lincoln, "lies in the homes of its people." In other words, the state of the union is determined by the state of the marriage union—the condition of our nation's marriages, families and homes.

By what yardstick can we accurately measure how our homes are doing? The prophet Amos stood by a wall that was straight or "plumb" according to God's own measure. That is the measure we need to apply to our homes and our nation.

Yet, even as far back as 1947, historian Carle Zimmerman wrote a chilling account of the factors that he said have led to the ultimate collapse of a civilization. In those ruins he found that marriage had lost its sacredness and was frequently broken by divorce. Women lost their inclination for childbearing, and the birth rate decreased. There was public disrespect for parents, parenthood and authority in general.

He also found that there had been an increase in juvenile delinquency, promiscuity and rebellion. Even people with traditional marriages refused to accept family responsibilities. Adultery was increasingly accepted. There was an increasing desire for, and spread of, sexual perversions of all kinds, including homosexuality.

Think about Zimmerman's study as you look at the state of our country today. Half of all new marriages now end in divorce. The birth rate has declined. Juvenile delinquency, sexual perversion and promiscuity are rampant.

Why is this happening? Because the state of the union is determined by the state of the marriage union. Are we destined to follow in the footsteps of cultures that have fallen because of all this? Our only hope is to rebuild the walls of both the home and the nation according to God's plumb line.

....

Discuss:
As you look into God's Word—our plumb line—is there an area of your life or an attitude in your marriage that needs to be "corrected" and brought into conformity with God's standard?

Pray:
Ask God to help you, as individuals and as a family, to represent Him and His standard well.

REBUILDING THE WALLS

"The wall of Jerusalem is broken down." When I heard these words, I sat down and wept and mourned for days; and I was fasting and praying before the God of heaven.

NEHEMIAH 1:3,4

What can we do about the state of our nation and our homes? Of course we can see that our own homes resist the drift toward ruin. We can also do as Nehemiah did. He wept, fasted and prayed—for four months!

Then he acted. After months of prayer, he had a plan that was etched on his heart and mind by the hand of God. Nehemiah saw the walls of Jerusalem rebuilt in 55 days. Even his enemies stood in disbelief at the achievement. God intervened and brought order, cooperation, and action out of what had been chaos for nearly 90 years.

America today is much like Jerusalem was then. Our nation's primary wall of defense—the family—lies in ruin and desperately needs rebuilding. As in Nehemiah's time, the task before us needs God's intervention as never before. We need to pray that:

- Christian marriages and families will exemplify the love of God to a perishing world.
- We in the church will have wisdom and courage in standing against divorce and the impact it is having on our families, while having compassion and love for those who suffer its devastation.
- Our children will marry wisely.
- The legacy we leave our children will not be one of materialism and spiritual apathy, but of caring concern for a world that needs to know Jesus Christ as Lord and Savior.
- God will bring the resources (money, talent, leadership, technology and manpower) to all who are striving to strengthen families.

Let's pray for the state of the union by praying for the state of the marriage union: *God, come and rebuild the wall. Come and repair all the broken pieces of our families today. Confuse our enemies, O Lord, and weaken their influence for evil! May Your favor be upon our families.*

Discuss:
In what areas does your family need rebuilding?

Pray:
Spend some time tonight in prayer with your mate. Go through the prayer needs listed above. Pray that Jesus Christ will be Lord first in your own home, then in every Christian home, to the glory of God.

NOTES ON BEING GOOD

Thanks be to God that...you became obedient from the heart to that form of teaching to which you were committed.

ROMANS 6:17

One day our son Samuel, then eight, typed out a treatise titled: "HOW TO BE GOOD." Here is his own unedited work, shared with his permission:

HOW TO BE GOOD

1. Obay you parntes and GOD.
2. Do want other kids want to do.
3. Do not be selfish.
4. Be good to babbysearts.
5. Do want parntes say.
6. Do not cheat.
7. Play right.
8. Be a good player.
9. Dont be a por sport.
10. Do no cuse.

Not bad, is it? Who knows what triggered this active boy to jot down this inspired list? Samuel's conclusions are a child's perception of several of the Ten Commandments. And he may know them a little better than most adults.

When I look at the Ten Commandments, I see that the first two alone are a good summary of how to be good:

1. "You shall have no other gods before Me" (Exod. 20:3). While Israel was tempted to worship idols, I'm convinced that one of modern Christianity's worst forms of idolatry is materialism. Barbara and I constantly evaluate this issue because we don't want to leave a legacy of materialism for our kids.

Another form of idolatry is our worship of self-fulfillment. Careers, the number of children we decide to have, our attitudes about divorce—all have been sired by the personal rights movement.

2. "You shall not take the name of the Lord your God in vain" (v. 7). Taking God's name in vain is more than just using His name as a swear word. It means "to take His name to mean nothing." Even the way many Christians use the phrase "Praise the Lord" can become slang if we say it only out of habit. God is holy and sacred, the God to be feared. Swearing is thoughtlessly speaking of Him in a non-God-fearing way.

We know that these commandments (and the other eight as well) contain a moral snapshot of God's nature, holiness and goodness. Philosophers try to find out God's nature by reason. Believers discover who He is as they walk in obedience to His Word.

Discuss:
Read and discuss the Ten Commandments from Exodus 20:1-17
at your next family meal.

Pray:
That doing God's will may become an inner urge in your heart,
not just a dutiful observing of external commands.

HIDE AND SEEK

{Part One}

And they heard the sound of the Lord God walking in the garden in the cool of the day,
and the man and his wife hid themselves from the presence of the Lord God among
the trees of the garden.

GENESIS 3:8

emember playing "hide and seek" when you were a kid? My cousins and I usually played it just before dark. One kid was designated "It." While "It" covered his or her eyes (maybe) and counted out loud to 50 or 100, the rest of us scurried to our elusive hiding spots. Then "It" would try to find us before we dashed back to the safety of the "base," usually the trunk of a massive tree.

I remember being significantly better at hiding than I was at seeking. No one could find me. But after awhile, even the sheer joy of knowing that I had out-witted my buddies was overridden by my solitude. It was this loneliness that invariably would flush me out into the open.

In the same way, most of us are more adept at hiding than seeking in our rela-tionships. The human race is well trained in hiding—we've been doing it since the beginning of time. When Adam and Eve got into trouble in the Garden of Eden, the first thing they did was to run and hide. They hid from one another—the notorious fig leaf cover-up. Then they tried to conceal their disobedience by hiding from God.

From that point on, we've worn masks in our relationships, both with God and with other human beings. We hide because we are afraid to unmask our-selves and let people see us for who we really are. We feel that if others discov-er our faults, they'll reject us.

The problem is that God did not create us to hide. In the garden, He sought out Adam and Eve. And today He pursues us and challenges us to come out of our sinful, self-absorbed isolation and yield to being discovered both by Him and by our spouses.

....

Discuss:
Are you aware of keeping a part of your life
hidden from your mate or from God?

Pray:
To be truly "discovered" both by God and by your mate.

HIDE AND SEEK

{Part Two}

And you will seek Me and find Me, when you search for Me with all your heart.
JEREMIAH 29:13

In the previous devotion I spoke of hiding from God and each other. Why would anyone want to do this? Because we fear we'll be hurt. Intimate relationships can be painful.

No human relationship endures more hiding and hurting than marriage. It is within this most intimate of human associations that two people seek to know one another and be known. It is tragic that many people marry to stop being lonely, but soon find themselves lonelier than they were as singles.

I believe that 95 percent of all marriages suffer from isolation, and few people in marriage realize how desperately alone they really are. Often a husband and wife begin drifting apart so slowly that they hardly recognize the slide. Then, after a few years of hiding and poor communication, they realize that their once romantic love has grown stale. That's why many successful-looking marriages aren't much more than two successful people independently doing their own thing; they aren't friends and life-partners.

How do you defeat this drift to isolation?

I believe the most important thing you can do as a couple is to *regularly pray together*. Barbara and I began this spiritual discipline shortly after we were married in 1972, and I believe it's done more for our marriage than any other single thing. If there's a problem between us, we find that we either resolve the problem and pray, or go to sleep angry. Because of our commitment to end each day in prayer, we have learned to build bridges of understanding between us, forgive one another, and then pray.

Praying together keeps us from hiding from one another.

....

Discuss:
When was the last time you prayed together as a couple?
What keeps you from doing it now?

Pray:
Take turns praying for one another before you go to sleep tonight.
Ask God to help you develop this spiritual discipline in your relationship
with Him and one another.

A WIFE'S LIFE

Husbands, love your wives, just as Christ also loved the church and gave Himself up for her...and let the wife see to it that she respect her husband.

EPHESIANS 5:25,33

I'll never forget the discouragement, anger and pain expressed in a letter by a woman who attended one of our FamilyLife Conferences. She protested my unmitigated gall in referring to tired husbands. Then she gave me her daily schedule, plus a big piece of her mind:

5:30—Rise and start getting myself ready and put coffee on.
6:00—Start breakfast and get child's bag ready for day care.
6:30—Get hubby and kids up, fed and dressed for school.
7:00—Wash dishes.
7:15—Get kids on bus and finish dressing.
7:30—Leave for day care center and work. Coffee for breakfast.
8:00–4:00—Eight hours' work.
4:30—Back to day care, sometimes picking up something for supper.
5:15–11:00—Come home, start supper, load washer, help kids with lessons, listen to school tales. Fold clothes, wash dishes, run sweeper, baths for kids and me, flop in bed for next day.
Saturday—Clean house, do weekly shopping, prepare meals, wash dishes, get the kids cleaned up.
Sunday—Church, meals, do things around the house I neglected all week.

Of course in and around this schedule she had to work in trips to the doctor and dentist, attend PTA and other school programs, and receive occasional company that dropped by.

"And where is hubby all this time?" she wrote. "Glued to the paper or stuck in front of the TV. It's pretty hard to want to make love to a glob that finally unsticks himself from TV when I am semiconscious and look and feel like I've been drug through the brush backwards. Thanks for your help."

I wish this frustrated wife had included her name and address, because I wanted to write and apologize for sounding unsympathetic and insensitive.

I'd also like to speak with her husband.

Discuss:
How does your family share household chores and other responsibilities?
If you have two incomes, talk with your spouse about the real cost
to your relationship and family.

Pray:
Ask God to help you to be sensitive to the burden your wife carries. Ask Him
to show you how you can shoulder some of her burdens.

GOD'S MOMENTS FOR MOM

by Barbara Rainey

*And let us not lose heart in doing good, for in due time we shall reap if
we do not grow weary.*

GALATIANS 6:9

For me, being a mom is both my greatest joy and my area of greatest challenge and worry. But sometimes I believe God gives mothers special, fulfilling moments to keep us hanging in there.

One day my daughter Ashley and I went shopping, and as we came in carrying all the bags, a big bottle of cream rinse fell out of Ashley's arms, hit the garage floor and splattered everywhere. All I could say was, "Oh, Ashley!" Though I didn't form the words, my voice implied, "How could you be so careless?"

After cleaning up the mess I went inside and suggested that the kids help pick up the house a bit. Ashley made an uncharacteristic comment about the house being so messy it wouldn't make much difference anyway. My pride was offended at the truth of her statement, but I said nothing.

That night I found a note from Ashley: "Dear Mommy, I am sorry I called your house a messy place. Will you forgive me? And the rinse breaking. It was dumb. I hope you and I can go shopping again. Love you more than you can imagine. Love in Christ. Ashley."

One Christmas I received a similar note that also took me from the depths to the heights. I had bawled out Benjamin for messing up his bedroom. Afterward I said, "Benjamin, all you are going to remember about me is that I griped at you and I yelled about picking up your room."

That night he gave me a note that said, "Thank you for being a great mom. That's what I will remember the most. I love you, Benjamin."

Yes, being a mother can be challenging, hard, frustrating and lonely, but there are those priceless moments that come every day in the form of a note, a quick hug and a kiss, or something said as only a child can say it.

Discuss:
What part of being a parent do you find the most rewarding? Frustrating? Recall a time when one of your children made being a parent all worthwhile.

Pray:
Ask God to empower you with wisdom, equip you with patience and reward you with joy in the challenge of parenting.

THE EASIEST THING
TO DO IS NOTHING

"Let us not lose heart in doing good."

GALATIANS 6:9

It's no secret that America is in the midst of a spiritual and moral crisis. Polls today indicate that most Americans are deeply concerned about the direction our nation is heading. The real problem is a critical shortage of people who care enough to get off the sidelines and are determined to make a difference. Sometimes it only takes one person to turn the flow from negative to positive.

Take, for instance, Babe Ruth, the most famous baseball player of all time. The Babe finished his career in a slump, and according to one legendary story, he was jeered mercilessly one day in Cincinnati. As he made his customary trot off the field to the dugout, the fans began to yell obscenities at him. The booing intensified until a little boy jumped a fence and ran to his hero's side.

The child threw his arms around Babe's legs, crying as he fiercely hugged him. Moved by the young lad's display of affection and emotion, Ruth gently swept the boy upwards and into his arms. As they walked off the field, the man and boy cried together.

Suddenly, the hoots, howls and curses ceased. And the eerie silence was replaced by a thunderous ovation. Fans of all ages now began to weep. One small boy's courageous actions had changed the behavior of thousands of people.

I can't help but wonder how long the boy sat there listening to the cursing, angry crowd before he did something. Probably not very long.

And today, how much worse must our nation become before individuals are moved by compassion and conviction to get out of their seats and decide to make a difference?

As I pray for our nation and its families, I continue to sense that the battle will be won by laymen and women like you. As Paul says in Galatians 6:9, "Let us not lose heart in doing good."

....

Discuss:
In what ways are you concerned about the direction our country is headed?

Pray:
That God would burden your heart with the need to be involved in the battle.

TAKING A STAND

"You are the salt of the earth...You are the light of the world."
MATTHEW 5:13,14

*S*alt is a preservative, and light dispels darkness. As I see it, Christians need to take responsibility to lovingly confront the foolishness and wickedness that crosses our paths. You and I can't just turn our heads, acting like evil doesn't exist. We've got to step into the battle personally and confront it.

Recently Barbara and I were chaperoning a junior-high dance. I was a little late in getting there, and when I arrived I was told that, in a dark part of the dance floor a number of students were using some questionable dance moves.

I eased my way back toward the students in question and was amazed, shocked and embarrassed at what I saw. About two dozen kids were involved in a dance that looked like intercourse with clothes on.

I was faced with a dilemma—do something or do nothing. I was finally pushed over the edge and into action when two boys and a girl began a particularly vulgar move. I walked up to them, tapped the boys on the shoulder and said, "You've gone too far. This is indecent—knock it off!" As they backed away from the girl I looked her in the eyes and scolded her, "You shouldn't let boys treat you that way. It's immodest and vulgar. They are robbing you of your dignity as a young woman!"

It was interesting that those kids knew what they were doing was shameful. They just needed someone who cared enough to confront them.

For years our nation has trumpeted the value of "tolerance" above all other values. Tolerance says that there are no moral absolutes that govern us. That one person's beliefs are just as valid as another. Many adults would be shocked that I tried to "impose my standards" on those junior-high kids at the dance.

Unfortunately, this supposed ideal of tolerance has ushered in a culture that does not know right from wrong, and we're all sitting on the sidelines watching our culture slide.

....

Discuss:
What prevents you from taking a stronger public stand for morality?

Pray:
That God would give you the courage to be "salt" and "light" in our culture.

IS YOUR FAMILY PART OF GOD'S FAMILY?

For God so loved the world, that He gave His only begotten Son, that whoever believes in Him should not perish, but have eternal life.

JOHN 3:16

Years ago our family went on a vacation to Yosemite National Park. As we walked among giant Sequoia trees, we found one that was particularly enormous. A sign at its base read: "The Faithful Couple." A park ranger explained that this was actually *two* trees. Some 1,500 years ago two trees sprouted as seedlings about 15 feet apart. After some 800 years, their trunks grew close enough to touch, and began to fuse with each other. We all looked up, and sure enough, 40 or 50 feet above our heads we could see the two trees reappearing.

I thought, *What a perfect symbol of a godly family. The members are fused together as one, yet each has his or her individual identity. As they grow* upward *in their relationship with God, they grow* closer *to each other, and are able, like the mighty redwood, to withstand life's storm because they are one.*

That's the key to a great marriage—a commitment to growing closer to God. To experience this, however, you first must make sure you are part of God's family—that you have received Christ as your Savior and Lord.

Just as a marriage begins when two people make a personal commitment, so it is with your relationship with God. You need to turn to Him in repentance for your sin and place your faith in Christ for the forgiveness of those sins.

Establishing a relationship with God is the most important decision you will ever make. And let me tell you, your life will never be the same.

....

Discuss:

Have you received Christ as your Savior? Share at dinner tonight what led you to make that decision. How has your life changed since then?

Pray:

That your family members will be able to blend their individualities into a single, strong and firmly rooted tree in the vineyard of the Lord.

SINGING IN THE FIRE

For there our captors demanded of us songs, and our tormentors mirth, saying,
"Sing us one of the songs of Zion."

PSALM 137:3

*G*il Beers, former editor of *Christianity Today* magazine, told the story of an ancestor that you may want to remember the next time family trials put you to the test.* Beers's great-great-grandmother to the eighth great was Catharine duBois.

One day in 1663 a band of Minnisink Indians swept down from the Catskill Mountains and captured Catharine and her daughter, along with several other women and children.

After 10 days, the Indians, thinking they had avoided reprisal, decided to celebrate their success by putting Catharine and her daughter to death by fire. They placed the captives on a pile of logs and lit the torch to ignite them.

Instead of screaming at her tormentors and cursing them, or God, for her plight, Catharine duBois burst into song! It was a Huguenot hymn she had learned in France, and it was based on Psalm 137:3. The Indians were so taken by her bravery and by the song itself that they demanded another, then another. And while Catharine duBois was still singing, her husband and a search party burst upon the scene and rescued her.

Don't think this story is farfetched when applied to your household just because the little "fires" you face aren't usually life threatening. There are many situations when a little singing, a little humor, can extinguish the flames of a dispute or a bit of tension in the home. In fact, parents who are habitually humming or singing at their places of work are surprisingly empowered to defuse crises and problems.

Paul and Silas knew this principle. When they were cast into prison in the city of Philippi, they prayed and sang—and an earthquake jarred them out of jail! Don't underestimate the power of song to break open downcast hearts in your home.

....

Discuss:
Why do you think singing can have such an uplifting effect? Pull out an old hymnal and sing some songs at the dinner table tonight.

Pray:
Ask God to enable you to burst into songs of praise when the challenge of the moment would seem most disheartening.

*From "A Theology to Die By," *Christianity Today*, (February 6, 1987: 11.) Used by permission.

WHAT COMMUNICATES LOVE TO WOMEN?

{Part One}

So husbands ought also to love their own wives as their own bodies,...for no one ever hated his own flesh, but nourishes and cherishes it, just as Christ also does the church.

EPHESIANS 5:28,29

What would your wife do if you looked her in the eye one night and asked, "Sweetheart, what can I do to let you know that I love you? What communicates love to you?"

I know from experience that many wives would respond in one of several ways:

- Fall to the floor in shock, stunned that her husband would even ask.
- Run to the bathroom and return with a thermometer, certain that he must not be feeling well.
- Laugh cynically and change the subject, figuring that he's probably just joking.
- Frown with suspicion, knowing from experience that her husband is just trying to manipulate her so he can get something he wants.

I wish that didn't sound so cynical, but many men seem to lose their romantic ardor once they marry. Some men stop thinking of what communicates love to their wives and focus on trying to meet their own needs.

If you ask this question of your wife, she may not have an answer immediately. She probably hasn't had time to think about it. But she will be pleased you are interested in meeting her needs.

Once you learn the answer, you will need to follow through and demonstrate your love to her with no strings attached. Too often, as men, we think of romance as a means to an end—and that end is sex. We think, *If I do this for my wife, she'll really be responsive in bed tonight!*

If that's your attitude, your wife will sense it quickly. That's not sacrificial love. When you seek to please your wife in this area of romance, you've got to understand you need to deny your agenda and let the goal be solely to help her feel loved, nourished and cherished.

....

Discuss:

Ask your wife what makes her feel loved. Now c'mon, think about this one for a while. This could be really fun and educational!

Pray:

That you would be able to nourish and cherish her with no strings attached and no agenda of your own to fulfill.

WHAT COMMUNICATES LOVE TO WOMEN?

{Part Two}
by Barbara Rainey

"My beloved is mine, and I am his."

THE SONG OF SOLOMON 2:16

As Dennis wrote in the last devotional, the best way to learn what says "I love you" to your wife is to ask her. But to give you a little more help, we surveyed 800 people at our FamilyLife Marriage Conferences. Here is our top 10 list, in reverse order, of what communicates romantic love to women.

10. *Holding hands.* To a woman, this simple act communicates closeness. It says, "I want to be close to you and I like you."

9. *Massage.* Many women are reluctant to ask their husbands for foot rubs or back rubs because they know that most men tend to see massage as sexual foreplay. But women often enjoy massages with no strings attached.

8. *Acts of servanthood and sacrifice.* Sometimes it's as simple as opening the door for your wife or cleaning the dishes after dinner. When a husband denies himself, even in little ways, he tells her he cares about her and wants to make her feel special.

7. *A kiss.* It's interesting that men ranked this higher than women. I suspect women would rank kissing higher if they didn't know from experience that their husbands usually don't want to stop with a kiss.

6. *Taking a walk together.* Again, this is not usually high on men's lists. It's very relational. When you go for a walk with your husband, you are taking a break from daily responsibilities and distractions. You're away from the telephone and the television, away from children, away from work. It allows you to focus on the relationship in a nonthreatening way.

After looking at this part of the list, I was struck with how God has made women different from one another. And how, as a woman, different things communicate romantic love to me at different times. But we all have one thing in common: we want to feel that our husbands love us.

....

Discuss:
Look over this devotion with your wife and ask her,
"Which of these items most communicates love to you?"

Pray:
That God would develop within you the desire to communicate love to your wife without any expectation of her response.

WHAT COMMUNICATES LOVE TO WOMEN?

{Part Three}
by Barbara Rainey

"My beloved is mine, and I am his."

THE SONG OF SOLOMON 2:16

*C*ontinuing my top 10 list of romantic things you can do for your wife:

5. *Written notes, letters or cards.* Recently, I was cleaning our bathroom and I found an old note from Dennis: "Have you found all your little notes around that say how much I love you?" He had once left notes like this all around the house, and I had a great time searching for them. I had taped this one on a closet wall in the bathroom just to remind me what a wonderful husband I had.

4. *Going out on a date.* Again, a date means time away, with no kids — just the two of you. A wife likes to be the focus of her husband's attention. She enjoys having a block of time where she has him all to herself.

3. *Having special meals together.* You can put the kids to bed a little early and have a quiet candlelight dinner at home. You can pick up your wife at her office at noon and take her for a short picnic.

2. *Touch.* I'm not talking about sexual touch here, but hugging, cuddling and caressing without expectation of a later payoff.

Many women never received much physical affection from their parents. So they grow up with a longing for physical touch, and if all they get from their husbands is touch that is tied to sex, they will begin thinking, *He really doesn't love me that much. He just needs me for his own pleasure.*

And finally we come to the end of my list:

1. *Flowers.* Many men never understand the power of flowers on women, and I'm not sure if I understand it myself. I think flowers say, "You are special." I think perhaps it's because flowers are so frivolous — they will wilt and die in a few days, but for that brief period of time you see a constant bright reminder that your husband loves you.

You'll note that a few themes run through this list: Women want to feel special. They want you to show love without an expectation of sex. For women, romance = relationship.

Discuss:

Again, look through this list and ask your wife which items most communicates love to her. Talk about the equation: romance = relationship. Agree/disagree?

Pray:

That God will enable you to keep romance alive in your marriage.

STICKS AND STONES...

He who mocks the poor shows contempt for their Maker.
PROVERBS 17:5 (NIV)

When I was in first grade, a few friends and I began to choose who would be "in" and who would be "out." One of the first "outs" was Lois. She came from a poor family and couldn't dress as well as the others. She was also slow in class, which didn't help. So we quickly excluded her.

The "in" group rejected Lois as a person—slowly at first, but ruthlessly as the years passed. By the time we reached high school, she was the butt of countless jokes. When we were seniors, she had such an inferiority complex that I don't recall seeing her look up from the floor that entire year.

Years later I recognized my false values and my haughty, foolish evaluation of Lois. I wept when I thought about my cruelty to her. I asked God to forgive me for my arrogant, childish behavior. She was made in the image of God every bit as much as I was.

Peers can have poisonous tongues. William Hazlitt wrote, "A nickname is the hardest stone the devil can throw at a man." Some never forget the names they have been called.

Here are a few nicknames we've come across: Dummy, Pit-i-ful Paul, Messy, Fatso, Peewee, Runt, Brick-Brain, Ornery, Grasshopper Brain, Yo-Yo, Troublemaker, Slow Learner, Bones, Motor-Mouth, Sloppy, Sleepy, Devil's Daughter, Nerd, Turkey, Lardo, Bird Legs, Space Cadet, Rebellious, Simple Sally, Buzzard-Beak, Metal-Mouth, Freckle-Face, Weirdo and Geek. Names like these can really hurt.

The way your mate views himself today was heavily influenced by his peers as he grew up. Even today, your mate may be very peer-dependent. He may self-consciously wonder if he's wearing "just the right" outfit or using "just the right" lingo. He may doubt his ability to relate to your friends.

As we've said elsewhere in this devotional, you are a mirror to your mate. You can still stop those condemning voices from his past by replacing them with positive words in the present.

....

Discuss:
How did your peers view you as you grew up? What were your nicknames as you grew up? Share any feelings about those experiences with your spouse.

Pray:
That you will take the opportunity to build your mate's self-esteem with positive words.

THE PROVERBS 31 WOMAN

An excellent wife, who can find? For her worth is far above jewels.
PROVERBS 31:10

One of our favorite types of broadcasts on "FamilyLife Today" is the "Mom Check" day. We call some stay-at-home mothers we know around the country and just ask how their day is going.

I always enjoy asking these women how their houses look. A woman in Dallas with a new baby said, "Our bedroom's a disaster! Nicole's cradle is in there. The swing's in there. My desk has become a makeshift changing table. Diapers are all over. We've gotten 30 million gifts of girls' outfits, and the corners are filled with clothes."

We called my wife, Barbara, and she described the kitchen: "Oh, it's a mess, as always. Let's see, we still have blueberry muffins out. There are dishes in the sink and crumbs on the floor and laundry on the dining room table that I folded this morning. And a basket sitting on a chair that's mounded with ready-to-be-folded laundry."

Then there was Brenda, a friend in Portland. I loved her comment: "Our house is a wreck. The kitchen is filled with dirty dishes. But it's been a great day. My priorities have been in order."

I know that many people look upon the wife and mother described in Proverbs 31 as some sort of "Super Woman" who never did anything wrong. But let me ask you this: Do you think her home was dirty at times? Do you think she always folded her laundry?

While this woman was praised—"She looks well to the ways of her household, and does not eat the bread of idleness" (v. 27)—she was not perfect. The way I see it, her praise was based not on the neatness of her household but on the priorities she lived by.

One of the great tragedies of recent decades is that too many people judge the performance of a "housewife" by the tidiness of her home. We need to be able to pull back and know what's important. You may have a floor that needs to be mopped or a refrigerator that needs to be cleaned. You may have kids with sniffles. It all feels like it's pressing in on you.

But 10-15 years from now, what is going to matter? What will your kids recall most about you? Do you want to be remembered for the love you gave your children and the godly character you modeled for them?

....

Discuss:
How important is keeping a clean house to you? Why?

Pray:
Ask God to help you keep your perspective as you fulfill your responsibilities as wife and mother. Men, pray for your wives—then help them!

WHAT LEGACY ARE YOU LEAVING?

Remember the days of old, consider the years of all generations. Ask your father, and he will inform you, your elders, and they will tell you.

DEUTERONOMY 32:7

As we conduct FamilyLife Conferences across the country, I find that the concept of leaving behind a "legacy" is a bit unfamiliar to many couples. Old Testament families had a strong sense of the legacy of generations. In the text above, families contemporary with Moses had received a legacy from the past that they were urged to remember, giving them a sense of roots.

Some families in the twentieth century also take their heritages seriously. As one young lad approached his sixth birthday, he could tell something big was going to happen. A week before his birthday party, he noticed the garage door locked with a shiny new padlock. The day finally arrived, and he was awakened by an uncle who asked him to come downstairs to the kitchen where his parents, aunts, uncles, grandmother and grandfather were waiting.

They all walked out and formed a semicircle in front of the garage door. Then the boy's father unlocked the padlock and opened the door. Lying there was a section of a redwood tree, nearly five feet tall and one foot thick.

As the boy drew closer, he noticed the huge slice of wood had been carefully lacquered and polished. Then he saw little signs painted on the rings of the tree. One ring was labeled "The Emancipation Proclamation, January 1, 1863." Still another marker signified when his mother and father had met and married.

The more the boy studied the carefully labeled rings on that huge piece of redwood, the more he realized it not only contained a history of his family, but also a history of his race. His family understood the importance of helping a young man understand his origins.

Is it any wonder that this little boy—Alex Haley—grew up to write the best-selling novel *Roots*?

Discuss:
What legacy did you inherit from your parents? What legacy would you like to bequeath to your children?

Pray:
That you will be able to affirm the positives in your family of origin, negate all the negatives and leave a strong spiritual legacy for your children.

THE END OF EVERY MAN

It is better to go to a house of mourning than to go to a house of feasting,
because that is the end of every man, and the living takes it to heart.

ECCLESIASTES 7:2

*A*s this verse in Ecclesiastes reminds us, knowing that we will die someday should affect how we live today.

Unfortunately, many people never seem to understand what's important in life until they are faced with the end of it. A few years ago I received a
letter illustrating this truth:

Frank was a wonderful man, but he was also stern and stoic; he taught his
three boys to be strong, tough, no more tears, no more hugs and only
manly handshakes at bedtimes. He liked things done his way. He was not
a good listener.

Frank [developed] an incurable form of cancer that spread from his
legs to his lungs, spleen and various parts of his body. He was 43 years old.
Within days of learning he had cancer, he gave his life to Jesus. Frank
began to trust in Jesus Christ and go to Him for strength and courage.

Hugging and loving his sons became a daily absolute in their lives. He
shared from his heart with the boys, cried with them, told them how
proud he was of them and how very much he loved them. He became the
listening, loving husband every wife dreams of.

His last four months here on earth were filled with laughter and good
times with his family. Even though the cancer was taking over his body,
God gave him a quality life to the end. Frank prepared his family for his
death and for the task ahead of them, so that they, too, would one day
reach the goal and stand before the Throne.

Frank was fortunate to learn his true priorities while he still had a chance. I
can't help but think of Senator Paul Tsongas, who said after his third bout with
cancer: "I think of all the fathers who have young children and play golf all day
Saturday and Sunday. They've never had cancer. I think of the husbands who
never voice their affections for their wives. They've never had cancer."

Discuss:
What would you do if you learned you had only one year to live?

Pray:
That God would give you the ability to live by those priorities.

THE BATTLE BEFORE US

Suffer hardship with me, as a good soldier of Christ Jesus.

2 TIMOTHY 2:3

*P*arents, you are desperately needed in a major battle before us. The need was illustrated when I was asked to speak to junior high kids about sexual abstinence.

First I spoke to the girls. I introduced three senior high girls who were all taking a stand for virginity and purity. Two hundred junior high girls responded by breaking into spontaneous applause. They seemed hungry for a model other than Madonna.

The boys were different. When I introduced two high school students as young men who were committed to moral purity and to being virgins when they married, a group began laughing. They mocked the young men from the high school. It made me mad. I bristled and walked directly toward the hecklers and told them, "That attitude is exactly what is wrong with our nation—there's little or no respect for those who have standards."

As I thought about these kids getting married I was sobered for the next generation. What kind of homes will they create? What will their children be like? I couldn't help but wonder if law and order as we now know it would be considered the "good old days."

Private Dad and Private Mom, put on your battle fatigues and expect hardship and anguish in raising a kid who doesn't always do it right. Suffer hardship as a good parent-soldier who has to give up everyday pleasures to win the war. Lay aside those golf clubs, those civic activities.

Get involved in your children's battles. Be there for them. Know their battlefields. Carefully screen those with whom they go into battle—their peers. Prepare them for the war zone of their own adolescent sex drive. Talk about it even when you are both embarrassed.

Above all, don't stick your head in a foxhole and pretend the battle doesn't exist.

....

Discuss:
What are you doing to help your children win in the
battle for absolutes and values?

Pray:
That you and your family will be wise in battle and that God will grant you
victory in the battle for moral purity.

A CHRISTMAS I'LL NEVER FORGET

{Part One}

The Lord gave and the Lord has taken away. Blessed be the name of the Lord.

JOB 1:21

It was December 20, 1981. The kids were tucked in early, and Barbara and I were about to sit down for a nice, quiet meal.

The phone rang and the voice at the other end had a chilling soberness to it that I shall never forget. I learned that my good friend Mick Yoder and two of his boys had been in a tragic plane crash that afternoon in Greenville, South Carolina.

Mick and his wife, Helen, had just moved to Greenville in the summer to start a church there. Only months before, Barbara and I had said good-bye to the Yoders after working with them for nearly five years to help start the ministry of FamilyLife.

That morning, Mick had preached and led the Sunday service. Then he and his boys joined a couple for a plane ride. About two miles from the runway, a two-dollar part attached to the carburetor broke, and the plane lost all power. They missed the runway by only 10 feet and hit an embankment head-on.

Everyone survived the crash except for Mick's seven-year-old son, Benji. He died instantly.

The next morning, I kissed Barbara good-bye and flew to South Carolina. Nothing in all my years of ministry experience prepared me for what I beheld. Mick was in critical condition, with three of his four limbs broken. And Helen was numb from the emotional shock.

As I approached Mick's hospital bed, I was astounded at the number of tubes that made their way into his body. I leaned over his bed to attempt to comfort him by saying that hundreds around the country were praying and pulling for him.

Mick nodded and then acknowledged his response to the loss of Benji from Job 1:21: "The Lord gave and the Lord has taken away. Blessed be the name of the Lord."

And with those words, the sorrow that had left a lump in my throat now caused my eyes to well up with tears.

....

Discuss:

As a couple the kind of faith that it takes to make that kind of pronouncement. Do you feel you are at the point where you could make the same expression of faith?

Pray:

Ask God to help your faith grow. Pray that you will both become the man and woman that God wants you to be.

A CHRISTMAS I'LL NEVER FORGET

{Part Two}

O death, where is your victory? O death, where is your sting?

1 CORINTHIANS 15:55

*M*ick was the only pastor for this small church, so it fell upon me to conduct the graveside memorial services for Benji.

That day will forever be etched in my heart. There was a grayish-white coffin barely four feet long, holding the body of a seven-year-old boy. There was Benji's mom, Helen, with her 10-year-old son trying to stand strong and tall beside her. The rest of her family lay back in a hospital, broken and nearly crushed. All of life seemed to have stopped and stood still.

What positive words could man feebly utter in such a desperate moment? What could man possibly have to say to a mother who would wake up on Christmas morning and look at the unopened presents to a boy she loved? Humanly, that moment was filled with injustice, questions, despair and anger. It was grim and dark.

But in the midst of the darkness of death, the star of Bethlehem suddenly shone bright. As I read from the Scriptures, the hope of the gospel of Jesus Christ came and swallowed up the darkness. "O death, where is your victory?"

I will never forget the contrast of agony and joy that day. If the gospel of Jesus Christ can bring hope and comfort to those who have just lost a child, then He is all powerful. The tomb of Jesus Christ is empty. We can find forgiveness and peace with God because Christ is alive.

Many couples who lose a child, as Mick and Helen did, are never able to recover, and they end up divorcing. But somehow the Yoders were able to claim the victory that Christ promises. In fact, 14 months after Benji's death, Helen delivered a healthy baby girl. She and Mick named her Hope, as they claimed the promise of Jeremiah 29:11:

> "For I know the plans that I have for you," declares the Lord, "plans for welfare and not for calamity, to give you a future and a hope."

....

Discuss:
Do you believe God has your welfare in mind,
no matter what happens to you?

Pray:
Together that you will never lose hope in the midst of the
challenges and tragedies of life.

A LITTLE BIT OF GRACE

by Barbara Rainey

As a ring of gold in a swine's snout, so is a beautiful woman who lacks discretion.

PROVERBS 11:22

J think we wives need to give our husbands some grace...to not know how a woman feels, or how we function and operate as the other sex. I used to think, *Why doesn't Dennis just understand what I'm going through? Why doesn't he do things the way I want them done?* But I had to learn that he doesn't automatically know where I am emotionally, or what I expect in different situations, unless I tell him. And if I come across as judgmental, he'll get defensive. I need to bestow some grace.

I laugh thinking about one morning. I needed to leave about the same time the kids had to be out the door. I said to Dennis, "I really need your help this morning. Could you make breakfast for everybody?"

Now I was thinking he would do it like I did—prepare the meal, call the girls in and say "Here's your plate, do you want juice?" I'm real involved in serving them breakfast and talking to them.

Well, Dennis fixed them toast while watching the morning news on television. He fixed about 10 slices of toast, stacked them on a plate, and laid them on the table. When the kids got in the car they hadn't eaten. I said, "Why didn't you eat?" They said, "Where was the food?" Dennis assumed since the food was out, they would find it.

As I walked back in the house I realized Dennis's burden isn't the same as mine. I'm involved on an emotional level with the kids during breakfast, while he just wanted to complete the task while gearing up for a day at the office. He did what I asked. He just didn't do it like I would have.

I decided that I needed to give him some grace.

....

Discuss:

How have you been at communicating your feelings to your mate lately?
Are you bestowing grace?

Pray:

Ask the Lord to help you understand that your spouse may do things
differently than you, and give grace instead of condemnation.

BENT NAILS
AND REAL HOMES

For that which I am doing, I do not understand; for I am not practicing what I would like to do, but I am doing the very thing I hate. For I know that nothing good dwells in me...for the wishing is present in me, but the doing of the good is not.

ROMANS 7:15,18

It started with a beautiful seven-foot Scotch pine Christmas tree. The problem was its trunk—it was too big for our tiny tree stand. Then, after whittling it down, it was too short to reach the bottom of the stand. Barbara suggested I nail on an extension. So I attempted to drive two nails through a one-inch block of wood into the trunk. Simple plan, right? Wrong.

With a swift blow of the hammer, the first nail bent at a sharp angle as if it were being driven into a piece of petrified wood. When the second nail followed suit, I began to murmur under my breath that Christmas trees must be a pagan ritual after all.

Nail number three was a kissing cousin of the first two. Number four went flying into an azalea bush. That tree trunk could have been butter and I'm convinced number five would have bent—which it did. Do you believe in demon-possessed Christmas trees?

I threw the tree, flying needles and all, into the trunk of the car with the intent of taking this stupid, pagan, petrified thing back where I bought it. And then I looked at my horrified son, five-year-old Benjamin, who witnessed this display and probably thought that Christmas was about to be canceled. Just this once I should have taken W. C. Field's advice: "If at first you don't succeed, then quit! There's no use being a stupid fool about it!"

Nobody likes to fail, especially in front of a young child, but we can't avoid it. Just as the apostle Paul lamented, we want to do good, but we cannot always do it.

Real homes see a lot of failure. We might fool our friends and coworkers, but in the home there are only so many rugs to sweep things under, closets to hide things in and attic spaces to tuck away junk. What do you do when you blow it at home? Stuff it, or admit it and ask forgiveness for it?

....

Discuss:
What is your typical reaction to small failures around your home?

Pray:
Ask God for an authentic family that can be real and forgiving.

OUR MOST MEMORABLE CHRISTMAS GIFT

{Part One}

Present your bodies a living and holy sacrifice, acceptable to God.
ROMANS 12:1

Barbara and I recently were asked, "What is the most memorable Christmas gift you've ever given or received?" Instantly our minds raced backwards over invisible tracks and skidded to a stop at the same intersection: Our first Christmas together as a couple, in 1972.

Our Christmas tree that year was sparsely decorated with a dozen red ornaments. The small living room was quiet, but warm. A scant few presents lay scattered under the scotch pine.

Neither of us have any recollection of what prompted us, but evidently the Spirit of God wanted us to dedicate and commemorate our new life together in Jesus Christ. So we decided that before we would give each other our gifts, we would first give God the most valued gift we possessed: our lives.

The kitchen table became Barbara's altar, while I sat on the borrowed couch. Each of us, individually, spent some time writing out the "Title Deeds to Our Lives."

It was a time of counting the cost of being a committed follower of Jesus Christ. It meant relinquishing all rights and ownership of our lives to God. It was a practical application of Romans 12:1,2, which urges us to commit our lives totally to the Lord.

It wasn't easy, that bare-bones honesty with God. We wrote down all that we desired, all the things we thought were important, and said we wanted to give them to Him. Then, folding and placing those two sheets of paper in an envelope, we wrote on the outside: To God Our Father.

We sealed the envelope, and then we verbalized together in prayer what had already taken place privately on our sheets of paper.

There were no bells. No angelic choirs singing. No blinding light. Just the firm confidence that what we had done was right.

Eighteen years later we retrieved those documents from our safety deposit box and read them. And in the next devotion I'll show you what we found.

....

Discuss:
Have you ever written out a "Title Deed" to your life? What would prevent you from giving God total control of your life?

Pray:
That you would be able to wholeheartedly give your lives completely to Him.

OUR MOST MEMORABLE CHRISTMAS GIFT

{Part Two}

Now to Him who is able to do exceedingly abundantly beyond all that we ask or think, according to the power that works within us.

EPHESIANS 3:20

It was fascinating to read, 18 years later, the earnest commitment we had made as a young couple: At the top of our pages was a similar statement:

Contract with God

I hereby give all rights to God of the following things that I want:

Then came our lists (partial):

Dennis	**Barbara**
Nice big house with workshop, office	Children—at least one boy and one girl
To ski well	Dennis
Nice furniture and things	To live to see my children grow up
Sharp clothes	To be settled and stable
Security	To be an outstanding couple and family
Easygoing job	
Success in ministry and speaking ability	
Stay healthy	
A healthy, big family—several boys	
Barbara	

Reading the lists on those two pages, Barbara and I were immediately stunned by two things. First, we noticed how silly and shallow some of the things were that we deemed valuable and difficult to give up to God. I was struck by how much I was preoccupied with material things. Looking back over our years together, I found it fascinating how God had continuously sought to wean us from that which is perishable and replace our values with the imperishable: People and His Word.

We also were surprised at how much more God has given us than what we gave up. We immediately thought of Ephesians 3:20. Both of us feel we sacrificed nothing and have gained far more than we ever dreamed of.

....

Discuss:

Get alone with God and make your own list of things that are most important to you. Prayerfully formalize a contract with God giving Him total ownership and rights to your life. Sign and date your document.

Pray:

That God would give you discernment about your true priorities in life.

FRIENDSHIPS WITH OTHER WOMEN

Finally, brethren, rejoice, be made complete, be comforted, be like-minded.

2 CORINTHIANS 13:11

In my relationship with Dennis I am confident he understands me, my role and my struggles. We have spent endless hours talking together to create this rapport. He has been with me through many difficult times. He has been a "substitute mother" to the children when I've been out of the house, so he knows a great deal about that role and its responsibilities.

But there is a point beyond which he cannot go. Only another wife and mother can really share the pain I felt in childbirth, my struggles with understanding my role in marriage, or how some days I feel like I'm just a "Need Machine" that everyone comes to and pushes a button. Only a woman can join with me in prayer about issues like these. Other mothers can provide the support and motivation I need to carry the daily weight of bringing up children.

I need a deep affinity with two or three women, and I have it. It's wonderful. I am affirmed every time we talk by phone, get together or correspond. And when I feel good about myself, Dennis feels less pressure to try to meet all of my needs.

May I urge you men to encourage your wives to find at least one other woman with whom they can identify? This friendship should not take your place as her primary source of approval, but can supplement the self-image you are helping your wife build.

Here's another tip: Give your wife a weekend off to get away for a retreat with a friend. On Sunday evening, your wife will return with a better perspective of herself. She'll be encouraged and built up in ways that you, as a man, could never accomplish. This retreat is especially needed if your wife is occupied with young children or works outside the home, thus leaving little time to develop friendships.

Dennis and I encourage you to resist the tendency to be threatened by your wife's outside friendships with women. Give her time and encouragement to develop these friendships. You'll never regret it.

....

Discuss:

Discuss your wife's friendships. Too few? Too many? Right kind? Does she have enough time to pursue them? What are her friendship needs as a woman in the stage of life she is in right now?

Pray:

That God will give your wife at least one "soul mate" who can identify with her season of life.

THE "GREAT" LETTER

So that you may walk in a manner worthy of the Lord, to please Him in all respects, bearing fruit in every good work and increasing in the knowledge of God.

COLOSSIANS 1:10

One privilege of my ministry is to receive letters from people whose lives have been transformed by the love and grace of Jesus Christ. One of my favorites came from a wife and mother in Maryland, who wrote to tell of the discovery she made one day while listening to our radio program, "FamilyLife Today," while driving to work:

> I've been married to a terrific man for almost eight years and have two wonderful boys, five and one. But until last year, when I began to listen to your program regularly on my 30-mile commute to work, I never realized I had been short-changing my family and myself by not turning my marriage over to the Lord.
>
> Yes, I viewed myself as a Christian woman with decent moral standards, but I just wasn't allowing the Spirit of Jesus to work. I thought I needed to transform things all by myself. Disappointed with my drifting relationship, I became controlling, critical, and even resentful at times. I began to let down my "hedges" at work, and to become dangerously close to sacrificing everything I hold dear.
>
> When I tuned in to your "Building Your Mate's Self-Esteem" series, I couldn't believe it. Here was my life, coming over the radio. As I listened, I wept, realizing how I was tearing down my wonderful man, and subsequently robbing our family life of real happiness. I resolved to turn my marriage and family life over to the Holy Spirit, and to look for ways to encourage and lift up my husband.
>
> I have never been happier or more satisfied in my life. My marriage has been transformed and is happy, fun, and alive. I see my husband with new eyes and a renewed heart. My children must feel the strength and stability as they see their parents touch and support each other in daily life.

Like wheel alignments on a car, all of us are in need of correcting attitudes that are out of alignment with God's Word.

Discuss:

If appropriate, discuss a time in your marriage where you dropped your guard, even for a short time. What characterized your marriage? Your spiritual life? Share what you can do today to keep your hedges of protection strong.

Pray:

For one another that you would increase in the knowledge of God, and that you would "walk in a manner worthy of the Lord."

LAUGHTER IN THE WALLS

There is an appointed time for everything....A time to weep, and a time to laugh;
a time to mourn, and a time to dance.

ECCLESIASTES 3:1,4

The late Bob Benson once wrote that, when his kids grew up and left home, he and his wife would sit and listen to the "laughter in the walls." I love that phrase.

Do the walls of your home ring with laughter? Laughter and strong homes go together. A Christian couple should sooner be found guilty of having too much laughter than of having too little. Fun lifts us out of the daily ruts and assassinates the drab, the boring and the mundane. Laughter lightens loads and knits hearts together instantaneously.

God gave children a funny bone and giggle-box to balance all of those who are "overly intense." He gave our family kids who love to laugh, especially our daughter Rebecca. She lives to laugh. Her beaming smile and giggle is the all-time best. And when she gets going at the supper table, pandemonium breaks loose. Her giggle-box infects us all with uncontrollable, delicious delight. In fact, we've renamed her because of her love for laughter: "Rebecca Jean Joy Susie-Q Rainey."

My family taught me how to laugh. Our home was filled with practical jokes, teasing and surprises. I'll never forget my dad's laugh (the best) and my mom's sense of humor, which is still as sharp as ever. Some of my fondest memories are of laughing so hard the tears just streamed down our faces.

I remember the time my mom gave herself a Hoover vacuum cleaner for Christmas. She wrapped it and put it under the tree with this tag: To my dear wife from Ward.

Life is made up of pain. Disappointments. Pressure. Doubts. Trials. We are all sapped of strength by these dark, ominous clouds. But, like an exploding shaft of sunlight in a dark room, laughter illuminates life by reminding us not to be so serious.

Why not leave a little laughter in the walls of your home tonight?

....

Discuss:

How was laughter a part of your own home as a child? What laughter have you heard in your present home during the last two days? Is there enough "fun" in your own heart to spill over and infect other members of your family?

Pray:

That the God who calls life from the dead will fill your spirit with new optimism and joy.

THE FINAL WORDS
OF OBADIAH HOLMES

{Part One}

So teach us to number our days, that we may present to Thee a heart of wisdom.

PSALM 90:12

Obadiah Holmes was a godly man who, with his wife, raised eight children in the 1600s. On December 16, 1675, knowing his end was near, Obadiah sat down to write a final letter to his children. Little did he know that this amazing document would survive for another 10 generations. I recently came across this document and decided to use some excerpts from it here. The words of Psalm 90:12 take on new meaning when you read words like these:

My Dear Children:

A word or two unto you all who are near and dear unto me, and much on my heart as I draw near to my end and am not likely to see you nor speak to you at my departure. Wherefore I am moved to leave these lines for your consideration when I am gone and you shall see me no more.

Above all things in this world let it be your care to seek the Kingdom of Heaven and His righteousness first. Be you thoroughly convinced of that and, by actual transgressions, that you are sinners. Yet, know that such great love as cannot be expressed by man nor angels has the Lord sent and held forth: even his Son, his only Son, to save and deliver you from wrath....

My soul has been in great trouble for you, to see Christ formed in you by a thorough work of the Holy Spirit of the Lord that it may appear you are born again and engrafted in the true vine; so you, being true branches, may bring forth fruit unto God and serve Him in your generation. Wherefore, wait on Him with care and diligence; carefully read the Scriptures and mind well what is therein contained, for they testify of Him.

Obadiah Holmes started his letter with the most important issue in life: repentance from sin and faith in Jesus Christ. He knew that if his descendants missed Christ then they would miss life.

Discuss:

How will your descendants know what you lived for? How can you communicate the need for generations that follow you to repent and come to faith in Jesus Christ?

Pray:

That God would use you to lead your children to a saving knowledge of Christ and a closer walk with Him.

THE FINAL WORDS OF OBADIAH HOLMES

{Part Two}

That the generation to come might know, even the children yet to be born, that they may arise and tell them to their children, that they should put their confidence in God, and not forget the works of God.

PSALM 78:6,7

Obadiah Holmes evidently took these words from Psalm 78 to heart as he raised his nine children. Even their names were all taken from biblical characters. And in his last letter to these children he reminded them of the godly character he hoped they would carry on after his death:

And now my son, Joseph: Remember that Joseph of Arimathea was a good man and a disciple of Jesus; he was bold and went in boldly and asked for the body of Jesus, and buried it.

My son, John: Remember what a loving and beloved disciple he was.

My daughter, Hope: Consider what a grace of God hope is, and covet after that hope that will never be ashamed but has hope of eternal life and salvation of Jesus Christ.

My son, Obadiah: Consider that Obadiah was a servant of the Lord and tender in spirit, and in a troublesome time hid the prophets by fifty in a cave.

My son, Samuel: Remember Samuel was a chief prophet of the Lord, ready to hear his voice saying, "Speak, Lord, for thy servant heareth."

My daughter, Martha: Remember Martha, although she was encumbered with many things, yet she loved the Lord and was beloved of Him, for He loved Mary and Martha.

My daughter, Mary: Remember Mary who chose the better part that shall not be taken away and did hearken to the Lord's instructions.

My son, Jonathan: Remember how faithful and loving he was to David, that servant of the Lord.

My daughter, Lydia: Remember how Lydia's heart was opened, her care borne, her spirit made to be willing to receive and obey the apostle in what the Lord required, and was baptized, and entertained and refreshed the servants of the Lord.

....

Discuss:

What is the most important thing you could leave your children when you die?

Pray:

That your children would grow up to have an impact for Christ wherever they go.

THE FINAL WORDS OF OBADIAH HOLMES

{Part Three}

So then, my beloved, just as you have always obeyed,...work out
your salvation with fear and trembling.

PHILIPPIANS 2:12

*O*badiah Holmes and his wife gave their children a firm foundation in Christ. After speaking of this foundation in his final letter, he concluded with a list of challenging, practical ways to live out their faith:

Be you content with your present condition and portion God has given you. Make a good use of what you have by making use of it for your comfort (solace). For meat, drink or apparel, it is the gift of God. Take care to live honestly, justly, quietly with love and peace among yourselves, your neighbors and, if possible, be at peace with all men.

In what you can, do good to all men, especially to such as fear the Lord. Forget not to entertain strangers, according to your ability; if it be done in sincerity, it will be accepted, especially if to a disciple in the name of a disciple. Do to all men as you would have them do to you.

If you would be Christ's disciples, you must know and consider that you must take up your cross and follow Him, through evil report and losses. But yet know, he that will lose his life for Him shall save it.

Thus, my dear children, have I according to my measure, as is my duty, counseled you. May the good Lord give you understanding in all things and by His Holy Spirit convince, reprove and instruct and lead you into all truth as it is in Jesus. So that when you have done your work here, He may receive you to glory. Now the God of truth and peace be with you, unto Whom I commit this and you, even to Him be glory forever and ever, Amen.

A powerful exhortation. Did it make a difference? Yes. Some 10 generations later, one of Obadiah's descendants is a man by the name of Dave Jones. Dave pastors a church in Georgia and, with his wife, Peggy, is impacting thousands of marriages through speaking at FamilyLife Marriage Conference.

Today, some 300 years later, Obadiah reminds us that nothing we leave our children will ever be as important as a conviction that God must be everything to them.

....

Discuss:
If you were to write a final letter to your children, what would you say?

Pray:
That God would help you "number your days," live your life for Christ and raise your children by His priorities.

ENDNOTES

January 1: Dennis and Barbara Rainey, *The New Building Your Mate's Self-Esteem* (Nashville, Tenn.: Thomas Nelson Publishers, 1995), pp. 42-45.

January 3: Dennis Rainey, *Staying Close* (Dallas, Tex.: Word Publishing, 1989), p. 11.

January 6: Ibid., pp. 201, 202.

January 12: Ibid., pp. 105, 106.

January 13: Ibid., pp. 106, 107.

January 14: Ibid., pp. 108.

January 15: Ibid., pp. 110, 111.

January 19: Rainey, *The New Building Your Mate's Self-Esteem*, pp. 70, 71.

January 20: Ibid., pp. 241-243.

January 21: Rainey, *Staying Close*, p. 163.

January 23: Rainey, *The New Building Your Mate's Self-Esteem*, pp. 175, 176.

January 25: Rainey, *Staying Close*, pp. 39-41.

January 28: Dennis Rainey with David Boehi, *The Tribute* (Nashville, Tenn.: Thomas Nelson Publishers, 1994), pp. 270, 271.

January 29: Ibid., pp. 272, 273.

January 30: Rainey, *The New Building Your Mate's Self-Esteem*, pp. 4, 5.

February 4: Ibid., pp. 115-117.

February 10: Dave Roever and Harold Fickett, *Welcome Home, Davey* (Dallas, Tex.: Word Publishing, 1986), pp. 125, 126, 128.

February 16: Rainey, *The New Building Your Mate's Self-Esteem.*, pp. 68, 69.

February 19: Rainey, *Staying Close*, pp. 119-121.

February 23: Ibid., pp. 121-123.

March 2: Ibid., p. 113.

March 5: Ibid., pp. 215, 216.

March 8: Ibid., p. 156.

March 9: Ibid., pp. 12, 13.

March 10: Ibid., pp. 13, 14.

March 13: Ibid., pp. 57, 58.

March 14: Ibid., p. 164.

March 15: Rainey, *The Tribute*, pp. 66, 67.

March 16: Rainey, *The New Building Your Mate's Self-Esteem*, pp. 15, 16.

March 17: Ibid., pp. 17, 18.

March 18: Ibid., pp. 19, 20.

March 21: Rainey, *Staying Close*, pp. 49, 51.

March 27: Ibid., p. 182.

April 1: Ibid., p. 41.

April 2: Ibid., pp. 195, 196.

April 13: Ibid., pp. 97, 98.

April 19: Ibid., pp. 49, 50.

April 21: Rainey, *The New Building Your Mate's Self-Esteem*, pp. 239, 240.

April 28: Rainey, *The Tribute*, pp. 32, 33.

April 29: Ibid., pp. 38, 39.

April 30: Ibid., pp. 48, 49.

May 8: Rainey, *Staying Close*, pp. 143, 144.

May 14: Rainey, *The Tribute*, pp. 28-31.

May 17: Rainey, *Staying Close*, pp. 62, 63.

May 24: Ibid., pp. 227 ff.

May 25: Ibid., pp. 230, 231.

May 26: Ibid., 231, 232.

May 27: Ibid., p. 229.

May 28: Ibid., p. 132.

May 29 Ibid., p. 132, 133.

June 7: Douglas Botting, *The Second Front* (Alexandria Va.: Time-Life, Inc., 1978), pp. 140, 141.

June 9: Rainey *Staying Close*, pp. 162-165.

June 10: Ibid., pp. 156,157.

June 14: Rainey, *The Tribute*, pp. 147, 148.

June 15: Ibid., pp. 148-150.

June 18: Rainey, *The New Building Your Mate's Self-Esteem*, pp. 222, 223, 226.

June 23: Rainey, *The Tribute*, pp. 46, 47.

June 25: Rainey, *Staying Close*, pp. 254-256.

June 29: Ibid., pp. 5 ff.

July 5: Ibid., pp. 42, 43.

July 14: Rainey, *The New Building Your Mate's Self-Esteem*, pp. 260-262.

July 15: Rainey, *Staying Close*, p. 58.

July 16: Ibid., pp. 241-245.

July 23: Ibid., pp. 30, 31.

July 31: Rainey, *The New Building Your Mate's Self-Esteem*, pp. 101, 102.

August 1: Rainey, *Staying Close*, pp. 177, 178.
August 4: Ibid., pp. 203 ff.
August 5: Ibid., p. 206.
August 6: Ibid., pp. 191, 192.
August 7: Ibid., pp. 208, 209.
August 10: Rainey, *The New Building Your Mate's Self-Esteem*, pp. 113, 114.
August 15: Rainey, *Staying Close*, pp. 230, 231.
August 16: Ibid., pp. 231, 232.
August 17: Rainey, *The New Building Your Mate's Self-Esteem*, pp. 44-45.
August 20: Rainey, *Staying Close*, p. 59.
August 21: Rainey, *The New Building Your Mate's Self-Esteem*, pp. 237, 238.
August 22: Rainey, *Staying Close*, p. 87.
August 26: Rainey, *The Tribute*, pp. 94-104.
August 27: Rainey, *Staying Close*, p. 86.
September 6: Rainey, *The New Building Your Mate's Self-Esteem*, pp. 65-67.
September 9: Rainey, *Staying Close*, pp. 173-177.
September 11: Ibid., p. 97.
September 14: Ibid., pp. 98-100.
September 17: Rainey, *The New Building Your Mate's Self-Esteem*, pp. 67, 68.
September 23: Rainey, *Staying Close*, p. 72.
September 24: Rainey, *The New Building Your Mate's Self-Esteem*, pp. 158, 159, 164, 165.
September 25: Ibid., pp. 166, 167.
September 30: Rainey, *The Tribute*, pp. 184, 186.
October 7: Rainey, *Staying Close*, p. 180.

October 9: Rainey, *The Tribute*, pp. 67, 68.
October 12: Rainey, *The New Building Your Mate's Self-Esteem*, pp. 258-260.
October 13: Rainey, *Staying Close*, pp. 219, 220.
October 19: Ibid., pp. 67, 68.
October 20: Ibid., p. 72.
October 23: Rainey, *The New Building Your Mate's Self-Esteem*, pp. 141, 142.
October 24: Ibid., pp. 142-144.
October 25: Ibid., pp. 144-146.
October 26: Rainey, *Staying Close*, pp. 192, 193.
October 31: Ibid., pp. 95, 96.
November 1: Ibid., pp. 190, 191.
November 3: Rainey, *The New Building Your Mate's Self-Esteem*, pp. 98, 99.
November 5: Rainey, *Staying Close*, pp. 178, 179.
November 17: Ibid., pp. 21, 22.
November 27: Rainey, *The New Building Your Mate's Self-Esteem*, pp. 52, 53.
December 6: Rainey, *Staying Close*, pp. 6, 7.
December 7: Ibid., p. 172.
December 10: Ibid., pp. 133, 134.
December 11: Rainey, *The Tribute*, pp. 59-62.
December 15: Rainey, *The New Building Your Mate's Self-Esteem*, pp. 92, 93.
December 17: Rainey, *Staying Close*, pp. 268, 269.
December 26: Rainey, *The New Building Your Mate's Self-Esteem*, pp. 195, 196.

Renew Your Commitment.

You've been working on the most important commitment of your life—spending time with God and with your spouse. No doubt you've learned a lot of things about your mate that will help the two of you grow closer together for years to come. You've also learned a lot about God's Word and how much it means to study the Bible with each other. But don't let it stop here—lay the next block in the foundation of your marriage by beginning the HomeBuilders Couples Series®. It will help you keep your marriage as strong, as dynamic, as solid as the day you said "I do."

Building Your Marriage
By Dennis Rainey
Help couples get closer together than you ever imagined possible.
•Leader's Guide
ISBN 08307.16130
•Study Guide
ISBN 08307.16122

Building Your Mate's Self-Esteem
By Dennis & Barbara Rainey
Marriage is God's workshop for self-esteem.
•Leader's Guide
ISBN 08307.16173
•Study Guide
ISBN 08307.16165

Building Teamwork in Your Marriage
By Robert Lewis
Help couples celebrate and enjoy their differences
•Leader's Guide
ISBN 08307.16157
•Study Guide
ISBN 08307.16149

Resolving Conflict in Your Marriage
By Bob & Jan Horner
Turn conflict into love and understanding.
•Leader's Guide
ISBN 08307.16203
•Study Guide
ISBN 08307.16181

Mastering Money in Your Marriage
By Ron Blue
Put an end to conflicts and find out how to use money to glorify God.
•Leader's Guide
ISBN 08307.16254
•Study Guide
ISBN 08307.16246

Growing Together In Christ
By David Sunde
Discover how Christ is central to your marriage.
•Leader's Guide
ISBN 08307.16297
•Study Guide
ISBN 08307.16289

Life Choices for a Lasting Marriage
By David Boehi
Find out how to make the right choices in your marriage.
•Leader's Guide
ISBN 08307.16262
•Study Guide
ISBN 08307.16270

Managing Pressure in Your Marriage
By Dennis Rainey & Robert Lewis
Learn how obedience to God will take pressure off your marriage
•Leader's Guide
ISBN 08307.16319
•Study Guide
ISBN 08307.16300

Expressing Love in Your Marriage
By Jerry & Sheryl Wunder and Dennis & Jill Eenigenburg
Discover God's plan for your love life by seeking God's best for your mate.
•Leader's Guide
ISBN 08307.16661
•Study Guide
ISBN 08307.16688

FAMILYLIFE CONFERENCES

FamilyLife Conferences are bringing meaningful, positive change to thousands of couples and families every year. The conferences, offered throughout the country, are based on solid biblical principles and are designed to provide couples and parents—in just one weekend—with the practical skills to build and enhance their marriages and families.

The FamilyLife Marriage Conference gives you the opportunity to slow down and focus on your spouse and your relationship. You will spend an insightful weekend together, doing fun couples' projects and hearing from dynamic speakers on real-life solutions for building and enhancing oneness in your marriage.

The FamilyLife Parenting Conference will equip you with the principles and tools you need to be more effective parents for a lifetime. Whether you're just getting started or in the turbulent years of adolescence, you'll learn biblical blueprints for raising your children.

FAMILYLIFE TODAY
RADIO PROGRAM

Over 1,000,000 listeners are tuning in weekly to "FamilyLife Today," recently given the 1995 National Religious Broadcasters Radio Program Producer of the Year Award. FamilyLife Executive Director Dennis Rainey, and Co-host Bob Lepine, provides a fast-paced half-hour of interviews and practical biblical issues your family faces.

So tune in this week and take advantage of this unique opportunity to be encouraged in your marriage and family. Call **1-800-FL TODAY** for the times and stations near you.

Dennis Rainey & Bob Lepine, Hosts.

FOR MORE INFORMATION

For more information on the FamilyLife Conferences, call FamilyLife at **1-800-999-8663**. To receive the HomeBuilders Couples Series® and other resources, call **1-800-FL TODAY**. For your marriage ... for your children ... for yourself ... for a lifetime.

FAMILYLIFE™
Bringing Timeless Principles Home

P.O. Box 23840 • Little Rock, AR 72221-3840
(501) 223-8663 • 1-800-999-8663

A ministry of Campus Crusade for Christ